INDIGENOUS KNOWLEDGE AND EDUCATION

Sites of Struggle, Strength, and Survivance

Edited by
MALIA VILLEGAS
SABINA RAK NEUGEBAUER
KERRY R. VENEGAS

Harvard Educational Review
Reprint Series No. 44

Copyright © 2008 by the President and Fellows of Harvard College

All rights reserved. No part of this publication may be reproduced or transmitted in any form or by any means, electronic or mechanical, including photocopy, recording, or any information storage and retrieval systems, without permission in writing from the publisher.

Library of Congress Control Number 2007941190

ISBN 978-0-916690-48-9

Published by Harvard Educational Review,
an imprint of the Harvard Education Publishing Group

Harvard Educational Review
8 Story Street
Cambridge, MA 02138

Cover Design: Nancy Goulet
Cover Art: *Yakkity Yak Ravens* was created by Sugpiaq/Alutiiq watercolor artist Helen Simeonoff, who is originally from Kodiak, Alaska, and spends her summers in her mother's village of Afognak, Alaska, which was destroyed in the 1964 earthquake.

The typefaces used in this book are ITC New Baskerville for text and Adobe Hypatia Sans Pro for display.

DEDICATION

To fulfill the promise of this book,
we dedicate this volume to those who have come
before us and have paved the pathway ahead of us.
We would like specifically to honor the memories of
Dr. Vine Deloria Jr., Dr. Beatrice Medicine, and
Reverend Chief David Salmon, three Elder scholars
whose service and commitment to education
we seek to emulate and advance.

Contents

Acknowledgments — vii

Editors' Introduction — 1

PART ONE   Sites of Struggle — 7

Fundamental Considerations: The Deep Meaning of Native American Schooling, 1880–1900
    DAVID WALLACE ADAMS — 9

Mexico: Indianismo and the Rural School
    RAMÓN EDUARDO RUIZ — 40

Literary Colonialism: Books in the Third World
    PHILIP G. ALTBACH — 55

The Use of Argumentation in Haitian Creole Science Classrooms
    JOSIANE HUDICOURT-BARNES — 65

The Struggle and Renaissance of Indigenous Knowledge in Eurocentric Education
    MARIE BATTISTE — 85

PART TWO   Sites of Strength — 93

No Longer Overlooked and Undervalued? The Evolving Dynamics of Endogenous Educational Research in Sub-Saharan Africa
    RICHARD MACLURE — 95

Beyond the Methods Fetish: Toward a Humanizing Pedagogy
    LILIA I. BARTOLOMÉ — 125

Aboriginal Education: The School at Strelley, Western Australia
    KENNETH LIBERMAN — 148

Nicaragua 1980: The Battle of the ABCs
FERNANDO CARDENAL, S.J., AND VALERIE MILLER   155

Tribal Sovereigns: Reframing Research in American Indian Education
K. TSIANINA LOMAWAIMA   183

Sites of Strength in Indigenous Research
GREGORY A. CAJETE   204

PART THREE   Sites of Survivance   209

American Indian Geographies of Identity and Power:
At the Crossroads of Indígena and Mestizaje
SANDY MARIE ANGLÁS GRANDE   211

Education as Transformation: Becoming a Healer among the
!Kung and the Fijians
RICHARD KATZ   243

Serving the Purpose of Education
LEONA OKAKOK   268

"Not Bread Alone": Clandestine Schooling and Resistance in the
Warsaw Ghetto during the Holocaust
SUSAN M. KARDOS   287

Community Education: To Reclaim and Transform What Has Been
Made Invisible
MUNIR FASHEH   320

"Yakkity Yak" and "Talking Back": An Examination of Sites of
Survivance in Indigenous Knowledge
BRYAN MCKINLEY JONES BRAYBOY   339

About the Contributors   347

About the Editors   351

Acknowledgments

We would like to express our heartfelt appreciation to all of those whose time and energy went into publishing this volume, including the Editorial Board of the *Harvard Educational Review*, Laura Clos, Douglas Clayton, Dody Riggs, all of the authors, and artist Helen Simeonoff, whose work in image and in story symbolizes the vision of this volume. We also want to acknowledge our families, friends, and mentors who supported us in this endeavor.

Editors' Introduction

Education reflects what a society values through the development of a set of experiences where we share our histories and ways of understanding with our youth. With this book, we offer an opportunity to explore a collective vision of education; to examine existing ways of thinking about education; and to consider the role of schooling in helping our children achieve a sense of belonging and self in relationships with others and with our world. There are many ways we could frame this exploration, especially in light of growing concerns about our youth, as well as recent successes in Indigenous movements, like the enactment of the United Nations Declaration on the Rights of Indigenous Peoples on September 13, 2007.[1]

We begin by highlighting the possibilities that exist in education if we are willing to adopt a different orientation, a new way of thinking about ourselves and our world. Our aim is to demonstrate that Indigenous Knowledge in education offers a way to support our children and improve our communities by making central issues of power, place, and relationships. We present examples of Indigenous Knowledge in education in order to underscore the "humanness" of education, which comes through in both specific and universal expressions. Each reveals different vantage points or perspectives from which to think about the purpose of education and the nature of learning.

We spent months combing through fifty years of *Harvard Educational Review* (*HER*) archives to identify articles that engaged questions of knowledge and epistemological beliefs, that offered insight into the importance of local and Indigenous ways of knowing, and that provided examples of how communities were forming their education systems according to a specific set of values and ways of knowing. We invite all readers — Indigenous and non-Indigenous, researcher and researched, student and teacher — to consider the articles and essays we have compiled here and we hope that those who have not thought much about education's epistemological roots will find this volume a useful entry point for considering the role of Indigenous Knowledge in education. We also hope that Indigenous scholars and others well-versed in the field of Indigenous education will find this volume a useful tool for engaging a broader audience and attempting to identify some of the domains, practices, and possibilities for Indigenous Knowledge in education. In this introduction, we have three goals: (1) to introduce the concept of Indigenous Knowledge; (2) to explain why it is important to engage this topic in education; and (3) to help our readers understand why the concepts of "sites of struggle, strength, and survivance" are central to this discussion.

Introducing the Concept of Indigenous Knowledge

While Mi'kmaq scholar Marie Battiste (2002) critiques European scholars' demand for a definition of terms such as Indigenous Knowledge, she offers a way of thinking about this concept that is useful here:

> Indigenous knowledge . . . is the expression of the vibrant relationships between the people, their ecosystems, and the other living beings and spirits that share their lands. (p. 42)

In this conception, "the expression of the vibrant relationships" is an essential. Knowledge is neither an object that can be possessed, controlled, or owned, nor is it something that belongs only to a "traditional" past. Knowledge is living, dynamic, active, and fundamentally about our connections to each other and our world. Bryan Brayboy (2005) captures the "fixed" and "dynamic" tensions inherent in this conception of knowledge that are reflected in the nature of Indigenous culture:

> Culture is simultaneously fluid or dynamic, and fixed or stable. Like an anchor in the ocean, it is tied to a group of people and often a physical place. For many Indigenous people, culture is rooted to lands on which they live as well as to their ancestors who lived on those lands before them. However, just as the anchor shifts and sways with changing tides and the ebbs and flows of the ocean, culture shifts and flows with changes in contexts, situations, people, and purposes. (p. 434)

The very expression of Indigenous Knowledge is inextricably linked to the relationships in which it is situated. Thus, the significance of this kind of knowledge lies in both being and acting — being in relationship to and acting in relationship with. In education, these two are companions that complement each other and fulfill our capacity to know.

Indigenous Knowledge in Education

Indigenous Knowledge in education provides a means of living out one's understanding. It manifests neither simply in having knowledge nor in the performance of a particular task, but in a process of applying learning to a purpose that is meaningful to oneself, and to the relationships between the teacher and learner and between the learner and the world. The teacher in this sense can include non-humans and one's environment:

> Education is, at its essence, learning about life through participation and relationship in community, including not only people, but plants, animals, and the whole of Nature. (Cajete, 1999, p. 26)

The articles in this book have implications that could apply to many communities, in that they draw attention to key questions about the epistemological bases of education. They also offer a great deal to communities specifically working to develop Indigenous institutions of education because they raise cautions about specific arenas (e.g., the power of written text and publishing, the role of local research), point to resources and possible areas of promise (e.g., our connections as humans, models of local control and social movements), and offer examples of communities engaging issues of knowledge and place in education.

We can understand Indigenous Knowledge more firmly through its application in education practice and research because it is dynamic and lived – it comes about through experience in the world. The articles in this volume were chosen in part because they detail educational initiatives in a range of geographic regions, which highlights the role of local places. They are situated in one of three conceptual "sites" in order to emphasize the universal ways of making meaning of human experiences of struggle, strength, and survivance. Their educational agendas occur in various realms, which draws attention to the importance of the relationships and social contexts that reflect the vantage points and perspectives of the educators, community members, and institutions involved in each case.

Sites of Struggle, Strength, and Survivance

This volume is divided into three sections — Sites of Struggle, Sites of Strength, and Sites of Survivance. This language was inspired by the work of Maori scholar Graham Hingangaroa Smith (2004):

> It is argued that successful transformation for Maori aspirations must be developed in multiple sites. In this sense transformative struggle is not to be seen as a singular struggle but as many struggles, developed in many different sites, and often by differently skilled people. Transformation must be "won" in many places and often requires many issues having to be confronted at the same time. (Abstract)

"Sites" in this sense has several connotations. It suggests physical space or a particular place where Indigenous education emerges out of local ways of knowing that are grounded in the values and insights of a local community. From this perspective, education is by nature inextricably connected to the terrain where it originates. When relocated, this local knowledge generated by and endogenous to a "site" is altered and becomes something different than what it was at its inception. Sites can also refer to human experience, as in a site of pain or happiness, and can evoke the idea of our role, our "place" in relationships with others and to a way of being in the world.

The section titles are also significant. In selecting the contents of this volume, we found three central themes that these *HER* articles converged around. The first — struggle — identifies the articles that address what aspects of education are at issue when we consider concepts like knowledge and local or place-based ways of knowing (e.g., authority in truth, identity, and our student's sense of worth). It was also essential to frame this discussion of struggle by pointing to Native or Indigenous peoples' struggles as a major premise of this collection. We can learn a great deal about the trials of our present educational context by considering the Indigenous experience in education. The concept of the second section — strength — is used to identify examples of groups or communities naming sources of strength and taking action to foster education based on their own ways of knowing about themselves in the world. And the third section category — survivance — describes the human drive for education and the important purpose of exploring worldviews and epistemologies in education.

Conclusion

In selecting this collection of works from the *Harvard Educational Review*, we acknowledge that there are many important works being developed today in the area of Indigenous Knowledge. Nevertheless, we felt it important to present a work that acknowledges that kernels of Indigenous Knowledge have been present over time and that they exist in pockets across the academy and the globe. While we envision this volume as an opportunity to invite all educators to consider Indigenous Knowledge in education, we believe that the seminal text on Indigenous Knowledge should be largely written and developed by Indigenous scholars. To reflect this belief, we invited three established scholars in the field of Indigenous Knowledge to contribute essays speaking to sites of struggle, strength, and survivance.

We end by asking readers to be open to the possibilities of Indigenous Knowledge — specifically as it relates to the concepts of place, power, and education — for the work we do with all children, for Indigenous communities, and for the ways we think about our responsibilities as teachers and learners. We offer the cover art as a metaphor for the themes we see within this volume. The multiple visions of a raven embodies our message regarding the importance of examining knowledge in education from diverse perspectives. These three distinct images echo the sites of struggle, strength, and survivance that are the framework of this book. This community of ravens faces the light, and we invite you to face it too in order to seek a new way of being an educator. Invoking the distinction Yup'ik scholar Angayuqaq Oscar Kawagley makes between supporting students to *make a living* and to *make a life*, Ray Barnhardt (2005) reminds us:

> [Indigenous knowledge] serve[s] as the basis for a pedagogy of place that shifts the emphasis from teaching about local culture to teaching through the culture as students learn about the immediate places they inhabit and their connection to the larger world within which they will make a life for themselves. . . . As Indigenous people reassert their world views and ways of knowing in search of a proper balance between . . . "two worlds," they offer insights into ways by which

we can extend the scope of our educational systems to prepare all students to not only make a living, but to make a full-filling and sustainable life for themselves. (pp. 113–114)

Notes

1. *Indigenous* (with a capital *I*) is used here to refer to Native communities throughout the world who assert their sovereignty as peoples — or as unique cultural groups — because of their status as the original inhabitants of the land, whether or not this sovereignty has been acknowledged by other nations.

References

Barnhardt, R. (2005). Creating a place for Indigenous Knowledge in education: The Alaska Native Knowledge Network. In G. Smith & D. Gruenewald (Eds.), *Place-based education in the global age: Local Diversity* (pp. 113–133). Hillsdale, NJ: Lawrence Erlbaum.

Battiste, M., & Henderson, J. Y. (2002). *Protecting Indigenous Knowledge and heritage: A global challenge.* Saskatoon, Saskatchewan: Purich.

Brayboy, B. M. J. (2005). Toward a tribal critical race theory in education. *The Urban Review, 37,* 425–446.

Cajete, G. (1994). *Look to the mountain: An ecology of Indigenous education.* Skyland, NC: Kivaki Press.

Smith, G. H. (2004). *"Transforming institutions": Ambiguities of theory and practice within the academy.* Paper presented at the annual meeting of the American Educational Research Association, San Diego, CA.

PART ONE

Sites of Struggle

Struggle can be a problematic term. It can raise visions of militancy and rigidity. It can conjure up the image of an ongoing battle or even of one completed in the past. But struggle in the sense we are using it here is more like a current — rising and falling, shifting across place and time, changing in terms of place and players.

The first section of this book illustrates various sites of struggle. From the struggle to maintain and hold on to intrinsic, holistic ways of knowing, learning, and doing, to the struggle to define a new vision of what being Indigenous means, these articles illustrate the history and the actions of a struggle for the recognition and affirmation of knowledge through identity, culture, and education.

In "Fundamental Considerations: The Deep Meaning of Native American Schooling, 1880–1900," David Wallace Adams illustrates a historical site of struggle in his examination of the deeper meaning and impact of generations of forced assimilation as educational policy. Ramón Eduardo Ruiz also offers a historical examination of struggle in "Mexico: Indianismo and the Rural School." However, he uses a national context to paint a portrait of people in post-revolutionary Mexico who are struggling to recognize and assert an Indigenous identity and knowledge in education after generations of colonization. In "Literary Colonialism: Books in the Third World," Phillip G. Altbach's description of "Third World 'book hunger'" discusses site of struggle in an international (and often overlooked) context, demonstrating how publishing rights are an extension of the colonization of knowledge and describing what actions can challenge and change this paradigm. Josiane Hudicourt-Barnes moves into a more intimate site of struggle in "The Use of Argumentation in Haitian Creole Science Classrooms." She examines the struggle against preconceived ideas of deficiency by presenting a portrait of how the culture, language, and knowledge of Haitian students actually predisposes them to practice reflective, sophisticated scientific inquiry.

In the final outcome, struggle is not always about success or progress, but about motion. The essays in this collection demonstrate the motion of trying out ideas and stretching the conversation about what constitutes knowledge, ability, and the language of educational discourse. They also speak to the desire and the basic human right to choose how to exist in the world, and to recognize the validity of one's own language, culture, and history in making that choice.

In the final essay of this section, "The Struggle and Renaissance of Indigenous Knowledge in Eurocentric Education," Mi'kmaq scholar Marie Battiste considers the way struggle has played out in sites of higher education. As she notes, in the complete absence of Indigenous Knowledge systems in higher education, the struggle to recognize and assert the role of Indigenous Knowledge is "an urgent agenda that has been the source of a renaissance in Indigenous scholarship to effect educational reform." But this struggle is not one of asserting power over either Indigenous or colonial systems of knowing and thinking in order to suppress one and raise the other. Rather, Battiste's vision is of finding a way to generate a new relationship between the two systems of knowledge that together can create power and develop "an educational system that is a place of connectedness and caring."

Finally, these articles should not be seen as prescriptives nor as warnings; rather, they offer a brief glimpse at various points into the ways, means, and locations of the struggle to identify and affirm knowledge on its own terms. More than just a "fight," the act of struggle creates an opportunity for examination and reassessment and a chance to reflect on larger questions and issues.

As you read through this section, we ask you to consider the following questions that we grappled with in developing it:

- What is the struggle for Indigenous Knowledge in education and how are culture, language, and identity implicated?
- How does the act of struggle relate to the building of healthy and holistic ways of knowing, being, and learning? How does the act of struggle teach us about who we are, prompt us to question what we want to be, and push us to consider what is possible in education?
- Where are the current and future sites of struggle and how can communities meet them and learn from them?

Fundamental Considerations: The Deep Meaning of Native American Schooling, 1880–1900

DAVID WALLACE ADAMS

> This they tell, and whether it
> happened so or not I do not know;
> but if you think about it,
> you can see that it is true.
> — from *Black Elk Speaks* by John Neihardt

"These are great evils; and it must be added that they appear to me to be irremediable." Alexis de Tocqueville used these terms to characterize the ways that the young republic treated its native peoples in his now classic *Democracy in America*. Tocqueville's judgment was not the result of casual speculation. In his tour of America he had observed firsthand the tragic consequences that occurred when Indian societies stood in the path of "the most grasping nation on the globe."

> At the end of the year 1831, while I was on the left bank of the Mississippi, at a place named by Europeans Memphis, there arrived a numerous band of Choctaws. . . . These savages had left their country and were endeavoring to gain the right bank of the Mississippi, where they hoped to find an asylum that had been promised them by the American government. It was then the middle of winter, and the cold was unusually severe; the snow had frozen hard upon the ground, and the river was drifting huge masses of ice. The Indians had their families with them, and they brought in their train the wounded and the sick, with children newly born and old men upon the verge of death. They possessed neither tents nor wagons, but only their arms and some provisions. I saw them embark to pass the mighty river, and never will that solemn spectacle fade from my remembrance. No cry, no sob, was heard among the assembled crowd; all were silent. Their calamities were of ancient date, and they knew them to be irremediable. The Indians had all stepped into the bark that was to carry them across, but their dogs remained upon the bank. As soon as these animals perceived that their masters were finally leaving the shore, they set up a dismal howl, and plunging all together into the icy waters of the Mississippi, swam after the boat.[1]

Tocqueville understood all too well that removal was at best only a temporary solution to the "Indian problem." As White settlers pushed ever westward, oblivious and contemptuous of Indian ways and treaty agreements, the same uneven confrontation between the two races would be repeated on succeeding frontiers, and with the same results. Indian removal only postponed the long-term question of what place, if any, the Native American would have in the American empire. The keen-eyed Frenchman was pessimistic: "I believe that the Indian nations of North America are doomed to perish, and that whenever the Europeans shall be established on the shores of the Pacific Ocean, that race of men will have ceased to exist."[2]

Throughout the nineteenth century, two visions of the Indian's future struggled for dominance in the minds of policymakers. One of them predicted, as Tocqueville's did, that the Indian was doomed to extinction. In this vision Indians, like characters in a Cooper novel, would retreat ever deeper into the forest in an attempt to live out their last days as a dying race in accordance with ancestral customs. According to this view, even if the hand of philanthropy were extended by a beneficent government, the "Red Man" would be either unable or unwilling to grasp it. Reinforced by the frontier mentality of Indian-hating and the continued call for land concessions, this attitude prevailed all too often in the councils of Washington. But a second and contradictory vision is also evident throughout the course of Indian-White relations. From this perspective, Indians, like most other members of the human family, were creatures of environmental and historical circumstance, fully capable of being transformed and assimilated once exposed to the "superior" influences of White society. This was clearly the view of the Congress in 1819, when it created a "civilization fund" to support missionaries on the frontier. The House Committee on Indian Affairs exhorted the Congress thus: "Put into the hands of their children the primer and the hoe, and they will naturally, in time, take hold of the plow; and as their minds become enlightened and expand, the Bible will be their book, and they will grow up in habits of morality and industry, leave the chase to those of minds less cultured, and become useful members of society."[3]

By midcentury, the Indian's fate was still unresolved, and, by 1880, the time for postponement had run out. The earlier policies of removal had now reached their logical conclusion in the form of the Indian reservation. Now, with the near extinction of the buffalo, with renewed demands by Whites for Indian land, and with the iron rails of the locomotive snaking their way across the vast stretches of prairie, it was clear that the days of the Indian were numbered. Census figures told the story. The Indian population continued to decline with each decade: 1850–400,764; 1860–339,421; 1870–313,712; 1880–306,543; 1890–248,253.[4] It was in this context that policymakers moved aggressively to assimilate the Indian into the mainstream of American life. Their efforts were greatly aided by the rise of several organizations devoted specifically to the reform of Indian policy, notably the Indian Rights Association, the Lake Mohonk Conference, and the Women's National Indian Association. These groups, together with the older Board of Indian Commissioners, led a well-coordinated effort to solve the "Indian problem" along humanitarian lines.[5]

Much of this assimilation campaign focused on education. Annual congressional appropriations for Indian education rose from $75,000 in 1880 to nearly $3 million in 1900.[6] In 1891 Congress declared that school attendance for Indian children should be compulsory. Two years later it added teeth to the measure by authorizing the Indian Bureau to "withhold rations, clothing, and other annuities" from those parents who resisted sending their children to school.[7] While these measures held weight only where schools were in existence, they provided the legal basis for stricter enforcement of school attendance. In fact, between 1880 and 1900 the number of Indian children enrolled in school more than quadrupled from 4,651 to 21,568, the latter figure representing over one-half of all Indian children of school age.[8] By 1900, Congress had created a network of Indian schools composed of 147 reservation day schools, 81 reservation boarding schools, and 25 off-reservation boarding schools.[9]

This dramatic growth in Indian schooling reflects the sublime faith that Americans in general, and reformers in particular, placed in schools as agencies for social cohesion and assimilation. The extent of that faith is captured by Annie Beecher Scoville, a missionary to the Sioux, in her remarks at Lake Mohonk in 1901. Having observed the government's feverish efforts to construct schools among the Sioux, she observed:

> If there is an idol that the American people have, it is the school. What gold is to the miser, the schoolhouse is to the Yankee. If you don't believe it go out to Pine Ridge, where there are seven thousand Sioux on eight million acres of land incapable of supporting these people, and find planted over that stretch of territory thirty-two schoolhouses, standing there as a testimony to our belief in education. There is something whimsical in planting schoolhouses where no man can read, far from the highways, unneighbored by farms, and planted, not at the request of the Sioux, but because we believed it was good for them! It is a remedy for barbarism we think, and so we give the dose. Uncle Sam is like a man setting a charge of powder. The school is the slow match. He lights it and goes off whistling, sure that in time it will blow up the old life, and of its shattered pieces he will make good citizens.[10]

My purpose in this article is to reveal the fundamental considerations that underlay the late nineteenth-century campaign for the establishment of Indian schools. To characterize this campaign as merely another use of the common school as an instrument for assimilation misses, in my view, the deeper historical significance of the determined crusade to school the Native American in the ways of White society. I will examine the subject from three interpretive vantage points, and while I will occasionally discuss life in Indian schools for the purpose of illustration, my primary focus will be on the rhetoric of reform. This article, then, is largely a study of reformers' motives and how those motives were translated into educational policy.

The Protestant Ideology

The first interpretive perspective I will utilize is that of the so-called Protestant ideology.[11] In the work of John Higham, Carl Kaestle, and David Tyack and Elizabeth Hansot, ideology is seen as a set of interconnected and mutually reinforcing beliefs and values that provide members of a given society with a sense of who they are as a collective cultural enterprise and where they fit into the historical scheme of things.

Using this broad definition, historians have undertaken the difficult task of sorting out the various strands of American ideology that gave rise to the common school in the first half of the nineteenth century. The result has been an emerging consensus around the importance of three seminal elements in American thought: Protestantism, capitalism, and republicanism. Briefly stated, the thesis is that the pan-Protestant values of common-school reformers — the importance of Bible reading, individual salvation, and personal morality — were conveniently linked to the secular values inherent in nascent capitalism; namely, the emphasis on personal industry, the sanctity of private property, and the ideal of "success." The fusion of religious and economic values made the dominant ideology powerful enough, but when these ideals were incorporated into a larger vision of national destiny — an aspect of republican thought that went beyond idealizing constitutional democracy as a form of government — the ideology assumed truly mythic proportions. As Higham notes: "America began to be seen as the spiritual center of Christendom. Thus, the Protestant ideology, instead of enshrining a single creed, exalted a sacred place."[12] By providential intention, America had a millennial destiny to impose its system onto those who stood in the path of its march to the Pacific. And if Protestantism, capitalism, and republicanism constituted the core of the ideology, the common school was seen as the natural instrument for transmitting it to rising generations of American youth.[13]

The question before us is the following: Can the Protestant ideology, which played such an important role in defining the goals of the common-school movement in the first half of the nineteenth century, also aid us in understanding the aims of Indian education in the last two decades of that century? At first, one might think not. Higham argues, for instance, that in the late nineteenth century the integrating force of the Protestant ideology gradually began to wane and give way to the more intensified and cohesive force of "technical unity."[14] Tyack and others have clearly established how this development manifested itself in the sphere of education, where a new generation of educational leaders labored to apply the principles of centralization, specialization, standardization, and meritocracy to all aspects of school life.[15] The quest for the "one best system" makes for an important story, yet it would be a misreading of the period to assert that the rise of educational bureaucracies somehow condemned evangelical Protestants to playing bit parts in the new educational drama. Quite the contrary. As demonstrated by Robert T. Handy, Protestantism in post–Civil War America continued to be an "aggressive dynamic form of Christianity that set out confidently to confront American life at every level, to permeate, evangelize, and Christianize it."[16] Most important, Protestants continued to wield immense influence over the course of the nation's schools. William J. Reese argues correctly that "American Evangelical Protestants of the turn of the century could still rejoice that the schools were safely theirs."[17]

Particularly significant to this story is the fact that those involved in reshaping the nation's Indian policy were firmly rooted in the Protestant tradition and, more to the point, were thoroughly imbued with the three cardinal elements of that ideology: Protestantism, capitalism, and republicanism. Indeed, by slightly recasting these three themes into Protestantism, individualization, and Americanization, we are provided with a useful angle for understanding late nineteenth-century Indian schooling. As it turns out, all three themes figured prominently in discussions concerning Indian education.

The importance placed on individualization stemmed from the belief that the greatest barrier to the Indians' assimilation was their attachment to the tribal community over and above their own individual advancement. This attachment reflected two aspects of Indian society that reformers viewed as particularly loathsome: the Indians' longstanding adherence to communal values and their general disdain for the White man's work ethic. The problem was especially acute given the fact that many reservations were almost totally dependent upon government rations for day-to-day subsistence.

With the eradication of the buffalo and the rise of the reservation system, hunting-oriented economies all but collapsed. Young warriors who had once been honored for their hunting skill were now reduced to gathering at the agency for bi-weekly distributions of flour, sugar, coffee, and periodically, beef. What was particularly infuriating to reformers was that, in the face of such humiliating dependency, all too many Indians remained contemptuous of what Whites saw as the only path to self-respecting manhood; namely, the endless toil associated with eking out an existence from the soil. The situation was even more complicated by the Indian's lack of desire to accumulate more wealth than his neighbors; and indeed, once he did accumulate it, to squander it in elaborate gift-giving ceremonies.[18] It followed that a major objective of policymakers was to convert the Indian child to the ideal of the self-reliant man. This effort took two forms: industrial training and the inculcation of values.

In boarding schools, which accounted for a majority of Indians enrolled, half of the student's day was devoted to some form of manual or industrial training. This practice followed from the belief, as expressed by one school superintendent, that "the best education for the aborigines of our country is that which inspires them to become producers instead of remaining consumers." He maintained that although acquiring rudimentary academic skills was surely important, it was even more fundamental to teach the Indian child how to work: "A string of textbooks piled up in the storehouses high enough to surround a reservation if laid side by side will never educate a being with centuries of laziness instilled in his race."[19] Because policymakers believed that the Indian's future depended upon the schools' success at transforming hunters into farmers, it followed that boys were taught those skills required for self-sufficient farming: plowing, planting, harvesting, fence-building, stock-raising, wagon-making, harness-making, carpentry, and blacksmithing. Likewise, Indian girls were taught skills deemed appropriate for the rural housewife and mother: cooking, cleaning, and sewing.[20]

Individualization also entailed persuading the student to embrace a cluster of related values and beliefs that, taken together, served to portray capitalism as a model social order and the rugged individualist as an ideal personality. For U.S. Senator Henry Dawes, the solution to the Indian problem was to "teach him to stand alone first, then to walk, then to dig, then to plant, then to hoe, then to gather, and then to *Keep*" — the last step being a vital one.[21] Similarly, Merrill Gates reminded those at Lake Mohonk in 1896 that the primary challenge to philanthropy was to awaken "wants" in the Indian. Then, and only then, Gates argued, could the Indian be coaxed "out of the blanket and into trousers and trousers with a *pocket that aches to be filled with dollars*"! [emphasis added][22] Commissioner of Indian Affairs John Oberly believed that the Indian student should be taught the "exalting egotism of American civilization, so that he will say 'I' instead of 'We,' and 'This is mine' instead of 'This is ours.'"[23] Thus did educators seek to create in the Indian student's mind the mental and moral concept of possessive individualism. In textbooks, classrooms, workshops, and sermons, the importance of the key American values of industriousness, thrift, perseverance, and acquisitiveness was continually drummed home. For the students at Phoenix Indian School, the message of individualism came in the form of a poem, "There's Always a Way," printed in the school newspaper:

> There's always a way to rise, my boy,
> Always a way to advance;
> Yet the road that leads to Mount Success
> Does not pass by the way of chance
> But goes through the stations of Work and Strife,
> Through the valley of Persevere.
> And the man that succeeds, while others fail,
> Must be willing to pay most dear.[24]

The Protestant ideology also required that the Indian child be Christianized and, ideally, Protestantized. Reformers invariably dismissed the Indian's native religion as a hodgepodge of barbaric rites and ceremonies totally

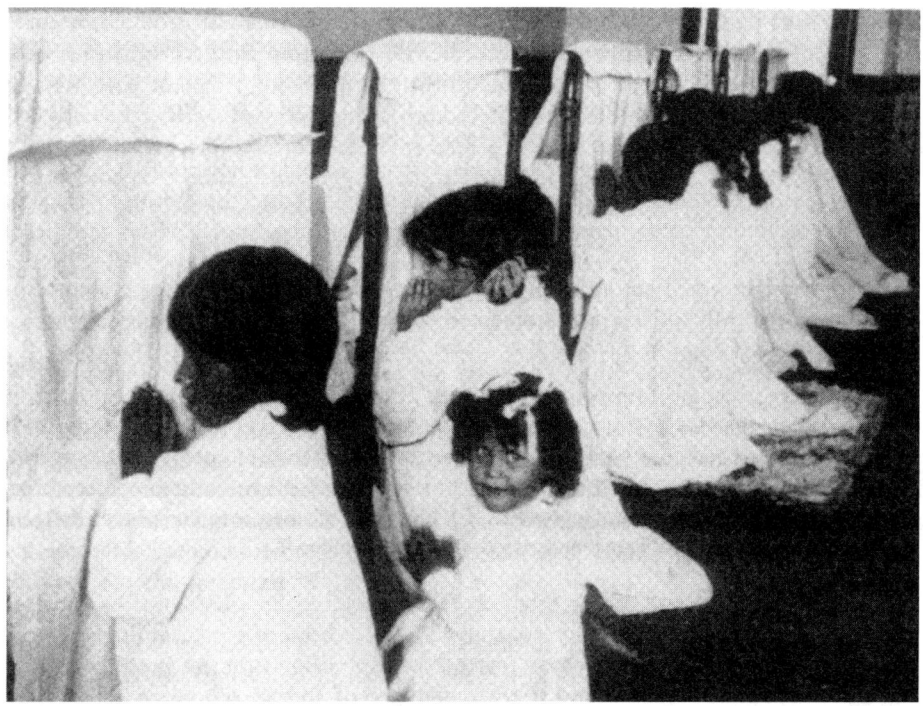

"Good Night," Phoenix Boarding School, 1900.

devoid of any moral content. Beyond this, native beliefs were condemned for encouraging in Indians a naive and childish tendency to seek spiritual meanings and truth in the natural world, for their failure to acknowledge any association between religious activity and material advancement, and finally, for their acceptance of polygamous marriage and extended kinship relationships as legitimate and desirable social arrangements.[25] What reformers were objecting to was the fact that Native American religions reinforced and reflected the values and cultural patterns of Indian life, something they were committed to erasing.[26]

It followed that the religious aims of Indian schooling fell into two categories. On the one hand, reformers believed that Indian children should be introduced to essential Christian doctrine, and in the process come to feel the "pulsing life-tide of Christ's life." On the other hand, they should be subjected to a rigorous program of moral training. It was in this realm that the religious and acquisitive values of Protestant America were to be given complementary expression. Indian children must be taught to love their neighbor, but they must also be told about "the road that leads to Mount Success."[27]

The Christian message was communicated in a number of ways. In day schools, it came in the form of *McGuffey Readers,* classroom prayers, and hymn singing. In boarding schools, it was expressed in the form of Sunday church services, nightly prayer meetings, and a host of religious clubs. Native American autobiographies from this period clearly show that the Protestant impulse profoundly influenced life in Indian schools. For instance, Jason Betzinez, an Apache, tells us that his introduction to Christianity came at Carlisle Indian School in Pennsylvania, where, as a result of attending church on Sundays and frequent prayer meetings, the "influence became stronger and stronger as I came to understand English better. It changed my whole life."[28] Similarly, Thomas Wildcat Alford, a Shawnee, who on the eve of departure for a distant boarding school was instructed by tribal chiefs not to listen to the White man's preaching, also fell under the spell of the evangelical promise. At first, Alford was able to resist the religious onslaught, "but as time passed," he explains, "and the interest of my teachers became stronger, their pleas more insistent, I could not ignore the subject. I began to consider the religious beliefs and to study the Gospel of Jesus Christ." In time, he wrote, he came to know "deep in my soul that Jesus Christ was my Savior."[29] Don Talayesva, a Hopi boy who attended an off-reservation school in Riverside, California, tells us of being torn between his ancestral Hopi beliefs and the White man's religion. He remembers conjuring up this sermon for the school YMCA meeting:

> Well, my partners, I am asked to speak a few words for Jesus. I am glad that I came to Sherman and learned to read and cipher. Now I discover that Jesus was a good writer. So I am thankful that Uncle Sam taught me to read in order that I may understand the Scriptures and take my steps along God's road. When I get a clear understanding of the Gospel I shall return home and preach it to my people in darkness. I will teach them all I know about Jesus Christ, the Heavenly Father, and the Holy Ghost. So I advise you boys to do your best and pray to God to give us a good understanding. Then we will be ready for Jesus to come and take us up to heaven. I don't want any of my friends to be thrown into the lake of hell fire where there is suffering and sorrow forever. Amen.[30]

These passages should not be taken as representative responses to the Christian message; many students, to the exasperation of school officials, stubbornly adhered to their native beliefs. These passages simply illustrate the extent to which the evangelical spirit permeated the atmosphere of Indian schooling.

When policymakers turned to the third aim of Indian schooling — Americanization — they were primarily addressing the issue of the Indian's future political status. Two issues were involved here: the status of the tribal unit as a collective political entity (that is to say, tribal sovereignty), and the individual Indian's citizenship status. In the minds of reformers the two issues were inextricably linked: the elimination of tribal sovereignty would facilitate the individual Indian's entry into citizenship. The political sovereignty of Indian tribes had, in fact, been eroding steadily throughout the nineteenth century. By 1871, when Congress declared that the government would no longer conduct its relations with Indians by treaty, the process was nearly complete; henceforth, Indians were to be regarded as mere "wards" of the government.[31] Meanwhile, the Indian reservation was an anomaly in the American system. Only when Indians were separated from the larger tribal unit, the government held, would they be truly fit for citizenship. Congress could simply declare them citizens, but was hesitant to do so. Most policymakers agreed with Commissioner of Indian Affairs Ezra Hayt, who contended that Indians needed "a long tutelage before launching them into the world to manage their own affairs."[32] On two questions, then, reformers were in agreement: First, the Indians' connections to their tribal unit and the reservation had to be severed if they were to be absorbed into the larger body politic; and second, the government had a special responsibility to prepare them for citizenship. In this matter the schools would have a special role to play.

Education for citizenship focused on language instruction and political socialization. The connection between language and citizenship stemmed from the belief that, along with all citizens, the Indian child should be compelled to read, write, and speak the English language. As Commissioner of Indian Affairs J. D. C. Atkins argued in 1887: "If we expect to infuse into the rising generation the leaven of American citizenship, we must remove the stumbling blocks of hereditary customs and manners, and of these language is one of the most important elements." According to Atkins, "no unity or community of feeling can be established among different peoples unless they are brought to speak the same language and thus become imbued with the like ideas of duty."[33] That same year, John Riley, Superintendent of Indian Schools, echoed the sentiments of his superior. Teaching English to the Indian, he argued, would reduce the Indian's prejudice toward the White man's ways, would enhance the Indian's understanding of the "spirit of the laws and institutions under which they are to live," and finally, would lessen their vulnerability to "unprincipled white men."[34] The bottom line was that Indians, as a colonized people, could legitimately be expected to take on the tongue of their conquerors. Again, according to Atkins, citizenship required a certain amount of cultural absorption and "nothing so surely and perfectly stamps upon an individual a national characteristic as language." Besides, Atkins continued, "this language, which is good enough for a white man and a black man, ought to be good enough for the red man."[35]

If the issue of language was largely instrumental, the real focus of citizenship education was the Indian's political socialization. On the one hand, this meant instruction in the rights and duties of citizenship and in the principles of the U.S. Constitution. No less important, however, was the need to awaken a "fervent patriotism" in Indian students. They should, according to Commissioner Morgan, "be taught to look upon America as their home and upon the United States Government as their friend and benefactor."[36] The campaign to win the Indian's political allegiance was in part carried out in the traditional U.S. History course.[37] Beyond textbook instruction, schools were encouraged to teach students patriotic songs, political recitations, and, perhaps most important, involve them in patriotic rituals, including the celebration of national holidays.

Since boarding-school students wore special government uniforms and were subjected to a daily routine of marching and drilling, these patriotic rituals occasionally assumed elaborate proportions. When President William McKinley visited Phoenix Indian School in 1901, for example, the entire student body performed a highly disciplined marching routine before lining up in front of the President, who looked on from the reviewing stand. "There they stood for an instant, 700 pairs of eyes gazing sharply and intently at the 'great father,'" the school newspaper reported, and then at the sound of a bugle, the Indians roared in unison: "I give my head and my heart to my country; one country, one language, and one flag."[38]

In remote outposts, patriotic rituals were more modest, but equally pointed. A Hopi memoir describes an observance at a reservation boarding school in the Southwest: "In May we had a decoration celebration. We stuck little flags in our caps, took bunches of flowers, and marched out to the graves of two soldiers who had come out here to fight the Hopi and had died."[39] In another school, students were asked to participate in a political pageant celebrating the day that Europeans first set foot on the shores of the New World. An Indian student, dressed as Columbus, recited the lines:

> Then boomed the Pinta's signal gun!
> The first that ever broke
> The sleep of the new world — the sound
> Echoing to forest depths profound,
> A continent awoke![40]

A continent awoke? From what? This question suggests another line of investigation, one that explores the idea that reformers, in their discussion of Indian policy in general and Indian schooling in particular, were forced to draw upon images more fundamental than those generated by the Protestant ideology, images at least as old as that fateful day in 1492, when Columbus and his band of voyagers first confronted not only a New World, but, as Tzvetan Todorov has put it, "the question of the other," the people Columbus called *Indios*.[41]

The Civilization-Savagism Paradigm

When Europeans, and later, European-Americans, first encountered the Native American's "otherness," they made a distinction between Indians and Whites that by the late eighteenth century had become the central reference point for explaining the cultural chasm that separated the two races. The basic idea was that peoples on the globe were at various stages in their evolution from "savagism" to "civilization." As the theory went, while the Whites were for the most part civilized, Indians were still largely savages. There was room for minor variations where particular groups or societies were involved, but the generalization was said to be true in the main. Because Indians — and here the images came flooding forth — indulged in barbaric religious practices, relied on hunting and gathering for subsistence, were disdainful of private property and wealth, and generally lived out their lives in pagan ignorance of all things civilized, they were culturally worthless. Sometimes noble, sometimes ignoble, they were nevertheless savages.[42]

Central to the civilization–savagism paradigm was the concept of historical process. History was seen as the story of man's progressive movement toward the ideal of civilization. If one wished to see the process unfold, one had only to look at America. Near the end of his life Jefferson wrote to a friend:

> Let a philosophic observer commence a journey from the savages of the Rocky Mountains, eastwardly towards our sea-coast. These he would observe in the earliest stage of association living under no law but that of nature, subsisting and covering themselves with the flesh and skins of wild beasts. He would next find those on our frontiers in the pastoral state, raising domestic animals to supply the defects of hunting. Then succeed our own semi-barbarous citizens, the pioneers of the advance of civilization, and so in his progress he would meet the gradual shades of improving man until he would reach his, as yet, most improved state in our seaport towns. This, in fact, is equivalent to a survey, in time, of the progress of man from the infancy of creation to the present day.[43]

Just as savagery must give way to civilization, Jefferson and his contemporaries reasoned, so Indian ways must give way to White ways. Whether Indians as a people would survive remained an open question. Jefferson seems to have genuinely hoped and believed that they would. In any event, traditional Indian ways were destined to perish. The alternatives before them were clear: civilization or extinction.[44]

Throughout the nineteenth century, the idea of civilization remained a fixed reference point in all discussions of the Indian question. Coincidentally, in 1877, just as the movement to reform Indian policy was getting under way, the idea received impressive scholarly support with the appearance of Lewis Henry Morgan's *Ancient Society*.[45] A cultural evolutionist, Morgan identified seven stages in the path to human progress: lower savagery, middle savagery, upper savagery, lower barbarism, middle barbarism, upper barbarism, and civilization. On Morgan's scale, North American Indians fell somewhere between middle savagery and middle barbarism, depending upon the particular attributes of a given culture. Numerous factors determined where Morgan placed various societies on his categorical scale, but three were deemed to be of particular importance in the passage to civilization: the acceptance of monogamous marriage and the nuclear family as the basic unit in society, the reliance on agriculture as the basis for subsistence, and a firm belief in private property as the proper basis for economic and social organization. Morgan found Indian societies wanting in one or more of these criteria. Nevertheless, he was convinced that Indians, with proper guidance from a benevolent government, were fully capable of acquiring civilized ways and eventually being absorbed into the mainstream of American life.[46]

Late nineteenth-century reformers subscribed not only to the law of civilized progress, but also to its corollary, that the Indians' only hope for survival depended upon their assimilation into mainstream American society. According to Commissioner of Indian Affairs Henry Price: "Savage and civilized life cannot live and prosper on the same ground. One of the two must die."[47] As Secretary of the Interior Carl Shurz pointed out, time was of the essence: "To civilize them, which was once only a benevolent fancy, has now become an absolute necessity, if we mean to save them." Indians were a dying race.[48]

Since Indians were on the brink of extinction, the civilization–savagism paradigm posed a question that was of immense importance to the Indians' destiny: Must the process of social evolution be as painstakingly slow for Indians as it had been for Whites? No, reformers answered; where human progress was involved, historical time was to be measured in relative rather than absolute terms. Moreover, the school could be the instrument for hastening the evolutionary process. As Commissioner Morgan pointed out, a civilizing education was capable of carrying a single generation of Indian youth across "the dreary chasm of a thousand years of tedious evolution."[49] Addressing the Lake Mohonk Conference, U.S. Commissioner of Education William Torrey Harris concurred:

> But shall we say to the tribal people that they shall not come to these higher things unless they pass through all the intermediate stages, or can we teach them directly these higher things, and save them from the slow progress of the ages? In the light of Christian civilization we say there is a method of rapid progress. Education has become of great potency in our hands, and we believe that we can now vicariously save them very much that the white race has had to go through. Look at feudalism. Look at the village community stage. . . . We have had our tribulation with them. But we say to lower races: we can help you out of these things. We can help you avoid the imperfect stages that follow them on the way to our level. Give us your children and we will educate them in the Kindergarten and in the schools. We will give them letters, and make them acquainted with the printed page. With these comes emancipation from mere personal authority, from the authority of the master, from the authority of the overseer and the oracle. With these comes the great emancipation, and the school will give you that.[50]

Schools, then, could not only civilize; they could civilize quickly.

It should be clear by now that where the education of Indians was concerned, fundamental and unique considerations come into play that are unaccounted for in the Protestant ideology. To be sure, there is nothing in the first interpretation that contradicts the one emerging here. Indeed, one might reasonably argue that nineteenth-century discussions on the fate of the Indian were simply the by-product of the historical forces unleashed by one of the most consequential strands in the Protestant ideology; namely, the belief that it was America's destiny to extend European-American institutions and ways of life across the continent. Moreover, the doctrine of progress was certainly as deeply embedded in the tradition of evangelical Protestantism as it was in the Enlightenment tradition of Jefferson. The fact remains, however, that when policymakers turned their attention to the Indian question, they invariably shifted to a frame of reference and a descriptive language tailor-made for the occasion — they shifted to the civilization–savagism model. Needless to say, to define the Indian's "otherness" in terms of savagery was more than a little self-serving. To dismiss the Indian as a savage was surely a convenient means of legitimizing the history of Indian-White relations, a history that, if viewed objectively, might cast a shadow over the righteous pretensions of the American empire.

It should be noted that the Protestant ideology, including its educational prescriptions (Protestantization, individualization, and Americanization), was certainly relevant to the discussion of what it would take to civilize the Indian. When policymakers spoke of Christianizing Indians, they always assumed that their conversion would be an important step in civilizing them as well. Thus, Merrill Gates proclaimed at Lake Mohonk that introducing the Indian to Christianity could "do in one generation most of that which evolution takes centuries to do."[51] And although the reformers preferred that Protestantism prevail over Catholicism in the battle for the Indian's heart and soul, most saw the Indian's conversion from paganism to any Christian faith as progress. Even Herbert Welsh, well known for his anti-Catholic sentiment, could appreciate the fact that "the great religious bodies, the Roman communion on the one side, and the Protestant communions on the other, should try to recognize the value of each other's work, at least as an instrument of civilization."[52] Citizenship education was regarded as a civilizing force as well. Instruction in the rights and duties of citizenship would prepare the Indian child for full participation in the political life of one of the most civilized nations on earth. As for language instruction, Commissioner Atkins was convinced that "the first step to be taken toward civilization, toward teaching the Indians the mischief and folly of continuing in their barbarous practices, is to teach them in the English language."[53] Finally, the Indian's individualization would surely advance the cultural elevation process. "There is an utter barbarism in which property has almost no existence," claimed Merrill Gates. "The tribal organization tends to retain men in such barbarism. It is a great step gained when you awaken in an Indian the desire for the acquisition of property of his own, by his own honest labor."[54] In this respect, as in others, the Protestant ideology shaped reformers' thinking as to what they must teach the Indians if they were to civilize them.

The idea of civilization, however, remained a fundamental frame of reference for discussions on Indian education. Its impact on the overall direction of Indian schooling can be illustrated in three ways. First, it set the boundaries for one of the most troublesome questions confronting the Indian Bureau: What type of institution — the day school, the reservation boarding school, or the off-reservation boarding school — was best suited to accomplish the Indian child's transformation? This question forced policymakers to return to first principles. In time, they would conclude that the civilizing process could be carried out most effectively if it were conducted in an environment isolated from the countervailing influence of savagery, that is, at a distance from the tribal community. By the late 1870s, this resulted in a general preference for the reservation boarding school over the day school. The problem with the day school, officials in the field complained, was that although children were taught the curriculum of civilization during the day, they were instructed in the ways of savagery at night. By removing children from the camp and cloistering them in a boarding school for nine months of the year, the civilizing process could be carried on much more efficiently.[55]

By the early 1880s, however, the enthusiasm for reservation boarding schools had begun to wane. Students, it seemed, still felt the pull of traditional life beyond the school fence, and they frequently ran away. Furthermore, during the annual summer vacation, many students suffered severe cases of "relapse." More than one Indian agent would observe "how soon they seem to forget all they have been taught, after they return to camp."[56] According to another agent:

> Immediately following the close of the school the children laid aside the clothing furnished them and donned the kind the camp Indians wear. A number of them continue to come about the agency, but not a word can one be induced to speak in English. They attend our Sabbath services, but they can not be prevailed upon to sing, while in school the majority of them sing elegantly. These are some of the reasons why the results of the school are not satisfactory to me. I really believe that one year's schooling away from the influence of the camp Indians would do the child more good than four at the agency.[57]

A good number of policymakers and reformers agreed. The result was the creation of a new institution, the off-reservation boarding school, where students were schooled in the ways of Whites for an uninterrupted period of five years before returning home. As it turned out, both types of boarding schools, reservation and off-reservation, would remain the cornerstone of the Indian school system for years to come. One thing remained certain: in order for savagism to be countermanded, the Indian child had to be educated in an isolated environment. Hence, by 1900 close to 85 percent of Indian children enrolled in school were attending boarding schools.[58]

A second impact of the idea of civilization on Indian schooling can be seen by examining the nature of the educational program itself; namely, the sheer comprehensiveness of it. A close examination of the institutional life of

Indian schools reveals that they were waging an all-out assault on the child's "otherness." For the war against savagery to be successful, reformers decided, it must be waged uncompromisingly on every aspect of the child's being. Thus, while their bronze skin would never wash white, the Indian children could otherwise be taught to look, dress, eat, walk, and think like civilized Whites. The alteration process can be seen in the following account of the opening day at Pine Ridge boarding school in South Dakota, about 1880. The description was written by Julia McGillycuddy, wife of the government's agent, Valentine McGillycuddy.

> On the opening day, hundreds of curious Indians — bucks, squaws, and children — hung about the building wondering just what was going to happen to the 200 youngsters sequestered within it. McGillycuddy advised pulling down the shades at the windows in the large bathroom on the ground floor to exclude the gaze of the inquisitive.
>
> The first step toward civilizing these primitive children was to purge them of various uncleanliness. The several bathrooms as well as the laundry were the scenes of activity, the hair-cutting to be accomplished first, followed by a bath which would include washing the heads as a labor-saving device.
>
> In each bathroom a teacher armed with shears was prepared to begin operations. Curious peepers stood close to the windows on the ground floor, deeply regretful of the drawn shades which barred their observation of the activities carried on behind them. There the matron seated a small boy and taking a lousy braid in one hand, raised the shears hanging by a chain from her waist. A single clip and the filthy braid could be severed. But unfortunately, at that moment a breeze blew back the shade from the window. The previously baffled effort of a youngster plastered against the casing on the outside of the window was now rewarded by a fleeting glimpse of his playmate seated in the chair and a tall lean woman with a pair of shears in her hand prepared to divest the boy of his hair — Delilah bringing calamity upon an embryo Samson.
>
> Like a war whoop rang out the cry: *"Pahin kaksa, pahin kaksa!"* The enclosure rang with alarm, it invaded every room in the building and floated out on the prairie. No warning of fire or flood or tornado or hurricane, not even the approach of an enemy could have more effectively emptied the building as well as the grounds of the new school as did the ominous cry. "They are cutting the hair!" Through doors and windows the children flew, down the steps, through the gates and over fences in mad flight toward the Indian villages, followed by the mob of bucks and squaws as though all were pursued by a bad spirit. They had been suspicious of the school from the beginning; now they knew it was intended to bring disgrace upon them.
>
> McGillycuddy's raised hands, his placating shouts, and his stern commands were less effective than they had been on occasions of threatened outbreak. He was impotent to stem the flight. He calmed the excited teachers, assuring them that the schoolhouse would soon again be filled with children. But their faces expressed disappointment as well as chagrin over the apparent failure of his attempt to civilize the Sioux.[59]

All this was necessary, we are expected to understand, because Indians were too savage to know what was good for them. This leads us to a third implication of the civilization ideal — namely the belief that the student must be made to embrace the essential elements of the civilization–savagism paradigm. The Indian child must come to know what Whites already knew — that Whites were civilized and Indians were savages. The entire boarding school experience, of course, implied this message, but occasionally the point had to be made outright. At Hampton Institute in Hampton, Virginia, for instance, where Indians were educated along with Blacks, it appears to have permeated the entire curriculum.[60] Thus, the following section of a student's examination was published in the school newspaper under the heading "Work and Fun in the Geography Class":

9. To what race do we all belong?
9. The Human race.
10. How many classes belong to this race?
10. There are five large classes belonging to the Human race.
11. Which are the first?
11. The white people are the strongest.
12. Which are the next?
12. The Mongolians or yellows.
13. The next?
13. The Ethiopians or blacks.
14. Next?
14. The Americans or reds.
15. Tell me something of the white people.
15. The Caucasian is away ahead of all of the other races — he thought more than any other race, he thought that somebody must made the earth, and if the white people did not find that out, nobody would never know it — it is God who made the world.[61]

An underlying assumption of the civilization–savagism paradigm was that although Indians were at the bottom of the ladder of civilization, the ladder could eventually be climbed. The proper note to be struck, then, was one that simultaneously inspired both humiliation and hope in the student. In 1893, Philip Garrett, an influential member of the Indian Rights Association, attempted to strike just this note when addressing the graduating class of Carlisle Indian School. Garrett began by reminding his audience that their race had been "thrown by the providence of God in the pathway of a mighty and resistless tide of civilization." Since the only path of survival was to adopt civilized ways, Garrett continued, the Indian would have to make the best of a difficult situation. Indeed, they ought to be thankful for their situation. Left to their own resources and the painstakingly slow process of social evolution,

Bobtail and son, Cheyenne, Carlisle Indian Boarding School, circa 1900.

they might have been mired in the backwaters of savagery for several generations. Instead, a benevolent government was offering them a different and brighter prospect: Students had a "unique opportunity to show the marvelous change that can be wrought in a single generation by the aid of good schools, and the lessons of centuries."[62]

As one considers these statements, the question comes to mind: What were the ultimate concerns that drove reformers to make such statements? The answer, in part, no doubt lies in the fact that they truly believed them. As philanthropic spokesmen for Protestant America, they appear to have been utterly convinced that the Indian's only hope for survival lay in embracing White civilization. But there was another, perhaps more fundamental, consideration at work as well. And this leads us to still another perspective on the meaning of Indian schooling.

Taking the Land

This third perspective begins with the rude fact that in the beginning Indians possessed the land and Whites desperately wanted it. On the proposition that Indian land would eventually become White land there was never any serious debate. Both the Protestant ideology and the civilization–savagism paradigm presupposed and demanded it. In the meantime, the question of how the great transfer of real estate might be managed loomed large.[63]

The problem facing policymakers in Jefferson's time was how to dispossess Indians of large tracts of land without doing undue violence to their philanthropic ideals. Their ingenious solution to this dilemma was rooted in the conviction that it required much more land to support a nomadic hunting society than a like-sized population of sedentary farmers. Thus, the willingness of Indians to sell their land would be directly proportionate to their ability to acquire civilized ways. Moreover, in the civilizing process, they would be drawn inevitably into the White economy; they would come to hunger for the goods of Whites just as the White man hungered for Indian land. The pieces of the puzzle began to fall into place. "When [Indians] shall cultivate small spots of earth, and see how useless their extensive forests are," Jefferson wrote, "they will sell from time to time, to help out their personal labor in stocking their farms, and procuring clothes and comforts from our trading houses."[64] On another occasion he remarked: "While they are learning to do better on less land, our increasing numbers will be calling for more land, and thus a coincidence of interests."[65] The so-called "coincidence of interests" between the two races amounted to this: Indians possessed the land and needed civilization; Whites, on the other hand, had civilization but needed land. The philanthropic solution to the Indian question was now clear: a fair exchange whereby Whites would give the Indians civilization in return for land cessions — land the Indians would no longer require once they were civilized. This was the basis for an Indian policy characterized by one historian as "expansion with honor."[66]

As it turned out, there was very little honor to be had. The White hunger for land was far in excess of congressional willingness to fund civilization programs. Moreover, Native Americans proved to be less enthusiastic about committing cultural suicide than the Jeffersonians had surmised. The result was that Indian nations were first simply moved farther West, and in time were concentrated on reservations so that Whites might circumvent them in their rush across the continent. But the march of civilized progress was not to be stopped; eventually, even the reservation itself was looked upon as a new source of land. As Henry Pancoast, cofounder of the Indian Rights Association, noted in 1882: "The rush of Western settlement grows more and more; an enormous army pours forth continually into our Eastern seaports to spread itself over the West. How can we keep these still places in the midst of the current, a bit of stone age in the crush and fever of American enterprise?"[67] The answer, of course, was that it would be impossible; the only solution was civilization, which, once accomplished, would free up more land. As Commissioner Morgan reminded philanthropists in 1892: "A wild Indian requires a thousand acres to roam over, while an intelligent man will find a comfortable support for his family on a very small tract."[68]

Thus, while reformers were earnestly striving to save Indians from extinction by a process of assimilation, they were also mindful of the fact that under the reservation system Indians still possessed more land than they would ever need once they were transformed into farmers. Some reformers were even willing to challenge the idea that the Indians really owned the land to begin with. In the words of Lyman Abbott:

> It is sometimes said that the Indians occupied this country and that we took it away from them; that the country belonged to them. This is not true. The Indians did not occupy this land. A people do not occupy a country simply because they roam over it. They did not occupy the coal mines, nor the gold mines, into which they never struck a pick; nor the rivers which flow to the sea, and on which the music of a mill was never heard. The Indians can scarcely be said to have occupied this country more than the bisons and the buffalo they hunted. Three hundred thousand people have no right to hold a continent and keep at bay a race able to people it and provide the happy homes of civilization. We do owe the Indians sacred rights and obligations, but one of those duties is not the right to let them hold forever the land they did not occupy and which they were not making fruitful for themselves or others.[69]

Not all reformers went as far as Abbott, but all were convinced that the reservation system should be abandoned.

I do not mean to create the impression that reformers were primarily motivated by their desire to dispossess Indians of their land. Their opposition to the reservation system was rooted in several factors, not the least of which was the fact that it forestalled the Indian's absorption into national life. As we can see from the discussion above, however, the issues of land and national economic growth clearly figured into their considerations. In any event, the reservation system came under increasing attack in the 1880s from reformers, and, not surprisingly, from Western land interests, who had their own reasons for wanting to abolish the Indian reservation.

The result of this unholy alliance was one of the most important and devastating pieces of Indian legislation of the late nineteenth century — the General Allotment Act of 1887, more commonly called the Dawes Act after its chief sponsor, Senator Henry Dawes of Massachusetts. The Dawes Act authorized the President to select those reservations he deemed suitable for allotment, after which the following provisions came into effect: First, the reservation would be divided into individual allotments, the head of each family receiving 160 acres, with smaller allotments made to unmarried women and orphans. Second, to protect the new landholders from land-hungry Whites, title to the land would be held by the government for a period of twenty-five years, after which it would pass to its lawful owner. Third, holders of allotments would be granted U.S. citizenship. Finally, the surplus, unalloted lands would be sold off to Whites, the funds gained therefrom to be spent for the Indians' benefit, mainly for education.[70] Reformers looked upon the Dawes Act as a major milestone in their crusade to solve the Indian problem. In a single piece of legislation they believed they had found the mechanism to smash tribalism, transform hunters into farmers, and grant the Indians U.S. citizenship. Even the selling of the surplus lands would facilitate the process; as White settlers established productive homesteads on the available lands, they would inevitably prove to be positive role models for their Indian neighbors.[71]

Against this background, the campaign to educate the Indians takes on new meaning. First, allotment enables us to understand why educators placed so much emphasis on individualization and citizenship training — both were essential if the Indians were going to survive in their new citizen-farmer roles. Without such preparatory education, reformers pointed out, allotment would prove to be a cruel hoax. "Put an ignorant and imbruted savage on land of his own, and he remains a pauper, if he does not become a vagrant and a thief," claimed Lyman Abbott.[72] Charles Painter, lobbyist for the Indian Rights Association, agreed: "The reservation walls being down" he said, "and the retraining power of the agent broken, he [the Indian] and his children will become a race of wanderers and beggars, unless they are met . . . with influences wise enough and large enough to teach them the nobility of manhood and the uses of freedom." Painter then added: "There is now scope and hope for the schoolmaster."[73] The Dawes Act, then, helped to remind educators of what they must teach Indians if they were to survive and prosper as citizens.

A second connection between education and allotment stems from the fact that, in theory, the allotment process was to be set into motion on a given reservation only when the President, with the advice of the Indian Bureau, deemed a given Indian population capable of making the transition to a freeholding agricultural economy. Since surplus lands could not be sold until allotment was completed, it followed that educating Indians was a necessary preliminary to divesting them of excess lands. The connection between education and surplus lands would provide Commissioner Morgan with one of his most effective arguments for funding Indian education.

> [The] great economical fact is that the lands known as Indian reservations now set apart by the Government for Indian occupancy aggregate nearly 190,000 square miles. This land, for the most part, is uncultivated and unproductive. When the Indians shall have been properly educated they will utilize a sufficient quantity of those lands for their own support and will release the remainder that it may be restored to the public domain to become the foundation for innumerable happy homes; and thus will be added to the national wealth immense tracts of farming land and vast mineral resources which will repay the nation more than one hundred fold for the amount which it is proposed shall be expended in Indian education.[74]

Third, the issue of Indian land loss was inextricably connected to the school's efforts at citizenship education. The point here is that school officials occasionally felt compelled to address the issue that was at the heart of so much Indian–White conflict — the fact that Whites had nearly succeeded in dispossessing the Indians of the entire continent. The objective was to persuade the students to accept the idea that it was inevitable and entirely justified that the Indians lose their ancestral lands to a more progressive people. Some students did in fact come to internalize this point of view, as evidenced by this account of Indian–White relations by a Hampton pupil:

> Centuries ago we undoubtedly held full control over this fair land — this vast domain from east to west. Bodily we were free to roam, but our freedom of thought lay dormant as we slumbered heavily by the camp-fires of prosperity. What did the fertile valleys, the rich plain, the mineral treasures concealed in the hillsides mean to us? They simply told us that here was a good hunting ground, and there a good site for temporary habitation. But when the white man came he put everything in a new light. He saw how everything in nature could render him a service. 'Twas not long before we saw his engines making their way across our domains west-ward. Mountains were in his way, but he climbed them. Rivers were there, but he crossed them. When he was killed by our arrows, he, as it were, sprang up from his own ashes. He brought with him civilization and freedom. These constituted the power which made him a most formidable adversary. Our wanderings along his track proved a hindrance to his progress and we were driven away until finally we found ourselves penned on reservations with nothing to do and nothing to expect. . . . Since then we have entered upon a stage of civilization which brings with it problems hard for us to handle. This is our past.[75]

One suspects that such sentiments were relatively rare among Indian students, but this passage illustrates the ultimate political purpose to which the civilization theme might be applied. The civilization–savagism paradigm called for establishing political and cultural hegemony over Indians as a first step to their incorporation into American life. In the instance above, the process may be said to have merely reached its logical conclusion.[76]

School officials also made concerted efforts to win student support for the Dawes Act. Just two years after its enactment, Commissioner Morgan instructed school superintendents to observe annually the anniversary of the law's passage, along with other national holidays. The occasion might be used, explained Morgan, "to impress upon Indian youth the enlarged scope and opportunity given them by this law and the new obligations which it imposes."[77] For the next decade or so, especially at larger off-reservation schools, special efforts were made to celebrate the day with speeches, dramatic sketches, and elaborate pageants. In 1890, the Carlisle celebration of "Franchise Day" required students to listen to a recitation of a poem titled "A Message from Carlisle Students to the Indians." Apparently written by one of the school staff, but read by a student, the purpose of the poem was to dispel Indian fears that the Dawes Act, despite its promise of citizenship, was in reality nothing but a scheme to dispossess the Indian of more real estate. As the poem admits, taking land from the Indian was an old American story.

> You say we are poor, though a splendid dominion
> Of forests and rivers and mountains of gold
> Were ours, e'er the greed of the white man detained it;
> You are sorry and grumble that now it is sold.

The poem continues by pointing out that the government was now offering the Indian redress:

> Redress in this way, that though we as a Nation
> No more may hold sway o'er a boundless domain,
> Though tribes may be scattered like leaves of the maple
> And the pipes of our councils be smoked not again.
>
> Yet prospects more pleasant than these in the future
> And riches far better, our people may see,
> When learning, shall bring us a wealth more resplendent
> Than title to millions can possibly be.

Education, then, would compensate for the past dispossession of Indian lands, and presumably for those lost as a consequence of the Dawes Act as well.

> But welcome the ruin, if now by our losses,
> We gain thousand fold in a better estate.
> A man may be chief in the empire of reason.
> Education, not land, makes a citizen great.[78]

Celebrations of the Dawes Act were intended to evoke in students a genuine enthusiasm for the provision of the bill that awarded citizenship to allottees. One student responded:

> Now we are citizens
> We give him applause;
> So three cheers, my friends,
> To Senator Dawes![79]

For those students converted to the idea of civilization and the Protestant ideology, the Dawes Act indeed gave them something to celebrate. For others, those still not won over to the White man's way of thinking, the price of citizenship must have appeared too severe: the further loss of the tribal estate.[80]

Conclusion

This essay has been an attempt to peel away the layers of meaning behind the late nineteenth-century effort to school Native Americans in the ways of

"American Progress," chromolithograph, issued by George Crofutt, 1873.

Whites. My investigations have caused me to conclude that while the Protestant ideology tells us a great deal about the aims of Indian schooling during this period, it leaves a good deal unexplained as well. In particular, it leaves unexplained reformers' preoccupation with the concept of civilization and its counterpart, savagism. It also fails to make any direct connection between the objectives of Indian schooling and the most fundamental fact of Indian–White conflict, the fact that Whites were aggressively dispossessing Native Americans of their land. It might be argued that I have engaged in a bit of hairsplitting: that while the Protestant ideology failed to address the Indian question directly, its glorification of the American empire certainly implied the cultural inferiority of people who stood in its path; and that the Indian's loss of land was always rather blatantly assumed — in short, the handwriting was on the wall. Perhaps so, but this does not explain away the fact that when policymakers went about the business of designing an Indian school system, both the civilization–savagism paradigm and the issue of land possession became the fundamental points of reference for discussion. It is entirely understandable that this should be so. Although Protestant ideology might provide the necessary spiritual and ideational energy to propel the American empire westward, ever deeper into Indian country, it could not address in precise terms what it was about the Indians' "otherness" that justified systematic political and cultural subjugation, including the taking of their land.

Still, it was not irrelevant either. The Protestant ideology helped shape policymakers' ideas of what it meant to be civilized, of what Indians must become if they were to be saved from extinction. In the end, I would argue, the Protestant ideology, the civilization–savagism paradigm, and the White hunger for Indian land were all mutually reinforcing and hopelessly intertwined as factors influencing the educational campaign to assimilate the Indian.

A visual depiction of historical forces at work can be seen in George A. Crofutt's chromolithograph "American Progress," published in 1873 after an earlier painting by John Gast, and issued with an accompanying text, in which Crofutt sought to capture the quintessential spirit and meaning of the American experience.[81] At center stage is one of the most powerful icons of nineteenth-century America, Columbia, who, with the "Star of the Empire" on her forehead, drifts majestically westward over the American landscape. In one hand she carries the "talking wires" of the telegraph, a symbol of American progress, and in the other a large volume, which one would expect to be the Bible. Closer inspection, however, reveals the inscription "Schoolbook."

Crofutt's print can be read at several levels. On the one hand, it is an attempt to dramatically show a persistent strain in the Protestant ideology — the idea that America is a sacred place with a millennial destiny. But "American Progress" is about the idea of civilization as well; it is about the triumph of civilization over Indian savagism. Indeed, one can scarcely look at it without calling to mind Jefferson's vision of America as a panoramic representation of "the progress of man from the infancy of creation to the present day." In fact, the accompanying text relates:

> On the right of the picture is a city, steamships, manufactories, schools, and churches, over which beams of light are streaming and filling the air — indicative of civilization. The general tone of the picture on the left declares darkness, waste and confusion. From the city proceed the three great continental lines of railway, passing the frontier settlers' rude cabin, and tending toward the Western Ocean. Next to these are the transportation wagons, overland stage, hunters, gold seekers, pony express, the pioneer emigrant and the war-dance of the "noble red man." Fleeing from "Progress," and towards the blue waters of the Pacific, which shows itself on the left of the picture beyond the snow-capped summits of the Sierra Nevadas, are the Indians, buffaloes, wild horses, bears, and other game, moving Westward — ever Westward the Indians, with their squaws, papooses, and "pony lodges," . . . as they flee from the presence of the wondrous vision. The "Star" is *too much for them*.[82]

And finally, of course, there is the land. As the Indian is pushed off the canvas of American life, the land remains for the taking.

Crofutt's print is a depiction of the national myth of the day. But let us imagine that he had issued the print several years later, let us say 1883. Would the vision have been altered? Probably little would have been changed, except that now Columbia, with an outstretched arm, would be seen offering the

"Schoolbook" to the "vanishing American." For the schoolbook contained within it the Americanizing lessons of Christianity, capitalism, and republicanism. The schoolbook would save the Indian from extinction. If only Indians would accept the gift of the book, they would come to enjoy the blessings of civilized progress. But even then — and this was always clearly understood — they must continue to give up the land. Such was the deep meaning of Indian education.

Notes

1. Tocqueville, *Democracy in America,* Vol. 1 (1835; rpt., New York: Alfred A. Knopf, 1980), p. 340.
2. Tocqueville, *Democracy,* p. 342.
3. For an overview of nineteenth-century Indian-White relations, see Francis Paul Prucha, *The Great Father: The United States Government and the American Indians* (Lincoln: University of Nebraska Press, 1984), vol. 1; Wilcomb E. Washburn, *The Indian in America* (New York: Harper & Row, 1975), pp. 146–249; Arrell Morgan Gibson, *The American Indian: Prehistory to the Present* (Lexington, MA: D. C. Heath, 1980), pp. 249–484; Robert M. Utley, *The Indian Frontier of the American West, 1846–1890* (Albuquerque: University of New Mexico Press, 1984); Robert F. Berkhofer, Jr., *The White Man's Indian: Images of the American Indian from Columbus to the Present* (New York: Alfred A. Knopf, 1978); and Brian W. Dippie, *The Vanishing American: White Attitudes and U.S. Indian Policy* (Middletown, CT: Wesleyan University Press, 1982), pp. 3–196. The House Committee on Indian Affairs quotation is taken from Henry Warner Bowden, *American Indians and Christian Missions: Studies in Cultural Conflict* (Chicago: University of Chicago Press, 1981), p. 167.
4. Dippie, *The Vanishing American,* p. 200.
5. The assimilation campaign is examined in Francis Paul Prucha, *American Indian Policy in Crisis: Christian Reformers and the Indian, 1865–1900* (Norman: University of Oklahoma Press, 1976); Loring Benson Priest, *Uncle Sam's Stepchildren: The Reformation of United States Indian Policy, 1865–1887* (New Brunswick, NJ: Rutgers University Press, 1942); Frederick E. Hoxie, *A Final Promise: The Campaign to Assimilate the Indians, 1880–1920* (Lincoln: University of Nebraska Press, 1984); Henry E. Fritz, *The Movement for Indian Assimilation, 1860–1890* (Philadelphia: University of Pennsylvania Press, 1961); and Robert Winston Mardock, *The Reformers and the American Indian* (Columbia: University of Missouri Press, 1971). For the role of reform organizations, see, in addition to the above, William T. Hagan, *The Indian Rights Association: The Herbert Welsh Years, 1882–1904* (Tucson: University of Arizona Press, 1985); Vine Deloria, Jr., "The Indian Rights Association: An Appraisal" in *The Aggressions of Civilization: Federal Indian Policy Since the 1880's,* ed. Sandra L. Cadwalder and Vine Deloria, Jr. (Philadelphia: Temple University Press, 1984), pp. 3–18; Larry E. Burgess, "'We'll Discuss It at Mohonk'," *Quaker History,* 60 (Spring 1971): 14–28; Larry E. Burgess, "The Lake Mohonk Conferences on the Indian, 1883–1916," Diss., Claremont Graduate School, 1972; Helen M. Wanken, "'Women's Sphere' and Indian Reform: The Women's National Indian Association, 1879–1901," Diss., Marquette University, 1981. The role of the Board of Indian Commissioners is assessed in Robert H. Keller, Jr., *American Protestantism and United States Indian Policy, 1869–1882* (Lincoln: University of Nebraska Press, 1983), chap. 4; and Henry E. Fritz, "The Board of Indian Commissioners and Ethnocentric Reform, 1878–1893," in *Indian-White Relations,* ed. Jane Smith and Robert Kvasnicka (Washington, DC: Howard University Press, 1976), pp. 57–78.

6. *Annual Report of the Secretary of the Interior,* 1913, Administrative Reports, Vol. II, p. 183.
7. The legislative history on compulsory education for Indians during this period is traced in Theodore Fischbacher, *A Study of the Role of the Federal Government in the Education of the American Indian* (San Francisco: R and E Research Associates, 1974), pp. 125–131.
8. *Annual Report of the Commissioner of Indian Affairs,* 1900, House Doc. No. 5, 56th Cong., 2nd sess., 1900–1901, serial 4102, p. 643; and Laurence F. Schmeckebier, *The Office of Indian Affairs* (Baltimore: Johns Hopkins Press, 1927), p. 209.
9. Schmeckebier, *The Office of Indian Affairs,* p. 214.
10. *Proceedings of the Nineteenth Annual Meeting of the Lake Mohonk Conference,* 1901, pp. 17–18.
11. John Higham, "Hanging Together: Divergent Unities in American History," *Journal of American History,* 61 (June 1974): 5–28; Carl F. Kaestle, *Pillars of the Republic: Common Schools and American Society, 1780–1860* (New York: Hill & Wang, 1983), chap. 5; Carl F. Kaestle, "Ideology and American Educational History," *History of Education Quarterly,* 22 (Summer 1982): 123–138; and David Tyack and Elizabeth Hansot, *Managers of Virtue: Public School Leadership in America, 1820–1980* (New York: Basic Books, 1982), pt. 1.
12. Higham, "Hanging Together," p. 10; Kaestle, *Pillars of the Republic,* p. 76.
13. Kaestle argues that the Protestant ideology was largely composed of ten interlocking propositions:

> "the sacredness and fragility of the Republican polity (including ideas about individualism, liberty, and virtue); the importance of the individual character in fostering social morality; the central role of personal industry in defining rectitude and merit; the delineation of a highly respected but limited domestic role for women; the importance for character building of familial and social environment (within certain racial and ethnic limitations); the sanctity and social virtues of property; the equality and abundance of economic opportunity in the United States; the superiority of American Protestant culture; the grandeur of America's destiny; and the necessity of a determined public effort to unify America's polyglot population, chiefly through education." See Kaestle, "Ideology and American Educational History," pp. 127–128.

14. Higham, "Hanging Together," p. 23.
15. Tyack and Hansot, *Managers of Virtue,* pp. 94–180; Tyack, *The One Best System: A History of American Urban Education* (Cambridge: Harvard University Press, 1974), pts. 2, 4.
16. Handy, "The Protestant Quest for a Christian America, 1830–1930," *Church History,* 22 (March 1953): 10. See also Handy, *A Christian America: Protestant Hopes and Historical Realities* (New York: Oxford University Press, 1971), chaps. 3–4; and Winthrop S. Hudson, *American Protestantism* (Chicago: University of Chicago Press, 1961), pp. 109–127.
17. Reese, "The Public Schools and the Great Gates of Hell," *Educational Theory,* 32 (Winter 1982): 14. See also David B. Tyack and Thomas James, "Moral Majorities and the School Curriculum: Historical Perspectives on the Legalization of Virtue," *Teachers College Record,* 86 (Summer 1985): 513–535.
18. Reformers' assessments of the Indian's economic value system were both exaggerated and misinformed. Still, the sharing and cooperative tradition of most Indian societies is richly documented in ethnographic literature. See, for instance, De Mallie, "Pine Ridge Economy, Cultural and Historical Perspectives" in *American Indian Economic Development,* ed. Sam Stanley (The Hague: Monton Publishers, 1978), p. 250; Royal B. Hassrick, *The Sioux* (Norman: University of Oklahoma Press, 1964), pp. 36–37, 296; Edward P. Dozier, *Hano: A Tewa Indian Community in Arizona* (New York: Holt, Rinehart & Winston, 1966), pp. 88–89; Malcolm McFee, *Modern Blackfeet: Montanans on a Reservation* (New York: Holt, Rinehart & Winston, 1972), p. 46; and E. Adamson Hoebel, *The Cheyennes: Indians of the Great Plains* (New York: Holt, Rinehart & Winston, 1962), p. 94.
19. *Annual Report of the Commissioner of Indian Affairs,* 1886, House Exec. Doc. No. 1, 49th Cong., 2nd sess., 1886–1887, Serial 2467, pp. 221–222.

20. "Rules for Indian Schools," *Annual Report of the Commissioner of Indian Affairs,* 1890, House Exec. Doc. No. 1, 51st Cong., 2nd sess., 1890–1891, Serial 2841, pp. CXLVI, CLII.
21. *Journal of the Thirteenth Annual Conference with Representatives of Missionary Boards,* in the *Annual Report of the Board of Indian Commissioners,* 1883, House Exec. Doc. No. 1, 48th Cong., 2nd sess., 1883–1884, Serial 2191, pp. 731–732.
22. *Proceedings of the Fourteenth Annual Meeting of the Lake Mohonk Conference,* 1896, pp. 11–12.
23. *Annual Report of the Commissioner of Indian Affairs,* 1888, House Exec. Doc. No. 1, 50th Cong., 2nd sess., 1888–1889, Serial 2637, p. 89.
24. *Native American,* September 13, 1902, p. 1.
25. The Protestant missionary effort has been examined in Robert F. Berkhofer, Jr., *Salvation and the Savage: An Analysis of Protestant Missions and American Indian Response, 1787–1862* (New York: Atheneum, 1972); Bowden, *American Indians and Christian Missions;* and Keller, *American Protestantism and United States Indian Policy.*
26. Hopelessly ethnocentric, reformers had little appreciation for the richness and diversity of Native American religious life. For an introduction to this aspect of Indian societies, see Joseph Epes Brown, *The Spiritual Legacy of the American Indian* (Crossroad: New York, 1982); Ake Hultkrantz, *Belief and Worship in Native North America* (Syracuse: Syracuse University Press, 1981); Hultkrantz, *The Religions of the American Indians* (Berkeley: University of California Press, 1979); Hartley Burr Alexander, *The World's Rim: Great Mysteries of the North American Indians* (Lincoln: University of Nebraska Press, 1953); Sam D. Gill, *Native American Religions: An Introduction* (Belmont, CA: Wadsworth Publishing Co., 1982).
27. See the remarks of Merrill Gates in the *Proceedings of the Eleventh Annual Meeting of the Lake Mohonk Conference,* 1893, pp. 11–12; and Daniel Dorchester, "Moral Training in Indian Schools," *Annual Report of the Commissioner of Indian Affairs,* 1891, House Exec. Doc. No. 1, 52nd Cong., 1st sess., 1891–1892, Serial 2934, p. 542.
28. Betzinez, *I Fought with Geronimo* (Harrisburg, WV: Stackpole Co., 1959), p. 156.
29. Alford, *Civilization, as Told to Florence Drake* (Norman: University of Oklahoma Press, 1936), pp. 105–106.
30. Leo W. Simmons, ed., *Sun Chief: The Autobiography of a Hopi Indian* (New Haven: Yale University Press, 1942), pp. 116–117.
31. The changing legal status of the American Indian during this period is reviewed in Prucha, *American Indian Policy in Crisis,* chap. 11; Walter L. Williams, "From Independence to Wardship: The Legal Process of Erosion of American Indian Sovereignty, 1810–1903," *American Indian Culture and Research Journal,* 7 (1984): 5–32; and Alvin J. Ziontz, "Indian Litigation," in Cadwalder and Deloria, *Aggressions of Civilization,* chap. 7.
32. *Annual Report of the Commissioner of Indian Affairs,* 1878, House Exec. Doc. No. 1, 45th Cong., 3rd sess., 1878–1879, Serial 1850, p. 444. All Indians were granted citizenship by an Act of Congress in 1924. See Gary C. Stein, "The Indian Citizenship Act of 1924," *New Mexico Historical Review,* 47 (July 1972): 257–274.
33. *Annual Report of the Commissioner of Indian Affairs,* 1887, reprinted in Francis Paul Prucha, *Americanizing the American Indians: Writings by the "Friends of the Indian," 1880–1900* (Cambridge: Harvard University Press, 1973), pp. 201–203.
34. *Annual Report of the Commissioner of Indian Affairs,* 1887, House Exec. Doc. No. 1, 50th Cong., 1st sess., 1887–1888, Serial 2542, p. 763.
35. *Annual Report of the Commissioner of Indian Affairs,* 1887, reprinted in Prucha, *Americanizing the American Indians,* pp. 200–203.
36. *Annual Report of the Commissioner of Indian Affairs,* 1889, reprinted in Prucha, *Americanizing the American Indians,* p. 233; and "Instructions to Indian Agents in Regards

to Inculcation of Patriotism in Indian Schools," *Annual Report of the Commissioner of Indian Affairs*, 1890, House Exec. Doc. 1, 51st Cong., 2nd sess., 1890–1891, Serial 2841, p. CLXVII.

37. For the belief system of U.S. history texts during this period see Ruth M. Elson, *Guardians of Tradition: American Schoolbooks of the Nineteenth Century* (Lincoln: University of Nebraska Press, 1964); and Laurence M. Hauptman, "Mythologizing Westward Expansion: Schoolbooks and the Image of the American Frontier before Turner," *Western Historical Quarterly*, 8 (July 1977): 269–282.

38. Quoted in *Annual Report of the Commissioner of Indian Affairs*, 1901, House Exec. Doc. 5, 57th Cong., 1st sess., 1901–1902, Serial 4290, p. 524.

39. Simmons, *Sun Chief*, p. 99.

40. *Southern Workman*, March 1892, p. 42.

41. Todorov, *The Conquest of America: The Question of the Other*, trans. Richard Howard (New York: Harper & Row, 1984).

42. Nineteenth-century images of the Indian are examined in Ray Allen Billington, *Land of Savagery, Land of Promise: The European Image of the American Frontier* (New York: W. W. Norton, 1981); Elemire Zolla, *The Writer and the Shaman: A Morphology of the American Indian* (New York: Harcourt Brace Jovanovich, 1969), chaps. 4–7; Berkhofer, *The White Man's Indian*, pts. 1–3; Roy Harvey Pearce, *The Savages of America: A Study of the Indian and the Idea of Civilization* (Baltimore: The Johns Hopkins Press, 1965); Reginald Horsman, *Race and Manifest: The Origins of American Racial Anglo-Saxonism* (Cambridge: Harvard University Press, 1981), chaps. 6–10; and Thomas F. Gossett, *Race: The History of an Idea in America* (New York: Schocken, 1965), chaps. 3–4, 10.

43. Quoted in Pearce, *The Savages of America*, p. 155.

44. The philanthropic tradition in early federal Indian policy is treated in Bernard W. Sheehan, *Seeds of Extinction: Jeffersonian Philanthropy and the American Indian* (Chapel Hill: University of North Carolina Press, 1973); and Prucha, *The Great Father*, vol. 1, chapter 5.

45. Lewis Henry Morgan, *Ancient Society* (New York: Henry Holt & Co., 1877).

46. For a discussion of Morgan's ideas see Dwight W. Hoover, *The Red and the Black* (Chicago: Rand McNally, 1976), pp. 157–160; Berkhofer, *The White Man's Indian*, pp. 52–54; and Gossett, *Race*, pp. 248–251. The idea of social evolution also figured prominently in the works of sociologists Herbert Spencer and William Graham Sumner and historian Frederick Jackson Turner. However, in the hands of these writers there was little room for a happy resolution to the Indian story. See Richard Hofstadter, *Social Darwinism in American Thought* (Philadelphia: University of Pennsylvania Press, 1944; rpt. ed., Boston: Beacon Press, 1962), chaps. 2–3; David A. Nichols, "Civilization over Savage: Frederick Jackson Turner and the Indian," *South Dakota History*, 2 (Fall 1972): 383–405; and Robert F. Berkhofer, "Space, Time, Culture and the New Frontier," *Agricultural History*, 38 (January 1964): 21–30.

47. *Annual Report of the Commissioner of Indian Affairs*, 1881, House Exec. Doc. No. 1, 47th Cong., 1st sess., 1881–1882, Serial 2018, pp. 1–2.

48. Shurz, "Present Aspects of the Indian Problem," *North American Review*, No. 133 (July 1881): 7. See also *Annual Report of the Secretary of the Interior*, 1886, House Exec. Doc. No. 1, 49th Cong., 2nd sess., 1886–1887, Serial 2467, p. 4; and *Annual Report of the Commissioner of Indian Affairs*, 1888, House Exec. Doc. 1, 50th Cong., 2nd sess., 1888–1889, Serial 2637, p. 262. While reformers' statements on the possibility of Indian extinction may reflect the rising tide of social Darwinism, I would argue that they were much more rooted in the Jeffersonian tradition that hoped for a philanthropic resolution of the Indian question. For the impact of social Darwinism on American thought, see Hofstadter, *Social Darwinism in American Thought;* and Robert Bannister, *Social Darwinism: Science and Myth in Anglo-American Social Thought* (Philadelphia: Temple University

Press, 1979). This is also an underlying theme in Stephen Jay Gould's *The Mismeasure of Man* (New York: W. W. Norton, 1981.
49. *Annual Report of the Commissioner of Indian Affairs,* 1891, House Exec. Doc. No. 1, 52nd Cong., 1st sess., 1891–1892, Serial 2934, p. 5.
50. *Proceedings of the Thirteenth Annual Meeting of the Lake Mohonk Conference of Friends of the Indian,* 1895, pp. 36–37.
51. *Proceedings of the Fourteenth Annual Meeting of the Lake Mohonk Conference of Friends of the Indian,* 1900, reprinted in Prucha, *Americanizing the American Indians,* p. 339. See also Herbert Welsh, *Four Weeks Among Some of the Sioux Tribes of Dakota and Nebraska Together with a Brief Consideration of the Indian Problem* (Philadelphia: Horace F. McCann, 1882), p. 21.
52. Welsh, "The Meaning of the Dakota Outbreak," *Scribner's Magazine,* April, 1891, p. 452. Welsh's anti-Catholicism came through in his efforts to end the government's support for contract schools (missionary schools supported by congressional funds) when Catholics began to capture an increasing percentage of appropriations. See Francis Paul Prucha, *The Churches and the Indian Schools, 1888–1912* (Lincoln: University of Nebraska Press, 1979), chap. 3.
53. *Annual Report of the Commissioner of Indian Affairs,* 1887, reprinted in Prucha, *Americanizing the American Indians,* p. 203.
54. *Annual Report of the Secretary of the Interior,* 1885, House Exec. Doc. No. 1, 49th Cong., 1st sess., 1885–1886, Serial 2378, p. 777.
55. *Annual Report of the Secretary of the Interior,* 1880, House Exec. Doc. No. 1, 46th Cong., 3rd sess., 1880–1881, Serial 1959, p. 7.
56. *Annual Report of the Commissioner of Indian Affairs,* 1879, House Exec. Doc. No. 1, 46th Cong., 2nd sess., 1879–1880, Serial 1910, p. 174.
57. *Annual Report of the Commissioner of Indian Affairs,* 1889, House Exec. Doc. No. 1, 51st Cong., 1st sess., 1889–1890, Serial 2725, p. 119.
58. *Reports of the Department of Interior,* 1909, Administrative Reports, Vol. II, p. 89. For selected aspects of the boarding school story see David Wallace Adams, "Schooling the Hopi: Federal Indian Policy Writ Small, 1887–1917," *Pacific Historical Review, 48* (August 1979): 335–356; Wilbert H. Ahern, "The Returned Indians: Hampton Institute and Its Indian Alumni, 1879–1893," *Journal of Ethnic Studies, 10* (Winter 1983): 101–124; Robert A. Trennert, "From Carlisle to Phoenix: The Rise and Fall of the Indian Outing System, 1878–1930," *Pacific Historical Review, 52* (August 1983): 267–291; Trennert, "Educating Indian Girls at Nonreservation Boarding Schools, 1878–1920," *Western Historical Quarterly, 13* (July 1982): 271–290; Margaret Connell Szasz, "Federal Boarding Schools and the Indian Child: 1920–1960," *South Dakota History, 7* (Fall 1977): 371–384; and Sally J. McBeth, *Ethnic Identity and the Boarding School Experience of West-Central Oklahoma American Indians* (Washington, DC: University Press of America, 1983).
59. McGillycuddy, *McGillycuddy, Agent: A Biography of Dr. Valentine T. McGillycuddy* (Stanford: Stanford University Press, 1941), pp. 205–206.
60. Hampton's Indian work is examined in Frances Greenwood Peabody, *Education for Life: The Story of Hampton Institute* (New York: Doubleday, Page and Co., 1918); David Wallace Adams, "Education in Hues: Red and Black at Hampton Institute, 1878–1893," *South Atlantic Quarterly, 76* (Spring 1977): 159–176; William H. Robinson, "Indian Education at Hampton Institute," in *Stony the Road: Chapters in the History of Hampton Institute,* ed. Keith L. Schall (Charlottesville: University of Virginia Press, 1977), pp. 1–33; and Joseph Willard Tingey, "Indians and Blacks Together: An Experiment in Biracial Education at Hampton Institute, 1878–1923," Ed.D. Diss., Teachers College, Columbia University, 1978.
61. *Southern Workman,* February, 1885, p. 20.
62. *Red Man,* March–April, 1893, p. 4.

63. See Wilcomb E. Washburn, "The Moral and Legal Justifications for Dispossessing the Indians," in *Seventeenth-Century America: Essays in Colonial History*, ed. James Morton Smith (Chapel Hill: University of North Carolina Press, 1959), pp. 15–32; and Arrell Morgan Gibson, "Philosophical, Legal, and Social Rationales for Appropriating the Tribal Estate, 1607 to 1980," *American Indian Law Review*, 12 (1985): 3–37. The link between dispossession and education is briefly but perceptively analyzed by Lawrence A. Cremin in his *American Education: The National Experience, 1783–1876* (New York: Harper & Row, 1980), pp. 230–242.
64. Quoted in Gibson, "Philosophical, Legal, and Social Rationales," p. 14.
65. Quoted in Gibson, *The American Indian*, p. 272.
66. Berkhofer, *The White Man's Indian*, pp. 134–145.
67. Pancoast, *Impressions of the Sioux Tribes in 1882 with Some First Principles in the Indian Question* (Philadelphia: Franklin Printing House, 1883), pp. 6–7.
68. Thomas J. Morgan, "A Plea for the Papoose," reprinted in Prucha, *Americanizing the American Indians*, p. 249.
69. *Proceedings of the Third Annual Meeting of the Lake Mohonk Conference*, 1885, reprinted in Prucha, *Americanizing the American Indians*, pp. 33–34.
70. The literature on the Dawes Act is especially rich. See Prucha, *The Great Father*, vol. 2, chap. 26; Prucha, *American Indian Policy in Crisis*, chap. 8; Hoxie, *A Final Promise*, pp. 70–81, chap. 5; Priest, *Uncle Sam's Stepchildren*, pt. 4; D. S. Otis, *The Dawes Act and the Allotment of Indian Lands*, ed. Francis Paul Prucha (Norman: University of Oklahoma Press, 1973); Leonard A. Carlson, *Indians, Bureaucrats, and Land: The Dawes Act and the Decline of Indian Farming* (Westport, CT: Greenwood Press, 1981). Two excellent case studies are Donald J. Berthrong, *The Cheyenne and Arapaho Ordeal: Reservation and Agency Life in the Indian Territory, 1875–1907* (Norman: University of Oklahoma Press, 1976); and William T. Hagan, *United States–Comanche Relations: The Reservation Years* (New Haven: Yale University Press, 1976), chaps. 9–12.
71. In 1881, Indians owned 155,632,312 acres. By 1900, the number had dwindled to 77,865,373. Prucha, *American Indian Policy in Crisis*, p. 257.
72. *Proceedings of the Sixth Annual Meeting of the Lake Mohonk Conference of Friends of the Indian*, 1888, reprinted in *Annual Report of the Commissioner of Indian Affairs*, 1888, House Exec. Doc. No. 1, 50th Cong., 2nd sess., 1888–1889, Serial 2637, p. 780.
73. *Proceedings of the Fifth Annual Meeting of the Lake Mohonk Conference of Friends of the Indian*, 1887, reprinted in *Annual Report of the Commissioner of Indian Affairs*, 1887, House Exec. Doc. No. 1, 50th Cong., 1st sess., 1887–1888, Serial 2542, p. 959.
74. *Annual Report of the Commissioner of Indian Affairs*, 1889, reprinted in Prucha, *Americanizing the American Indians*, p. 237.
75. *Talks and Thoughts*, February, 1904, p. 4.
76. T. J. Jackson Lears, "The Concept of Cultural Hegemony: Problems and Possibilities," *American Historical Review*, 90 (June 1985): 567–593.
77. "Instructions to Indian Agents in Regard to Inculcation of Patriotism in Indian Schools," p. CLXVII.
78. *The Red Man*, March, 1890, p. 5.
79. Quoted in Cora Folsom, "Memories of Old Hampton," Cora Folsom Papers, Hampton Institute.
80. While the focus of this paper is essentially on the meaning behind policymakers' assimilation efforts, it should be noted that students responded to these efforts in a variety of ways. While some cooperated with the educational program, others resisted. In the latter instance, arson, running away from school, and subtle forms of passive resistance all proved effective. Another response was to selectively embrace some aspects of the program while rejecting other strands, thereby constructing a kind of personal syncretic resolution of potentially conflicting value systems, all the while attempting

to maintain a sense of personal and ethnic identity. The subject of student response is treated in Michael C. Coleman, "The Mission Education of Francis La Flesche: An Indian Response to the Presbyterian Boarding School in the 1860's," *American Studies in Scandinavia, 18* (1986): 67–82; Coleman, "The Responses of American Indian Children to Presbyterian Schooling in the Nineteenth Century: An Analysis through Missionary Sources," *History of Education Quarterly* (forthcoming); Sally J. McBeth, *Ethnic Identity and the Boarding School Experience of West-Central Oklahoma American Indians* (Washington, DC: University Press of America, 1983), esp. pp. 127–134; David Wallace Adams, "The Federal Indian Boarding School: A Study of Environment and Response, 1879–1918," Ed.D. Diss., Indiana University, 1975, chaps. 5–6; and Wilbert H. Ahern, "The Returned Indians: Hampton Institute and Its Indian Alumni, 1875–1893," *Journal of Ethnic Studies, 10* (Winter 1983): 101–124. An important perspective can be gained from consulting Indian autobiographies. Especially good are Luther Standing Bear, *My People the Sioux* (1928; rpt. Lincoln: University of Nebraska, 1975); Simmons, *Sun Chief;* Louise Udall, ed., *Me and Mine: The Life Story of Helen Sekaquaptewa* (Tucson: University of Arizona Press, 1965); Francis La Flesche, *The Middle Five: Indian Schoolboys of the Omaha Tribe* (Madison: University of Wisconsin Press, 1963); Jim Whitewolf, *The Life of a Kiowa Apache Indian* ed. Charles Brandt (New York: Dover, 1969); and Harold Courlander, *Big Falling Snow: A Tewa-Hopi Indian's Life and Times and the History and Traditions of His People* (Albuquerque: University of New Mexico Press, 1978).

81. The text is reprinted in Wilcomb E. Washburn, ed., *The Indian and White Man* (Garden City: Anchor Books, 1964), pp. 128–130. Charles Burgess has used the Gast painting as a point of departure for his discussion of the late nineteenth-century compulsory school-attendance movement in "The Goddess, the School Book, and Compulsion," *Harvard Educational Review, 46* (May 1976): 199–216.
82. Washburn, *The Indian and the White Man*, p. 129.

The first two photographs in this article are provided courtesy of the National Archives. The third is provided courtesy of the Library of Congress.

Mexico: Indianismo and the Rural School

RAMÓN EDUARDO RUIZ

Out of the Revolution ignited by the creole Francisco Madero (1910–1913), there emerged a struggle to vindicate the Indian, long-forgotten by the rulers of Mexico. A phenomenon of the twenties and thirties, the *indianista* movement pictured the Indian as a leading element of Mexican society and culture. Nowhere were the tenets of *indianismo* outlined more clearly than in the ideas of the reformers who built a rural school system for the peasants.

Nationality and the Indian

During "the last ten years [the 1910's] . . . not fighting but thinking has been our occupation. Violent deeds are only the signs of our mental effort to fathom the truth of our reality and of our ideals," wrote Moisés Sáenz, intellectual figure and Under-Secretary of Education in the twenties.[1] An era of national introspection emerged with the Revolution, as Mexicans began to analyze themselves and their society. "What are we? What would we like to be?" asked Sáenz (29, pp. 26–27).[2] "What is the right of the white man, of the mestizo . . . , of the Indian in the scheme of things" (28, pp. 8–9)? Specifically, there were two questions: what was the Mexican nationality, and what was the place of the Indian in society?

For the artists the answer was a simple one. The masses, Indian by "race," brown by color, peasant by class, were the essence of revolutionary Mexico. So Rivera, Orozco, and Siqueiros turned for inspiration to the peasant, depicting on canvas and wall his struggle for justice and equality. What the artist painted, the writer put into words. The literature of Mariano Azuela and his friends spoke of villages and peasants; of battles waged by cotton-clad warriors against the forces of city and greed. The brown peasant exemplified strength and virtue; city, landlord, and foreigner were his enemies. The lawmakers of 1917, too, recognized the Indian by giving a place in the national Constitution to the *ejido*, a village land system dating back to the pre-Conquest (34, pp. 60–61).

The issue, however, was not as simple for the architects of the national program of education, for the answers given would determine its orientation, and this was a matter of public concern. Public opinion, furthermore, was divided on this question for the character of the nationality was a sensitive issue among Mexicans, hybrids of Indian and Spanish stock. Some thought themselves Spaniards, or basically European; others boasted that they were "pure" Indian. And after all, what were Mexicans by race, ideals, and culture? Fundamentally, the question was whether the relationship established by the Conquest — equality of races in theory but with the Spaniard superior in practice — still existed; or whether in four centuries one group had risen at the expense of the other. Had the Indian by sheer weight of numbers and loyalty to tradition overcome the Spaniard, or, had the European triumphed over the Indian? The answer to this question would determine the nationality of Mexico, which the reformers sought zealously to define. On this issue of nationality, subject to diverse interpretations, the reformers split into two general groups: the Europeanists (for want of a better term), and the Nationalists or *indianistas* as they were popularly called.

Equally important was the place of the Indian in society — second of the two questions. The census of 1921, the last to use race as a classification, had reported that there were 4,000,000 Indians in Mexico.[3] There were more than eighty groups, some small and relatively unimportant, others — like the Aztecs — numerous and significant. They were distinct in language, folklore, and culture. A few remained in the nomadic stage; some were barbarous and war-loving; the great majority farmed for a living (30, p. 170). With some exceptions, the Indian lived in poverty, the victim of disease, malnutrition, and superstition.

Urban society, the aristocracy, and the majority of reformers looked upon the Indian as a problem.[4] In a material sense he lived on the margin of the national economy, a status detrimental to his welfare and to that of the Republic. Ways had to be found to raise his living standards and to encourage his aspirations. On this point reformers were in substantial agreement; but they split over how to carry out this rehabilitation.

The Conservatives and the Issues

The attitude of the Europeanists on the issues of nationality and the Indian was clear: the character of Mexico had been fixed by the European, by the Western world, wrote José Vasconcelos, dean of the Europeanists and former Minister of Education (37, pp. 24–25). If the soil of Mexico had given birth to indigenous civilizations, independent of the old world, they had fallen before the stronger, more virile culture of the Spaniards, and were now merely of historical interest. Now the land belonged to the mestizo, physical offspring of conqueror and Indian, but heir of the European civilization.

As to what should be done about the Indian, the Europeanists felt that after four centuries of interbreeding, the Indian was a dying segment of the population — a subject for redemption and nothing more. Their gospel was the "incorporation of the Indian into society," a society on the European mold. If the Indian could be made over in the image of his mestizo neighbor, Western in thought, the problem would be solved.[5] Since the Indian and his culture were anachronisms in the twentieth century, the Mexican of the future had to look for guidance and inspiration to the Western world, not to his indigenous heritage (43).

Like Roosevelt's New Deal, the program of the Europeanists was conceived in terms of recovery rather than radical social change. The reforms which they envisaged accepted the Western capitalism of the Diaz regime, modified here, strengthened there.[6] They stood for the protection of the private property of the middle class. In general, the Europeanists were urban, rather than rural-minded, more linked with commerce and business — and later industry — than with agriculture. Their crusade stressed the rights of the individual and the virtues of Western democracy, which were alien to the Indian. In the light of the doctrine of the twenties and thirties, they aimed at conservative reform.

The Indianistas

These views found no support among the *indianistas*. To them the nationality was Indian. Since three out of four Mexicans still lived in rural villiges, the traditional home of the Indian, the great Mexican majority was Indian, wrote Manuel Gamio, distinguished anthropologist and Under-Secretary of Education under Calles (15).[7] While the Spaniard had triumphed militarily and as an individual, his civilization had not been transmitted to the Indian. The Spaniard had always been a minority, and even the mestizo was more Indian than European. So why not accept reality — intellectually, artistically, and otherwise — and build around it (28, p. 14)? If the nationality was Indian, the Indian had a vital role to play, declared the *indianistas*. As heir to the pre-Columbian past, he had much to give the present; for, eulogized Sáenz in one of his sentimental moments, the Indian represented a "civilization so high and delicate that at times one wonders if . . . the coming of the white man . . . was not a pity rather than a blessing" (31, pp. 72–73).[8] There was, moreover, no reason to deny the continuing existence of the Indian, as some did. "We gain nothing and lose much by trying to argue that Mexico has no Indians," announced Sáenz. "Indeed . . . this attitude is responsible for the neglect in which . . . [the] Indians . . . have been left" (30, pp. 169, 175).

The *indianistas* were a mixed lot, bound together by a common interest in rural life, a Jeffersonian faith in agriculture, and a belief in the masses. Their ranks included rural educators, anthropologists, farm experts, here and there a renegade historian, and a strange collection of artists and writers, antiquarians and romanticists. When the political climate favored *indianismo*, which happened rarely, politician, general, and businessman echoed its sentiments. But the businessman was hardly a friend, for he had cast his lot with commerce, and later with industry, traditional rivals of agriculture. At the head of the *indianista* movement was the rural expert, usually the anthropologist or the specialist on rural education, who came to know and admire the qualities of the peasants. Intellectuals with an intimate sense of rural life, they were the links between the reality of the countryside and the *indianismo* of the printed page.

Ironically, what was lacking in the leadership was the Indian himself. With few exceptions, the *indianista* movement, never an organized affair, was the child of intellectuals interested in rural problems who were certainly not Indian. Even at the grass roots the Indian seldom joined the crusade.[9] Once educated, however, — and therefore no longer an Indian in the Mexican sense — he often returned as a teacher or rural expert, having learned and adopted the doctrines of *indianismo*. But this was acquired or imposed doctrine, not something indigenous. While the Indian of the village usually joined in the folk festivals sponsored by a cultural mission and supported the native language program this was not always the case. The village was often indifferent, as Ralph Beals pointed out in *Cheran* (1, p. 111).[10] Yet the symbol of *indianismo*, if it had one, was Zapata, the Indian agrarian chieftain, whose struggle for land and schools was an important phase of the Revolution.[11]

Usually out of power, and therefore free of any responsibility, the *indianistas* frequently allowed sentiment to get the better of reason. Still they were an influential and vocal minority. Their writings left a mark on social and economic theory and their activities colored the agrarian era of the twenties and thirties.

Historically speaking, *indianismo* came into its own with the Revolution; but its roots were old. The beginnings were laid in the pre-Columbian era, by the scores of Indian uprisings of the colonial period, and by Las Casas and his priestly cohorts, whose defense of the Indian was a cult. Certainly, the Hidalgo and Morelos uprisings had characteristics later associated with *indianismo*. Throughout the nineteenth century — especially in the early 1830's, later during La Reforma, and even under the Díaz regime — there were vocal individuals of *indianista* leanings. Still the movement was a more recent phenomenon.

The Rationale of Indianismo

There were many factors behind the *indianista* concept of nationality. Foremost was a rising group spirit, an impulse for nationalism emerging after centuries of neglect and exploitation. In a symbolic sense, the rediscovery of the Indian gave substance to the desire to stand alone, to be free of Europe and independent of the United States, as Redfield asserted (25, p. 138).[12] The new nationalism was a revolt against Spain, the colonizer and master, four centuries after the Conquest. It was an emotional repudiation of centuries of imitation, a reaction against Comte and Spencer, against the prejudices of Western society categorizing the Indian, and Mexicans generally, as inferior people. Viewed from this angle, *indianismo* was pride of race — racial chauvinism in some cases. For as Antonio Díaz Soto y Gama boasted to a group of visiting students from the United States: "We prefer the Indian blood that runs in our veins to the small amount of white blood from European extraction" (11, p. 179).[13]

With *indianismo* there came an awakened interest in folk language, folk customs, and folk personality. The new interest stressed things native, using the Indian as a symbol of individual honor and pride, ideals sought by that generation. "We must take advantage of what the country gives us: men of dark skin . . . to govern us, *tequila, charanda,* and *aguardiente* . . . the beverages of a cane as noble as the grape," José Rubén Romero had his Pito Pérez say. "Were the clerics to use *aguardiente* in place of wine for mass, they would be humble and kind to their flocks."

Basically, *indianismo* was a belief in the simple agrarian economy of the peasant, long forgotten by an industrialized world. The Indian's communal system offered a way out of the dilemma posed by a lingering quasi-medieval colonial system on one side and capitalism on the other. By fusing the communal village with collectivism the peasant would get the benefits of Western technology and avoid the dangers of capitalism or the limitations of an antiquated colonial system. Perhaps, in the final analysis, behind the cotton *calzones,* the *huaraches,* and the *ejido* lay an attack — Marxian or otherwise — on capitalism or what passed for it in Mexico (24, p. 21; 33, p. 422). The *ejido* — and the rural school — represented *indianismo* in the countryside (22, p. 18).

No surprise was it, therefore, to find Ramón Beteta, still the idealistic school teacher, suggesting in 1935 that Mexico revise her land system in order to substitute the small communal holding for private property. He saw no reason why land reform should be used to create an agrarian bourgeoisie which, though new to Mexico, was antiquated elsewhere. To redistribute the land and not to go ahead with its socialization he considered a dangerous step. Unless carried to its logical conclusions, declared Beteta, the Revolution had won a Pyrrhic victory (3, pp. 100–102).

Conservative hostility to *indianismo* was born of this attempt to meddle with the economic status quo. The conservative reformer had no quarrel with a weak and numerically insignificant group that suggested a return to a nebulous and ill-defined "Indian culture," and raised no protest when the Secretariat of Education subsidized mural art critical of the middle class. But here was an attack on private property in the guise of a cultural crusade, and conservatives rallied to protect the old order.

In the light of this picture, the Church-school issue of the twenties and thirties, which divided reformers, takes on new meaning. In general the conservatives remained loyal Catholics or at least gave lukewarm support to the Church. With some exceptions, they were ready to accept the Church as vital to the future of Mexico and some were willing to accept modification of Article 3 of the Constitution which dealt with education. After all, the Church gave tacit approval to the status quo and, since the days of Juárez, had posed no threat to the middle class. So long as the Church refrained from political intrigue harmful to the social order, which it was willing to do if its own position was not threatened, the conservatives were ready to share education with the Church.

On the other hand, the *indianistas* considered the Church a vested partner of the status quo, thus a logical target. If the school was to achieve its purpose — the transformation of society — the Church, as constituted, had to go. As Sáenz wrote, "if religion is to function in a constructive way in the life of our peoples, the Church-to-be must be willing to deal with the realities of the present life in accordance with the *social* and *political* ideals [italics mine] for which we are striving." There could be no enduring harmony while there existed an ambivalence between present and future life, between material and spiritual values (28, pp. 15–16). Viewed from this perspective, *indianismo* was an extension, with collectivist undertones, of the anti-clericalism of the nineteenth century, which was rooted in the struggle for power between Church and State.

Further, unlike traditional anti-clericalism, which was neither anti-Catholic nor anti-Christian, *indianismo* denied both the faith and the Church. The village — so ran the argument — while deeply religious, was neither Christian nor Catholic; its faith was a strange mixture of pagan rite and Catholic worship, both degenerate and misunderstood. Christianity, instead of replacing the ancient cults, had merged with them. "Why not accept this fact and blend the two?" asked Sáenz. For "out of pagan feeling and Christian conception and practice, a new manner of religion may come about where a complete synthesis of life will be realized" (28, pp. 15–16). Or as Gamio asserted, the destruction of many aspects of pre-Conquest worship was regrettable, not especially because of their religious character, "but . . . because of the originality, the significance, and the rare beauty in the art which pre-Columbian mythology [had] created." Nothing since the Conquest had artistically equalled or surpassed "the decoration of the Maya temples, the bas-reliefs of Palenque, the plumed serpents of Teotihuacán, [and] a thousand other marvels." Since the mixture of Catholic dogma and pre-Hispanic pantheism had not produced anything equal to that art born of the union of esthetics and mythology in the ancient world, why not replace "classic occidental mythology" with courses in school on the mythology of the new world (17, pp. 388–389).

What these *indianistas* asked was that the Church support their social order and accept the school's right to blend pagan worship with Catholicism.

While the conservative reformer was familiar with the paganism of the village and with anti-clericalism, this was asking much of him. He balked and gave his support to the Church.

The Indigenistas

On the question of nationality, there was general agreement among the *indianistas*. But when the immediate problems of the Indian population faced them, they drifted into three ill-defined groups or wings: romanticists, radicals, and moderates.

For the romanticists — the antiquarians, folklorists, artists, and poets — *indianismo* was, in practice, the cult of the lyrical and little else.[14] Having accepted *indianismo* in theory, the romanticists had nothing to offer. Their idealized Indian had scant relation to the flesh-and-blood Indian in the countryside. Their Indian inspired the artist, was eulogized as quaint, furnished material for "scientific investigation," or was displayed in museum cases. Because their interest was the sentimental, the romanticists' role in *indianismo* was theoretical and minor.

While the radicals were often also guilty of stressing the lyrical, their weakness was the impracticality of their social and economic proposals. They called for total reform: confiscation of haciendas, collectivization of land, socialized education. They dealt in wholesale condemnations and categorical imperatives, leaving no room for compromise.[15] With little actual experience in rural affairs, with no clear understanding of the cultural factors involved, they, like the romanticists, had little to offer beyond doctrine. The radical was an agitator, a dreamer with only a sketch of a program vast and intricate which would require the careful planning of every detail.

The practical reformers were in the moderate wing. They were reformers who forsook the city to work with Indian groups in the village, who saw that the nationality issue was meaningless unless there were tangible benefits for the Indian, and who envisaged an agrarian nation with a place for the Indian as well as for the machine. They gradually came to be known as *indigenistas*, and the philosophical, often lyrical, *indianismo* of earlier years gave way to their "scientific" *indigenismo*, a movement concerned primarily with alleviating the socio-economic plight of the Indian. It was the *indigenistas* who laid out the educational program for the Indian, partly on the basis of Gamio's experiments at San Juan de Teotihuacán (16).

Indigenismo and the Rural School

The task of the practical *indigenistas* was to help the Indian raise his living standards, to make him a part of the national stream of life. Of primary importance was the matter of approach or method, which in turn called for intimate knowledge of Indian characteristics. From this problem arose the question of what are Indian characteristics, or, more succinctly, "What is an Indian?" The racial classification — which, in the census of 1921, defined an Indian as one of "more or less pure" blood — had proved inadequate; how could one decide who was "pure blooded" after four hundred years of racial intermixing? Further, the Indian question was not one of blood, but the plight of a group or segment of society, declared the *indigenistas*. So the census of 1930, while still taking race into account, adopted the new socio-economic definition put forth by the *indigenistas*.[16] For the Indian life revolved around Indian things: the planting stick instead of the plow, corn in place of wheat, the *rebozo* or *sarape* for the coat, and usually a native language spoken in preference to Spanish.[17] Racially, he was more "Indian" than Spaniard. In a psychological sense, he was conscious of being Indian, a feeling that had not diminished over the centuries, as Robert Redfield reported in *Chan Kom Revisited*.[18] By this classification, an Indian, merely by a change in economic and intellectual status, became a mestizo.

Reform had to take the characteristics of the Indian into account, insisted the *indigenistas*. A meaningful education had to serve each Indian group according to its needs and this would effect, paradoxically, a real national unity, by lifting all groups to one plane of civilization (38, p. 154). The policy of "incorporation" ignored group differences. As the agrarian and political programs had demonstrated, there was little logic in "incorporation." If the rural majority demanded an agrarian program that would break up large land holdings and divide them among the people, many of the Indians did not need this. Unlike his neighbors, the Indian had held on to his tiny plot of land. To benefit him, the agrarian program had to increase the size of his land, improve his agricultural techniques, and encourage cooperative farming (30, p. 176). Where matters of political organization were involved, the Indian, unlike his apolitical neighbor, had an organization of his own worthy of respect and consideration; it dated back to the pre-Columbian era, wrote Luis Chávez Orozco, Under Secretary of Education and Chief of the Department of Indian Affairs in the late thirties (8). The Indian considered the politician from outside an invader of the worst sort. Gamio argued that the Indian had been corrupted politically by western society; and, in fact, the closer he lived to centers of occidental culture the more corrupt he was (17, p. 389).

According to the *indigenistas*, the formula of the Europeanists not only ignored the characteristics of the Indian, but rejected what Gamio called "static and dynamic" values. The static values were the long-forgotten higher arts and social practices of the pre-Columbian age, which had once been of great significance and could be again. The dynamic values were the pre-Columbian practices, tools, and beliefs which still persisted in the modern era (17, p. 386).

Among the chief "static" values of the Indian were architecture, sculpture, work in precious metals, his mythology, and an innate sense of democracy. In the opinion of Gamio, they might be revived because the "mental processes of the Indian" resembled those of his ancestors. By adapting them to modern conditions, these "static" values could be restored to the life of today (17, pp. 386–387). The "dynamic" values were found in housing, food, clothing, agriculture, tools, domestic equipment, and, generally speaking, in the material things of indigenous life. There were survivals also in the intellectual concepts of the Indian, in his aesthetics, his religious ideas, and in his interpretations of cosmic phenomena and sickness. Some survivals were of intrinsic value, even though they might appear degenerate. The useful ones were to be cultivated. Folk arts, now corrupted by the tourist trade, could be restored to their original authentic character. Villages and towns could be laid out as they were before the Conquest, with houses placed on small plots of land surrounded by orchards and cultivated fields — a more hygienic and picturesque plan than the compact block of buildings that the Spaniards introduced (17, pp. 391–392).

The *indigenistas* denied, however, that they wanted to return to the planting stick, the medicine man, and the mud hut. As they said, they did not want to "indianize" Mexico; there was no project to restore pre-Columbian life, for that would exterminate the Indian in the event that such an absurd scheme could be carried out. But certainly this was not a program to "Europeanize" the Indian, to uproot him from his traditions and his environment. The goal was "mexicanization" — the catch-word — the blending of all strains into a Mexican society enriched by the contribution of the Indian (19, p. 637; 6). *Indigenistas,* said Gamio, "wish . . . to offer . . . [the Indian] . . . a harmonious combination of the best . . . of his pre-Hispanic and colonial legacy, . . . and the best elements in western culture" adapted to his needs (17, pp. 392–393). Incorporation was a false god. It not only threatened to change the way of life of the Indian, his tools and techniques, but it ignored all that he stood for. If the Indian was to have status in society, "incorporation" had to be a mutual process (30, p. 178). The Indian had to play an important role in the social and economic life of the Republic, else reform was nothing but the "conqueror's design for a vanquished people whose spirit and way of life he had sworn to destroy." This was the warning of the anthropologist Daniel F. Rubín de la Borbolla (27, p. 97).

No matter what the goal was, reconstruction had to start with the reality of the Indian world, declared the *indigenistas*. Should the nation later decide upon industrialization, great care should be taken lest the factory system be imposed artificially upon native agrarianism. It would be a national calamity to reject the farm for the factory before either the Indian or the rest of the country was prepared for it (2, pp. 35–36). The question, said Celerino Cano, an educator of note, was not how to impose an alien system upon the wreckage of the old, but how to integrate the new with the old (4, p. 261). Reform, President Cárdenas declared, had to respect the Indian as an individual and to recognize his traditions and sentiments (6).

The function of the school was to make the modern world intelligible to the Indian; it proposed to link the primative with the modern. For unless this were done, declared the *indigenistas,* the tools of Western civilization could have little impact upon the village. Thus, the curriculum emphasized subjects of immediate value to the community: agriculture, animal husbandry, craftsmanship, rural hygiene, native languages, and academic disciplines geared to local utilitarian needs. But according to the *indigenistas,* the purpose was not to perpetuate peasant status; it was to help the Indian to improve his social and economic position. In the teaching of language, the objective was not to keep the Indian ignorant of Spanish, but to teach him Spanish through his own language. The *indigenistas* believed that one learned a second language with more facility after having mastered his own (12, p. 60). Above all else, the goal of education was to give the individual a sense of his own value, to justify his world to him, and, ultimately, to erase the myth of inferiority from the national conscience. With this in mind, the curriculum stressed the study of the pre-Hispanic heritage, so that the Indian might find inspiration for greatness in the record of his own past (17, p. 389).

Unlike the conservative reformers, the *indigenistas* did not look upon education as an answer to all problems. They thought it senseless to hope to build a nation through education. That was for populations united by historic, racial, cultural, and economic bonds, where education bound more closely existing ties. But the Mexicans were not a united people; their differences were too fundamental for education to harmonize (38, p. 129). For the *indigenistas,* then, education was only one aspect of a reform program all social.

Nor would it have been logical otherwise. The *indigenistas* had in mind a larger reform than the conservatives. To them the school was a political organism, an instrument to use against the status quo. The school could never be neutral; it had to take a stand and, by the reasoning of *indigenismo,* on all issues, particularly socio-economic ones.[19] It was no accident that the collectivist-minded *indigenistas* found their bible in John Dewey.

The Facts of Reality

Theory was one thing and practice something else, for the *indigenistas* seldom had political power during the twenties and thirties. Yet their infrequent moments of power came at crucial times in the history of rural education: at the start of the national movement in 1921, again in the mid-twenties, and during the reform administration of President Cárdenas, 1934–1940.

The first opportunity came with the legislation of 1921 which established a Federal Secretariat of Education with a Department of Indian Culture and Education. For three years the Department sought to organize schools for the Indians patterned on the *indigenista* philosophy of education. The experiment collapsed in 1924 when Vasconcelos — then Secretary of Education — merged the Department with that of Rural Schools.

A second, more limited opportunity, followed almost immediately, when Gamio, then Sáenz, served as Under Secretaries of Education under President Calles, 1924–1928. Gamio held his appointment briefly, but Sáenz stayed in office until 1930. Sáenz did much to implement *indigenista* doctrines. Perhaps the salient experiment of the time was the founding of a school for Indians in Mexico City: *La Casa del Estudiante Indígena*. This school had two purposes: to train leaders for Indian communities, and to demonstrate to the doubting people of the capital that Indians were human beings with an intellectual capacity equal to their own. But while the students proved there ability easily — much to the astonishment of some residents of the capital — they refused to return home upon graduation. So in the end the parents lost their children to urban centers and the rural communities did not profit from the experiment. To remedy this failing, *La Casa del Estudiante Indígena* was replaced by a number of similar schools built in rural areas where students could remain in contact with the village. Unfortunately, President Calles and his successors had little sympathy for this idea, and these schools got only what was left of funds and personnel after the needs of other institutions had been met. By 1935 they were on the verge of collapse.

There was a final opportunity under President Cárdenas after 1935. His administration — firmly supporting *indigenismo* — improved the quality of Indian schools, multiplied their number, placed neighborhood primary schools under their direction, and organized a Department of Indian Education to supervise them. Then, in a bold departure from past practice, the President organized an Autonomous Department of Indian Affairs to handle all Indian problems. Both the Department of Indian Education and the Office of Cultural Missions — the pet of the Secretariat of Education — were placed under it. Finally, in another precedent-shattering step, the administration recognized both the Spanish and Indian languages as official for rural schools.

The Cardenista period was the epoch of *indigenismo*. Although the Department of Indian Affairs, and some of the policies, lived on through the administration of President Ávila Camacho, they were never the same again. In 1946, President Alemán, who dissented from the *indigenista* approach, disbanded the Department and most of the reforms of the thirties lapsed. The *indigenistas,* who decline in number day by day, have not had a major opportunity since 1946.

Indigenismo and *indianismo* were products of their times, — of the postrevolutionary decade and the world depression of the twenties and thirties. So long as nineteenth-century Europe was strong and prosperous, Mexicans imitated Europe; when World War I and depression destroyed the model and brought chaos to Mexico, Mexicans rejected the outside world. The United States experienced a similar, if somewhat more limited, reaction in the depression years of the New Deal. The WPA artist and writer took inspiration from "American" ways. Both *indigenismo* and *indianismo* were products of an era that believed in government planning, of an era that saw the Soviet experiment receive world recognition, and a planned New Deal launched in the United States.

A swing to conservatism came during the forties, and grew strong after 1943. World War I had created new problems, and made Mexican industrialization almost inevitable. By 1949, when Jesús Silva Herzog was writing that the Revolution was only a matter of historical interest, the *indianismo* of yesterday was a forgotten phenomenon, and *indigenismo* no longer a movement of national significance (32, pp. 13–14). Industrialization and conservatism were the keynotes of this age; the agricultural objectives of the Revolution were in disrepute. With industrialization there was no time to worry about the Indian and his special characteristics; the Republic of the future needed technicians and mechanics, not artisans or small farmers. Nor was there need, or sympathy, for the government planning of the depression years. The reforms of the post-war years aimed to create a country able to support industry. All else was secondary.

Both *indianismo* and *indigenismo* had lost their force. Their followers no longer had their revolutionary fervor, and many of their reforms had failed when put to a practical test. The school of the *indigenistas* had faced a dilemma. As designed for life in the village, it was accused of preparing the children of the peasant for the life of the peasant; if its program sought to avoid this charge, it was said to have no practical meaning for the people of the village. In 1940, the last year of the *indigenista* experiment, the problem had been "solved" by making urban and rural curricula fundamentally the same, with some concessions to environment (42, pp. 193–194). But according to Beals, the school, having lost contact with the rural reality, made no impact on the village (1, p. 175). There were other weaknesses. As an ideology, *indianismo* ignored the diversity of the Indian groups. While the *indigenistas* avoided this error, their movement touched only a narrow segment of the rural population: the Indian as defined by the anthropologist. Neither *indianismo* nor *indigenismo* had contributed a well-rounded, practical solution to the problems of the typical mid-twentieth century Mexican.

Yet both made significant contributions. By furnishing a platform for political debate, by raising issues for public airing, they strengthened the cause of reform. They upheld the dignity of the Indian, the value of the village; thus giving recognition to both. The problems of the countryside were brought into national focus. Whatever its failures, the school the *indigenistas* built was closer to reality than any that had ever been designed in Mexico.

Notes

1. See (29, pp. 26–27) and also Ramos (23, pp. 47–48, 53–54) who writes: "In reality, there was born in those years a phenomenon that we could call the rediscovery of Mexico."

2. For a full discussion of this question see (41).
3. See (44, p. 62). The category "race" was not used in the censuses of 1895, 1900, and 1910. In 1921 Manuel Gamio was writing that of the approximately 16 million Mexicans, some 10 to 12 million were more Indian than white (15).
4. To quote Vasconcelos: "The founders of the United States were fortunate in not finding in this territory a very large Indian population, and so it was easy for them to push the Indian back" (38, p. 87). This was written before Vasconcelos had given up reform.
5. According to Vasconcelos, "what we call 'mestisaje,' is bound to be the rule" (38, pp. 94–95). See also (35, p. 73), (39), and (25, p. 142).
6. According to Villareal, the solution to the Indian problem lay with the *hacendados* and industrialists. Once they had guarantees for their property, and freedom to work, they would care for the Indians (40).
7. See also (30, p. 14) and (5).
8. See also (29, p. 16) were Sáenz says, "When Spain came, the world was virgin. On every side life was crushed, the spirit fled, the flavor and aroma of living was destroyed: government, religion, tradition, rite, a culture."
9. "In Mexico, the rabic *indianistas* are the Whites; the Indians, as a general rule, never speak of their caste" (36, p. 188).
10. See Redfield also (25, p. 138).
11. Vasconcelos believed that the Zapata movement "contained the seeds of an Indian revival over the whole extent of the country" (38, pp. 89–90).
12. See also Tannenbaum (33, pp. 420–421, 423) and Ramos (23, pp. 47–48, 53–54). Ramos points out that the publication of Oswald Spengler's *Decline of the West* favored the concentration of Mexican thought on its immediate problems. An excellent expression of the new nationalism is the title of an early work by Manuel Gamio (14).
13. See also (28, p. 5) and (35, p. 286).
14. "We, the supposedly civilized, must incorporate ourselves . . . [with the Indian], the sad and dispossessed Lord of the Earth, the authentic man of Mexico . . ." (21, p. 29). Bolio urged that a model Maya village be built in Yucatan that would preserve Maya architectural forms, whose schools would teach Maya and glorify tradition and folklore.
15. Lombardo Toledano suggested that, in place of the traditional political units, whose foundations rested on nothing better than colonial precedent, Mexico be divided into Indian republics based on ethnic characteristics. He recommended that his "Union of Socialist Republics of Mexico" collectivize the land, give it to the Indian, and expel the mestizos and creoles. "Our Revolution," he lamented, "has demogogic aspects only, exalting nationalism and offering nothing better than folklore." There was still an Indian question. "We have a magic formula: the incorporation of the Indian into civilization. But to which of many local civilizations . . . ?" Why not face reality; "no matter how much we want to be Spaniards . . . , we are Indians" (20).
16. For literature on this point see (7), (18, pp. 11–15), (10, p. 247), (13, p. 64), and (33, pp. 413–420).
17. While the *rebozo* and the *sarape* are European in historical origin, they are now identified almost exclusively with the Indian. For a discussion of what Indian characteristics are see (9, pp. 77–80), (18, pp. 11–15), and (33, pp. 413–420).
18. See (26, p. 74) and also (25, p. 133).
19. Hübner said, "The teacher will be a soldier." "The text, a rifle. The school a field battery" (19, pp. 420–422). Said Gamio, "Above all, I would repeat the importance of the economic factor in Mexican education as a fundamental in the success or failure of whatever project is undertaken . . ." (38, p. 154).

References

Beals, R. *Cherán: a Sierra Tarascan village.* Washington, D.C.: U.S. Govt. print. off., 1946.

Beteta, R. Social forces in Mexican life. In H. C. Herring and K. Terrill (Eds.), *The genius of Mexico.* New York: The Committee on Cultural Relations with Latin America, 1931. Pp. 33–45.

Beteta, R. Some economic aspects of Mexico's six-year plan. In H. C. Herring and H. Weinstock (Eds.), *Renascent Mexico.* New York: Covici, Friede, 1935. Pp. 88–109.

Cano, C. El antecedente filosófico-social. *Revista Mexicana de Educación,* 1940, I, 257–262.

Cárdenas, L. *El Nacional,* May 15, 1937.

Cárdenas, L. *Excelsior,* April 15, 1940.

Caso, A. Definición del indio y lo indio. *América Indígena,* 1948, 8, 237–247.

Chávez Orozco, L. *Las instituciones democráticas de los indígenas Mexicanos en la época colonial.* Mexico: Instituto Indigenista Interamericano, 1954.

Cline, H. F. *The United States and Mexico.* Cambridge: Harvard Univer. Press, 1953.

Comas, J. *Ensayos sobre indigenismo.* Mexico: Instituto Indigenista Interamericano, 1953.

Díaz Soto y Gama, A. The agrarian movement in Mexico. In H. C. Herring and K. Terrill (Eds.), *The genius of Mexico.* New York: The Committee on Cultural Relations with Latin America, 1931. Pp. 177–184.

Fuente, J. de la. Ocho años de experiencia en el medio rural. *Revista Mexicana de Educación,* 1940, 1, 57–67.

Fuente, J. de la. Definición, pase y desaparición del indio en México. *América Indígena,* 1947, 7, 63–69.

Gamio, M. *Forjando patria (pronacionalismo).* Mexico: Porrúa Hermanos, 1916.

Gamio, M. Las pretendidas razas inferiores de México. *El Universal,* March 4, 1921.

Gamio, M. (Ed.) *La población del valle de Teotihuacán.* Mexico: Dirección de Talleres Gráficos, 1922.

Gamio, M. Static and dynamic values in the indigenous past of America. *The Hispanic American Historical Review,* 1943, 23, 386–393.

Gamio, M. *Consideraciones sobre el problema indigena.* Mexico: Instituto Indigenista Interamericano, 1948.

Hübner, M. E. *México en marcha.* Chile: Edición Zig-zag, 1936.

Lombardo Toledano, V. *Excelsior,* Nov. 19, 1935.

Mediz Bolio, A. La hora del indio. *Política Social,* 1936, 1.

Portes Gil, E. *The Mexican schools and the peasantry.* Mexico: Ministry of Foreign Relations Press, 1936.

Ramos, S. Las tendencias actuales de la filosofía en México. In Latin-American studies, I. *Intellectual trends in Latin America.* Austin: Univer. of Texas Press, 1945. Pp. 44–54.

Redfield, R. *Tepoztlán a Mexican village.* Chicago: Univer. of Chicago Press, 1930.

Redfield, R. The Indian in Mexico. *The Annals of the Amer. Acad. of Polit. Sci.,* 1940, 208, 132–143.

Redfield, R. *A village that chose progress; Chan Kom revisited.* Chicago: Univer. of Chicago Press, 1950.

Rubin de la Borbolla, D. F. El problema indígena de México. *Educación,* 1940.

Sáenz, M. *Mexico, an appraisal and a forecast.* New York: The Committee on Cultural Relations with Latin America, 1929.

Sáenz, M. The genius of Mexican life. In H. C. Herring and K. Terrill (Eds.), *The genius of Mexico.* New York: The Committee on Cultural Relations with Latin America, 1931. Pp. 3–30.

Sáenz, M. Indian Mexico. In H. C. Herring and H. Weinstock (Eds.), *Renascent Mexico.* New York: Covici, Friede, 1935. Pp. 168–178.

Sáenz, M., and Priestly, H. I. *Some Mexican problems.* Chicago: Univer. of Chicago Press, 1926.
Silva Herzog, J. La revolución Mexicana ya es un hecho histórico. *Cuadernos Americanos,* 1949, 47, 7–16.
Tannenbaum, F. Agrarismo, indianismo, y nacionalismo. *The Hispanic American Historical Review,* 1943, 23, 394–423.
Tannenbaum, F. *Mexico, the struggle for peace and bread.* New York: Knopf, 1950.
Urrea, B. (Luis Cabrera). *Veinte años después.* Mexico: Ediciones Botas, 1937.
Vasconcelos, J. *La tormenta, segunda parte de Ulises Criollo.* Mexico: Ediciones Botas, 1937.
Vasconcelos, J. *La raza cósmica.* Mexico: Espasa-Calpe Mexicana, 1948.
Vasconcelos, J., and Gamio, M. *Aspects of Mexican civilization.* Chicago: Univer. of Chicago Press, 1926.
Véjar Vásquez, O. *Excelsior,* Sept. 13, 1942.
Villareal, A. I. *Excelsior,* Nov. 22, 1938.
Zea, L. *Conciencia y posibilidad del Mexicano.* Mexico: Secretaría de Educación Pública, 1952.
Conferencia pedagógica. Mexico: Sindicato Nacional de Trabajadores de la Educación, 1945.
La escuela nacional. *Excelsior,* Oct. 10, 1941.
Resumen del censo general de habitantes de 30 de Noviembre de 1921. Mexico: Dirección de Estadística Nacional, 1928.

Literary Colonialism:
Books in the Third World

PHILIP G. ALTBACH

The products of knowledge are distributed unequally. Industrialized countries using a "world" language — notably, the United States, Britain, France, and to a lesser extent, West Germany and the Soviet Union — are at the center of scientific research and scholarly productivity. These same countries dominate the systems which distribute knowledge; they control publishing houses and produce scholarly journals, magazines, films and television programs which the rest of the world consumes. Other countries, especially those in the Third World, are at the periphery of the international intellectual system.[1]

This essay will examine the relationship between industrialized and developing countries by looking at a small but important aspect of this relationship — the world of books and publishing. The discussion is predicated on several ideas. First, the unequal distribution of intellectual products results from a complex set of factors including historical events, economic relationships, language, literacy and the nature of educational systems. Second, industrialized nations have benefited from their control of the means for distribution of knowledge and have at times used their superiority to the disadvantage of developing countries. Third, patterns of national development, the direction and rate of scientific growth, and the quality of cultural life are related to issues of intellectual productivity and independence. Third World nations have not often paid sufficient attention to these issues because of their overwhelming concern with more immediate problems of development.

There are not enough books to meet the rapidly growing needs of the developing countries. The shortage is not a problem which can be solved simply by printing vast quantities of books, but a complex issue which involves a number of national needs, from printing technology to research support. Some Third World countries lack the technical facilities for mass production of books, and some lack indigenous authors to write on subjects of national concern in languages that most literate citizens understand. Even where books exist to serve a national culture, they often cost more than individuals or even institutions can afford.

At present, there is a shortage of books for 70 percent of the globe.[2] The nature of the Third World "book hunger," as Barker and Escarpit have recently called it, can be seen in the fact that the 34 industrialized countries with only 30 percent of the population produce 81 percent of the world's book titles.[3] Although literacy rates in these nations are higher than in developing countries, the rates alone do not begin to account for the disparity in book production.

Figures for Asia dramatically illustrate the book gap. In 1967 the 18 developing countries of the region with 28 percent of the world's population, accounted for only 7.3 percent of the total number of book titles and 2.6 percent of the total number of copies produced per year, and half of these were textbooks.[4] This represents only 32 book titles per million population, while in Europe the average was 417 per million.

Not only are too few books produced in developing countries, but the kinds of books published may not serve national priorities. For example, only 10 percent of all book titles published in India are concerned with pure and applied sciences. By comparison, 54 percent of the books published in the Soviet Union and 25 percent in the United States are on scientific subjects. While nations differ in the types of books they read, it is clear that India and other Third World nations need more scientific books than they now are publishing. As we shall see, many of the books used in the Third World are imported from the industrialized countries or are reprinted or translated volumes of Western origin, and such books may not be appropriate for developing countries' needs.

Book publishing does not function in a vacuum; it is related to other elements in a society and has international dimensions as well.[5] The following discussion will not analyze all elements of publishing in developing countries — a complex process in any society. Rather, it will treat those particular weaknesses of Third World publishing which perpetuate the dependent position in which most developing nations find themselves.

This is not to say that Third World publishing is totally dependent on industrial cultures or that accomplishments have not been achieved. Indeed, given the odds against creative independent publishing, a number of developing nations have made impressive gains. Nor should it be inferred that industrialized nations have manipulated Third World publishing solely for their own national interests and economic gain. Third World dependence on industrial nations for intellectual products results from a complex set of interrelated factors.

The colonial past remains a major influence on the intellectual and educational life of many developing areas and has had considerable impact on publishing as well. Traditional intellectual institutions atrophied under colonialism. Employment in the modern sector was linked to knowledge of the colonial language and to European education. Gradually, the colonial language became the medium for commerce, politics, science and government.

Colonial languages have been used as a means of national unification in a number of Third World nations, particularly those in which no one indigenous language commands the loyalty of the entire population. In addition, ruling elites in Third World countries have often used the colonial language to protect their own privileged position. As long as only 10 percent or less of a population has access to the language of political and economic control, that language represents a source of power.

The colonial language has also been the medium for scholarship. The continued domination of the highest levels of the educational system by Western languages has resulted in a paucity of technical and scholarly books in indigenous languages. English or French continues to be a key to graduate education and to research studies in the Third World, even in countries with some commitment to indigenous languages.

Furthermore, libraries and institutions, which comprise the bulk of the market for scholarly and non-fiction books, are accustomed to buying books in European languages. Even where classes are conducted in the indigenous language, a Western language is usually necessary for library research. Thus, authors wishing to write for a national audience and to reach their intellectual peers generally write in a European language.

Even in Indonesia, one of the few former colonies which has made a concentrated and fairly successful effort to promote the use of an indigenous language, *Bahasa Indonesia,* indigenous scholarly books and advanced textbooks do not yet exist and materials in English are widely used. It is my estimate that in India, about half of the book titles are published in English, while only 2 percent of the population is literate in English. In both Anglophone and Francophone Africa, virtually all books are published in the metropolitan language. In many former colonies the 80 to 95 percent of the population who do not know English or French are effectively barred from the higher levels of education.[6]

Publishers are an integral part of this colonial tradition. Indian publishers, for example, do not follow a consciously neocolonialist policy of trying to maintain foreign influence on the subcontinent. Rather, they perceive that the largest market for books is in English and that, in fact, the only national market is for such material. Hence, a complex web of economic and intellectual relationships and traditions makes it difficult to stop publishing in European languages.

In most countries, the home for intellectual activity is the university. Even in the industrialized nations, intellectual journals probably would not survive were it not for the academic market of university libraries and individual scholars. In the West, scholarly books are often published by non-profit university presses and universities, especially those in the United States, emphasize research and publication as the main criteria for promotion and academic success. Faculty members are allowed time for research activities with funding often available.

In developing countries, research is not always a fundamental part of the academic enterprise and scholarly publication is not always seen as a key to professional advancement, largely because the nineteenth century British and French institutions — models for many Third World universities — did not emphasize research. In addition, many faculty members are too busy with heavy teaching loads, or with such external responsibilities as advising government agencies to pursue research interests.

Conditions for research are often poor: funding is negligible; laboratories and computer facilities are rare; and while universities in developing countries are fairly well-endowed by local standards, library facilities on the level of Western institutions are often lacking. Faculty salaries are seldom high enough to cover the price of books and journals and, what is perhaps most important, colleagues and students provide little impetus for research within the university. Without the material resources and the academic subculture to stimulate research and writing, Third World universities contribute less than they might to the production of research and knowledge.

For those intellectuals outside the university structure the situation is worse. While the economic rewards for intellectual work are not great in any country, they are particularly meager in the Third World. In general, intellectuals lack adequate working conditions and can obtain little public financial support for their work. Few journals and publishing houses exist to provide outlets for scholarly writing. Due to low literacy levels in developing nations, there is only a small audience for either scholarly or non-scholarly work. With neither public support nor a large book-buying public, very few intellectuals can support themselves solely on the basis of their writing or research.[7]

Therefore, Third World intellectuals tend to look toward a Western audience. If there is prestige in publishing, it lies in writing for such Western journals as *Encounter* or *Les Temps Modernes,* or in having a book published in London, New York, or Paris. Publication abroad may bring money and the opportunity to communicate with other Third World intellectuals, since communication seldom runs directly between one developing country and another but is mediated through advanced nations.

There is little circulation of books or journals among Third World nations, even between those with the same language. It is significant that *Jeune Afrique,* an influential African journal with a multinational circulation, is published in Paris. The enterprising Nigerian publisher, Joseph Okpaku, came to New York to start his Third Press, which specializes in African and black subjects. It is perhaps indicative of the difficulties involved in regional publishing that it is often easier to travel between Dakar or Abidjan and Paris than between various African capitals.

The economics of publishing concerns much more than the cost of producing a book in a particular country. Rates of literacy, reading habits of the population, government policy toward books, copyright regulations and the nature of libraries are all part of the economic equation.[8] For example, low literacy rates, low per capita purchasing power and a diversity of languages — all common in Third World nations — contribute to a limited market for books. Many of the smaller developing countries find it economically impossible to publish most kinds of books because the internal market is simply too small. Even in such large nations as Nigeria, India and Indonesia, only some textbooks, certain kinds of popular fiction, and religious books are profitable to publish. Although labor costs are lower than in the West, total costs are high since print runs are small and distribution is difficult.

Book distribution may be the single most serious dilemma of publishing in the Third World. Dan Lacy divides the problem into three elements: (a) the actual demand for books as distinguished from the need; (b) the network of distribution, for example, booksellers and wholesalers; (c) the means of conveying information about books, such as reviews, advertising and book-trade journals. Low reader density, great distances between settlements, and poor transportation facilities make book distribution in developing countries particularly difficult.[9] Just as developing countries themselves are at the periphery of the world's knowledge system, regions outside of capital cities, especially rural areas, which are often completely without access to books, periodicals or newspapers, are at the periphery of knowledge systems within these nations.[10]

An important part of the Third World's cultural dependency stems from political and trade relationships with industrialized nations.[11] Industrialized nations export their products, in this case, books and expertise, to the developing countries. Foreign aid programs, while seeking to provide help to developing countries, often deepen existing patterns of dependence.[12] Knowledge, then, is a part of the neocolonial relationship.

Commercial arrangements built up over years of colonialism persist in many developing countries. Branches of British and French publishers continue to operate in the Third World, and in some places dominate the publishing scene.[13] The advantages of foreign firms — expertise, the backing of foreign capital and a worldwide distribution network — have made the emergence of indigenous publishers even more difficult than might otherwise have been the case.

In general, French and British firms have dealt in commercially successful and uncontroversial textbooks, which constitute the overwhelming proportion of the book market in most Third World countries. These firms have published few original works by local authors and many of their products are printed in Britain or France. In recent years, American publishers have followed the same pattern, establishing themselves in developing areas particularly where United States foreign aid programs have been active. The balance, however, is not entirely negative. Foreign firms provided an early base for publishing and increasingly have taken legal responsibility for training indigenous individuals as workers in the industry.

Foreign aid programs have had an impact on publishing in developing countries. While the United States has sponsored the largest aid effort, other countries have also engaged in aid programs. For example, the English Language Book Scheme (ELBS), sponsored by Britain, each year sells more than 1 million copies comprising several hundred titles, intended mainly for use as college and university textbooks. On a considerably smaller scale, West Germany and the Soviet Union have also sponsored intellectual assistance, including aid to publishing.

Foreign aid, particularly intellectual assistance, cannot be separated from the policy goals of the donor country or, for that matter, from the policies and orientation of the recipient nation's government. The American rationale for book-related aid programs has involved both the technical importance of books in the development process and the ideological elements of anti-communism.[14] Between 1950 and 1964, the United States Information Agency assisted in the production of 9,000 editions and printed 80 million copies in 51 languages.[15]

The Indo-American Textbook Program (PL480) was one of the largest American efforts. Under the PL480 program more than 1,000 different textbooks were reprinted in English for use by Indian college and university students, and more than 4 million copies were distributed at subsidized prices. Although the titles were predominantly in the natural sciences, the reprints included many topics in the social sciences and humanities. The Indian government gave full approval to the program and a joint Indo-American committee selected the textbooks. With the recent cooling in Indo-American relations and changing U.S. foreign aid priorities, textbook aid has virtually ended in India.

Like similar programs in other countries, the Indo-American Textbook Program had certain negative results. In some fields, particularly the social sciences, American books were not relevant to the Indian situation, and the orientations of American social scientists reflected their own ideological biases. Yet the subsidized books tended to drive their more expensive unsubsidized domestic counterparts off the market. The artificially low prices for American books gave buyers a distorted sense of the real cost of books. Finally, several subsidiaries of U.S. publishers were able to establish themselves in the Indian market through the aid programs and their growth may have retarded the development of indigenous Indian publishing.

Yet not all aspects of foreign book programs are pernicious. Aid programs place inexpensive books in the hands of students and can make textbooks in a range of disciplines quickly available. Such programs often provide technical assistance, printing or other equipment to local publishers and sponsor translations into indigenous languages. It is necessary, however, to evaluate such programs carefully. Do aid programs help Third World publishers to establish strong roots and to bring out relevant locally-written books? Or do they circulate materials which the industrialized countries think will win them influence at the cost of discouraging the development of local publishing? The answers to such questions are complicated, but certainly require more attention at the planning and implementation stages of aid programs than they have been given to date.

Another aspect of intellectual neocolonialism is the impact of Western research on the developing countries. Most research, particularly in technology and the natural sciences, is done in the West. Despite some efforts at research in the Third World, it is likely that this monopoly will persist — if anything, the developing countries will lag farther and farther behind. It is not that scholars in the Third World do not have the ability to do research; in India, such individuals as M. N. Srinivas and André Bétille in sociology have done outstanding work. But, as we noted earlier, the universities do not stress research and funds are seldom available to finance it.

In fact, Western scholars have done much of the research on the Third World, and indigenous scholars often must learn about their own political system or agricultural situation through the writings of their Western counterparts. Certainly much of the Western scholarship has been useful and reasonably accurate; but as long as knowledge about the nature of society in developing countries is mediated through Western sources, it is suspect for all the possible methodological and ideological biases, misperceptions and other problems such mediation may entail.[16] In addition, much scholarship and interpretation concerning the Third World is published in the West, and accessible only with difficulty in the developing countries themselves.

A final problem which developing countries face in their quest for intellectual independence is that of copyright, which traditionally has worked to the advantage of the industrialized nations and only now is beginning to change.[17] Copyright regulations have made it difficult and expensive for Third World nations to translate and publish materials originally appearing in the West. Western publishers have often preferred to export their own books rather than to license reprinting in developing nations because larger profits could be realized. Recently, changes in international copyright arrangements have permitted developing countries to reprint and/or translate educational materials more freely than before and at modest cost.[18] These changes, made when the industrialized nations began to realize that copyright agreements were being violated with increasing frequency, will no doubt help the developing countries to obtain the printed materials they need at prices they can afford.

In a situation of drastic inequality, there is a limited amount that the Third World can do to establish independence immediately. Yet there are a number of strategies Third World nations can use to increase the independence of their intellectual life generally and of their publishing in particular.

A few Third World nations have attempted radical solutions to the problem of dependency. The best known examples, China and Tanzania, have stressed an ideology of self-sufficiency to redirect the educational system and intellectuals toward a completely indigenous orientation. These efforts have been strengthened by severing many intellectual and cultural ties with industrialized nations, by forcing intellectuals to become involved with the day-to-day problems of the peasantry through work in villages, and by stressing practical technology in schools and colleges. While it would seem from available reports that both China and Tanzania have achieved some success in reorienting intellectual life, it remains to be seen how effective these experiments will be in the long run.[19]

Other Third World nations have used more modest means to achieve some degree of intellectual independence and indigenous cultural development. Some countries have stressed the use of a national language as a means of cultural unification. Others have severely limited the importation of Western films and, in some cases, books, in order to stress indigenous values. A few countries have allocated funds to projects, such as the National Book Trust in India, which promote local authorship, cultural development and publishing. Finally, many Third World countries have nationalized textbook publishing to ensure that these books reflect values and orientations appropriate for national development. But with few exceptions, these efforts have been piecemeal. There has been little cooperation among Third World nations in joint cultural programs or even in sharing information and publications.

The following suggestions are intended to provide some ideas which can be easily implemented and which may help to ameliorate the existing inequalities in the world of books and publishing. These suggestions are realistic in the sense that no major changes in the relationships between industrialized and Third World nations are required to implement them. Clearly, more radical solutions to the problems of inequality are needed to effect basic change. But to suggest modest reforms is not to deny the need to radically restructure the relationship between the rich and poor nations.

As a first step, communications between Third World nations should be improved so that common problems and issues can be discussed directly without being mediated through institutions and publications in the industrialized nations. This is particularly important on a regional basis, for example, among the nations of Francophone Africa and of Southeast Asia. As a part of communications development, Third World countries must also create viable means of book distribution among themselves, and between themselves and the industrialized nations.

With the strengthening of indigenous publishing and internal distribution facilities in the Third World, intellectuals need not publish their work abroad. Such an effort should include financial and technical assistance from the public sector when necessary. Foreign scholars working in developing nations should publish their findings in the countries where they conduct their research. In this way local publishing will be strengthened and relevant research will be available to local audiences. The intellectual infrastructure in many Third World countries needs to be strengthened in other ways. Libraries, journals which review books, and bibliographical and publicity tools for publishing should be supported.

In addition, major national policy questions which relate directly to books, including the language of instruction in the educational system, levels of literacy and the ownership of the publishing apparatus, must be solved by Third World governments with an understanding of their implications for the balance of intellectual production. Part of any language reform effort should be assistance to publishing in indigenous languages. Finally, Third World leaders must carefully evaluate foreign aid programs to ensure that their nations benefit without local publishing industries or intellectual autonomy being undermined.

These are but a few suggestions for the solution of a complex problem. While publishing is a small part of the relationship between industrialized and developing countries, Third World nations can institute reforms in the publishing process because massive financial investments are not required and power politics are not involved. Through understanding the complexities of the issue, individuals in both industrialized and developing countries may be able to begin exploring constructive solutions.

Notes

1. The "center-periphery" concept has been most fully developed by Edward Shils. See his *The Intellectuals and the Powers and Other Essays* (Chicago: University of Chicago Press, 1972).
2. Ronald Barker and Robert Escarpit, *The Book Hunger* (Paris: UNESCO, 1973), p. 16.
3. Barker and Escarpit, p. 16.
4. *Book Development in Asia: Report on the Production and Distribution of Books in the Region* (Paris: UNESCO, 1967), p. 25.
5. This point is elaborated in Philip G. Altbach, "Publishing and the Intellectual 'System,'" *Annals of the American Academy of Political and Social Science* (1975, in press).
6. Latin America is an exception in this regard since either Spanish or Portuguese is the language of a great majority of the population and a larger regional market for books exists. The two publishing giants of the region, Mexico and Argentina, have fairly effectively used this linguistic unity to build thriving publishing industries.
7. Edward Shils, *The Intellectual Between Tradition and Modernity: The Indian Situation* (The Hague: Mouton, 1963).
8. Datus Smith, Jr., *A Guide to Book Publishing* (New York: Bowker, 1966). See also Herbert Bailey, Jr., *The Art and Science of Book Publishing* (New York: Harper and Row, 1970).
9. Dan Lacy, "Practical Considerations, Including Financial, in the Creation, Production, and Distribution of Books and Other Educational Materials," in *The Mohonk Conference*, ed. Francis Keppel (New York: National Book Committee, 1973), pp. 55–66.
10. The developing countries are not alone in this situation, although it is much more serious in these countries. In the United States, for example, few good bookstores exist outside of the major metropolitan areas and university campuses.
11. For a more general discussion of neocolonialism, see Philip G. Altbach, "Neocolonialism and Education," *Teachers College Record,* 72 (1971), 543–558.
12. Tibor Mende, *From Aid to Recolonization: Lessons of a Failure* (New York: Pantheon, 1973).
13. John Nottingham, "Establishing an African Publishing Industry; A Study in Decolonization," *African Affairs,* 68 (1969), 139–144.

14. Curtis Benjamin, *Books as Forces in National Development and International Relations* (New York: National Foreign Trade Council, 1964). See also Stanley Barnett and Roland Piggford, *Manual on Book and Library Activities in Developing Countries* (Washington, D.C.: Agency for International Development, 1969).
15. Benjamin, p. 72.
16. An example of the possible effects of Western interpretations is the widespread notion of the key role of the middle classes in promoting stability and development in the Third World. Such a notion, while perhaps correct in some respects, fits neatly into the ideological predispositions and interests of American foreign policy, and has become, over the years, the dominant interpretation of American social science. While some social scientists in both the United States and in the Third World disagree with this interpretation, it has had a great influence on thinking in developing countries.
17. See N. N. Gidwani, ed., *Copyright: Legalized Piracy?* (Bombay: Indian Committee for Cultural Freedom, 1968). Also Barker and Escarpit, pp. 88–102.
18. *Records of the Conference for Revision of the Universal Copyright Convention* (Paris: UNESCO, 1973).
19. For discussion of recent trends in Chinese education, see M. Bastid, "Economic Necessity and Political Ideals in Educational Reform During the Cultural Revolution," *China Quarterly*, No. 42 (1970), 16–45; and P. Seybolt, "China's Revolution in Education," *Canadian and International Education*, 1 (1972), 29–41.

This article is part of a larger investigation of publishing, focusing on developing countries in general and India in particular. See Philip G. Altbach, *Indian Publishing in Context* (Delhi: Oxford University Press, 1975); Philip G. Altbach, "Publishing in Developing Countries," *International Social Science Journal*, 26 (1974), 458–473; and Philip G. Altbach, "Publishing and the Intellectual 'System,'" *Annals of the American Academy of Political and Social Science* (1975, in press). I am indebted to Sheila McVey for her comments of an earlier draft of this article.

The Use of Argumentation in Haitian Creole Science Classrooms

JOSIANE HUDICOURT-BARNES

The lack of minority participation in science is a concern in many circles. As Oakes (1990) points out, "Blacks and Hispanics each constitute about 2 percent of the scientific workforce[, and] schooling rests at the heart of the issue" (pp. v–vi). This concern highlights research in which cultural diversity is seen as either a barrier to learning or a resource to build on in learning and teaching. In this article I critique one body of research on science learning by providing counterexamples to understand cultural differences in language and cognitive abilities. Previous cross-cultural research in this area has assumed that the "sense-making" resources of children from diverse language and cultural communities differ from those central to scientific inquiry, which leads to the conclusion that this difference is a barrier to learning that must be overcome by instructional means.

I propose instead that cultural differences can enrich the learning situation when the teacher moves away from a uniform "top-down" view of content and incorporates students' existing knowledge in science teaching. In this article, I give examples of teachers who used discourse practices common in Haiti to leverage scientific argumentation in their classrooms. As the students' argumentation style became more animated, teachers reflected on their own practice and the relevance of the science content for their students.

Much work has been undertaken to discover and document why minority and linguistic-minority students lag behind their mainstream peers in science and mathematics. Research and evaluation using statistical analysis and test scores (National Science Foundation, 1996) only inform us about the existence of differences among children, but do little to enlighten teachers and policymakers about the obstacles these students face in the classroom. "Low expectations" or "not wanting to act White" are often blamed for minority underachievement (Belluck, 1999). Different aspects of this problem need closer scrutiny, in particular the assumptions underlying comparative methods of investigation.

By employing certain methodologies, researchers assume that identical responses are obtained by asking children from diverse communities the same question. When differences are found, they are attributed to the children's ability and knowledge, rather than to their interpretation of the purposes and intentions of the task or of the experimental situation in general. A group of studies coming out of the University of Miami exemplifies this type of cross-cultural investigation, resulting in descriptions of Haitian students in fairly negative terms as to their scientific ability (Lee & Fradd, 1996; Lee, Fradd, & Sutman, 1995). In an analysis of data from interviews with Haitian students, the research associated the poor quality of the children's responses to features of Haitian culture. For example, Lee, Fradd, and Sutman describe cognitive strategies of Haitian students in this manner:

> Haitian Creole students displayed a pattern of strategy use different from that of the other 3 groups (Latino, white Anglo, Black English speakers). Instead, they used more incipient strategies, such as observation and imitation. . . . The students also used nonverbal signals such as looking down, hiding their faces with hands, or displaying long pauses. . . . Haitian Creole students reported little use of strategies. They appeared not to understand the question of strategy use, or responded on several occasions with "Nothing" or "No." (1995, p. 808)

Lee et al. further claim that patterns of interaction that are culturally congruent with Haitian culture could be considered inconsistent with the norms of discourse and task engagement in science. This research corpus is the only group of articles making claims about Haitian immigrants' cognitive skills. Researchers and staff at the Chèche Konnen Center at TERC[2] have had experiences with public school students in Haitian bilingual classrooms in Massachusetts that are quite different from those described by Lee et al.

The Chèche Konnen Center, which conducts classroom research and professional development, is dedicated to improving science education for children from linguistically, culturally, racially, and socioeconomically diverse backgrounds. *Chèche Konnen* means "search for knowledge" in Haitian Creole. The first group of teachers and students affiliated with the center in 1988 gave it this name. At the center we are studying and documenting the intellectual and language traditions that children from diverse backgrounds bring to science, and seeking ways to use these as the basis for teaching and learning in science. We use a "teaching as inquiry" model of professional development in which teachers conduct their own investigations to learn scientific theory and practice; examine issues of language, culture, and race in education; and explore their students' ideas and sense-making practices and their own teaching practices.

Lee et al.'s claims left us puzzled about the validity of their methods because our own experiences with Haitian immigrant students did not point us in the direction of cognitive deficiencies or lack of congruence with the practices of science. As has been amply demonstrated by sociolinguistic research, questions and other verbal interactions are interpreted differently, depending on social context (Labov, 1972). I argue that the types of measures used in defining what constitutes knowledge and cognitive skill are often too shallow and ethnically biased to inform the dialogue on diversity.

I became involved with the Chèche Konnen Center's work as a teacher-collaborator when it first began, and subsequently left classroom teaching to work in research and professional development with the group at TERC. As a teacher I taught a self-contained middle school class with children ranging in age from twelve to fourteen who had recently arrived from Haiti. The students' skills varied from preliterate to middle school levels. I worked to adapt my practice to whoever was in the class, and I was constantly searching for resources that would help me respond adequately to their needs. When the two researchers (Ann Rosebery and Beth Warren) who had a grant to improve science teaching in bilingual classes approached me, I was happy to join what I thought would be a good support group. They observed my science classes twice a week and met with me after school each time to discuss the class and make plans on how to proceed. In the first two years many of the classes were audiotaped. In subsequent years most classes were videotaped.

Three years later the group received a larger grant to work with more bilingual teachers, and I was invited to join the research staff. In addition to having researchers observe, videotape, and transcribe, the science classes, there were summer seminars and biweekly evening meetings where teachers would learn science and discuss their practice. Although the research team was directing the content of the work, the teachers' voices always strongly influenced the center's work.

Throughout our fourteen-year history, Chèche Konnen researchers have recorded, videotaped, transcribed, and analyzed science courses in Haitian bilingual classrooms. We find that when Haitian children are in culturally familiar environments in classrooms focused on practicing science, the type of behavior they exhibit toward the acquisition of knowledge and the search for scientific meaning is deeply congruent with the practice of authentic scientific research (Ballenger, 1997; Conant, Rosebery, Warren, & Hudicourt-Barnes, 2001; Rosebery, Warren, & Conant, 1992; Warren & Rosebery, 1996). In contrast to the findings of Lee et al. (1995), which claim that Haitian children are "nonverbal" or "using incipient strategies," we find that the Haitian children participate in animated and sophisticated arguments about scientific phenomena. We think their participation mirrors everyday Haitian culture and is congruent with a scientific search for meaning and the construction of knowledge.

Cazden (1988) describes the traditional pattern of classroom interaction as a three-part sequence named the IRE: teacher initiation, student response, and teacher evaluation. In most cases, the teacher initiates discussion with a question, the student volunteers to answer by raising his/her hand, and the teacher chooses a child who has a hand up. The teacher's aim is to ascertain if the children have learned what has been taught, and the teacher offers evaluative comments such as "right" or "not yet" to assess student responses. These kinds of questions and answers would be considered inappropriate in any context other than school and the military.

In a traditional classroom and in the military there are issues of power and control. One individual is in charge of controlling the speech event, and allows and disallows certain types of responses:

> In typical classrooms, the most important asymmetry in the rights and obligations of teacher and students is over control of the right to speak. To describe the difference in the bluntest terms, teachers have the right to speak at any time and to any person; they can fill any silence or interrupt any speaker; they can speak to a student anywhere in the room and in any volume or tone of voice. And no one has the right to object. (Cazden, 1988, p. 54)

The limits of the students' right to speak are usually defined by each classroom teacher, as are the rules of politeness and the definitions of competence.

As a result of this most commonly used pattern, the classroom conversations are teacher centered and often involve a fraction of the students who believe they may have the right answer. In many classrooms, some students would rather remain silent than subject themselves to possible negative teacher evaluations. In mainstream classrooms, students whose cultural and linguistic knowledge differs from the teacher's patterns of acceptable responses tend to withdraw from participation. Hemphill (1986) found that middle school working-class girls used less complex syntax, more silences, and more minimal responses in formal discussions than in informal discussions.

In recent years the influence of constructivist thinking has required changes in teachers' stances toward classroom conversations. Inquiry-based teaching and collaborative groups in classrooms require that the teacher step outside the role of academic authority and take part in the "finding out" (Barnes & Todd, 1995). Gallas (1995) describes classroom science talks: "The children co-construct and build together ideas about seminal questions through real dialogue, and the teacher listens and reflects without immediately agonizing over what ought to be said" (p. 11). However, we must acknowledge that, even with this more open stance toward science discussions in constructivist classrooms, cultural differences exist. These need not be seen as a detriment to learning but as a resource on which teachers can rely to open up views of scientific meaning and discourse (Warren, Ballenger, Ogonowski, Rosebery, & Hudicourt-Barnes, 2001).

The classroom conversations quoted in this article were influenced by this inquiry-based stance, but they vary in style according to their chronology and their historical position in the Chèche Konnen research corpus. The teachers in the science conversations presented here capitalized to varying degrees on a conversational style of argumentation in Haitian culture (although neither they nor the Chèche Konnen researchers may have been totally aware of this until later). The first conversation quoted here represents the beginning of the Chèche Konnen Center's work. At that time our interest in classroom conversation was not as strong as our interest in teaching students to "do science" and "make sense" of their work. Classroom talks were recorded as evidence of learning and sense-making. We were interested in what the students had to say because we wanted to know what they were learning and how to proceed with teaching. Later, by the second conversation quoted here, we had decided to open up classroom discourse to increase student participation because we thought that discussions were important building blocks in science learning. In the second conversation, the teacher was speaking with the students as if he were one of them. This was a pivotal conversation in our work because it told us that Haitian children in an informal setting have some prior knowledge and experience in their discourse skills that can be useful in science class. This class became the model that the third teacher had in mind when he deliberately planned to open up his classroom discussions to permit more diverse participatory structures. Arguments about science became events that we celebrated because the students were enthusiastic about scientific phenomena and anxious to arrive at answers or conclusion to their questions.

Argumentation is an essential skill in the development of scientific knowledge (Latour & Woolgar, 1986). In any scientific endeavor, the researcher, working within a theoretical framework, constructs claims based on evidence developed through scientific practices (such as experimentation, fieldwork, historical reconstruction, and modeling). Arguments are what scientific research is all about: searching for truth, presenting a position as fact, defending and redefining that position in the face of challenges.

Argumentative discussion is a major feature of social interaction among Haitian adults. In the Haitian style of discussion, though some cultural features are added, argumentation is the same as that found in the scientific community; this has proven to be a great resource for teachers who attempt not only to teach science but to practice science in the classroom in ways similar to those of scientists (Ballenger, 1997; Conant et al., 2001; Rosebery et al., 1992; Warren & Rosebery, 1996). In this article, I provide evidence that by middle school age, children arriving from Haiti are skilled at argumentation and that these skills can be harnessed effectively to teach and learn science.

Haitian Discourse Practices:
Bay Odyans as Preparation for Scientific Research

As a natural process of language acquisition and socialization, children growing up in Haiti are part of a culture that is essentially oral. Rather than being read to at bedtime, children are included in evening encounters of whole villages or neighborhoods, or of their extended family, where language becomes entertainment. These encounters can be joyful, theatrical, defiant, creative, and participatory (Naudillon, 2001). Folklorist Wolkstein (1978) recorded many of these sessions and described the children as most often being integrated into the adult circle, and occasionally forming their own circles on the side and creating their own entertainment.

Consider this quote from Paul Brodwin's book, *Medicine and Morality in Haiti*:

> Every day scores of public buses leave Port-au-Prince bound for the provincial towns of southern Haiti. Conversation is impossible for the first hour as the bus crawls through the impossibly congested neighborhood of Kafou, on the expanding western fringe of the city. Finally breaking free of the urban sprawl, the bus picks up speed in the verdant agricultural plain near Leogane, still planted in sugar after 300 years. The landscape changes yet again during the long climb up the mountainous spine of the southern peninsula, stretching away from the city into the Caribbean Sea. Cooled by the fresh mountain air, this is when people — total strangers when they boarded the bus — start to talk.
>
> The first exchange I remember went something like this. A woman sighs loudly and thanks Jesus, but someone else breaks in with a pointed joke, "It wasn't Jesus, it was our driver who saved us." "But we are all children of God," responds the woman amid scattered laughter. Then an aggressive voice pushes the debate further: "Are you a child of God? Then why do you say that we Catholics worship the devil?" A murmur stirs the passengers. . . . The first speaker protests, "No, it's not all Catholics. But there are those who deal with 'other things.'" The conversation then explodes into a free-for-all about the sincerity of converts to Protestantism and about Catholics who are morally upright as opposed to those who need "other things." (1996, pp. 1–2)

The social event described above is one of everyone's favorite activities in Haiti: *Bay odyans*.[3] A literal translation of bay odyans would be "give talk," and it could be loosely translated as "chatting." But whereas a chat involves a certain focus on the relationships of the people involved, in odyans the focus is on the words or the stories. The word chat usually has an intimate or friendly connotation, while bay odyans has a public connotation. Most households in Haiti are still very low tech; instead of watching television for entertainment, Haitians talk. Adults and children spend a remarkable amount of time in conversation. People drop in on each other, sit down wherever it is comfortable, and just talk. Sometimes the group is made up of friends and family members, at other times the members of the group don't know each other, as in the bus conversation above. People "bay odyans" in medical offices, while waiting for transportation, among a group of outdoor merchants and their clients, at places of work, under streetlights at night in the cities, at wakes and parties.

Bay odyans, or *lodyans*, can follow different formats, which may include storytelling, telling jokes and riddles, reminiscing about the good old days, or arguments or *diskisyon* (discussion). The richness of Haiti's oral tradition was described by Haitian folklorist and theoretician Jean Price Mars in 1928:

"Tales, legends, riddles, songs, proverbs, beliefs thrive here with an extraordinary exuberance, generosity and openness. . . . They constitute in an unexpected and startling fashion the raw material of our spiritual unity" (translated and quoted in Arthur & Dash, 1999, pp. 300–301). Recent Haitian writers (Anglade, 1999; Desquiron, 1995) describe the storytelling style of lodyans as a literary genre unlike any other, born of the oral nature of Haitian literature. Anglade (1999) claims that it is a significant creation of Haitian society comparable to other unique cultural creations of the Haitian people, such as the Vodou religion, the Creole language, marketing systems created by women, and the pairing of crops in agriculture. Anglade and Desquiron each published a book of short stories that they considered lodyans in a written form, stories about the good old days with an odd twist and a social type of humor. Desquiron (1995) describes these stories as nonlinear, meandering like a stream, unhurried in reaching conclusions.

As a middle school teacher in a Haitian bilingual program, I realized that my immigrant students felt the need for these oral events and occasionally asked if we could just sit and talk. There were times when a child would entertain the class with captivating oral skills, and other times when I would want to stop discussions because religious topics (not appropriate for public schools) would dominate our talk. I also remember having to forbid discussions about soccer that would occur immediately after recess because they were so animated that it was difficult for the boys to restrain themselves. My students who were respectful, shy, and quiet in some situations were verbally skilled in others. In order to help students master scientific concepts, I began to investigate the use of bay odyans in the science classroom.

I focus here on one particular type of bay odyans that I believe can be marshaled productively in learning and teaching science: diskisyon, or arguments, such as the one presented in the Brodwin example above. In everyday life, arguments most often center around religion, soccer, and politics. Haitian children often observe and participate in arguments. I propose that bay odyans is a linguistic event in which various participants in the group may take on certain roles, as in theater.

Life as theater is a concept used by social psychologists to underline the regularity of human behavior. Social encounters follow certain regular scripts, for each of us follows a certain pattern and type of interpretation (Billig, 1996). In Haitian social interaction we often come upon animated discussions that may seem like fights to non-Creole-speaking outsiders but that are entertaining to the participants. During these bay odyans discussions, one of the speakers voluntarily or involuntarily takes the role of a theoretician and makes a statement. In the example above, the first speaker involuntarily starts the discussion by thanking Jesus for her safety on the bus. A challenger follows the theoretician, questioning her thankfulness to Jesus, and suggests that the safety of the passengers is in the hands of the bus driver. The challenge excites the rest of the group and provokes laughter, expressions of surprise, or enthusiasm. The challenger in this religious argument asks the theoretician how she can reconcile the Protestant views that all people are children of God, yet Catholics are said to worship the devil. An argument then follows, through which divergent points of view are supported or disputed with evidence or logic. In most cases, funny interjections, laughter, and theatrical gestures punctuate the argumentation.

The theoretician or proponent of the idea has the burden of remaining calm and defending his point. Throughout the argument he may have to support his position with evidence or the force of logic, and narrow his generalizations and claims. In the bus conversation, the Protestant woman has to clarify the idea of Catholics as devil worshippers by adding that not all Catholics fall into that category. The challenger's role is often more theatrical and is directed toward both the theoretician and the audience. The challenger's counter argument is considered both a tool to arrive at the truth and entertainment for the audience. The other members of the group may watch and goad the group on for a while or take over one of the two main roles.

Bay Odyans in the Science Classroom

The following conversations took place in three different classrooms with three different teachers in two different schools. Both schools were located in an urban school district in Massachusetts that received new immigrants from Haiti every year. The teachers were participating in Chèche Konnen's professional development and research projects. They met with researchers about science content and read research on science teaching during a one-week summer seminar, and twice a month during the school year. The researchers observed classes and videotaped classroom discussions weekly. On occasion the researchers chose classroom segments that they found interesting and viewed and discussed them with the teachers at professional development sessions.

The students in the following examples ranged in grade from fifth to eighth and in age from ten to fourteen. They did not have identical educational histories, yet all of them had been in the United States for fewer than three years. Some of the students had limited experience in school; some could not read or write Creole; all were learning English.

These classes had no science textbooks because there were no appropriate books available in Haitian Creole. The teachers, by having to use primary sources of information and through their participation in the Chèche Konnen Center's professional development seminar, were propelled into the exciting role of being co-learners and co-researchers with the students (Warren & Rosebery, 1995).

The three classroom transcripts are presented here chronologically. The teachers have different participatory styles. The first is challenging the class while assuming a more traditional "teacher" role, while the other two are primarily involved in supporting the challengers. The variations in participatory styles reflect changing discourse practices of Chèche Konnen Center teacher collaborators. As our research and teaching practices evolve, there is movement away from the traditional IRE patterns of teacher-student interaction and toward the informal patterns of social interaction — in this case more towards a bay odyans type of discussion as it naturally occurs in Haitian society. The conversations were in Haitian Creole, and the Creole transcript is accompanied by an English translation, with my interpretation of the interaction. The names of the participants have been changed.

Example One: "It's invisible, and what am I?"

This example is from an early period of the Chèche Konnen Center (academic year 1991–1992), when the focus of our work was essentially on the science content. I was the seventh/eighth-grade teacher in a Haitian bilingual program. While in this position I participated as a teacher collaborator in the Chèche Konnen Project, whose goal was the improvement of science education for bilingual students. We wanted to make the content relevant to the students, and to this end we incorporated the study of sound from a scientific point of view with the production of a play that involved the whole school. While the goal of the study was to develop students' understanding of aspects of sound, like pitch and volume, we capitalized on these students' knowledge of and affinity for drum rhythms to support learning.

The following discussion was not a planned lesson. The students in this example were studying sound while also preparing a drumming and dance performance (see Conant et al., 2001, for a more detailed discussion of this example). Several of the students had been using software that provided a graphic display of sound waves picked up by a microphone attached to a computer. A portion of the wave could be frozen on the screen and printed. When the students hit a drum near the microphone, they saw a sound wave of the stroke on the screen. The transcript of the conversation begins after I asked the students to explain what the computer screen was showing. The sound probe had been in use in the classroom for a while, but I felt unsure whether it was anything more than a toy to the students.

The question being discussed was, What is being represented by the computer?

	Speaker	Creole Utterance	English Translation
1	Paul *Offers a response*	Lam son an	The sound wave
2	Teacher *Requests clarification*	E kouman l fé li nan kompitè a e m pa wè l devan zye m?	And why is it in the computer and I cannot see it with my eyes?

	Speaker	Creole Utterance	English Translation
3	Paul *Proposes that although sound waves are invisible they can be picked up by the computer*	Paske l'envisib. Kompitè a ka pran l.	Because it is invisible. The computer can grab it.
4	Jean-Pierre *Tries to challenge Paul but offers a challenge that is theatrical rather than content oriented*	Li envisib mwen menm sa m ye?	It's invisible, and what am I?
	Jean Pierre's utterance successfully brings in the audience	LAUGHTER	
5	Teacher *Redirects attention to sound waves*	Li envisib. Yeah. E pou ki sa yo rele li lam menm jan ak . . . yes?	It is invisible. Yeah. And what, why do they call it wave just like . . . yes?
6	Marilia *Responds to teacher*	Paske li fè tankou yon lam lamè.	Because it looks like an ocean wave.
7	Teacher *Approves of response*	Yeah. Li fè yon fòm tankou yon, li fè tankou yon lam lamè.	Yeah. It has a shape like a, it is like an ocean wave.
8	Jean-Pierre *Offers funny description of sound wave*	Tan kou yon majigridi.	Like a scribble.
	Audience is satisfied	LAUGHTER	
9	Teacher *Asks for more clarification*	Men kisa li ye? Ki kote lam sa ye? Nou wè li nan kompite a, epi lè li devan zye nou nou pa wè li. Ki kote li ye konsa?	But what is it? Where is that wave? We see it in the computer, then in front of our eyes we can't see it. Where is it?
10	Mireille *Responds to teacher*	Nan èr la.	In the air.
15	Reginald *Returns to original question*	Kijan kompitè a pran son an nou pa ka tande l?	How can the computer take the sound and we can't hear it?
16	Teacher *Challenges Reginald's questions*	Nou pa tande son an?	You can't hear the sound?
17	Reginald *Amends his assumption*	Nou ka tande li, nou pa ka wè li.	We can hear it, we can't see it.
18	Teacher *Returns to theoretician's proposal*	Gen yon moun ki di li envizib. Eske gen yon lòt moun ki ka di yon bagay sou sa?	Someone said it was invisible. Is there anyone else who can say something about that?
19	Jean-Pierre *Finally responds in a serious manner with a specific disagreement*	Nou pa ka tande son an. Apa yo di nou ka tande l.	We cannot hear the sound. They have just said we can hear it.
21	Paul	Nou pap tande l.	We won't hear it.
22	Jean-Pierre	Nou pa tande son an.	We don't hear the sound.

	Speaker	Creole Utterance	English Translation
23	Teacher *Questions both Paul's and Jean-Pierre's statements*	Ou pa tande?	You don't hear?
24	Jean-Pierre	Non.	No.
25	Teacher *Narrows the question*	Lè yo bat tanbou an ou pa tande l?	When they play the drum you don't hear it?
26	Jean-Pierre *Appears unsure about responding*	M tande le yo bat tanbou "but"	I hear when they play the drum, but
27	Teacher *Narrows the question*	Sa ki parèt nan kompitè a ou pa tande l?	You don't hear what shows on the computer?
28	Jean-Pierre	Non.	No.
29	Paul *Responds with a theory*	Kompitè a pa gen "baf."	The computer has no "baf."
30	Teacher *Asks for clarification*	Li pa gen kisa?	It has no what?
31	Paul *Uses a word that is actually a mispronunciation of the word "bass" he has seen on stereos*	Baf.	Baf.
32	Jean-Pierre *Plays with the word ("baf" can mean "slap"). Playful challenge with no attempt to resolve current issue*	Baf yo konn bay moun yo? LAUGHTER	The "baf" you hit people with?
33	Teacher *Asks for clarification*	M pa konprann non. Sak baf la?	I don't understand. What is "baf"?
34	Student *Suggests that they can't "hear" because the computer has no speaker*	Wo palè.	A speaker.

As the teacher in this discussion, I fill the role of the challenger, but I also behave like a traditional teacher in an IRE pattern: I ask most of the questions, repeat students' statements, and also prod students to clarify their positions. However, this discussion is somewhat more natural than a traditional IRE because no hands are raised, no students are called on individually, and divergent talk is allowed.

One interesting character in this discussion is Jean-Pierre. Since I was not providing any of the theatrical features ordinarily offered by a challenger, he has taken them up. Jean-Pierre is asking questions that are aimed at challenging the theoretician (Paul in this case) but are also intended as entertainment for the class. When he says, "It's invisible, and what am I?" he may be saying that Paul should not call something he sees on the computer screen invisible, but he is most likely trying to get a laugh from the class/audience. He is playful and funny.

Paul is the theoretician who says that sound waves are invisible, and he is trying to explain what the computer is showing. Jean-Pierre's response sounds like a challenge and provokes laughter, but the seriousness of his contributions advancing the discussion is unclear. Most of Jean-Pierre's utterances relate to some word in the theoretician's utterance and the class appreciates them, but he rarely gets close to the core subject of the discussion. He is in the theatrical mode until number 19, when he is serious and disagrees with the previous speaker. In number 32, Jean-Pierre again throws a funny challenge at Paul, the theoretician.

While the interaction in this class is not as free as in a naturally occurring discussion, my acceptance of students' speaking out without having to raise their hands and be called on, and of Jean-Pierre's recurrent remarks, show that I recognize this behavior as "normal." In a traditional IRE discussion, Jean-Pierre would have been considered disruptive and would probably have been asked to stop talking or leave the classroom. In this classroom, his role is accepted by the teacher and appreciated by the students. He is paying attention, he is participating, his peers enjoy his participation, and he does not keep the class from arriving at a reasonable conclusion for the problem being discussed.

Example Two: "How long does it take for a snail to grow?"

This example comes from a unit in which seventh- and eighth-grade students were studying pond life during the 1992–1993 school year. The teacher was a young Haitian man at the beginning of his teaching career, who was participating in the Chèche Konnen seminars on biology. The students had gone to a local pond and collected plant and animal samples for classroom observation. One boy, Steve, has told the group that he had taken about ten snails home in a jar and that after three weeks he had many more, about thirty, which he believed to be three generations of snails (see Warren & Rosebery, 1996, for more discussion of this example as a form of scientific argumentation).

The following transcript begins where Danielle repeats Steve's claim and challenges him to discuss how long it takes for snails to have babies. All of the students have observed snails and have become knowledgeable about their reproduction and growth cycles. They use their newly acquired expertise to question Steve's claim, which doesn't fit with what they have observed.

	Speaker	*Creole Utterances*	*English Translation*
1	Danielle *Challenges a claim Steve made earlier*	Ou di ou gen 30 kalmason. Nan konben tan ke chak kalmason fè pitit? Kankou, eske yon kalmason ki gen, si l fèt jodi a, èske demen li ka al fè pitit?	You say you have 30 snails. How long does each snail take to have babies? Like, does a snail that is, if it is born today, could it make babies tomorrow?

	Speaker	Creole Utterances	English Translation
2	Ameli *Supports the challenge*	Yes, Steve!	Yes, Steve!
3	Teacher *Supports the challenge*	Bon kesyon.	Good question.
4	*Class shows satisfaction for the situation*	{Commotion, students cry out, some hoot}	
5	Steve *Makes his claim more specific*	Mwen menm, m di sa! Mwen di konsa lè yo grandi. Mwen di lé yo grandi yo fè pitit.	I myself said that! I said when they grow. I said when they grow they have babies.
6	Teacher *Asks for more specificity*	Ok timoun te m di yon bagay. Sa se yon bagay ke m ta renmen konnen paske nou menm n'ap fè rechèch sou sa. M ta renmen konnen. Bon kèsyon. Steve reponn.	Ok kids let me say something. That's something I would like to know because we are also researching it. I'd like to know. Good question. Steve, respond!
7	Steve *Calmly repeats his claim that snails must grow before they reproduce*	Ok, mwen menm, men sa m te di, mwen menm, lè [ ] te poze m kèsyon sa, [ ] te mande eske menm lè pitit yo fenk fèt la, eske menm lè a yo al fè pitit anko? Mwen menm m te di non. Mwen menm m te di sa se lè yo grandi, yo vin fè pitit, paske ke, m konn mete . . .	Ok, Myself, here is what I said when . . . asked me that question . . . asked me whether just as the babies are born can they at that same time also have babies. I, myself, had said no. I myself said it will be when they grow that they will have babies because sometimes I put . . .
8	Danielle *Wants to push Steve into a narrower claim*	Kite m mande ou yon kesyon ankò anvan ou fin reponn.	Let me ask you a question again before you finish answering.
9	Steve *Asks for time*	Ou p ap rèt tann mwen fini?	You could not wait till I finish?
10	Danielle *Reformulates her challenge in a more precise form*	Anvan ou reponn li konsa, 'te m mande ou yon bagay pandan ou di sa. Kankou si ou di konsa ke yo fè pitit, e sa ou te di m, nan konben tan pou yon kalmason grandi?	Before you respond in that way, let me ask you something while you are saying it. Since you said that they had babies, and what you said, how long does it take for a snail to grow?
11	Steve *Acknowledges not knowing*	Koman m fè konnen?	How do I know?
12	Danielle	Eben, Steve . . .	Well, Steve . . .
13	Steve *Offers a general statement to explain his inability to respond to the challenge*	Kalmason toujou piti.	Snails are always small.

The teacher supports the validity of Danielle's question of how long it takes for a snail to grow, become sexually mature, and reproduce, and the rest of the students validate it as a fun challenge to Steve's claim. Steve remains calm and maintains that he has already stated that they must first grow before they have babies. Danielle refines her question to ask, "How long does it take for snails to grow?"

Warren and Rosebery's (1996) analysis of this portion of classroom conversation proposes that Danielle is asking what model of snail development underlies Steve's claim. She is basically saying to Steve that in science you cannot propose an observation that is inconsistent with other observations previously made unless you have strong evidence to support your claim. In effect her comment can be paraphrased as, "You cannot claim to have three generations of snails in your jar in a few days unless you can tell us how long it takes for a snail to reach sexual maturation and reproduce." Steve feels like he does not have enough information to answer the question, and calmly responds, "How do I know? Snails are always small."

In this discussion we notice that the teacher's role is merely to support the discussion as valid. The interaction is between Steve as the theoretician and Danielle as the challenger. The rest of the students show their enthusiasm for the challenge. Steve does not respond to the challenge very strongly. Danielle's arguments against his claim are powerful, to the point of not even giving him time to fully answer her questions. He restates what he has said, then gives up.

Example Three: "The bathrooms in Haiti have mold; the bathrooms here don't get moldy."

In this example, a group of fifth- and sixth-grade students have been observing and discussing the growth of mold (see Ballenger, 1997, for more discussion of this example). The teacher had been coteaching with an English as a Second Language teacher. As a participant in the Chèche Konnen professional development and research project, he had watched a video of the previously quoted discussion and discussed the importance of this kind of talk in the science class. As he watched the video of the snail discussion, he realized that it looked very much like discussions that commonly occur among Haitians. The following year he made a conscious decision to encourage the type of interaction that occurs naturally in a bay odyans situation in his science discussions.

The discussion in the example is about the conditions that favor or permit the growth of mold. The students have been watching mold grow on slices of bread in the classroom, and they are trying to draw inferences from their life experience about where mold will or will not grow. One of the students has already mentioned that mold grows easily in bathrooms, and Manuelle takes the position that mold doesn't grow in all bathrooms.

	Speaker	Creole Utterance	English Translation
1	Manuelle *Offers a generalization*	Twalèt Ayiti ap fè limon Twalèt isi yo pa konn fè limon. *{Whoops and commotion}*	The bathrooms in Haiti have mold. The bathrooms here don't get moldy.
2	Ernst *Challenges using counterevidence*	Oooo, kijan fè pen an fè limon?	OOOO, how come the bread gets moldy?
3	Teacher *Restates the challenge to the generalization*	Timoun, kite m di yon bagay. OK all right li di twalèt isit pa fè limon. Ou menm ou di ou pa dakò. Eksplike.	Children, let me say something. She said the bathrooms here don't get moldy, you say you don't agree. Explain.
4	Ernst *Restates his challenge*	Kijan fè pitit la di konsa pen-l lan fè limon?	How come the kid said that her bread got moldy?
5	Teacher *Invalidates the challenge*	Li pap pale de pen l'ap pale de twalèt.	She is not talking about bread, she is talking about bathrooms.
6	Ernst *Offers counter generalization*	Twalèt fè limon.	Bathrooms get moldy.
7	Manuelle *Wants the genralization narrowed*	Se pa tout moun.	Not everybody's.
8	Teacher	Esplike, esplike.	Explain, explain.
9	Manuelle *Offers evidence for her point*	Eske ou wè twalèt anba a konn fè limon?	Does the bathroom downstairs grow mold?
10	Ernst *Accepts her point with reserve*	Non, paske yo klin li.	No, because they clean it.
11	Manuelle *Takes the comment as a point in favor of her argument*	Enben se sam di ou la. Mwenm menn twalèt lakay mwen pa fè limon paske m klin li. *{Commotion}*	Well, that's what I'm saying. The bathroom at my house does not have mold because I clean it.
12	Jerry *Offer a possible experiment to settle the issue*	Mr. I., sak fè li pa fè limon an se paske li toujou lave l lakay li. Se pou ou fè yon eksperyans. Pinga ou lave twalèt la, pinga ou lave rido a. Rido a ap gen limon. L'ap fè limon rido a.	Mr. I, the reason it doesn't grow mold in her house is because she always cleans it. You should do an experiment. Do not clean the bathroom, do not clean the shower curtain. The curtain will have mold. The curtain will grow mold.
13	Pierre *Predicts results*	Li toujou fè limon. Chak tan li fè limon yo lave l.	It always makes mold. Every time it makes mold, they clean it.

	Speaker	Creole Utterance	English Translation
14	Manuelle *Offers an explanation*	M konn ap dòmi manman m leve m pou m lave twalèt la.	Sometimes I am asleep, my mother wakes me up to clean the bathroom.

Manuelle originally said that mold doesn't grow as much in U.S. bathrooms as in bathrooms in Haiti. The students find the claim fun to confront, as evidenced by the commotion her comment generates. Ernst attempts to challenge her claim by offering that mold is growing on the bread in the classroom. When the teacher dismisses the bread as appropriate evidence, Ernst restates his position to clarify that mold is generally something that grows in bathrooms. Ballenger's (1997) analysis of this segment interprets Manuelle's response as an attempt to discuss science against the background of her personal values: she has no mold in her bathroom because she is good at cleaning. In the video, we could see her in a posture of pride, shaking her head with authority. The difference between her opinion that mold only grows in some bathrooms and Ernst's position that mold can grow in any bathroom brings Jerry to offer the possibility of an experiment in which the frequency of bathroom cleanings would be a variable.

The teacher serves as moderator, acknowledges that there is a conflict, and encourages Manuelle to defend her position. Manuelle is a strong theoretician who is challenged at first by Ernst, and later by others in the class. Her statement that bathrooms grow mold in Haiti but not in the United States is immediately taken up by Ernst and brings on sounds of excitement in the classroom. Ernst's counter example as a challenger is not a sufficient argument against Manuelle's claim, because he focuses on the fact that mold does grows in the United States because the class saw it grow on bread. When the teacher asks that the discussion remain on the subject of bathrooms, Ernst simply states that bathrooms get moldy. After the 11th turn the class seems to think that Manuelle is winning the argument and shows it with noisy restlessness. At that point Jerry takes over the role of the challenger and offers an experiment that would prove that mold does grow in the United States.

Bay Odyans as an Intellectual Resource in the Science Class

In each of these conversations, Haitian students presented their ideas about the scientific topics they have been studying. In each case, the conversation was in their native language with a teacher who was competent in that language. The teacher was not the single center of the conversation. These conversations moved away from a controlled dialogue in which the teacher asked all the questions and the children must provide satisfactory answers, and moved toward a group attempt to come to conclusions about observed scientific phenomena. The teacher assumed that all of the children involved were attempting to make sense of the subject. In every one of the classes the children were involved in a prolonged, multifaceted study of a subject. The students' beliefs and ideas were used as theories to be examined, tested, and explored in many ways. The teachers were not assumed to be the single, authoritative source of information. The argumentation skills the children brought from home were a powerful intellectual resource as they made sense of diverse ideas and data.

These data stand in contrast to Lee et al.'s (1996) research in science education that aims to measure the cognitive skills of students from various linguistically and culturally diverse communities. To do so, they constructed a set of tasks and trained teachers to administer the tasks to children. The teachers learned the protocol in order to attempt to elicit certain types of language from the children. By choosing teachers of the children's ethnic group, the researchers presumably felt that they had covered the "language and culture" aspects of the tasks. Their measures of achievement, however, were defined in terms of White, middle-class standards. They primarily used a question-and-answer situation, which for most middle-class students is a familiar format. For other children, this format can be strange, confusing, and, to some, even threatening (Boggs, 1985; Cazden, 1988; Heath, 1983). The results of these tasks — and the way they have been interpreted — imply incorrectly that Haitian children are nonverbal. In our experience, however, we have typically found Haitian children to be both highly competent and highly verbal. We suggest that tasks that are designed to elicit Western literate modes of language will inevitably find discrepancies in the performance of children from diverse backgrounds. It would be a mistake to equate these discrepancies with a lack of cognitive or linguistic ability. We worry that this kind of research does not make visible the considerable intellectual and verbal fluency of these children, and therefore lacks a necessary foundation on which to design instruction.

Labov's (1972) classic research on children who speak Black English vernacular gave us an example of different verbal performances by the same child in different situations. Labov concluded that "the social situation is the most powerful determinant of verbal behavior and that the adult must enter into the right social relation with a child if he wants to find out what a child can do" (p. 212).

The Haitian teachers participating in the Chèche Konnen seminars were inspired by Karen Gallas' idea of opening up the range of discourses allowed in science discussions. They were able to move away from the front of the classroom to position themselves in a circle and allow the students' cultural background to permeate the science class. By moving away from the authoritarian stance of a traditional teacher, they allowed the bay odyans tradition to support scientific argumentation. In a traditional classroom where knowledge always resides in the teacher's mind, many students fall silent as they try to guess the teacher's expectations. The case could be even more extreme with Haitian children. Many Haitians are so used to being socially slighted that their first response to a question is not even to try to answer it, but to figure out why the question is being asked. A child's silence and lack of response may have its own particular meaning. The interpretation of silence by the interviewer is subjective.

These classroom discussions reflect a type of inquiry that undergirds scientific research. Scientists do not usually work in isolation, but within a group of researchers and graduate students. They spend time daydreaming, joking and arguing informally about their ideas and their results (Feynman, 1985; Root-Bernstein, 1989; Wolpert & Richards, 1997).

The students in the above examples also are engaged in authentic scientific thinking and discussion of scientific phenomena. Although the classroom discussions involved fun, laughter, interjections, interruptions, and theatrical gestures, they accomplished the goals of scientific arguments: observations were discussed, generalizations were attempted and narrowed, knowledge was clarified. The teaching and learning environment was designed to provide the students with an opportunity to build on their knowledge, beliefs, and skills in ways that are similar to those of scientists. They are not dealing with a teacher who already knows all the answers and asks all the questions. Rather, they theorize with the teacher, ask questions, explore the meanings of their questions, make claims, and offer evidence and arguments to support their claims. All of this is accomplished because the teacher assumes a position of respect for the knowledge and sense-making resources of the students. The professional development seminars offered by the Chèche Konnen center encouraged the teachers to take a learner's stance and a researcher's purpose. The teachers learned science during the seminars and discussed their learning with the group of teachers and researchers. Later they approached the same issues with their students with the same open-ended attitude; for instance, in the second example the teacher says, "I would like to know because we are also researching it." In other instances, the teacher's questions are generally about clarifying points or asking for evidence. As our work became more focused on classroom discourse, "bay odyans" skills emerged as an asset that the children had and were able to build on in science discussions.

Some educators who hold a more rigid view of science language may question my characterization of the classroom talk here as scientific inquiry. Some teachers have very specific ideas about when children should speak and what they should say. It is possible that these teachers may fail to engage students because they ignore the fact that in order for genuine learning to take place the students need to integrate new skills and knowledge with what they bring from home. To be "responsive to the children and responsible to the subject matter" (Ball, 1997, p. 776), we must be able to hear children's diverse voices and create opportunities for them to pursue their ideas and questions. The rigidity of a traditional classroom interaction with predefined responses following a question-answer format ignores the learner's involvement in learning (Cazden, 1988; Lemke, 1990). It may mean that children from families of non-Western traditions are shut out of classroom participation and that skills from other traditions are devalued and subtracted from children's cognitive repertoires, and therefore also made unavailable to their fellow students.

We must question research that characterizes children of Haitian descent as incompetent — that is, lacking language and cognitive skills — in thinking scientifically. We must question the assumptions such research makes about the neutrality or objectivity of the tasks and analytic methods it uses in constructing interpretations of complex social interactions between teachers or researchers and students. We must look instead for evidence of competence in situations where children are able to display what they know and what they can do.

Notes

1. The development of this article was funded by the U.S. Department of Education, Office of Educational Research and Improvement, Cooperative Agreement No. R306A60001-96 to the Center for Research on Education, Diversity and Excellence, University of California, Santa Cruz; the National Science Foundation, REC 0106194; and the Spencer Foundation. The original data collection was funded by the National Science Foundation, RED-9153961. The data presented, the statements made, and the views expressed are solely the responsibility of the author. No endorsement by the funding agencies should be inferred.
2. The Chèche Konnen Center is a research group at TERC, a not-for-profit education research and development organization based in Cambridge, Massachusetts. Our mission is to improve mathematics, science, and technology teaching and learning. Directed by Ann Rosebery and Beth Warren, and working in collaboration with public school teachers on issues of language and culture in science teaching and learning, the Chèche Konnen Center for Science Teaching and Learning is funded by the National Science Foundation, ESI-9555712.
3. *Lodyans* and *odyans* are variants of the same word. Variations due to regional or educational background are accepted in both spoken and written Creole.

References

Anglade, G. (1999). *Les blancs de mémoire*. Québec: Les Editions du Boréal.
Arthur, C., & Dash, M. (1999). *Libète: A Haiti anthology*. Princeton, NJ: Markus Wiener.
Ball, D. L. (1997). What do students know? Facing challenges of distance, context, and desire in trying to hear children. In T. Biddle, T. Good, & I. Goodson (Eds.), *International handbook on teachers and teaching* (pp. 769–817). Dordrecht, Netherlands: Kluwer Press.
Ballenger, C. (1997). Social identities, moral narratives, scientific argumentation: Science talk in a bilingual classroom. *Language and Education, 11*, 1–14.
Barnes, D., & Todd, F. (1995). *Communication and learning revisited*. Portsmouth, NH: Boynton/Cook Heinemann.
Belluck, P. (1999, July 4). Reason is sought for lag by Blacks in school effort. *New York Times*, p. 1.
Billig, M. (1996). *Arguing and thinking: A rhetorical approach to social psychology* (2nd ed.). Cambridge, Eng.: Cambridge University Press.

Boggs, S. T. (1985) *Speaking, relating, and learning: A study of Hawaiian children at home and at school.* Norwood, NJ: Ablex.

Brodwin, P. (1996). *Medicine and morality in Haiti.* Cambridge, Eng.: Cambridge University Press.

Cazden, C. B. (1988). *Classroom discourse.* Portsmouth, NH: Heinemann.

Conant, F., Rosebery, A., Warren, B., & Hudicourt-Barnes, J. (2001). The sound of drums. In E. McIntyre, A. Rosebery, & N. Gonzalez (Eds.), *Building bridges: Linking home and school* (pp. 51–60). Portsmouth, NH: Heinemann.

Desquiron, J. (1995). *Je me souviens.* Port-au-Prince, Haiti: Les Editions Henri Deschamps.

Feynman, R. (1985). *What do you care what other people think?* New York: Bantam Books.

Heath, S. B. (1983). *Ways with words: Language, life, and work in communities and classrooms.* Cambridge, Eng.: Cambridge University Press.

Hemphill, L. (1986). *Context and conversational style: A reappraisal of social class differences in speech.* Doctoral dissertation, Harvard University.

Gallas, K. (1995). *Talking their way into science.* New York: Teachers College Press.

Labov, W. (1972). *Language in the inner city: Studies in the Black English vernacular.* Philadelphia: University of Pennsylvania Press.

Latour, B., & Woolgar, S. (1986). *Laboratory life: The social construction of scientific facts.* Princeton, NJ: Princeton University Press.

Lee, O., & Fradd, S. (1996). Interactional patterns of linguistically diverse students and teachers: Insights for promoting science learning. *Linguistics and Education, 8,* 269–297.

Lee, O., & Fradd, S. (1998). Science for all, including students from non-English-language backgrounds. *Educational Researcher, 27,* 12–21.

Lee, O., Fradd, S., & Sutman, F. (1995). Science knowledge and cognitive strategy use among culturally and linguistically diverse students, *Journal of Research in Science Teaching, 32,* 797–816.

Lemke, J. (1990). *Talking science.* Norwood, NJ: Ablex.

National Science Foundation. (1996). *Foundations: The challenge and promise of K-8 science education reform.* Arlington, VA: National Science Foundation.

Naudillon, F. (2001). *Rupture et irruption dans la lodyans.* Paper presented at the Haitian Studies Association Conference, St. Michael's College, Burlington, Vermont.

Oakes, J. (1990). *Lost talent: The underparticipation of women, minorities, and disabled persons in science.* Santa Monica, CA: Rand.

Root-Bernstein, R. S. (1989). How scientists really think. *Perspectives in Biology and Medicine, 32,* 472–488.

Rosebery, A., Warren, B., & Conant, F. (1992). Appropriating scientific discourse: Findings from language minority classrooms. *Journal of the Learning Sciences, 2*(1), 61–94.

Warren, B., Ballenger, C., Ogonowski, M., Rosebery, A., & Hudicourt-Barnes, J. (2001). Rethinking diversity in learning science: The logic of everyday languages. *Journal of Research in Science Teaching, 38,* 1–24.

Warren, B., & Rosebery, A. (1995). Equity in the future tense: Redefining relationships among teachers, students, and science in linguistic minority classrooms. In W. Secada, E. Fennema, & L. Adajian (Eds.), *New directions in mathematics education* (pp. 298–328). New York: Cambridge University Press.

Warren, B., & Rosebery, A. (1996). "This question is just too, too easy!" Perspectives from the classroom on accountability in science. In L. Schauble & R. Glaser (Eds.), *Innovations in learning: New environments for education* (pp. 97–125). Hillsdale, NJ: Erlbaum.

Wolkstein, D. (1978). *The magic orange tree and other Haitian folktales.* New York: Schocken Books.

Wolpert, L., & Richards, A. (1997). *Passionate minds: The inner world of scientists.* Oxford, Eng: Oxford University Press.

The Struggle and Renaissance of Indigenous Knowledge in Eurocentric Education

MARIE BATTISTE

To understand the suppression of Indigenous humanities in universities and the media is to replay colonial encounters in a freshly critical key. This effort of thinking, unthinking and rethinking has of course in so many places proven almost unthinkable. It has been a prohibited activity. It has also been taken as a sign of backwardness and deficiency to be ignored or ridiculed in social and educational encounters between Indigenous peoples and those intent on displacing, enslaving, assimilating or eliminating them. Thinking in Indigenous languages and Indigenous ways has until very recently fared spectacularly badly in those elite institutions explicitly and traditionally dedicated to thinking, namely universities. And the consequence of elite ignorance, resistance and refusal have been felt within school systems that take their cues and key features of their curricula from their educational "betters" within mainstream knowledge hierarchies. (Battiste, Bell, Findlay, Findlay, & Henderson, 2005, p. 11)

Distinct knowledges matter and generate deep struggle in education systems that cannot be avoided. The struggles of Indigenous students and scholars in the global Eurocentric academy are multiple, diverse, and complex, yet are largely intertwined with Eurocentric systems and their knowledge. In this brief overview, my purpose is to present the unfolding struggle to recognize and affirm Indigenous Knowledge (IK)[1] as a distinct knowledge system, with its own concepts of epistemology and scientific and logical validity, within contemporary education systems. This struggle demands an urgent agenda to effect educational reform — reform that has been the source of a renaissance in Indigenous scholarship — and to protect and enhance Indigenous heritage and livelihood damaged by colonial assimilation projects, neglect, diminishment, and racism.

In the global educational crisis facing Indigenous peoples[2] articulated over the past thirty years,[3] a convergence of Indigenous scholars who have pursued research through graduate work in universities and with their Elders, knowledge keepers, and leaders has drawn attention to the fatal abeyance of IK in the education of Indigenous peoples (see, Battiste, 1986, 1998; Battiste, Bell, & Findlay, 2003; Memmi, 1965; Said, 1992). Beginning with the early efforts to educate Indigenous people at Harvard College and Dartmouth College, assimilation strategies cultivated in governmental policy, educational systems, and teacher-training institutions around the world have had a long and devastating history of forcing Eurocentric values, beliefs, and knowledge on Indigenous peoples, and of displacing Indigenous knowledge, languages, and cultures. The results of these assimilationist strategies are multigenerational educational failures among Indigenous peoples and educational outcomes well below the national average. While school records are incomplete and fragmented, outcome measures on Indigenous students, in Canada and the U. S., have demonstrated that Indigenous peoples have the lowest record of achievement and employment among the citizens in those countries (Battiste, 2005; McConaghy, 2002).

The failings of those systems and practices are well known, as are their implications for Indigenous peoples in the loss and erosion of their languages and knowledge systems (Parliament of Canada, 1996). Compulsory English-language instruction and a prohibition on speaking Indigenous languages are part of an assimilationist strategy that resulted in great linguistic losses worldwide. Indigenous peoples who have lost their language due to government assimilationist policies face a great challenge. There is evidence that language loss is not purely linguistic but also involves the socialization of language and knowledge, ways of knowing, and nonverbal and verbal communication — the core tools of Indigenous knowledge and capacity within Indigenous cultures. Currently, the colonial and neocolonial models continue to offer publicly funded schools and their students a fragmented, negative, and distorted picture of Indigenous peoples in history, textbooks, and curricula. These models characterize IK as primitive, backward, or superstitious, causing Indigenous peoples to be viewed as deficient and requiring remedies that renew the assimilation cycles of European knowledge and languages and that destroy Indigenous peoples' self-esteem and self-confidence.

Despite this realization, few schools and universities have made IK a priority in educating Indigenous students, much less teaching all students about diverse knowledge systems; instead the focus is on fragmented cultural practices that make visible Aboriginal peoples' artistry, powwows, and archival and museum work, which perpetuates notions of Indigenous peoples as historical and local, not contemporary and global with a knowledge system that has value for all. Few teacher-training institutions have developed any insight into the diversity of the knowledge foundations of Indigenous peoples or decolonization of knowledge, often treating IK as though it were a matter of race or culture, or multicultural and cross-cultural education (Battiste et al., 2005). Indigenous Knowledge needs to be treated as a distinct knowledge system that is equal to Western thinking, rather than being invisible to Eurocentric scholarship and knowledge, to its development theories, and to its global science. Indigenous Knowledge comprises many diverse systems of knowledge, mostly unexplored by Eurocentrism and still being unraveled by Indigenous academics around the globe. Consequently, IK has not been captured and stored in a systematic way by Eurocentric educational systems and publishing companies. Indeed, in most cases there has been a concerted effort to erase it. Therefore, when Eurocentric educators encounter cultural difference, they have very little theory, scholarship, research, or tested practice to draw on in order to engage Indigenous learning in a way that is not assimilative or racially defined; their teaching is thus not informed by international conventions and declarations[4] or by best practices that have been shaped by a respect for IK and cultural diversity (Battiste et al., 2005). This absence creates unmanageable abeyances linked directly to Eurocentrism. The initial educational struggle for Indigenous educators, then, is to sensitize the Eurocentric consciousness in general and educators in particular to the colonial and neocolonial practices that continue to marginalize and racialize Indigenous students. The second struggle is to convince them to acknowledge the unique knowledge and relationships that Indigenous people derive from place, from their homeland, and that are central to their notions of humanity and science and passed on in their own languages and ceremonies.

Indigenous Knowledge is being revealed both nationally and internationally as an extensive and valuable knowledge system. It is not only a remedy to the continuing failures of the education system, but also the opening to understanding distinct knowledges that the twenty-first century education must learn to operate in. Unlike critical race theory, antiracism theory, and postcolonial critique, all of which focus on reforming Eurocentrism, when respectfully presented, IK provides a positive approach to dealing with self-doubt and low self-esteem among Indigenous populations and a balanced perspective of the socio-historic reality in which we all live (Battiste, 2000). The question "What *is* Indigenous knowledge?" is usually asked in order to understand a cognitive system that is alien to those who ask, thus underscoring the prevailing hegemony and monopoly of Eurocentrism in universities and colleges. According to the categories used by Eurocentric knowledge, IK is understood as a transcultural (or intercultural) and transdisciplinary source of knowledge; however, Indigenous peoples view their knowledge as distinct and separate from Eurocentric knowledge. Indigenous Knowledge comprises the complex set of languages, teachings, and technologies developed and sustained by Indigenous civilizations. Often oral and symbolic, it is transmitted through performance and the structure of Indigenous languages and passed on to the next generation through oral tradition in modeling, ceremonies, problem-solving, and animation, rather than through the written word. Indigenous Knowledge is typically embedded in the cumulative experiences and teachings of Indigenous peoples rather than in a library or in journals of applied research.

Indigenous Knowledge does not mirror classic Eurocentric orders of life or languages. It is a distinct knowledge system in its own right with its own internal consistency, diversities, and ways of knowing. Literature on the topic of IK and pedagogy is emerging, although it is limited in scope and depth, particularly in the North American context. What literature exists does attempt to clarify the nature of IK, its frameworks, and its contributions to educational reform and disciplinary research, and to explore the ethical considerations for the use of that knowledge (see Battiste & Henderson, 2000).

Indigenous Knowledge is a growing field of inquiry, particularly for those interested in innovation and success in Indigenous education. The educational successes acknowledge the distinctiveness of and the attempts to balance the knowledge systems. They seek a respectful way of converging Eurocentric and IK systems, including both the human and physical sciences. This is a struggle with the few pedagogical or theoretical structures and an opportunity, one that has consumed most of my professional career. In the past twenty years, my educational achievement and that of others in the universities and colleges is directly related to our understanding of Eurocentric knowledge (EK) systems. In graduate studies, I discovered that EK was not the solution but the problem. EK discriminates against IK systems and students as much as racism. Finding a satisfactory solution to the Eurocentric educational challenge is the necessary first step in remedying the failures of the existing educational system that affect Indigenous students, and in bringing about a fair and just educational system that acknowledges, respects, and builds on both Indigenous and Eurocentric knowledge systems. Such rethinking of education from the perspective of IK and learning ways of being and knowing is of crucial value to both Indigenous and non-Indigenous educators who seek to understand the failures, dilemmas, and contradictions inherent in past and current educational policy and practice for Indigenous students.

The recognition and intellectual activation of Indigenous Knowledge today is an act of remediation and renaissance by Indigenous people. These struggles are a regeneration of educational integrity, where success has been found in affirming and activating the holistic systems of Indigenous Knowledge. These practices reveal the utility, wealth, and richness of Indigenous languages, worldviews, teachings, and experiences to animate educational achievement. Once again, language is the most significant factor in the restoration, regeneration, and survival of Indigenous Knowledge. Educators of Indigenous students cannot stand outside of their languages to understand Indigenous knowledge. Where Indigenous languages, heritages, and communities are respected, supported, and connected to Elders and holistic learning, educational successes among Indigenous students can be found. These connections both nourish student learning and ensure their comprehension of the worldviews and heritage of their people. Indigenous languages are irreplaceable resources in any educational reforms.

The UN Declaration of the Rights of Indigenous Peoples affirmed that Indigenous people have the international right to establish and control their institutions and educational systems, and to provide education in their own languages in a manner appropriate to their cultural methods of teaching and learning (*Supra* note 9, Article 14). They have a right to their Indigenous Knowledge. They have a right to revitalize, use, develop, and transmit to future generations their "histories, languages, oral traditions, philosophies, writing systems and literature" (Article 13(1)). They have "the right to maintain, control, protect, and develop their cultural heritage, traditional knowledge, and traditional cultural expressions, as well as the manifestation of their science, technologies and cultures" (Article 31). States cannot discriminate against Indigenous peoples' cultures, traditions, histories, and aspirations in education (Article 14(2) and Article 15) and, in conjunction with Indigenous peoples, are required to take effective measures to provide an education to Indigenous students in their own culture and language (Article 14(3)). These rights are not new international law (*Supra* note 9), they constitute the "minimum standards for the survival, dignity, and well-being of the indigenous peoples of the world" (Article 43). The Declaration merely codifies the existing global consensus on the education of Indigenous students. Through intellectual and educational self-determination, Indigenous academics are developing and will continue to develop new analyses, pedagogies, and methodologies to decolonize themselves, their students, their communities, and their institutions (Findlay, 2003; Grande, 2004; Lomawaima & McCarty, 2006; McConaghy, 2002; Smith, 1999).

The traditional Eurocentric view of Indigenous peoples and their heritage as exotic objects that have nothing to do with science and progress is over. This prejudicial view will now have to compete with international law and the intellectual nexus of postcolonial and poststructural theories that underscore the importance of IK and languages. In this new context, the immediate pedagogical struggle for educators is how to balance colonial legitimacy, authority, and disciplinary capacity of EK with IK. What is obvious to committed educators teaching Indigenous students is that any attempt to decolonize schools and actively resist colonial paradigms is a complex, transformative, and daunting context-breaking praxis. In the past, it was easier for educators to ignore this struggle based on their vision of the superiority of Eurocentric thought. In the context of education reform, however, this balancing of distinct knowledges cannot be achieved without the schools acknowledging the silent curriculum of Eurocentric knowledge transmission and instructional pedagogy.

To effect reform, educators need to make a conscious decision to nurture Indigenous Knowledge, its dignity, identity, and integrity by making a direct change in school philosophy, policy, pedagogy, and practice. They need to develop missions and purposes that carve out time and space to affirm and connect with the wisdom and traditions of Indigenous Knowledge. They need to teach holistic and humanistic connections to local and collective relationships. They need to make educational opportunities for students to come together in community with people who bring out their holistic better selves.

In those few exceptional universities that have acknowledged the Indigenous Knowledge issue, the struggle becomes developing "transsystemic" analyses and methods that reach beyond the two distinct systems of knowledge to create fair and just educational systems and experiences. This is part of the ultimate struggle, a regeneration of new relationships among and between knowledge systems, as scholars competent in both knowledge systems seek to converge and reconcile them. Only when these analyses and methods in thought and behavior are made can we create a truly "higher" educational system that is a place of connectedness and caring, a place that honors the heritage, knowledge, and spirit of every Indigenous student and contributes to the building of transsystemic knowledge for all students.

Notes

1. Indigenous knowledge is systemic, covering both what can be observed and what can be thought. It has many names: "folk knowledge," "local knowledge or wisdom," "nonformal knowledge," "culture," "indigenous technical knowledge," "traditional ecological knowledge," and "traditional knowledge."
2. *Indigenous* is the international global term, while *Aboriginal* is local to Canada and *Native American* local to the United States. The issues here are not local but global.
3. The education of Native Americans is in a deplorable state with the overall status falling well below that of other Americans (*Senate Subcommittee Report, Indian Education: A National Tragedy, A National Challenge* (1969); *Indian Education Act* (1972); the *Native American Languages Act* (1990); *Indian Nations At Risk: An Educational Strategy for Action* (1992); the *White House Conference on Indian Education* (1992); *Bilingual Education Act of the Elementary and Secondary Education Act* (1994); and the *Executive Order of August 1998 on Indian Education* (1998)). Canada and Australia have the same failures (*The Report of the Royal Commission on Aboriginal Peoples* (1996), and *Factors Affecting Performance of Aboriginal and Torres Island Strait Islander Students at Australian Universities: A Case Study* (1996)). New Zealand had the same failures but they are correcting it with Maori language nests and Kaupapa Maori education (Smith, 2000).
4. UN *Declaration on the Rights of Indigenous Peoples* (2007), UN Doc. A/61/L.67; *International Covenant on Economic, Social and Cultural Rights* (1967) G.A. Res. 2200; *Convention on Biological Diversity* (1992); International Labour Organization *Convention on Indigenous and Tribal Peoples in Independent Countries*, 1989 (No. 169) 28 I. L. M. 1382; Mataatua Declaration on Cultural and Intellectual Property Rights of Indigenous Peoples (1993), First International Conference on the Cultural and Intellectual Property Rights of Indigenous Peoples, 12–18 June, 1993, Whakatane, Aotearoa Draft ms.; Indigenous Declaration of the Rights of Indigenous People (1993); Saskatoon Declaration of Indigenous Cultural Restoration and Policy Recommendations (1996); UNESCO *The World Conference on Science for the Twenty First Century: A New Commitment* (1999); UN Draft Principles and Guidelines for the Protection of the Heritage of Indigenous Peoples (2001) E/CN.4/Sub.2/1995/26 and E/CN.4/Sub. 2/1995/31; Draft Inter-American Declaration on the Rights of Indigenous Peoples; UNESCO Universal

Declaration on Cultural Diversity (2001); UNESCO World Conference on Cultural Policies, Mexico City (1982); UNESCO *Recommendation Concerning Education for International Understanding, Co-operation and Peace and Education relating to Human Rights and Fundamental Freedoms* (1974); UNESCO *Convention Against Discrimination in Education* (1960).

References

Battiste, M. (1986). Cognitive assimilation and Micmac literacy. In J. Barman, Y. Hébert, & D. McCaskill, (Eds.), *Indian education in Canada: The legacy. Vol. I.* (pp. 23–44). Vancouver, Canada: UBC Press.

Battiste, M. (1998). Enabling the autumn seed: Toward a decolonized approach toward Aboriginal knowledge, language and education. *Canadian Journal of Native Education, 22*(1), 16–27.

Battiste, M. (Ed.). (2000). *Reclaiming Indigenous voice and vision.* Vancouver, Canada: UBC Press.

Battiste, M. (2005). State of Aboriginal learning: Background paper for the "National dialogue on Aboriginal learning," Canadian Council on Learning. Retrieved November 3, 2007, from http://www.ccl-cca.ca/NR/rdonlyres/210AC17C-A357-4E8D-ACD4-B1FF498E6067/0/StateOfAboriginalLearning.pdf

Battiste, M., Bell, L., Findlay, I. M., Findlay, L., & Henderson, J. Y. (2005). Thinking place: Animating the Indigenous humanities in education. *Australian Journal of Indigenous Education* [Special Edition], *34*, 11.

Battiste, M., Bell, L., & Findlay, L. M. (2003). Decolonizing education in Canadian universities: An interdisciplinary, international, Indigenous research project. *Canadian Journal of Native Education, 26*(2), 82–95.

Battiste, M., & Henderson, J. Y. (2000). *Protecting Indigenous Knowledge and heritage: A global challenge.* Saskatoon, Saskatchewan: Purich Press.

Findlay, I. (2003). Working for postcolonial legal studies: Working with the Indigenous humanities [Special Issue]. *Law, Social Justice, and Global Development Journal, 1,* 1–15.

Grande, S. (2004). *Red pedagogy: Native American social and political thought.* Lanham, MD: Rowman and Littlefield.

Lomawaima, K. T., & McCarty, T. L. (2006). *"To remain an Indian": Lessons in democracy from a century of Native American education.* New York: Teachers College Press.

McConaghy, C. (2002). *Rethinking Indigenous education: Culturalism, colonialism, and the politics of knowing.* Flaxton, Australia: Post Pressed.

Memmi, A. (1965). *The colonizer and the colonized* (H. Greenfield, Trans.). New York: Orion Press. (Original work published 1957)

Parliament of Canada. (1996). *The Report of the Royal Commission on Aboriginal Peoples.* Retrieved November 3, 2007, from http://www.parl.gc.ca/information/library/PRBpubs/prb9924-e.htm

Said, E. (1992). *Culture and imperialism.* Cambridge, MA: Harvard University Press.

Smith, G. H. (2000). Maori education: Revolution and transformative action. *Canadian Journal of Native Education, 24,* 57–73.

Smith, L. T. (1999). *Decolonizing methodologies: Research and Indigenous peoples.* London: Zed Books.

PART TWO

Sites of Strength

For many, the word "strength" expresses ideas of endurance, sturdiness, or the ability to resist. In the context of Indigenous communities, strength also refers to purpose, power, and action — more specifically, community action. Hence, this section describes strength as it relates to the communal and action-oriented nature of Indigenous Knowledge. It draws the reader's attention to several sites of strength — communities taking action in the realms of knowledge and learning.

Richard Maclure opens this section with "No Longer Overlooked and Undervalued? The Evolving Dynamics of Endogenous Educational Research in Sub-Saharan Africa," an article that emphasizes the centrality of endogenous research — that is, the role of the local community in determining the direction of educational research and generating germane and sustainable answers to educational challenges. Further developing the links between power and action, Lilia Bartolomé's "Beyond the Methods Fetish: Toward a Humanizing Pedagogy" describes the role of "culturally responsive pedagogy" and the importance of humanizing educational experiences. Her proposed pedagogy is a call to deconstruct existing power dynamics in order to empower subordinated students. In "Aboriginal Education: The School at Strelley, Western Australia," Kenneth Liberman describes an exemplary effort by Aboriginal people in Strelley, Australia, to advance the values and goals of their community through educational self-governance. This dedication to local quests for empowerment and protection against foreign domination resonates in "Nicaragua 1980: The Battle of the ABCs," Fernando Cardenal and Valerie Miller's discussion of the 1980s Literacy Crusade in Nicaragua. They describe the literacy campaign — and the collective, collaborative fashion in which communities came together to organize and educate themselves — and thus contribute to the conceptualization of knowledge as a vehicle for political action. K. Tsianina Lomawaima's "Tribal Sovereigns: Reframing Research in American Indian Education" discusses the importance of situated scholarship and the need for communities to consider local goals for research and education in order to become self-governing and self-authoring — defining the terms of inquiry and action from a community base.

This section is capped off by, "Sites of Strength in Indigenous Research," a new work by renowned Indigenous scholar Gregory A. Cajete, who provides several crucial vantage points from which to examine strength as it relates to research and action in Indigenous communities. His discussion of research reflects the importance of Indigenous scholars studying and examining their own communities, while his focus on action represents a call for a process of social consciousness that can lead to collective movement and transformation. Cajete demonstrates that the strength of Indigenous Knowledge has relevance for diverse educational contexts, yet the knowledge source must be the local community of Indigenous scholars and communities themselves.

As you read through this section, we ask you to consider the following questions, which shaped the development of this book:

- How is strength perceived and how does it emerge, or come to be, in Indigenous contexts?
- What is the relationship or difference between power *over* and power *with*?
- How do varying perspectives of the same "site" (e.g., research or community) help us conceptualize strength?

No Longer Overlooked and Undervalued? The Evolving Dynamics of Endogenous Educational Research in Sub-Saharan Africa

RICHARD MACLURE

Obstacles to the Development of Endogenous African Educational Research

During the two decades following the success of independence movements across much of the African continent in the early 1960s, great hopes were invested in the rapid expansion of formal education systems. Yet since the end of the 1980s, education throughout sub-Saharan Africa has been persistently plagued by high rates of attrition, low achievement levels, shortfalls in infrastructure and learning materials, indications of poor teaching and low teacher morale, and disjunctions between school-based learning and subsequent job opportunities (United Nations Educational, Scientific and Cultural Organization [UNESCO], 2005). While the provision of universal access to basic education remains an as yet unattained imperative in most African countries, there is clearly also an urgent need to identify methods and strategies that will engender sweeping improvements in educational quality, relevance, and cost-effectiveness. It is now widely acknowledged that for this to occur, extensive ongoing programs of research are needed to shed light on the complexities of educational problems and to formulate appropriate policies of educational reform.

In many respects, existing knowledge of education systems and processes in sub-Saharan Africa is considerable. Yet most research published on education in sub-Saharan Africa has been produced by scholars and consultants who are employed in the universities, think tanks, and aid agencies of Northern countries.[1] Moreover, until quite recently, extensive public dissemination of endogenous educational research — studies that have been conducted by African researchers who live and work in their countries of origin — has been relatively scarce. This has been inevitable to some extent in light of the longstanding economic and sociopolitical travails that have afflicted African countries, and the vast technological and information disparities that exist between Northern countries and those of sub-Saharan Africa.

As elsewhere in the world, universities in Africa are ostensibly the main institutional foundations of autonomous national research. Yet despite the training and knowledge of their professorates, most university departments relegate independent scholarly research to a peripheral activity. The lack of financial and technical resources, the scarcity of journal subscriptions and recent books, and large student enrollments that necessitate heavy teaching loads have severely hampered the development and sustainability of endogenous research capacities within sub-Saharan African systems of higher education (Stren, 2001). With national universities generally overwhelmed by a combination of limited financial resources and steady growth in enrollment, scientific output from the whole of sub-Saharan Africa has been estimated at less than 1 percent of the world's output (International Development Research Centre/Association of Universities & Colleges of Canada [IDRC/AUCC], 2003). As a way to compensate, universities have customarily allowed for the creation of quasi-independent research centers that have attracted financial support from foreign backers and collaborative ties with Northern Africanist scholars. Institutes such as the Research Consultancy Bureau at Cape Coast University in Ghana and the Centre for Basic Research in Uganda have functioned essentially as consultancy firms, generating income for the universities that house them and complementing the relatively low university salaries of professors affiliated to these centers (Association for the Development of Education in Africa [ADEA], 1998). In fact, since adequate financial input for research is generally available through Northern-funded baseline studies and project evaluations, private research and evaluation consultancy groups have proliferated in sub-Saharan Africa. Yet as with all contracted research, the parameters of inquiry are defined by the contracting organizations, most of which are foreign to Africa. It is thus difficult for many otherwise well-trained researchers to establish their own independent research programs when they are understandably drawn to opportunity structures that offer attractive facilities and salaries (Association of African Universities & World Bank, 1997).

In light of the need to monitor and evaluate an array of processes and outcomes, specialized units have generally been established within African ministries of education to gather, analyze, and report on data pertaining to educational effectiveness and quality. Yet these ministries have rarely made effective use of the information they gather. As attested to in a recent comprehensive evaluation of aid to basic education, these ministries' failure to "link research to action is the most significant problem in the use of monitoring and evaluation in support of basic education" (Freeman & Faure, 2003, p. 51). A combination of factors, including staunch resistance to change and organizational cultures that impede the use of evaluative information, have rendered information gathering a frequently redundant and ineffective ministry exercise.

Given these political, financial, and ideological hindrances to the development of independent research, concerns have often been expressed that African educational research has been dislocated from national contexts and has become largely the prerogative of researchers and institutions situated in North America and Europe.

Nevertheless, despite the weakness of African universities and the general disinterest in the practical merits of research and evaluation, endogenous African educational research has been resilient and voluminous in many respects. Until recently, however, much of it was conducted in relative obscurity and appeared only in unpublished manuscripts or reports that had limited readerships, and thus was usually quickly forgotten. This "subterranean" reality of African educational research became clear to me personally in the early 1990s while I was working on the synthesis of a series of national inventories of educational research sponsored by the Educational Research Network of West and Central Africa (ERNWACA). To the delight of those involved, many unpublished reports and manuscripts were unearthed by the inventory exercise. Yet the very fact that so much research had languished unused clearly signaled that endogenous African educational research was generally being overlooked and undervalued by educational policymakers and international scholars (Maclure, 1997; Namuddu & Tapsoba, 1993). This in turn generated questions about the degree to which autonomous national research capacities could be developed and maintained, and whether independent educational research conducted by African scholars could influence African educational policymaking and reform.

The relationship between endogenous research and national educational policymaking in fact emerged as a central theme of the inventory synthesis report, which concluded by outlining three main recommendations to enhance the quality and visibility of African educational research: (a) that substantial support be directed to strengthen educational research capacities, largely through training and the establishment of partnerships among African scholars; (b) that concerted efforts be made to disseminate nationally conducted research through as many channels as possible — publications, databases, newsletters, enhanced library resources; and (c) that links and regular forums for communication be established between African educational researchers and educational policymakers (Maclure, 1997). These were challenging objectives, particularly in view of the entrenched fiscal and administrative constraints that had weakened African governments and university systems. It was clear, therefore, that achieving these ends would require substantial external financial and technical assistance.

Now, a decade later, with African governments and international development agencies galvanized by the Millennium Development Goal[2] of ensuring that all children complete a full course of primary schooling by 2015 (United Nations, 2000), and with the empirical knowledge base of African education an undoubtedly significant factor in shaping national policies and programs, it is useful to reexamine the current state of endogenous African educational research and to assess whether or not it continues to be overlooked and undervalued. To some extent this is a vastly presumptuous task. Given the enormous political, linguistic, and demographic diversity of sub-Saharan Africa and the breadth of education as a multidisciplinary field that engages many institutions and scores of researchers, it is next to impossible to undertake an in-depth and comprehensive assessment of the status of African educational research. Furthermore, given the continued heavy dependence of African educational research on foreign funding, there may be questions about the degree to which African educational research can be fully independent and reflective of African sensibilities and concerns.

Nevertheless, in this essay, I will attempt to piece together an overview of the evolving state of endogenous African educational research by examining two modalities of educational research, one that is characterized by the direct control of international financial and technical assistance agencies (which I will refer to more simply as donor agencies), and another that is conducted largely under the auspices of formally established research networks that promote a praxis approach whereby research is oriented toward fostering policy-related reflection and dialogue. As I will show, despite diverse constraints and limitations, African researchers, by using both approaches, have been able to make considerable advances in contributing to the available knowledge base of African education and in participating more effectively in discourses of educational policymaking.

The Donor-Control Approach: Research as Product

Over the last two decades, following the corrosive effects of structural adjustment policies and the advent of the Education For All movement catalyzed by the 1990 Jomtien Conference,[3] a number of multilateral donor agencies — notably the World Bank and UNICEF — and bilateral donors — including the United States Agency for International Development (USAID), the Canadian International Development Agency (CIDA), and the United Kingdom's Department for International Development (DFID) — have sought to transform themselves from functioning solely as sources of financial and material aid into purveyors of policy advice and catalysts of educational reforms in sub-Saharan Africa (King & Buchert, 1999; McGinn, 2000; Samoff, 1999). Consequently, in order to ensure the credibility of their advisory functions, they have become keenly attuned to the value of evidence-based research and the content and dissemination of ideas that impinge directly on policies of African education. Given their inevitable concerns about the efficacy and outcomes of their own programs of assistance to education, these organizations have become major producers as well as consumers of research on African education, with much of their attention centered on issues closely related to their own program mandates (Buchert, 1998; Samoff & Stromquist, 2001).

By and large, the objectives of donor-controlled inquiries are similar: to shed light on specific aspects or problems of education and to generate recommended courses of action for donor program staff and for host country counterparts (Reimers & McGinn, 1997).

To achieve these ends expeditiously, donors generally rely on a vast pool of education specialists, many of them African nationals, most of them hired on a contractual basis. While Africans are periodically designated as project leaders, they generally are appointed as coresearchers who work with or under the direction of Northern experts. Regardless of origin, however, education specialists who are involved in donor-controlled research and evaluation projects customarily share similar technical and disciplinary backgrounds. They usually hold graduate university degrees, often from Northern universities, and most have had previous and sometimes longstanding affiliation with donor agencies. Consequently, when collaborating on donor-controlled projects, they are generally bound together by mutual intellectual and professional perspectives that enable them to communicate easily and to work well together (Samoff, 1999).

With ample resources and expertise at their disposal, the World Bank and other major donors now wield substantial influence over the language and forms of inquiry and the overall orientation of applied educational research in most African countries. Although varying widely in terms of scope and quality, donor-controlled educational research has tended to generate or reinforce several common themes:

- Continued emphasis on the expansion of primary school placements and increased enrollment of girls, rural children, and other disadvantaged social groups (Tietjen, 1997; UNICEF, 2002; World Bank, 2000);
- Improved cost-effectiveness of education through more efficient fiscal and administrative capacities, and through the introduction of alternative "delivery" modalities, such as double-shift teaching and multigrade classrooms (Mattimore, Verspoor, & Watt, 2001; World Bank, 1999);
- Enhanced preservice and in-service teacher training as a way to foster improvements in the quality of classroom instruction and learning (Fiske, 1998; Gaynor, 1998; Perraton, Robinson, & Creed, 2001);
- Decentralized educational administration and strengthened local administrative systems and practices (Bray, 1996; Saunders, Riley, Craig, Poston, & Flynn, 2000; UNESCO, 2000; Watt, 2001);
- Combined support for and regulation of educational privatization and the establishment of autonomously managed community schools (Sosale, 2000; Watt, 2001; World Bank, 1999); and
- Enhanced donor coordination and emphasis on sectorwide strategies of educational assistance (Buchert, 1995; Freeman & Faure, 2003; Riddell, 2001).

While it is impossible to offer any comparative insights into the nature and content of donor-controlled research on these various issues, there is nonetheless a general tendency to focus on factors that are crucial to the continued expansion and improved efficiency of formal schooling. This is in line with a common donor agenda of specifying problems and prescribing solutions that generally include proposed system changes and external injections of financial and technical assistance. Yet this approach has attracted considerable criticism, particularly from Northern scholars (Reimers & McGinn, 1997; Samoff & Stromquist, 2001; Welch, 1998). As Samoff (1999) has argued, this approach to educational research is akin to a medical metaphor of inquiry in which education, particularly schooling, is regarded as a constellation of variables and outcomes that can be assessed through positivist methods determined in Northern institutional contexts. Because of this prescriptive approach, there rarely are indications of donor-controlled studies examining or questioning fundamental assumptions that relate to the purposes of education, to the cultural and linguistic dimensions of schooling, or to the social dynamics of classroom learning and interaction (Masemann, 1999; Welch, 1998).

At the heart of this medicalized approach to research is a power dynamic. Given the active involvement of donor agencies in the processes of knowledge accumulation and dissemination, and the corresponding dependence of African educational systems on foreign aid, agency-controlled research is essentially a top-down process (McNeely, 1995). Likewise, most of the principal authors of donor-controlled research that has focused on education in sub-Saharan Africa are non-Africans who are employed permanently in Northern institutions (Freeman & Faure, 2003). In line with the prescriptive research framework of the donor-control approach, the findings of donor agency studies are rarely subjected to extensive discussion outside of agency confines (Buchert, 1998). As such, African educational policymakers and other educational stakeholders — lower-level ministry bureaucrats, principals, teachers, and parents' associations — are generally regarded as recipients of validated knowledge that will facilitate the formulation and implementation of donor-proposed policy initiatives and reforms (Brock-Utne, 1995).

While donor agencies are frequently quite ready to embrace the language of stakeholder consultation and participation (Lavergne, 2004), and while there is clear indication of a growing African presence in donor-sponsored research and evaluation projects (even though there are still relatively few Africans functioning as principal researchers on these projects), ironically, in many instances the very *control* that donor agencies generally exercise over much of the process of knowledge production in Africa tends to hinder their effectiveness in influencing the perceptions and practices of those who work within education systems (Meier, 1999; Reimers & McGinn, 1997). Indeed, whether donor-agency studies have fostered major improvements in African education systems is a moot point (Freeman & Faure, 2003). For example, the goal of gender parity, particularly as it relates to the retention of girls in school and the quality of female learning, has proven elusive, as have questions about the long-term financial sustainability of expanding school systems and the faulty link between education and subsequent employment opportunities for the growing numbers of those leaving school. More recently, the HIV/AIDS pandemic, which has decimated the education profession in a number of southern African countries and left millions of children without parental support, has raised questions about alternative modalities of educational delivery that donor-directed studies have only recently begun to broach (World Bank, 2002).

Since the resolution of many abiding and looming problems depends substantially on coordinated actions by a range of educational stakeholders, there is growing acknowledgment of the need for a more symbiotic connection between researchers and policymakers, and for opportunities that enable stakeholders to share in the analysis of problems that they regularly confront (Reimers & McGinn, 1997). This has given rise to an alternative approach to endogenous African research, one that constitutes a combination of professional networking aiming to strengthen connections among African researchers and policymakers and the pursuit of research for purposes of collaborative reflection and policy-oriented dialogue. As I shall now discuss, it is this juxtaposition of networking and praxis-oriented research that appears to be augmenting the profile of endogenous African educational research as an increasingly significant factor in educational policy dialogue.

Networking and the Praxis Approach: Research as Social Learning and Policy Development

Just as ideas of grassroots participation and capacity-building have been integrated into the mainstream rhetoric of international development over the last two decades (Chambers, 1983; Clark, 1995), so too has the notion of research as a basis of stakeholder learning and dialogue crept into development-policy discourse (Buchert, 1998; Maclure, 2000; World Bank, 2004). This has been a key theme underlying efforts to "Africanize" educational research and to strengthen links between endogenous research and educational policymaking through the development and expansion of professional networks. Although heavily dependent on external financial aid, a key aim of networking has been to stimulate greater autonomy and solidarity among African educational researchers and to augment their influence on the praxis of policy formulation and implementation (Stren, 2001). To this end, for well over a decade, two professional networks have devoted singular attention to enhancing the capacities, the productivity, and the profiles of African educational researchers and to fostering regional communities of researchers and decisionmakers. As a result, both networks have attained prominence among African governments and donor agencies alike. A brief overview of these networks — one regional, the other covering the entire subcontinent — provides insights into an approach to educational research in sub-Saharan Africa that differs markedly from the conventional donor-control model.

The Educational Research Network of West and Central Africa (ERNWACA)

In 1988, with support from the International Development Research Centre (IDRC), a group of West African education specialists formally launched the Educational Research Network of West and Central Africa (ERNWACA).[4] The impetus for doing so was largely the sense of isolation and lack of supportive professional environments that these researchers and their colleagues had long experienced in their own countries. Conceived as a bilingual network of researchers in Francophone and Anglophone countries, ERNWACA has steadily expanded and is now a well-established professional association with national chapters in thirteen countries in West and Central Africa and a membership of approximately 250 researchers.[5] With its headquarters located in Bamako, Mali, ERNWACA is administered by a permanent coordinator who communicates regularly with national members and other significant parties, including officials in national ministries of education and donor-agency representatives, and with educational scholars in Northern countries who have an abiding interest in African education. ERNWACA widely circulates a semiannual network newsletter that provides information on recent publications and colloquia, on forthcoming activities, and on the accomplishments of prominent West African educational researchers. Although initially relying heavily on the financial assistance of IDRC, ERNWACA has successfully broadened its base of support to include funding from USAID, UNICEF, UNESCO's Regional Bureau for Education in Africa, the German Foundation for International Development, the Swiss Development Corporation, and PLAN International.

In expanding its presence among educational researchers, ERNWACA has also helped to highlight their work and strengthen their connections with policymakers. Two types of ERWNACA activities have been especially notable in this process: (a) its inventories of existing educational research in member countries, and (b) its support for workshops, meetings, and projects that have enhanced the visibility of educational researchers and served as channels of communication between researchers and policymakers. What follows is a brief overview of these two sets of activities.

The First ERNWACA Inventory: Two Decades of Post-Independence Educational Research

At the time of ERNWACA's formation, deliberations that immediately preceded and followed the 1990 Jomtien Conference on Basic Education for All frequently alluded to the imperative of strengthening the knowledge base for educational policymaking and reform (UNESCO, 1990; World Bank, 1988). Consequently, as a first tangible step in establishing a semblance of community among educational researchers across extensive national and linguistic boundaries, ERNWACA commissioned its newly created national chapters to undertake inventories of the published and unpublished products of educational research in each member country. Supported financially by IDRC and USAID, researchers in seven countries — Benin, Burkina Faso, Cameroun, Ghana, Mali, Sierra Leone, and Togo — embarked on a yearlong process of compiling and analyzing educational research manuscripts, reports, and publications.[6] By combing ministry archives and the libraries of universities and teacher-training colleges, the ERNWACA teams in each country uncovered a total of more than one thousand studies dating from the late 1960s to 1991. More than half of these included unpublished student theses and empirically grounded research papers. While the research uncovered encompassed an extensive range of topics, it was nonetheless possible to group the studies into thematic categories that revealed a broad pattern of an emerging educational crisis that has since become entrenched throughout much of the subcontinent. Very briefly, drawing from a selection of references cited in the national inventories, the findings in each category were as follows.

– Classroom Teaching and Learning: Shortcomings and Constraints

Over the years, teachers and their pupils have confronted a host of adversities: tenuous connections between the norms of family life and schooling (Essindi, 1977; Sow, 1985); severe deficiencies in infrastructures and materials that have undermined possibilities for effective teaching and fruitful learning (Wokwenmendam, 1981); pedagogical practices that have borne little relation to teacher training (Amegnonam, 1986; Mouthe, 1985); and curricular rigidities that have stifled innovation and reform (Diare, 1990; Koomson, 1990; Tetteh, 1989).

– Schooling and the Challenge of Community Engagement

Studies within this thematic cluster revealed two common findings related to community and schooling: persistent failures to establish sustainable income-generating cooperative and farm schools, and perennial difficulties in maintaining effective community management of local schools. Underlying these problems were the complex economic and socio-political dimensions of community life (Dougna, 1986; Rasera, 1986), and the contradictions between the professional and bureaucratic underpinnings of formal schooling and the decentralization of authority for purposes of community engagement in schools (Bediaku-Adu, 1987; Camara, 1987; Cisse, 1984; Gyilime, 1986).

– Education and Post-Educational Livelihoods

Another group of studies underscored the frequent disjuncture between formal schooling and the socio-cultural and economic contexts of local societies for reasons related to both educational supply and demand. On the supply side, there have been pronounced discontinuities between school curricula and labor market realities that have been shaped by weakened economies and the imposition of structural adjustment measures (Hode, 1987; Obanya, 1989). On the demand side, popular perceptions regarding the link between formal schooling and subsequent modern-sector employment remained largely constant, despite rising levels of unemployment among those leaving school (Megbemada, 1987).

– The Limits of Educational Innovation and Reform

The fourth broad category of research uncovered by the ERNWACA inventory project revealed the array of obstacles that has undermined efforts to fundamentally reform African school systems: weaknesses in planning (Gozo, 1977), lack of training and support for teachers and parent representatives (Konate, 1986), lack of consultation and local "ownership" of educational change (Sawadogo, 1984), and lack of recurrent resources for sustaining donor-sponsored innovations (Bockarie, 1979).

Implications of the First ERWNACA Inventory

Covering as it did only seven countries, the ERNWACA inventory was far from being an exhaustive survey of existing educational research in West Africa, let alone the rest of sub-Saharan Africa. Indeed, the lack of Nigerian involvement in the project was a significant caveat in what had been intended as a comprehensive review of educational research in the region. Most of the empirical research consisted of small-scale case studies that limited generalizability to broader political and economic problems affecting educational systems. It was also clear that diagnostic description far outweighed theoretical conceptualizations of educational issues, and that questions of validity and reliability were often ignored. This was not entirely surprising, however, since nearly two-thirds of the studies unearthed consisted of graduate student research essays and dissertations (the latter known as *mémoires* in Francophone countries). Other studies collated in the inventory included many unpublished seminar papers and a variety of technical reports, most of them earmarked for donor agencies and government ministries. Only 8 percent of the collated studies were published articles. The categories and breakdown of studies discussed in this first ERNWACA inventory are presented in Table 1.

For ERNWACA, this first inventory project underscored two key issues. First, despite the paucity of published research, this was an impressive volume of work that offered clear indication that African researchers had mapped out the terrain of many aspects of education in West and Central Africa. While there undoubtedly was room for capacity enhancement, this was ample evidence of a strong spirit of inquiry and evidence-based analysis that could provide fertile grist for the mill of African educational policymaking. Second, however, was the conundrum of a severe lack of dissemination. With the overwhelming proportion of endogenous educational research produced as unpublished theses and monographs that had languished in obscurity on archival shelves, it was clear that although many of these studies may have contributed to individual

TABLE 1
ERNWACA First Inventory: Types of Research Data

Types of Research	Frequency
Mémoires (French)	557
Theses (English)	89
Government Reports	146
Joint Agency Reports	7
Donor Agency Reports	55
Published Manuscripts	85
Seminar Papers	37
Unpublished Papers	80
TOTAL	1,056

career advancement, they had added little to the publicly available knowledge base of African education and to educational policy deliberations.

Fortunately, however, the collation of these studies by national ERNWACA teams, and the subsequent publication of the inventory synthesis report (Maclure, 1997), had a substantial effect in boosting the visibility of endogenous African educational research. With the assistance of USAID and ADEA, the synthesis report was translated into French and was circulated widely among international donor agencies and ministries of education. Although it is impossible to assess the impact of this first inventory project, it clearly heightened awareness among senior ministry personnel and educational researchers themselves of the untapped potential of endogenous research as a source for policy reflection and deliberation.[7]

The Second ERNWACA Inventory: Focus on Quality

Partly as a consequence of the first inventory's success in highlighting previously unknown endogenous research in several member countries, in 2002 ERNWACA undertook a second compilation of studies that focused primarily on the issue of educational quality. Although not as wide-ranging as the earlier inventory, this second project was undertaken by researchers in eleven countries and resulted in the collation of more than five hundred research reports. In a summary report of this second inventory project, Obanya (2003) summarized the main findings of the principal topics covered by the inventory. Briefly, drawing from selected references, these main findings are summarized below.

– Preschooling
This category of research consisted of a number of descriptive studies, several of which highlighted the importance of teachers' remuneration and work-

ing conditions (Agusiobo, 1999; Nchungong, 1996; Onuchukwu & Ifeanacho, 2001).

– Teaching Effectiveness

A notable issue discerned in these largely qualitative studies was the significance of teachers' personality traits over and above their formal academic qualifications. The importance of teacher morale, as exemplified by the attributes of empathy, creativity, and cheerfulness, were deemed essential for effective teaching (Alota, 1999; Goerke, 1995; Sawadogo, 1999).

– Rural-Urban Dichotomies

Although a wave of decentralization policies throughout Western Africa has been oriented toward transferring resources and administrative control of schooling to rural regions, partly in an effort to enhance local ownership of schools and to increase the relevance of schooling to community life, continuing differences in examination results and in rates of attrition and repetition indicate ongoing fundamental gaps in the quality of urban and rural schools (Madumere-Obike & Oluwuo, 2001; Tchegho, 2003).

– Gender and Education

Studies on this topic have generally indicated that increased female enrollment in schools does not signify a reduction in discrimination against girls. Prevailing patriarchal values and norms manifested in curriculum materials and in classroom interactions appear to discourage girls from excelling in subjects such as math and science, and tends to hasten female dropouts (Amin & Fonkeng, 2000; Azie, 1998; Eta, 2000; Sedel, 1999).

– Language of Instruction

Despite policy rhetoric that is largely supportive of the use of national languages for regular classroom instruction, the lack of resources for curriculum development, textbook publishing, and teacher training, coupled with evidence of lukewarm interest among parents and concerns about the politicization of language selection in multilinguistic regions, have thwarted full-scale institutionalization of national language instruction in the primary school systems of Western and Central Africa (Afiesimama, 1995; Doumbia, 2000; Haidara, 2000; Ogbonna, 2002; Ohiri-Aniche, 2002).

Implications of the Second ERNWACA Inventory

Compared to the earlier ERNWACA-sponsored inventory of educational research that had been conducted before 1991, this second compilation of studies carried out within the more recent ten-year period revealed a much lower proportion of graduate student dissertations: 31 percent versus 61 percent. The percentage of published work also increased in this later review: 19 percent, compared to the relatively meager 8 percent in the first inventory.

While a host of methodological factors prevents any definitive explanations for the differing levels of student work and published reports, particularly since Nigeria was included in the second review and not in the first, Obanya (2003) nonetheless has surmised that these differences might be due in part to an ironic combination of deteriorating graduate studies programs in West Africa and increased opportunities and incentives for researchers to publish their work.

Like the first inventory, this second compilation of studies highlighted the extensive volume of largely independent endogenous educational research that continues to be conducted in ERNWACA member countries. Much of this work remains unpublished, however, and there was no indication that any of these studies had had an impact on policy deliberations. As Obanya (2003) observed,

> This exercise demonstrates that some serious research on the quality dimensions of basic education is going on in West and Central Africa, even though a good deal of this work is not known because of the poor state of research communication and archival culture. (p. 36)

Nevertheless, through the very process of conducting an inventory of existing research, and by posting the summative report of the inventory on its website, ERNWACA has contributed to growing awareness of endogenous research that has been focusing on an array of educational issues.

Research and Policy Dialogue

In addition to bringing to light many unpublished studies and providing regular updates of national researchers and their activities, within the past ten years ERNWACA has helped to sponsor a number of national and regional studies that have been conducted expressly for the purpose of informing policy dialogue and decisionmaking. While it is beyond the scope of this essay to determine the degree to which any of these studies have actually *shaped* the formulation and implementation of the policies that they were intended to influence, it is clear that endogenous research undertaken under the auspices of ERNWACA has attained a visibility and legitimacy in educational policy dialogue that was clearly not evident in the early 1990s. This is exemplified in Table 2, which outlines a selection of ERNWACA-coordinated national and regional studies that were aimed specifically at contributing to the educational policy deliberations of ministries and international donor agencies (ERNWACA, 2005a, 2005b).

Since its inception, ERNWACA has been actively engaged in numerous meetings and conferences, most of which have brought together ERNWACA researchers with education ministry and donor agency personnel. Tables 3 and 4 present synopses of a series of national and regional meetings in 2004–05, most of which were devoted to educational policy dialogue (ERNWACA, 2005a, 2005b). As noted above, while it is not possible in this paper to demonstrate the degree to which researchers have affected the determination or modification of subsequent policies, suffice it to say that endogenous educational research has become increasingly an integral facet of educational policy dialogue in ERNWACA member countries.

As these studies and activities demonstrate, within the last ten years ERNWACA has established itself as a prominent association of African educational researchers that has a visible corporate presence in Western and Central Africa. Through a concerted effort to highlight and disseminate endogenous educational research, to sponsor studies that have a direct bearing on policy issues, and to strengthen links among educational researchers and policymakers within and among its member countries, ERNWACA has enhanced the profile of endogenous research in discourses related to educational policymaking.

The Association for the Development of Education in Africa

Working on a larger scale than ERNWACA is the Association for the Development of Education in Africa. Originally established in 1988 as the Donors to African Education under the direction of the World Bank, in the early 1990s the organization's statute as an exclusive "donors' club" was abandoned in favor of its reformulation as an association of African ministries of education. In contrast to ERNWACA, whose core purposes have been to reinforce educational research environments through research dissemination and enhanced communication and collaboration among researchers and policymakers in Western and Central African countries, ADEA has a much broader mandate.

Headquartered in the offices of the International Institute of Educational Planning in Paris, ADEA's principal mission for more than a decade has been to promote partnerships among stakeholders and to contribute to capacity-building within ministries of education for better management of educational policies. As such, a key objective has been to strengthen the knowledge base of ministries of education through policy-oriented research and systematic communication between researchers and ministry officials. With an annual budget that has recently surpassed U.S. $5 million, ADEA is bankrolled almost entirely by donor agencies (Universalia, 2005). Reflecting the contribution of international donors, ADEA's steering committee, which is responsible for the oversight and governance of the organization, is comprised of twenty-one donor-agency representatives and ten ministers of education. Yet despite this two-to-one imbalance, selected topics of research and policy dialogue are largely a function of the priorities of African ministers (Universalia, 2005).

In pursuing its mandate of enhancing policy through research, ADEA has sponsored three ongoing sets of activities that adhere to the shared praxis of strengthening the interconnections of research, policy, and practice.

TABLE 2
Recent Selected ERNWACA Studies: Topics and Countries

Complementarity between formal and nonformal education (Burkina Faso)
Study on the impact of armed conflict on the school system (Côte d'Ivoire)
Evaluation of the Ministry of Education's Scholarship Trust Fund for Girls (The Gambia)
Partnership dynamics in Koranic schools (Mali)
Study on conditions and quality of teachers (Niger)
Externally sponsored support for heightened girls' enrollment in primary schooling (Togo)
Factors affecting primary school pupil access and retention (Côte d'Ivoire and The Gambia)
Effects of community participation on access to and quality of basic education (Benin, Ghana, Guinea, and Mali)
Impact of conditionalities on educational reform policies (Benin, Ghana, Guinea, and Mali)

TABLE 3
National Colloquia Sponsored by ERNWACA, (2004–2005): Activity

Youth and HIV/AIDS conference (Cameroun)
Colloquium on teacher training (Cameroun)
Colloquium on policy-oriented participatory action research (Ghana)
Colloquium on HIV/AIDS in the education sector (Mali)
Colloquium on school management in the context of decentralization (Mali)
Colloquium on parental perceptions of education (Niger)
Colloquium on participatory action formative research (Nigeria)
Review of research and government policies on HIV/AIDS in the education sector (Senegal)

TABLE 4
Regional Activities Sponsored by ERNWACA or Involving ERNWACA Members from Two or More Countries (2004–2005): Activity

Colloquium on education, conflict, and perspectives for peace in Africa (Burkina Faso)
African Union Ministers of Education Conference (Algeria)
Governance, Equity, and Health Conference (Senegal)
UNESCO Regional Bureau for Education in Africa: "Dakar + 5 Education for All" Forum (Senegal)
Colloquium on the UN Girls Education Initiative (Senegal)
Colloquium on research and education sector policy implementation (Niger)
Colloquium on gender, education, and skills development (Mali)

– Research Working Groups

The most prominent aspect of ADEA is its research working groups. Each group is coordinated by one or two educational specialists employed in African or donor-country institutions (Table 5). Together the working groups constitute a mix of Africans and non-Africans who are specialists in different aspects of education and who can participate in defining the topics and parameters of specific research projects. In keeping with the evolving nature of issues and problems, three ad hoc working groups have recently been created and two of the original thirteen have been disbanded. In addition, the erstwhile Working Group on Female Participation has become an independent pan-African nongovernmental organization (NGO), the Federation of African Women Educators.

Although diverse in composition and in their terms of reference, the working groups share the functions of undertaking research on specific areas of potential innovation and reform and disseminating the results of research to an audience that consists primarily of ministerial and donor-agency officials who have interests and responsibilities in the areas of inquiry. The purpose of research, therefore, is instrumental: to influence the perspectives and attitudes of key officials and thus affect the formulation of national education policies. As described by Marope and Sack (2005), the research activities of the working groups have contributed significantly to "the pedagogy of policy formulation" (p. 10). A recent evaluation of ADEA notes several examples of working group research influencing national policies (Universalia, 2005). In Niger, an agreement between the Ministry of Education and the Ministry of Finance regarding improvements in the disbursement of the country's annual education budget was facilitated by a study conducted by the Working Group on Finance and Education. In Chad, a policy ratifying community hiring of school principals followed recommendations outlined in a report by the Working Group on the Teaching Profession. Similarly, research and advocacy conducted by the Working Group on Female Participation and the Working Group on Early Childhood Development have contributed to policy developments in several countries that focus specifically on gender equity and preschooling (Universalia, 2005).

As articulated in ADEA's formal vision statement, the approach to research as conducted by the working groups is one that promotes "the development of synergies and in some cases the active participation of stakeholders" (ADEA, 2003, p. 1). By conducting research not with the aim of producing policy and program blueprints but as a way to generate a fluid and iterative relationship between policy-oriented inquiry, analysis, and dialogue, the working groups have helped advance the engagement of senior African education policymakers in ongoing research activities, something often absent from conventional Northern and donor-controlled research projects. This has invariably had the

TABLE 5
ADEA Working Groups: Groups and Coordinating Institutions

Current Working Groups
Books and Learning Materials
    U.K.: Department for International Development
    South Africa: Read Educational Trust
Communication for Education and Development
    Benin: Comed Program-Wanad Center
Distance Education/Open Learning
    Mauritius: Tertiary Education Commission
Early Childhood Development
    Mozambique: Royal Netherlands Embassy
    Ghana: UNICEF House
Education Sector Analysis
    France: International Institute of Educational Planning
Education Statistics
    Netherlands: Ministry of Foreign Affairs
Finance and Education
    Senegal: Council for the Development of Social Science Research in Africa
    Canada: Canadian International Development Agency
Higher Education
    Ghana: Association of African Universities
Non-Formal Education
    Switzerland: Swiss Agency for Development and Cooperation
    U.K.: Commonwealth Secretariat
Teaching Profession
    U.K.: Commonwealth Secretariat
Female Participation
    Kenya: Federation of African Women Educators

Ad-Hoc Groups
HIV/AIDS and Education
    France: ADEA Secretariat
Quality of Education
    France: ADEA Secretariat
Postprimary Education
    France: ADEA Secretariat

Dissolved Working Groups
School Examinations
Education Research and Policy Analysis

effect of enhancing the profile and the relevance of endogenous African research as a basis of policy deliberation and decisionmaking.

– Meetings and Conferences

In tangent with working group activities that aim to link researchers to policymakers around key policy issues, over the past decade ADEA has organized six biennial meetings that have enabled researchers, ministers of education, senior bureaucrats, and donor agency representatives to convene and discuss policy-related issues in an informal, collegial fashion. By incorporating working group reports as key background documentation, these "Biennials" (as they are referred to within ADEA) have focused on different themes.[8] For example, the unifying theme of the 2003 Mauritius Biennial was The Quest for Quality: Learning from the African Experience. In keeping with this central theme, the three-day meeting consisted of a series of working group reports that were followed by roundtable discussions and informal exchanges, all focused on experiences shared by various countries concerning the challenges of strengthening educational quality in both formal and nonformal educational settings. ADEA organizers work to ensure that Biennial discussions do not dwell solely on diagnoses of educational problems, but instead move on to examine evidence of promising policies and practices, as well as the institutional and contextual factors that underlie successful educational innovations (Marope & Sack, 2005). By incorporating working group reports as key background documentation, the Biennials have provided opportunities for policymakers to reflect on what has been achieved, how and why achievements have occurred, and what opportunities and challenges must be confronted to guarantee effective policy development and implementation (Universalia, 2005).

A similar agenda underlies ADEA's Intra-African Exchange Program which organizes cross-national research visits that allow senior officials to observe educational innovations and to discuss possibilities for replication as well as corresponding constraints. Launched in 1996, the program is intended to use existing regional capacities to capitalize on the diversity of experiences and expertise.

In terms of a broader international profile, a notable highlight for ADEA was the Tenth World Congress of Comparative Education that took place in Cape Town in 1998. The first major comparative education conference to be held in Africa, the congress provided an opportunity for African researchers to present their peer-reviewed studies — many of them undertaken under the auspices of ADEA — and to interact with policymakers from elsewhere in Africa and from other parts of the world.

– Publications and Databases

In line with its aim to promote research as a basis for policy-oriented dialogue, the ADEA secretariat has compiled a catalogue of some two hundred African educational research publications and documents. Many of these are now available online. Most of the working group research reports are also included on the ADEA website (http://www.adeanet.org). In addition, the secretariat produces a quarterly newsletter that publicizes the activities of the ADEA working groups and a monthly broadsheet that offers information on recently circulated reports and publications and on educational initiatives in different countries. Both the newsletter and the broadsheet are produced on-line and are also widely distributed to ministries of education, universities, donor agencies, and NGOs.

Another form of dissemination, however, has not been successful. In the mid-1990s, with technical and financial assistance from USAID, the ADEA Secretariat established two comprehensive online databases that were intended to provide continent-wide information on education in Africa for ministries of education and donor agencies. The Statistical Profile of Education in sub-Saharan Africa (SPESSA) was said to be user-friendly, offering an interactive and graphics framework for multiple searches and uses (Hartwell, 1999). The Program and Project Information System on Education was similarly designed to provide up-to-date information on externally funded educational projects and programs in sub-Saharan Africa. Unfortunately, although the SPESSA was updated in 1999, neither database has been maintained and they have thus lapsed into redundancy. This was due in part to the lack of data emanating from many countries, which effectively thwarted possibilities for maintaining the currency of the databases. There were also indications that the databases were of little use to stakeholders in African countries where access to the Internet has often been slow and sporadic (Universalia, 2005).

The Merits and Limitations of Research Networking and the Praxis Approach

The studies, the reviews of research, and the range of dissemination activities carried out under the auspices of ERNWACA and ADEA by no means cover the extent of endogenous educational research conducted in sub-Saharan Africa. As mentioned at the outset of this essay, the breadth of education as a field of study does not allow for an in-depth, all-encompassing review of educational research in every African country. Nevertheless, the combination of networking and policy-oriented research that have been central to the mandates of these two professional associations have greatly enhanced endogenous African educational research in terms of its overall visibility and its relevance to educational policy deliberations throughout much of the subcontinent.

Three key factors have contributed to the success of these associations in augmenting the stature and influence of endogenous research. The first is the deliberate praxis orientation of the analytical work promoted and sponsored by these associations. To a large extent, this approach to research is rooted in a *raison d'être* that places less emphasis on standards of scientific rigor than it does on the social dynamics of research and the ensuing policy implications. By regarding research not as a meticulously collated and analyzed final "product" to be relayed to recipient decisionmakers, but rather as a catalyst of informed dialogue and negotiation among diverse educational policy stakeholders, these associations have attempted to situate research as an integral facet of educational policymaking and practice. From the perspective of this praxis approach to educational research, dialogue among key educational stakeholders that serves as the tangible link between knowledge creation and diffusion is as significant as the methodology of research and the content of knowledge acquired. Research, in other words, provides the springboard for collective learning and reflection that, once set in motion, may go beyond the parameters of the research itself.

This focus on collaborative stakeholder learning underscores a fundamental difference between the praxis orientation to research as exemplified by ERNWACA and ADEA and the more standardized procedures of donor-controlled research that generally focus on producing discrete research outcomes for purposes of formulating policy prescriptions and blueprints. The praxis approach is founded on the assumption that knowledge gathering and the utilization of knowledge are mutually reinforcing. Accordingly, there is a close symbiotic relation between inquiry, learning, and action, one not far from the precepts of participatory action research and the notion of indigenous knowledge as being "incarnated" in people's reflections and actions (World Bank, 2004). Indeed, as Marope (1999) has observed, this orientation is akin to a "self-study approach" that is meant to engage education officials in critically reviewing their own projects and programs. As such, "the development of a sustained culture of critical self-reflection . . . [takes] precedence over analytical sophistication" (p. 4).

A second critical factor, one that was not really foreseen when both ERNWACA and ADEA were first established, has been the advent of the Internet as a medium of dissemination. ADEA in particular has made effective use of this method of communication. Reports and publications, newsletters and news briefs, conference proceedings and *Who's Who* lists of African educational researchers are now regularly featured on ADEA's website and through ERNWACA's periodical electronic bulletins. The instantaneous nature of this form of communication and dissemination has greatly enhanced the visibility of African educational researchers and their work, not only among ministries of education and international donor agencies, but among Africanists and comparative education scholars in Northern countries. Indeed, given the universality and growing predominance of the Internet as a research tool in the North, there are indications that Northerners are becoming more knowledgeable about the scope and content of endogenous African educational research than are their African colleagues for whom access to the Internet is more expensive and cumbersome.[9] The advent of "networks of knowledge" (Stein, Stren, Fitzgibbon, & MacLean, 2001) that cross disciplinary, linguistic, organizational, and national lines, and that break free of formal, hierarchical structures in order to respond to broad social processes and policy issues, has proven to be enormously beneficial for African researchers. Through the combination of social capital and telecommunications afforded by research networks such as ERNWACA and ADEA, researchers in sub-Saharan Africa are attaining a greater and more independent voice in educational policy deliberations.

The third critical factor underlying the vibrancy of ERNWACA and ADEA has been a combination of dynamic leadership and sustained donor-agency support. Both of these associations have benefited from energetic and highly committed leaders. Since 1999, the regional coordinator of ERNWACA, Kathyrn Touré, has been indefatigable in developing links among educational researchers and decisionmakers, in encouraging the development of collaborative research projects, in disseminating research results, and in fundraising. Similarly, as the executive secretary of ADEA from 1996 to 2002, Richard Sack was instrumental in engaging ministries of education in the association's research activities and in promoting the dissemination of endogenous research as a vehicle for policy reform. His successor, ADEA's current Executive Secretary, Mamadou Ndoye, a former minister of education in Senegal, has likewise been described as having "considerable political and professional influence that helps him relate easily to donors and ministers alike . . . [and] being instrumental in facilitating dialogue and negotiating the numerous demands that are made on [ADEA]" (Universalia, 2005, p. 30). In large part because of such leadership, both ERNWACA and ADEA have been able to maintain a sustainable core of international financial and technical support.

Nevertheless, while networking and a praxis approach to research have undoubtedly raised the profile of endogenous educational research in sub-Saharan Africa, and while ministries of education appear more willing to heed the expertise of African educational researchers than they were before the early 1990s, evidence of the actual *impact* of endogenous African educational research on subsequent policy formulation and implementation remains sketchy and anecdotal.[10] To some extent this relates to the almost universal conundrum of the research/policy interface. Despite the proliferation of forums that have facilitated dialogue among African researchers and senior government officials, the formulation of African educational policies and the subsequent *implementation* of these policies are invariably constrained by extensive political, economic, technological, and sociocultural constraints. Lack of resources and weak systems of governance are major structural shortcomings that undermine the potential of praxis-oriented research from having an impact on educational policies and practices.

In addition, while ERNWACA and ADEA have benefited from the remarkable leadership of key individuals, particularly in terms of their organizational abilities and their collective energies in fostering communication and collaboration among researchers and decisionmakers, it is a truism that dynamic leadership is rarely sustainable. Likewise, sources of external financial support are finite, no matter how diversified they are. Without solid long-term institutional and financial foundations, the fortunes and accomplishments of professional networks in sub-Saharan Africa can quickly wane. This has been the fate of ERNWACA's counterpart — the Educational Research Network of East and Southern Africa (ERNESA) — which has lacked effective coordination in recent years, and therefore has lost most of its longstanding financial support.[11] This is clearly hazardous for African educational researchers who rely on network associations to provide them with significant opportunities to conduct and disseminate their research.

In addition, although research networks such as ERNWACA and ADEA can be highly effective in enhancing endogenous research capacity, they do not have the resources or the political influence to ensure long-term national institutional support for research within their member countries. In part this is because they are not bona fide *national* institutions. Despite the advantages of networking outlined above, ERNWACA and ADEA cannot singularly overcome problems associated with resource scarcity, political interference, and weak archival cultures that continue to render the conduct of independent research difficult in sub-Saharan Africa. While educational researchers and ministry officials have clearly benefited from their affiliations with these networks, there are others who have not been drawn into the orbits of these networks — particularly into inner circles of influence, such as membership in the ADEA working groups or participation in regional workshops and conferences (Universalia, 2005). For many outsiders, regionally and nationally conducted studies are still often either inaccessible or unknown. As Obanya (2003) has observed, the abiding lack of a culture of research communication continues to necessitate Herculean efforts to retrieve many endogenous research documents that are unpublished and excluded from databases.

In effect, professional networks are not fully grounded national institutions, and hence their ability to enhance research capacity and inculcate a culture of scholarly production and dissemination is constrained. Only through the strengthening of African universities, which are officially mandated to function as centers of teaching and research, coupled with reforms in systems of governance that are amenable to accommodating and supporting critical policy-oriented inquiry, will endogenous educational research be in a position to shift away from what has become an entrenched dependency on external financial and technical assistance. It is a dependency that is most obviously manifested through the direct involvement of African researchers in donor-controlled research and evaluation activities, but is also at issue under the auspices of research networks that must themselves rely on external assistance. Indeed, in the long run, if national universities have more resources to invest in strengthening their own institutional research capacities, regional and continental networking will likely become even more effective in facilitating the recognition and validation of endogenous African research.

Conclusion

The starting point of this essay centered on the following question: Is endogenous African educational research as overlooked and undervalued as it was over a decade ago when the first ERNWACA national inventories were conducted and ADEA was a fledgling offshoot of the Donors to African Education consortium? In broad terms the answer is mixed. Over the last ten years, a vast number of studies on education in Africa have been produced, many of them by African scholars working either individually or in partnership with Northern colleagues. Through various forms of networking, many of these studies have been widely disseminated and have attained substantial visibility. Yet the status of endogenous education research in much of sub-Saharan Africa remains ambiguous. Since most African universities are unable to function as major independent centers of social science research, African educational researchers have been highly dependent on funding from Northern sources. To a large extent, therefore, as outlined in this essay, the bulk of African educational research is currently being conducted in two distinctive ways: through studies that are commissioned and administered by international donor agencies in accordance with their own organizational mandates, and under the auspices of networks such as ERNWACA and ADEA that have promoted educational research as an essential process for enhancing the inevitable stakeholder discussions that underlie educational policies and practices. The differences in these two modalities of support entail fundamentally different purposes of research and consequently compel researchers to assume different roles and responsibilities. This then suggests that the status of endogenous African educational research must be qualified in terms of a postcolonial proviso: overlooked and undervalued — or recognized and appreciated — by *whom*?

Since the World Bank and other major donor agencies have assumed significant roles as knowledge producers and policy advisors to African governments, the donor-control approach to educational research is heavily funded and has thus become an attractive option for prominent African scholars. The studies these researchers undertake, sometimes as permanent agency staff members and at other times on a contractual basis, are obviously neither overlooked nor undervalued by the organizations for which they are undertaken. Nor are they overlooked by African governments that must negotiate the conditionalities of educational assistance programs with the agency sponsors of the studies in question. Indeed, in many respects there is little reason to critique the scope and quality of donor-controlled sector studies and program evaluations. The problem is not with the research per se — not the topics of inquiry, nor the methodologies that have been used, nor many of the findings that have resulted. Rather, as critics have frequently argued, it is the way agencies have so often attempted to *control* the entire progression of research from data collection and analysis to dissemination of results as a basis for policymaking and program implementation that is often flawed

(Reimers & McGinn, 1997; Samoff & Stromquist, 2001). Within this modality of research support, where terms of reference are determined by the donor-agency sponsors, there is relatively little scope for autonomous intellectual expression. Although African researchers are now frequently involved in eliciting information and producing research findings for aid agencies, they do not *own* the research, nor do they control its dissemination and utilization. To a large degree, donor control of research has generated a profound degree of external dependency.

In contrast, the alternative strategy of networking and the adoption of a praxis orientation to research has helped not only to augment the status of endogenous educational research among African policymakers, but also has fostered processes of subjective dialogue and learning that are as significant as the completion and delivery of a final document to stakeholder recipients. In so doing, as exemplified most strikingly by ADEA's working groups, the combined strategy of networking and a praxis approach to research has tended to expand the role of policy stakeholders from being recipients of research products to becoming partners in research processes. Underlying this approach is the fact that research and policymaking are practices that are not mutually exclusive, but can be conducted as interrelated and mutually beneficial activities.

Whether it is conducted within the framework of the donor-control approach or as part of a more associational, praxis-oriented approach, the work of many African educational researchers is no longer overlooked and undervalued among those who are engaged in deliberating on educational policies in sub-Saharan Africa. Yet in circumstances where the emphasis is on the social and pedagogical aspects of the research process, there is less of a propensity to strive for a fully polished "product" capable of being disseminated beyond forums of face-to-face discussion or relatively easy website postings. As a result, research that is valued for its praxis orientation is rarely recognized in the realm of international scholarship for which the publication of books, scholarly articles, and other peer-reviewed forms of dissemination are critical for validation. For those who advocate the value of applied research, this may not be seen as a critical issue, for in African countries where there are so many pressing educational challenges, peer-reviewed scholarship may appear to be a needless distraction. Yet in a world where the standards of international scholarship are largely defined in Northern countries, this has an inevitable effect on North-South power imbalances. In the long run, if there is to be a more level playing field in terms of the influence of educational research in sub-Saharan Africa, then there is a case to be made for increased efforts to transform a greater volume of endogenous educational research into peer-reviewed endogenous educational *scholarship*. To achieve this, however, will require not just the continuation of professional networking, but a more substantive strengthening of national institutions of research. In effect, while networking and praxis approaches have contributed significantly to African educational research, they must invariably be regarded as measures that precede the revitalization of African college and university systems as centers of endogenous research.

Notes

1. This is a commonly accepted term for high-income, or developed, countries, many of which are geographically situated in the northern hemisphere.
2. In September 2000, at the United Nations Millennium Summit, world leaders agreed to a set of eight time-bound Millenium Development Goals, which range from halving extreme poverty to halting the spread of HIV/AIDS and providing universal primary education, all by the target date of 2015.
3. In 1990 (March 5–9), delegates from 155 countries and representatives from over 150 organizations agreed at the World Conference on Education for All in Jomtien, Thailand, to universalize primary education and to greatly reduce illiteracy within a decade.
4. As Camerounian researchers were included in the network and because Cameroun is generally regarded as being situated in central Africa rather than in western Africa, the network included reference to the central region.
5. ERNWACA chapters exist in Benin, Burkina Faso, Cameroun, Côte d'Ivoire, The Gambia, Ghana, Guinea, Mali, Niger, Nigeria, Senegal, Sierra Leone, and Togo.
6. Three of the member countries — Nigeria, Niger, and Senegal — did not participate in this first network activity. The gap left by Nigeria was naturally significant, for it undoubtedly is a repository of a vast range of national research on education.
7. ADEA's former executive director, Richard Sack, once commented to me that on his trips to Africa he regularly distributed copies of the synthesis report to education ministers and senior ministry officials, and that this served as a useful reminder of the substantial "home-grown" talents of national researchers and the merits of them in policy dialogue.
8. The sequence of Biennials has been as follows:

    Implementation of Educational Reforms (France, 1993); *Formulating Education Policy: Lessons and experiences from Sub-Saharan Africa* (France, 1995); *Partnerships for Capacity Building and Quality Improvement* (Senegal, 1997); *What Works and What's New in African Education* (South Africa, 1999); *Reaching Out, Reaching All: Sustaining Effective Policy and Practice* (Tanzania, 2001); *Improving the Quality of Education* (Mauritius, 2003).

9. On several occasions within the past two or three years, through no prompting of my own, graduate students have referred to ERNWACA and ADEA studies that they have obtained from the Internet for inclusion in their term papers or seminar presentations.
10. An example of this localized connection between research and action is reflected in the experience of Tin Tua, a national NGO in Burkina Faso, which resuscitated a faltering state-supported literacy campaign in early 1990s and has since evolved into a federated system of community literacy centers and community-based primary schools. Underlying the dynamic of Tin Tua has been collaboration between a professor of linguistics, with an applied research background in adult education and Gulmancema, the *lingua franca* of the Gulma region of Burkina Faso, and local community leaders who were keen to revive and expand literacy training in their region (Faure, Maclure, Dao Sow, & Coulibaly, 2003).
11. Personal communication with IDRC personnel in Ottawa.

References

Association for the Development of Education in Africa [ADEA]. (1998). *Education research networks: Role and added value*. Retrieved January 26, 2005, from http://www.adeanet.org/newsletter/Vol10No3/en_10.html

ADEA (2003). *ADEA working groups: Taking stock, future prospects*. Retrieved January 26, 2005, from http://www.adeanet.org/newsletter/Vol15No1/V15N1_eng_coul.pdf

Afiesimama, A. (1995). Linguistic complexity in River's State: The position of language use in primary schools. In E. N. Emenanjo & O. M. Ndimele (Eds.), *Issues in African languages and linguistics: Essays in honour of Kay Williamson* (pp. 1–10). Aba, Nigeria: National Institute for Nigerian Languages.

Agusiobo, B. C. (1999). The early child-care curriculum development and implementation for functional education: Working towards the 21st century. *Nigerian Journal of Curriculum Studies, 6*, 3–9.

Alota, J. (1999). *Effects of teaching skills on pupils' performances*. Yaounde, Cameroun: École Normale Supérieure.

Amegnonam, K. (1986). *L'enseignement des sciences à l'école primaire: Formation et compétences des maîtres dans la recherche du materielle didactique au Togo*. Unpublished masters thesis, Division de la Formation des Personnels, Lomé, Togo.

Amin, M. E., & Fonkeng, G. E. (2000). Gender and the demand for primary education in Cameroun. *Advances in Gender Research, 4*, 5–17.

Association of African Universities and the World Bank. (1997). *Revitalizing universities in Africa: Strategy and guidelines*. Washington, DC: World Bank.

Azie, B. (1998). *Les déterminants des grossesses chez les jeunes filles des établissements sécondaires*. Abidjan, Côte d'Ivoire: École Normale Supérieure.

Bediaku-Adu, C. (1987). *The effects of parent-teacher coordination on the education of children in the Assin area*. Unpublished manuscript, University of Cape Coast, Cape Coast, Ghana.

Bockarie, S. L. (1979). *Curriculum diffusion project: Final report of the diffusion of core course projects in secondary schools*. Unpublished manuscript, International Development Research Centre, Ottawa.

Bray, M. (1996). *Decentralization of education: Community financing*. Washington, DC: World Bank.

Brock-Utne, B. (1995). Cultural conditionality and aid to education in East Africa. *International Review of Education, 41*, 177–197.

Buchert, L. (1995). From project to programme to sector-wide support: Some questions and concerns. *Prospects, 30*, 405–408.

Buchert, L. (1998). Education sector analysis in Africa: An evolving case in mutual North-South learning. *Prospects, 28*, 336–348.

Camara, S. (1987). *Attitudes des parents face à l'école malienne (auto-financement)*. Unpublished masters thesis, École Normale Supérieure, Bamako, Mali.

Chambers, R. (1983). *Rural development: Putting the first last*. London: Longman Group.

Cisse, B. S. (1984). *Les associations de parents d'élèves au Mali: Leurs perceptions sur l'école et sur leurs rôles et sur leur responsabilités dans le système scolaire malien*. Bamako, Mali: Rapport Institut International de Recherche et de Formation Éducation au Développement.

Clark, J. (1995). The state, popular participation, and the voluntary sector. *World Development, 23*, 593–601.

Diare, S. (1990). *Tentative d'analyse des causes de la déperdition scolaire: Cas des écoles de Hamdallaye Marche et mamadou Konate*. Unpublished masters thesis, École Normale Supérieure, Bamako, Mali.

Dougna, D. P. (1986). *Financement de l'éducation au Togo: Tendences et évolution*. Paris: Institut International de la Planification en Éducation.

Doumbia, A. T. (2000). L'enseignement du Bambara selon la pédagogie convergente au Mali : Théories et pratiques. *Nordic Journal of African Studies, 9*, 98–107.
Essindi, E. J. (1977). *Famille, école et éducation dans l'Afrique actuele.* Yaounde, Cameroun: École Normale Supérieure.
ERNWACA News # 8 (March, 2005). Retrieved March 1, 2005, from http://www.rocare.org/ERNWACA%20News_No.8.pdf
ERNWACA News # 9 (September, 2005). Retrieved September 20, 2005, from http://www.rocare.org/ERNWACA_News_No.9en.pdf
Eta, F. E. E. (2000). Dimensions of gender crisis in Nigerian education: A view from colleges of education. *The Nigerian Teacher Today, 8,* 13–19.
Faure, S., Maclure, R., Dao Sow, K. A., & Coulibaly, N. (2003). *Local solutions to global challenges: Toward effective partnership in basic education* (Country Study Report: Burkina Faso). The Hague: Netherlands Ministry of Foreign Affairs (Policy and Operations Department) for the Consultative Group of Evaluation Departments.
Fiske, E. B. (1998). *Education For All status and trends 1998: Wasted opportunities — When schools fail. Repetition and drop-out in primary schools.* Paris: UNESCO.
Freeman, T., & Faure, S. D. (2003). *Local solutions to global challenges: Toward effective partnership in basic education. Final Report.* The Hague: Netherlands Ministry of Foreign Affairs (Policy and Operations Department) for the Consultative Group of Evaluation Departments.
Gaynor, C. (1998). *Decentralization of education: Teacher management.* Washington, DC: World Bank.
Goerke, M. (1995). *Condition de l'enseignant: L'impact sur son rendement.* Lome, Togo: École Nationale Superieure.
Gozo, K. (1977). *L'inadequation du système d'enseignement togolais face au développement agricole.* Unpublished manuscript, Division de la Formation des Personnels, Lomé, Togo.
Gyilime, P. K. (1986). *The role of parent-teacher associations in the education of the Ghanaian child: A study of first cycle schools in the Kintampo education district.* Unpublished manuscript, University of Cape Coast, Cape Coast, Ghana.
Haidara, J. L. (2000). Introduction des langues nationales dans l'enseignement: Attitudes des maîtres de Bamako. *Nordic Journal of African Studies, 9,* 49–65.
Hartwell, A. (1999). SPESSA 1999: An easy way to access the most complete educational data for Africa. *ADEA Newsletter, 11,* 10.
Hode, M. N. (1987). *L'école nouvelle et la problematique de l'emploi en République populaire du Benin.* Unpublished masters thesis, École Nationale d'Administration, Cotonou, Benin.
International Development Research Centre & Association of Universities and Colleges of Canada (2003, May). *Research without (Southern) Borders.* Ottawa: Report of a roundtable, May 22–23.
Institut Pedagogique National. (1989). *Étude de la demande d'éducation en milieu rural au Mali.* Bamako, Mali: Rapport administratif.
King, K., & Buchert, L. (1999). *Changing international aid to education: Global patterns and national contexts.* Paris: UNESCO.
Konate, G. V. (1986). *L'instituteur face à la réforme du système éducatif voltaique: Réflexion à partir d'une enquête.* Unpublished masters thesis, Institut Pédagogique du Burkina, Ouagadougou, Burkina Faso.
Koomson, E. (1990). *A study of the factors that cause the incidence of dropout of pupils in juniour-secondary schools.* Unpublished manuscript, University of Cape Coast, Cape Coast, Ghana.
Lavergne, R. (2004). *Strengthening aid effectiveness: Principles, operational implications, and approaches.* Hull, Quebec: Canadian International Development Agency.

Maclure, R. (Ed). (1997). *Overlooked and undervalued: A synthesis of ERNWACA reviews on the state of educational research in West and Central Africa.* Washington, DC: Academy of Educational Development.

Maclure, R. (2000). NGOs and education in sub-Saharan Africa: Instruments of hegemony or surreptitious resistance? *Education and Society, 18,* 25–45.

Madumere-Obike, C. U., & Oluwuo, S. O. (2001). Strategies for effective participation of rural communities in primary school administration in Nigeria. *Nigerian Journal of Profession Studies in Education, 8,* 8–14.

Marope, P. T. M. (1999). The prospective stocktaking review of education in Sub-Saharan Africa. *ADEA Newsletter, 11,* 3–5.

Marope, P. T. M., & Sacks, R. (2005). *The pedagogy of education policy formulation: Working from policy assets.* Paper presented at the Comparative International Education Society Conference, Stanford University.

Masemann, V. L. (1999). Culture and education. In R. F. Arnove & C. A. Torres (Eds.), *Comparative education: The dialectic of the global and the local* (pp. 115–133). Lanham, MD: Rowman & Littlefield.

Mattimore, A., Verspoor, A., & Watt, P. (2001). *A chance to learn: Knowledge and finance for education in Sub-Saharan Africa.* Washington, DC: World Bank.

McGinn, N. F. (2000). An assessment of new modalities in development assistance. *Prospects, 30,* 437–450.

McNeely, C. L. (1995). Prescribing national education policies: The role of international organizations. *Comparative Education Review, 39,* 483–507.

Megbemada, Y. (1987). *"Jeunesse et emploi [Youth and employment]."* Paper presented at the National Seminar on Rural Youth Productivity and Assistance, Cotonou, Benin: l'Institut de Formation Sociale Economique et Civique.

Meier, W. (1999). *In search of indigenous participation in education sector studies in sub-Saharan Africa.* Unpublished manuscript, University of Ottawa, Ottawa.

Mouthe, J. (1985). *Analyses des resources utilisées dans le système éducatif Camerounais,* Unpublished manuscript, Centre National d'Éducation, Yaoundé, Cameroon.

Namuddu, K., & Tapsoba, J. M. S. (1993). *The status of educational research and policy analysis in sub-Saharan Africa: A report of the DAE working group on capacity-building in educational research and policy analysis.* Ottawa: International Development Research Centre.

Nchungong, C. (1996). *Improving the quality of teaching in Cameroun nursery schools.* Yaoundé, Cameroun: École Normale Supérieure.

Obanya, P. (2003). *Emerging trends in research on the quality of education: A synthesis of education research reviews from 1992 – 2002 in eleven countries of West and Central Africa.* Bamako, Mali : ERNWACA.

Obanya, P. (1989). Going beyond the educational reform document. *Prospects, 29,* 333–347.

Ogbonna, S. O. (2002). Parental preferences for medium instruction in primary schools: Implications for teaching Nigerian languages. *Universal Basic Education Forum, 1,* 22–35.

Ohiri-Aniche, C. (2002). The place of Nigerian languages in the new Universal Basic Education (UBE) scheme in Nigeria. *African Journal of Curriculum and Instruction, 1,* 4–16.

Onuchukwu, O., & Ifeanacho, M. J. (2001). Education versus indoctrination: A critical appraisal of nursery education in Port Harcourt. *Nigerian Journal of Professional Studies in Education, 5,* 4–13.

Perraton, H., Robinson, B., & Creed, C. (2001). *Teacher education through distance learning: Technology, curriculum, cost, evaluation: Summary of case studies.* Paris: UNESCO.

Rasera, J.-B. (1986). *Coût et financement de l'éducation au Benin.* Cotonou, Benin: Rapport de consultation.

Reimers, F., & McGinn, N. (1997). *Informed dialogue: Using research to shape education policy around the world.* Westport, CT: Praeger.

Riddell, A. (2001). *Sector wide approaches in education: Implications for donor agencies and issues arising from case studies of Zambia and Mozambique.* Stockholm: Swedish International Development Cooperation Agency.

Samoff, J. (1999). Education sector analysis in Africa: Limited national control and even less national ownership, *International Journal of Educational Development, 19,* 249–272.

Samoff, J., & Stromquist, N.P. (2001). Managing knowledge and storing wisdom: New forms of foreign aid? *Development and Change, 32,* 631–656.

Saunders, L., Riley, K., Craig, H., Poston, M., & Flynn, A. (2000). *Effective schooling in rural Africa (Report 2): Key issues concerning school effectiveness and improvement.* Washington, DC: World Bank.

Sawadogo, A. (1999). *Les innovations pédagogiques et leurs effets sur l'enseignement primaire burkinabe: Cas des classes multigrades et des classes à double flux.* Ouagadougou, Burkina Faso: École nationale d'administration et de magistrature.

Sawadogo, P. (1984). *La cooperative scolaire à l'école primaire.* Unpublished manuscript, Centre Pédagogique National, Ouagadougou, Burkina Faso.

Sedel, C. (1999). *Les rélations de genre et la scolarisation primaire en milieu rural Senoufo (nord de la Côte d'Ivoire).* Abidjan, Côte d'Ivoire: École 2000.

Sosale, S. (2000). *Trends in private sector development in World Bank education projects.* Washington, D.C.: The World Bank.

Sow, O. (1985). *Échec scolaire au Mali: Aspects socio-économiques.* Unpublished manuscript, École normale supérieure, Bamako, Mali.

Stein, J. G., Stren, R., Fitzgibbon, J., & MacLean, M. (Eds.) (2001). *Networks of knowledge: Collaborative innovation in international learning.* Toronto: University of Toronto Press.

Stren, R. (2001). Knowledge networks and new approaches to "development." In J.G. Stein et al. (Eds). *Networks of knowledge: Collaborative innovation in international learning* (pp. 133–150). Toronto: University of Toronto Press.

Tchegho, J.-M. (2003). *La décentralisation, l'éducation, l'unité nationale.* Yaoundé, Cameroun: Éditions Demos.

Tetteh, N. J. (1989). *A study of the causes of dropping out in first cycles schools in the Ningo traditional area.* Unpublished manuscript, University of Cape Coast, Cape Coast, Ghana.

Tietjen, K. (1997). *Educating girls in sub-Saharan Africa: USAID's approach and lessons for donors* (Technical Paper No. 54). Washington, DC: USAID, Health and Human Resources Analysis for Africa Project.

United Nations. (2000). *United Nations millennium declaration: Resolution adopted by the General Assembly.* New York: Author.

United Nations Children's Fund. (2002). *Quality education for all: From a girl's point of view.* New York: Author.

United Nations Educational, Scientific and Cultural Organization. (1990). *World declaration on education for all and framework for action to meet basic learning needs.* Paris: Author.

United Nations Educational, Scientific and Cultural Organization. (2000). *Education For All assessment 2000: Sub-Saharan Africa. Regional synthesis report.* Paris: Author.

United Nations Educational, Scientific and Cultural Organization. (2005). *EFA global monitoring report: The quality imperative.* Paris: Author.

Universalia. (2005). *Evaluation of the Association for the Development of Education in Africa (ADEA).* Ottawa: Author.

Watt, P. (2001). *Community support for basic education in sub-Saharan Africa.* Washington, DC: World Bank.

Welch, A. R. (1998). The cult of efficiency in education: Comparative reflections on the reality and the rhetoric. *Comparative Education, 34,* 157–175.

Wokwenmendam, Z. (1981). *Disponibilité des materiels didactiques et leur utilization dans l'enseignement du calcul et des sciences d'observation.* Unpublished manuscript, École normale superieure, Yaounde, Cameroun.

World Bank. (1988). *Education in Sub-Saharan Africa: Policies for adjustment, revitalization, and expansion.* Washington, DC: Author.

World Bank. (1988). *Education sector strategy.* Washington, DC: Author.

World Bank. (1999). *Education sector strategy paper.* Washington, DC: Author.

World Bank. (2000). *Effective schooling in rural Africa (Report 3): Case study brief on rural schooling.* Washington, DC: Author.

World Bank. (2002). *Education and HIV/AIDS: A window of hope.* Washington, DC: Author.

World Bank. (2004). *Indigenous knowledge: Local pathways to global development.* Washington, DC: Author.

I am most grateful to the editors of *HER* for their careful reading of earlier drafts of this paper and for their suggested revisions. In addition, I have very much appreciated Benjamin Piper's encouragement and helpful comments on earlier drafts.

Beyond the Methods Fetish: Toward a Humanizing Pedagogy

LILIA I. BARTOLOMÉ

Much of the current debate regarding the improvement of minority student academic achievement occurs at a level that treats education as a primarily technical issue (Giroux, 1992).[1] For example, the historical and present day academic underachievement of certain culturally and linguistically subordinated student populations in the United States (e.g., Mexican Americans, Native Americans, Puerto Ricans) is often explained as resulting from the lack of cognitively, culturally, and/or linguistically appropriate teaching methods and educational programs.[2] As such, the solution to the problem of academic underachievement tends to be constructed in primarily methodological and mechanistic terms dislodged from the sociocultural reality that shapes it. That is, the solution to the current underachievement of students from subordinated cultures is often reduced to finding the "right" teaching methods, strategies, or prepackaged curricula that will work with students who do not respond to so-called "regular" or "normal" instruction.

Recent research studies have begun to identify educational programs found to be successful in working with culturally and linguistically subordinated minority student populations (Carter & Chatfield, 1986; Lucas, Henze, & Donato, 1990; Tikunoff, 1985; Webb, 1987). In addition, there has been specific interest in identifying teaching strategies that more effectively teach culturally and linguistically "different" students and other "disadvantaged" and "at-risk" students (Knapp & Shields, 1990; McLeod, in press; Means & Knapp, 1991; Tinajero & Ada, 1993). Although it is important to identify useful and promising instructional programs and strategies, it is erroneous to assume that blind replication of instructional programs or teacher mastery of particular teaching methods, in and of themselves, will guarantee successful student learning, especially when we are discussing populations that historically have been mistreated and miseducated by the schools.

This focus on methods as solutions in the current literature coincides with many of my graduate students' beliefs regarding linguistic minority education improvement. As a Chicana professor who has taught anti-racist multicultural education courses at various institutions, I am consistently confronted at the beginning of each semester by students who are anxious to learn the latest teaching methods — methods that they hope will somehow magically work on minority students.[3] Although my students are well-intentioned individuals who sincerely wish to create positive learning environments for culturally and linguistically subordinated students, they arrive with the expectation that I will provide them with easy answers in the form of specific instructional methods. That is, since they (implicitly) perceive the academic underachievement of subordinated students as a technical issue, the solutions they require are also expected to be technical in nature (e.g., specific teaching methods, instructional curricula and materials). They usually assume that: 1) they, as teachers, are fine and do not need to identify, interrogate, and change their biased beliefs and fragmented views about subordinated students; 2) schools, as institutions, are basically fair and democratic sites where all students are provided with similar, if not equal, treatment and learning conditions; and 3) children who experience academic difficulties (especially those from culturally and linguistically low-status groups) require some form of "special" instruction since they obviously have not been able to succeed under "regular" or "normal" instructional conditions. Consequently, if nothing is basically wrong with teachers and schools, they often conclude, then linguistic minority academic underachievement is best dealt with by providing teachers with specific teaching methods that promise to be effective with culturally and linguistically subordinated students. To further complicate matters, many of my students seek *generic* teaching methods that will work with a variety of minority student populations, and they grow anxious and impatient when reminded that instruction for any group of students needs to be tailored or individualized to some extent. Some of my students appear to be seeking what María de la Luz Reyes (1992) defines as a "one size fits all" instructional recipe. Reyes explains that the term refers to the assumption that instructional methods that are deemed effective for mainstream populations will benefit *all* students, no matter what their backgrounds may be.[4] She explains that the assumption is

> similar to the "one size fits all" marketing concept that would have buyers believe that there is an average or ideal size among men and women. . . . Those who market "one size fits all" products suggest that if the article of clothing is not a good fit, the fault is not with the design of the garment, but those who are too fat, too skinny, too tall, too short, or too high-waisted. (p. 435)

I have found that many of my students similarly believe that teaching approaches that work with one minority population should also fit another (see Vogt, Jordan, & Tharp, 1987, for an example of this tendency). Reyes argues that educators often make this "one size fits all" assumption when discussing instructional approaches, such as process writing. For example, as Lisa Delpit (1988) has convincingly argued, the process writing approach that has been blindly embraced by mostly White liberal teachers often produces a negative result with African-American students. Delpit cites one Black student:

I didn't feel she was teaching us anything. She wanted us to correct each other's papers and we were there to learn from her. She didn't teach anything, absolutely nothing.

Maybe they're trying to learn what Black folks knew all the time. We understand how to improvise, how to express ourselves creatively. When I'm in a classroom, I'm not looking for that, I'm looking for structure, the more formal language.

Now my buddy was in a Black teacher's class. And that lady was very good. She went through and explained and defined each part of the structure. This [White] teacher didn't get along with that Black teacher. She said she didn't agree with her methods. But *I* don't think that White teacher *had* any methods. (1988, p. 287)

The above quote is a glaring testimony that a "one size fits all" approach often does not work with the same level of effectiveness with all students across the board. Such assumptions reinforce a disarticulation between the embraced method and the sociocultural realities within which each method is implemented. I find that this "one size fits all" assumption is also held by many of my students about a number of teaching methods currently in vogue, such as cooperative learning and whole language instruction. The students imbue the "new" methods with almost magical properties that render them, in and of themselves, capable of improving students' academic standing.

One of my greatest challenges throughout the years has been to help students to understand that a myopic focus on methodology often serves to obfuscate the real question — which is why in our society, subordinated students do not generally succeed academically in schools. In fact, schools often reproduce the existing asymmetrical power relations among cultural groups (Anyon, 1988; Gibson & Ogbu, 1991; Giroux, 1992; Freire, 1985). I believe that by taking a sociohistorical view of present-day conditions and concerns that inform the lived experiences of socially perceived minority students, prospective teachers are better able to comprehend the quasi-colonial nature of minority education. By engaging in this critical sociohistorical analysis of subordinated students' academic performance, most of my graduate students (teachers and prospective teachers) are better situated to reinterpret and reframe current educational concerns so as to develop pedagogical structures that speak to the day-to-day reality, struggles, concerns, and dreams of these students. By understanding the historical specificities of marginalized students, these teachers and prospective teachers come to realize that an uncritical focus on methods makes invisible the historical role that schools and their personnel have played (and continue to play), not only in discriminating against many culturally different groups, but also in denying their humanity. By robbing students of their culture, language, history, and values, schools often reduce these students to the status of subhumans who need to be rescued from their "savage" selves. The end result of this cultural and linguistic eradication represents, in my view, a form of dehumanization. Therefore, any discussion having to do with the improvement of subordinated students' academic standing is incomplete if it does not address those discriminatory school practices that lead to dehumanization.

In this article, I argue that a necessary first step in reevaluating the failure or success of particular instructional methods used with subordinated students calls for a shift in perspective — a shift from a narrow and mechanistic view of instruction to one that is broader in scope and takes into consideration the sociohistorical and political dimensions of education. I discuss why effective methods are needed for these students, and why certain strategies are deemed effective or ineffective in a given sociocultural context. My discussion will include a section that addresses the significance of teachers' understanding of the political nature of education, the reproductive nature of schools, and the schools' continued (yet unspoken) deficit views of subordinated students. By conducting a critical analysis of the sociocultural realities in which subordinated students find themselves at school, the implicit and explicit antagonistic relations between students and teachers (and other school representatives) take on focal importance.

As a Chicana and a former classroom elementary and middle school teacher who encountered negative race relations that ranged from teachers' outright rejection of subordinated students to their condescending pity, fear, indifference, and apathy when confronted by the challenges of minority student education, I find it surprising that little minority education literature deals explicitly with the very real issue of antagonistic race relations between subordinated students and White school personnel (see Ogbu, 1987, and Giroux, 1992, for an in-depth discussion of this phenomenon).

For this reason, I also include in this article a section that discusses two instructional methods and approaches identified as effective in current education literature: culturally responsive education and strategic teaching. I examine the methods for pedagogical underpinnings that — under the critical use of politically clear teachers — have the potential to challenge students academically and intellectually while treating them with dignity and respect. More importantly, I examine the pedagogical foundations that serve to humanize the educational process and enable both students and teachers to work toward breaking away from their unspoken antagonism and negative beliefs about each other and get on with the business of sharing and creating knowledge. I argue that the informed way in which a teacher implements a method can serve to offset potentially unequal relations and discriminatory structures and practices in the classroom and, in doing so, improve the quality of the instructional process for both student and teacher. In other words, politically informed teacher use of methods can create conditions that enable subordinated students to move from their usual passive position to one of active and critical engagement. I am convinced that creating pedagogical spaces that enable students to move *from object to subject position* produces more far-reaching, positive effects than the implementation of a particular teaching methodology, regardless of how technically advanced and promising it may be.

The final section of this article will explore and suggest the implementation of what Donaldo Macedo (1994) designates as an

> anti-methods pedagogy that refuses to be enslaved by the rigidity of models and methodological paradigms. An anti-methods pedagogy should be informed by a critical understanding of the sociocultural context that guides our practices so as to free us from the beaten path of methodological certainties and specialisms. (p. 8)

Simply put, it is important that educators not blindly reject teaching methods across the board, but that they reject uncritical appropriation of methods, materials, curricula, etc. Educators need to reject the present methods fetish so as to create learning environments informed by both action and reflection. In freeing themselves from the blind adoption of so-called effective (and sometimes "teacher-proof") strategies, teachers can begin the reflective process, which allows them to recreate and reinvent teaching methods and materials by always taking into consideration the sociocultural realities that can either limit or expand the possibilities to humanize education. It is important that teachers keep in mind that methods are social constructions that grow out of and reflect ideologies that often prevent teachers from understanding the pedagogical implications of asymmetrical power relations among different cultural groups.

The Significance of Teacher Political Clarity[5]

In his letter to North American educators, Paulo Freire (1987) argues that technical expertise and mastery of content area and methodology are insufficient to ensure effective instruction of students from subordinated cultures. Freire contends that, in addition to possessing content area knowledge, teachers must possess political clarity so as to be able to effectively create, adopt, and modify teaching strategies that simultaneously respect and challenge learners from diverse cultural groups in a variety of learning environments.

Teachers working on improving their political clarity recognize that teaching is not a politically neutral undertaking. They understand that educational institutions are socializing institutions that mirror the greater society's culture, values, and norms. Schools reflect both the positive and negative aspects of a society. Thus, the unequal power relations among various social and cultural groups at the societal level are usually reproduced at the school and classroom level, unless concerted efforts are made to prevent their reproduction. Teachers working toward political clarity understand that they can either maintain the status quo, or they can work to transform the sociocultural reality at the classroom and school level so that the culture at this micro-level does not reflect macro-level inequalities, such as asymmetrical power relations that relegate certain cultural groups to a subordinate status.

Teachers can support positive social change in the classroom in a variety of ways. One possible intervention can consist of the creation of heterogeneous learning groups for the purpose of modifying low-status roles of individuals or groups of children.[6] Elizabeth Cohen (1986) demonstrates that when teachers create learning conditions where students, especially those perceived as low status (e.g., limited English speakers in a classroom where English is the dominant language, students with academic difficulties, or those perceived by their peers for a variety of reasons as less able), can demonstrate their possession of knowledge and expertise, they are then able to see themselves, and be seen by others, as capable and competent. As a result, contexts are created in which peers can learn from each other as well.

A teacher's political clarity will not necessarily compensate for structural inequalities that students face outside the classroom; however, teachers can, to the best of their ability, help their students deal with injustices encountered inside and outside the classroom. A number of possibilities exist for preparing students to deal with the greater society's unfairness and inequality that range from engaging in explicit discussions with students about their experiences, to more indirect ways (that nevertheless require a teacher who is politically clear), such as creating democratic learning environments where students become accustomed to being treated as competent and able individuals. I believe that the students, once accustomed to the rights and responsibilities of full citizenship in the classroom, will come to expect respectful treatment and authentic estimation in other contexts. Again, it is important to point out that it is not the particular lesson or set of activities that prepares the student; rather, it is the teacher's politically clear educational philosophy that underlies the varied methods and lessons/activities she or he employs that make the difference.

Under ideal conditions, competent educators simultaneously translate theory into practice *and* consider the population being served and the sociocultural reality in which learning is expected to take place. Let me reiterate that command of a content area or specialization is necessary, but it is not sufficient for effectively working with students. Just as critical is that teachers comprehend that their role as educators is a political act that is never neutral (Freire, 1985, 1987, 1993; Freire & Macedo, 1987). In ignoring or negating the political nature of their work with these students, teachers not only reproduce the status quo and their students' low status, but they also inevitably legitimize schools' discriminatory practices. For example, teachers who uncritically follow school practices that unintentionally or intentionally serve to promote tracking and segregation within school and classroom contexts continue to reproduce the status quo. Conversely, teachers can become conscious of, and subsequently challenge, the role of educational institutions and their own roles as educators in maintaining a system that often serves to silence students from subordinated groups.

Teachers must also remember that schools, similar to other institutions in society, are influenced by perceptions of socioeconomic status (SES), race/

ethnicity, language, and gender (Anyon, 1988; Bloom, 1991; Cummins, 1989; Ogbu, 1987). They must begin to question how these perceptions influence classroom dynamics. An important step in increasing teacher political clarity is recognizing that, despite current liberal rhetoric regarding the equal value of all cultures, low SES and ethnic minority students have historically (and currently) been perceived as deficient. I believe that the present methods-restricted discussion must be broadened to reveal the deeply entrenched deficit orientation toward "difference" (i.e., non-Western European race/ethnicity, non-English language use, working-class status, femaleness) that prevails in the schools in a deeply "cultural" ideology of White supremacy. As educators, we must constantly be vigilant and ask how the deficit orientation has affected our perceptions concerning students from subordinated populations and created rigid and mechanistic teacher-student relations (Cummins, 1989; Flores, Cousin, & Diaz, 1991; Giroux & McLaren, 1986). Such a model often serves to create classroom conditions in which there is very little opportunity for teachers and students to interact in meaningful ways, establish positive and trusting working relations, and share knowledge.

Our Legacy: A Deficit View of Subordinated Students

As discussed earlier, teaching strategies are neither designed nor implemented in a vacuum. Design, selection, and use of particular teaching approaches and strategies arise from perceptions about learning and learners. I contend that the most pedagogically advanced strategies are sure to be ineffective in the hands of educators who implicitly or explicitly subscribe to a belief system that renders ethnic, racial, and linguistic minority students at best culturally disadvantaged and in need of fixing (if we could only identify the right recipe!), or, at worst, culturally or genetically deficient and beyond fixing.[7] Despite the fact that various models have been proposed to explain the academic failure of certain subordinated groups — academic failure described as *historical, pervasive,* and *disproportionate* — the fact remains that these views of difference are deficit-based and deeply imprinted in our individual and collective psyches (Flores, 1982, 1993; Menchaca & Valencia, 1990; Valencia, 1986, 1991).

The deficit model has the longest history of any model discussed in the education literature. Richard Valencia (1986) traces its evolution over three centuries:

> Also known in the literature as the "social pathology" model or the "cultural deprivation" model, the deficit approach explains disproportionate academic problems among low status students as largely being due to pathologies or deficits in their sociocultural background (e.g., cognitive and linguistic deficiencies, low self-esteem, poor motivation). . . . To improve the educability of such students, programs such as compensatory education and parent-child intervention have been proposed. (p. 3)

Barbara Flores (1982, 1993) documents the effect this deficit model has had on the schools' past and current perceptions of Latino students. Her historical overview chronicles descriptions used to refer to Latino students over the last century. The terms range from "mentally retarded," "linguistically handicapped," "culturally and linguistically deprived," and "semilingual," to the current euphemism for Latino and other subordinated students: the "at-risk" student.

Similarly, recent research continues to lay bare our deficit orientation and its links to discriminatory school practices aimed at students from groups perceived as low status (Anyon, 1988; Bloom, 1991; Diaz, Moll, & Mehan, 1986; Oaks, 1986). Findings range from teacher preference for Anglo students, to bilingual teachers' preference for lighter skinned Latino students (Bloom, 1991), to teachers' negative perceptions of working-class parents as compared to middle-class parents (Lareau, 1990), and, finally, to unequal teaching and testing practices in schools serving working-class and ethnic minority students (Anyon, 1988; Diaz et al., 1986; Oaks, 1986; U.S. Commission on Civil Rights, 1973). Especially indicative of our inability to consciously acknowledge the deficit orientation is the fact that the teachers in these studies — teachers from all ethnic groups — were themselves unaware of the active role they played in the differential and unequal treatment of their students.

The deficit view of subordinated students has been critiqued by numerous researchers as ethnocentric and invalid (Boykin, 1983; Diaz et al., 1986; Flores, 1982; Flores et al., 1991; Sue & Padilla, 1986; Trueba, 1989; Walker, 1987). More recent research offers alternative models that shift the source of school failure away from the characteristics of the individual child, their families, and their cultures, and toward the schooling process (Au & Mason, 1983; Heath, 1983; Mehan, 1992; Philips, 1972). Unfortunately, I believe that many of these alternative models often unwittingly give rise to a kinder and more liberal, yet more concealed version of the deficit model that views subordinated students as being in need of "specialized" modes of instruction — a type of instructional "coddling" that mainstream students do not require in order to achieve in school. Despite the use of less overtly ethnocentric models to explain the academic standing of subordinated students, I believe that the deficit orientation toward difference, especially as it relates to low socioeconomic and ethnic minority groups, is very deeply ingrained in the ethos of our most prominent institutions, especially schools, and in the various educational programs in place at these sites.

It is against this sociocultural backdrop that teachers can begin to seriously question the unspoken but prevalent deficit orientation used to hide SES, racial/ethnic, linguistic, and gender inequities present in U.S. classrooms. And it is against this sociocultural backdrop that I critically examine two teaching approaches identified by the educational literature as effective with subordinated student populations.

Potentially Humanizing Pedagogy: Two Promising Teaching Approaches

Well-known approaches and strategies such as cooperative learning, language experience, process writing, reciprocal teaching, and whole language activities can be used to create humanizing learning environments where students cease to be treated as objects and yet receive academically rigorous instruction (Cohen, 1986; Edelsky, Altwerger, & Flores, 1991; Palinscar & Brown, 1984; Pérez & Torres-Guzmán, 1992; Zamel, 1982). However, when these approaches are implemented uncritically, they often produce negative results, as indicated by Lisa Delpit (1986, 1988). Critical teacher applications of these approaches and strategies can contribute to discarding deficit views of students from subordinated groups, so that they are treated with respect and viewed as active and capable subjects in their own learning.

Academically rigorous, student-centered teaching strategies can take many forms. One may well ask, is it not merely common sense to promote approaches and strategies that respect, recognize, utilize, and build on students' existing knowledge bases? The answer would be, of course, yes, it is. However, it is important to recognize, as part of our effort to increase our political clarity, that these practices have *not* typified classroom instruction for students from marginalized populations. The practice of learning from and valuing student language and life experiences *often* occurs in classrooms where students speak a language and possess cultural capital that more closely matches that of the mainstream (Anyon, 1988; Lareau, 1990; Winfield, 1986).[8]

Jean Anyon's (1988) classic research suggests that teachers of affluent students are more likely than teachers of working-class students to utilize and incorporate student life experiences and knowledge into the curriculum. For example, in Anyon's study, teachers of affluent students often designed creative and innovative lessons that tapped students' existing knowledge bases; one math lesson, designed to teach students to find averages, asked them to fill out a possession survey inquiring about the number of cars, television sets, refrigerators, and games owned at home so as to teach students to average. Unfortunately, this practice of tapping students' already existing knowledge and language bases is not commonly utilized with student populations traditionally perceived as deficient. Anyon reports that teachers of working-class students viewed them as lacking the necessary cultural capital, and therefore imposed content and behavioral standards with little consideration and respect for student input. Although Anyon did not generalize beyond her sample, other studies suggest the validity of her findings for ethnic minority student populations (Diaz et al., 1986; Moll, 1986; Oaks, 1986).

The creation of learning environments for low SES and ethnic minority students, similar to those for more affluent and White populations, requires that teachers discard deficit notions and genuinely value and utilize students' existing knowledge bases in their teaching. In order to do so, teachers must confront and challenge their own social biases so as to honestly begin to perceive their students as capable learners. Furthermore, they must remain open to the fact that they will also learn from their students. Learning is not a one-way undertaking.

It is important for educators to recognize that no language or set of life experiences is inherently superior, yet our social values reflect our preferences for certain language and life experiences over others. Student-centered teaching strategies such as cooperative learning, language experience, process writing, reciprocal teaching, and whole language activities (if practiced consciously and critically) can help to offset or neutralize our deficit-based failure and recognize subordinated student strengths. Our tendency to discount these strengths occurs whenever we forget that learning only occurs when prior knowledge is accessed and linked to new information.

Beau Jones, Annemarie Palinscar, Donna Ogle, and Eileen Carr (1987) explain that learning *is* the act of linking new information to prior knowledge. According to their framework, prior knowledge is stored in memory in the form of knowledge frameworks. New information is understood and stored by calling up the appropriate knowledge framework and then integrating the new information. Acknowledging and using existing student language and knowledge makes good pedagogical sense, and it also constitutes a humanizing experience for students traditionally *de*humanized and disempowered in the schools. I believe that strategies identified as effective in the literature have the potential to offset reductive education in which "the educator as *the one who knows* transfers existing knowledge to the learner as *the one who does not know*" (Freire, 1985, p. 114, emphasis added). It is important to repeat that mere implementation of a particular strategy or approach identified as effective does not guarantee success, as the current debate in process writing attests (Delpit, 1986, 1988; Reyes, 1991, 1992).

Creating learning environments that incorporate student language and life experiences in no way negates teachers' responsibility for providing students with particular academic content knowledge and skills. It is important not to link teacher respect and use of student knowledge and language bases with a laissez-faire attitude toward teaching. It is equally necessary not to confuse academic rigor with rigidity that stifles and silences students. The teacher is the authority, with all the resulting responsibilities that entails; however, it is not necessary for the teacher to become authoritarian in order to challenge students intellectually. Education can be a process in which teacher and students mutually participate in the intellectually exciting undertaking we call learning. Students *can* become active subjects in their own learning, instead of passive objects waiting to be filled with facts and figures by the teacher.

I would like to emphasize that teachers who work with subordinated populations have the responsibility to assist them in appropriating knowledge bases and discourse styles deemed desirable by the greater society. However, this process of appropriation must be additive, that is, the new concepts and new discourse skills must be added to, not subtracted from, the students' existing background knowledge. In order to assume this additive stance, teachers must discard deficit views so they can use and build on life experiences and language styles too often viewed and labeled as "low class" and undesirable. Again, there are numerous teaching strategies and methods that can be employed in this additive manner. For the purposes of illustration, I will briefly discuss two approaches currently identified as promising for students from subordinated populations. The selected approaches are referred to in the literature as culturally responsive instructional approaches and strategic teaching.

Culturally Responsive Instruction: The Potential to Equalize Power Relations

Culturally responsive instruction grows out of cultural difference theory, which attributes the academic difficulties of students from subordinated groups to cultural incongruence or discontinuities between the learning, language use, and behavioral practices found in the home and those expected by the schools. Ana María Villegas (1988, 1991) defines culturally responsive instruction as attempts to create instructional situations where teachers use teaching approaches and strategies that recognize and build on culturally different ways of learning, behaving, and using language in the classroom.

A number of classic ethnographic studies document culturally incongruent communication practices in classrooms where students and teachers may speak the same language but use it in different ways. This type of incongruence is cited as a major source of academic difficulties for subordinated students and their teachers (see Au, 1980; Au & Mason, 1983; Cazden, 1988; Erickson & Mohatt, 1982; Heath, 1983; Philips, 1972). For the purposes of this analysis, one form of culturally responsive instruction, the Kamehameha Education Project reading program, will be discussed.

The Kamehameha Education Project is a reading program developed as a response to the traditionally low academic achievement of native Hawaiian students in Western schools. The reading program was a result of several years of research that examined the language practices of native Hawaiian children in home and school settings. Observations of native Hawaiian children showed them to be bright and capable learners; however, their behavior in the classroom signaled communication difficulties between them and their non-Hawaiian teachers. For example, Kathryn Hu-Pei Au (1979, 1980) reports that native Hawaiian children's language behavior in the classroom was often misinterpreted by teachers as being unruly and without educational value. She found that the children's preferred language style in the classroom was linked to a practice used by adults in their homes and community called "talk story." She discusses the talk story phenomenon and describes it as a major speech event in the Hawaiian community, where individuals speak almost simultaneously and where little attention is given to turn taking. Au explains that this practice may inhibit students from speaking out as individuals because of their familiarity with and preference for simultaneous group discussion.

Because the non-Hawaiian teachers were unfamiliar with talk story and failed to recognize its value, much class time was spent either silencing the children or prodding unwilling individuals to speak. Needless to say, very little class time was dedicated to other instruction. More important, the children were constrained and not allowed to demonstrate their abilities as speakers and possessors of knowledge. Because the students did not exhibit their skills in mainstream accepted ways (e.g., competing as individuals for the floor), they were prevented from exhibiting knowledge via their culturally preferred style. However, once the children's interaction style was incorporated into classroom lessons, time on task increased and, subsequently, students' performance on standardized reading tests improved. This study's findings conclude that educators can successfully employ the students' culturally valued language practices while introducing the student to more conventional and academically acceptable ways of using language.

It is interesting to note that many of the research studies that examine culturally congruent and incongruent teaching approaches also inadvertently illustrate the equalization of previous asymmetrical power relations between teachers and students. These studies describe classrooms where teachers initially imposed participation structures upon students from subordinated linguistic minority groups and later learned to negotiate with them rules regarding acceptable classroom behavior and language use (Au & Mason, 1983; Erickson & Mohatt, 1982; Heath, 1983; Philips, 1972). Thus these studies, in essence, capture the successful negotiation of power relations, which resulted in higher student academic achievement and increased teacher effectiveness. Yet there is little explicit discussion in these studies of the greater sociocultural reality that renders it perfectly normal for teachers to automatically disregard and disrespect subordinated students' preferences and to allow antagonistic relations to foment until presented with empirical evidence that legitimizes the students' practices. Instead, the focus of most of these studies rests entirely on the cultural congruence of the instruction and not on the humanizing effects of a more democratic pedagogy. Villegas (1988) accurately critiques the cultural congruence literature when she states:

> It is simplistic to claim that differences in languages used at home and in school are the root of the widespread academic problems of minority children. Admittedly, differences do exist, and they can create communication difficulties in the classroom for both teachers and students. Even so, those differences in language must be viewed in the context of a broader struggle for power within a stratified society. (p. 260)

Despite the focus on the cultural versus the political dimensions of pedagogy, some effort is made to link culturally congruent teaching practices with equalization of classroom power relations. For example, Kathryn Au and Jana

Mason (1983) explain that "one means of achieving cultural congruence in lessons may be to *seek a balance between the interactional rights of teachers and students,* so that the children can participate in ways comfortable to them" (p. 145, emphasis added). Their study compared two teachers and showed that the teacher who was willing to negotiate with students either the topic of discussion or the appropriate participation structure was better able to implement her lesson. Conversely, the teacher who attempted to impose both topic of discussion *and* appropriate interactional rules was frequently diverted because of conflicts with students over one or the other.

Unfortunately, as mentioned earlier, interpretations and practical applications of this body of research have focused on the *cultural* congruence of the approaches. I emphasize the term *cultural* because in these studies the term "culture" is used in a restricted sense devoid of its dynamic, ideological, and political dimensions. Instead, culture is treated as synonymous with ethnic culture, rather than as "the representation of lived experiences, material artifacts and practices *forged within the unequal and dialectical relations* that different groups establish in a given society at a particular point in historical time" (Giroux, 1985, p. xxi, emphasis added). I use this definition of culture because, without identifying the political dimensions of culture and subsequent unequal status attributed to members of different ethnic groups, the reader may conclude that teaching methods simply need to be ethnically congruent to be effective — without recognizing that not all ethnic and linguistic cultural groups are viewed and treated as equally legitimate in classrooms. Interestingly enough, there is little discussion of the various socially perceived minority groups' subordinate status vis-à-vis White teachers and peers in these studies. All differences are treated as ethnic cultural differences and not as responses of subordinated students to teachers from dominant groups, and vice versa.

Given the sociocultural realities in the above studies, the specific teaching strategies may not be what made the difference. Indeed, efforts to uncritically export the Kamehameha Education Project reading program to other student populations resulted in failure (Vogt et al., 1987). It could well be that the teachers' effort to negotiate and share power by treating students as equal participants in their own learning is what made the difference in Hawaii. Just as important is the teachers' willingness to critically interrogate their deficit views of subordinated students. By employing a variety of strategies and techniques, the Kamehameha students were allowed to interact with teachers in egalitarian and meaningful ways. More importantly, the teachers also learned to recognize, value, use, and build upon students' previously acquired knowledge and skills. In essence, these strategies succeeded in creating a comfort zone so students could exhibit their knowledge and skills and, ultimately, empower themselves to succeed in an academic setting. Teachers also benefitted from using a variety of student-centered teaching strategies that humanized their perceptions of treatment of students previously perceived as deficient. Ray McDermott's (1977) classic research reminds us that numerous teaching approaches and strategies can be effective, so long as trusting relations between teacher and students are established and power relations are mutually set and agreed upon.

Strategic Teaching: The Significance of Teacher-Student Interaction and Negotiation

Strategic teaching refers to an instructional model that explicitly teaches students learning strategies that enable them consciously to monitor their own learning. This is accomplished through the development of reflective cognitive monitoring and metacognitive skills (Jones, Palinscar, Ogle, & Carr, 1987). The goal is to prepare independent and metacognitively aware students. This teaching strategy makes explicit for students the structures of various text types used in academic settings and assists students in identifying various strategies for effectively comprehending the various genres. Although text structures and strategies for dissecting the particular structures are presented by the teacher, a key component of these lessons is the elicitation of students' knowledge about text types and their own strategies for making meaning before presenting them with more conventional academic strategies.

Examples of learning strategies include teaching various text structures (i.e., stories and reports) through frames and graphic organizers. *Frames* are sets of questions that help students understand a given topic. Readers monitor their understanding of a text by asking questions, making predictions, and testing their predictions as they read. Before reading, frames serve as an advance organizer to activate prior knowledge and facilitate understanding. Frames can also be utilized during the reading process by the reader to monitor self-learning. Finally, frames can be used after a reading lesson to summarize and integrate newly acquired information.

Graphic organizers are visual maps that represent text structures and organizational patterns used in texts and in student writing. Ideally, graphic organizers reflect both the content and text structure. Graphic organizers include semantic maps, chains, and concept hierarchies, and assist the student in visualizing the rhetorical structure of the text. Beau Jones and colleagues (1987) explain that frames and graphic organizers can be "powerful tools to help the student locate, select, sequence, integrate and restructure information — both from the perspective of understanding and from the perspective of producing information in written responses" (p. 38).

Although much of the research on strategic teaching focuses on English monolingual mainstream students, recent efforts to study linguistic minority students' use of these strategies show similar success. This literature shows that strategic teaching improved the students' reading comprehension, as well as their conscious use of effective learning strategies in their native language (Avelar La Salle, 1991; Chamot, 1983; Hernandez, 1991; O'Malley & Chamot, 1990; Reyes, 1987). Furthermore, these studies show that students, despite limited English proficiency, were able to transfer or apply their knowledge of specific learning strategies and text structure to English reading texts. For example, Jose Hernandez (1991) reports that sixth-grade limited English proficient students learned, in the native language (Spanish), to generate hypotheses, summarize, and make predictions about readings. He reports:

> Students were able to demonstrate use of comprehension strategies even when they could not decode the English text aloud. When asked in Spanish about English texts the students were able to generate questions, summarize stories, and predict future events in Spanish. (p. 101)

Robin Avelar La Salle's (1991) study of third- and fourth-grade bilingual students shows that strategic teaching in the native language of three expository text structures commonly found in elementary social studies and science texts (topical net, matrix, and hierarchy) improved comprehension of these types of texts in both Spanish and English.

Such explicit and strategic teaching is most important in the upper elementary grades, where students are expected to focus on the development of more advanced English literacy skills. Beginning at about third grade, students face literacy demands distinct from those encountered in earlier grades. Jeanne Chall (1983) describes the change in literacy demands in terms of stages of reading. She explains that at a stage three of reading, students cease to "learn to read" and begin "reading to learn." Students in third and fourth grade are introduced to content area subjects such as social studies, science, and health. In addition, students are introduced to expository texts (reports). This change in texts, text structures, and in the functions of reading (reading for information) calls for teaching strategies that will prepare students to comprehend various expository texts (e.g., cause/effect, compare/contrast) used across the curriculum.

Strategic teaching holds great promise for preparing linguistic minority students to face the new literacy challenges in the upper grades. As discussed before, the primary goal of strategic instruction is to foster learner independence. This goal in and of itself is laudable. However, the characteristics of strategic instruction that I find most promising grow out of the premise that teachers and students must interact and negotiate meaning as equals in order to reach a goal.

Teachers, by permitting learners to speak from their own vantage points, create learning contexts in which students are able to empower themselves throughout the strategic learning process. Before teachers attempt to instruct students in new content or learning strategies, efforts are made by the teacher to access student prior knowledge so as to link it with new information. In allowing students to present and discuss their prior knowledge and experiences, the teacher legitimizes and treats as valuable student language and cultural experiences usually ignored in classrooms. If students are encouraged to speak on what they know best, then they are, in a sense, treated as experts — experts who are expected to refine their knowledge bases with the additional new content and strategy information presented by the teacher.

Teachers play a significant role in creating learning contexts in which students are able to empower themselves. Teachers act as cultural mentors of sorts when they introduce students not only to the culture of the classroom, but to particular subjects and discourse styles as well. In the process, teachers assist the students in appropriating the skills (in an additive fashion) for themselves so as to enable them to behave as "insiders" in the particular subject or discipline. Jim Gee (1989) reminds us that the social nature of teaching and learning must involve apprenticeship into the subject's or discipline's discourse in order for students to do well in school. This apprenticeship includes acquisition of particular content matter, ways of organizing content, and ways of using language (oral and written). Gee adds that these discourses are not mastered solely through teacher-centered and directed instruction, but also by "apprenticeship into social practices through scaffolded and supported interaction with people who have already mastered the discourse" (p. 7). The apprenticeship notion can be immensely useful with subordinated students if it facilitates the acceptance and valorization of students' prior knowledge through a mentoring process.

Models of instruction, such as strategic teaching, can promote such an apprenticeship. In the process of apprenticing linguistic minority students, teachers must interact in meaningful ways with them. This human interaction not only assists students in acquiring new knowledge and skills, but it also often familiarizes individuals from different SES and racial/ethnic groups, and creates mutual respect instead of the antagonism that so frequently occurs between teachers and their students from subordinated groups. In this learning environment, teachers and students learn from each other. The strategies serve, then, not to "fix" the student, but to equalize power relations and to humanize the teacher-student relationship. Ideally, teachers are forced to challenge implicitly or explicitly held deficit attitudes and beliefs about their students and the cultural groups to which they belong.

Beyond Teaching Strategies: Towards a Humanizing Pedagogy

When I recall a special education teacher's experience related in a bilingualism and literacy course that I taught, I am reminded of the humanizing effects of teaching strategies that, similar to culturally responsive instruction and strategic teaching, allow teachers to listen, learn from, and mentor their students. This teacher, for most of her career, had been required to assess her students through a variety of closed-ended instruments, and then to remediate their diagnosed "weaknesses" with discrete skills instruction. The assessment instruments provided little information to explain why the student answered a question either correctly or incorrectly, and they often confirmed perceived student academic, linguistic, and cognitive weaknesses. This fragmented discrete skills approach to instruction restricts the teacher's access to existing student knowledge and experiences not specifically elicited by the academic tasks. Needless to say, this teacher knew very little about her students other than her deficit descriptions of them.

As part of the requirements for my course, she was asked to focus on one Spanish-speaking, limited English proficient special education student over the semester. She observed the student in a number of formal and informal contexts, and she engaged him in a number of open-ended tasks. These tasks included allowing him to write entire texts, such as stories and poems (despite diagnosed limited English proficiency), and to engage in "think-alouds" during reading.[9] Through these open-ended activities, the teacher learned about her student's English writing ability (both strengths and weaknesses), his life experiences and world views, and his meaning-making strategies for reading. Consequently, the teacher constructed an instructional plan much better suited to her student's academic needs and interests. And even more important, she underwent a humanizing process that allowed her to recognize the varied and valuable life experiences and knowledge her student brought into the classroom.

This teacher was admirably candid when she shared her initial negative and stereotypic views of the student and her radical transformation. Despite this teacher's mastery of content area, her lack of political clarity blinded her to the oppressive and dehumanizing nature of instruction offered to linguistic minority students. Initially, she had formed an erroneous notion of her student's personality, worldview, academic ability, motivation, and academic potential on the basis of his Puerto Rican ethnicity, low SES background, limited English proficiency, and moderately learning-disabled label. Because of the restricted and closed nature of earlier assessment and instruction, the teacher had never received information about her student that challenged her negative perceptions. Listening to her student and reading his poetry and stories, she discovered his loving and sunny personality, learned his personal history, and identified academic strengths and weaknesses. In the process, she discovered and challenged her deficit orientation. The following excerpt from this student's writing exemplifies the power of the student voice for humanizing teachers:

My Father

I love my father very much. I will never forget what my father has done for me and my brothers and sisters. When we first came from Puerto Rico we didn't have food to eat and we were very poor. My father had to work three jobs to put food and milk on the table. Those were hard times and my father worked so hard that we hardly saw him. But even when I didn't see him, I always knew he loved me very much. I will always be grateful to my father. We are not so poor now and so he works only one job. But I will never forget what my father did for me. I will also work to help my father have a better life when I grow up. I love my father very much.

The process of learning about her student's rich and multifaceted background enabled this teacher to move beyond the rigid methodology that had required her to distance herself from the student and to confirm the deficit model to which she unconsciously adhered. In this case, the meaningful teacher-student interaction served to equalize the teacher-student power relations and to humanize instruction by expanding the horizons through which the student demonstrated human qualities, dreams, desires, and capacities that closed-ended tests and instruction never captured.

I believe that the specific teaching methods implemented by the teacher, in and of themselves, were not the significant factors. The actual strengths of methods depend, first and foremost, on the degree to which they embrace a humanizing pedagogy that values the students' background knowledge, culture, and life experiences, and creates learning contexts where power is shared by students and teachers. Teaching methods are a means to an end — humanizing education to promote academic success for students historically under-served by the schools. A teaching strategy is a vehicle to a greater goal. A number of vehicles exist that may or may not lead to a humanizing pedagogy, depending on the sociocultural reality in which teachers and students operate.

The critical issue is the degree to which we hold the moral conviction that we must humanize the educational experience of students from subordinated populations by eliminating the hostility that often confronts these students. This process would require that we cease to be overly dependent on methods as technical instruments and adopt a pedagogy that seeks to forge a cultural democracy where all students are treated with respect and dignity. A true cultural democracy forces teachers to recognize that students' lack of familiarity with the dominant values of the curriculum "does not mean . . . that the lack of these experiences develop in these children a different 'nature' that determines their absolute incompetence" (Freire, 1993, p. 17).

Unless educational methods are situated in the students' cultural experiences, students will continue to show difficulty in mastering content area that is not only alien to their reality, but is often antagonistic toward their culture and lived experiences. Further, not only will these methods continue to fail students, particularly those from subordinated groups, but they will never lead to the creation of schools as true cultural democratic sites. For this reason, it is imperative that teachers problematize the prevalent notion of "magical" methods and incorporate what Macedo (1993) calls an anti-methods pedagogy, a process through which teachers 1) critically deconstruct the ideology that informs the methods fetish prevalent in education, 2) understand the intimate relationships between methods and the theoretical underpinnings that inform these methods, and 3) evaluate the pedagogical consequences of blindly and uncritically replicating methods without regard to students' subordinate status in terms of cultural, class, gender, and linguistic difference. In short, we need

> an anti-methods pedagogy that would reject the mechanization of intellectualism . . . [and] challenge teachers to work toward reappropriation of endangered dignity and toward reclaiming our humanity. The anti-methods pedagogy adheres to the eloquence of Antonio Machado's poem, "Caminante, no hay camino, se hace camino al andar." (Traveler, there are no roads. The road is created as we walk it [together])." (Macedo, 1993, p. 8)

Notes

1. The term "technical" refers to the positivist tradition in education that presents teaching as a precise and scientific undertaking and teachers as technicians responsible for carrying out (preselected) instructional programs and strategies.
2. "Subordinated" refers to cultural groups that are politically, socially, and economically subordinate in the greater society. While individual members of these groups may not consider themselves subordinate in any manner to the White "mainstream," they nevertheless are members of a greater collective that historically has been perceived and treated as subordinate and inferior by the dominant society. Thus it is not entirely accurate to describe these students as "minority" students, since the term connotes numerical minority rather than the general low status (economic, political, and social) these groups have held and that I think is important to recognize when discussing their historical academic underachievement.
3. "Chicana" refers to a woman of Mexican ancestry who was born and/or reared in the United States.
4. "Mainstream" refers to the U.S. macroculture that has its roots in Western European traditions. More specifically, the major influence on the United States, particularly on its institutions, has been the culture and traditions of White, Anglo-Saxon Protestants (WASP) (Golnick & Chinn, 1986). Although the mainstream group is no longer composed solely of WASPs, members of the middle class have adopted traditionally WASP bodies of knowledge, language use, values, norms, and beliefs.
5. "Political clarity" refers to the process by which individuals achieve a deepening awareness of the sociopolitical and economic realities that shape their lives and their capacity to recreate them. In addition, it refers to the process by which individuals come to better understand possible linkages between macro-level political, economic, and social variables and subordinated groups' academic performance at the micro-level classroom. Thus, it invariably requires linkages between sociocultural structures and schooling.
6. Elizabeth Cohen (1986) explains that in the society at large there are status distinctions made on the basis of social class, ethnic group, and gender. These status distinctions are often reproduced at the classroom level, unless teachers make conscious efforts to prevent this reproduction.
7. For detailed discussions regarding various deficit views of subordinated students over time, see Flores, Cousin, and Diaz, 1991; also see Sue and Padilla, 1986.
8. "Cultural capital" refers to Pierre Bourdieu's concept that certain forms of cultural knowledge are the equivalent of symbolic wealth in that these forms of "high" culture

are socially designated as worthy of being sought and possessed. These cultural (and linguistic) knowledge bases and skills are socially inherited and are believed to facilitate academic achievement. See Lamont and Lareau, 1988, for a more in-depth discussion regarding the multiple meanings of cultural capital in the literature.

9. "Think-alouds" refers to an informal assessment procedure where readers verbalize all their thoughts during reading and writing tasks. See J. A. Langer, 1986, for a more in-depth discussion of think-aloud procedures.

References

Anyon, J. (1988). Social class and the hidden curriculum of work. In J. R. Gress (Ed.), *Curriculum: An introduction to the field* (pp. 366–389). Berkeley, CA: McCutchan.

Au, K. H. (1979). Using the experience text relationship method with minority children. *The Reading Teacher, 32,* 677–679.

Au, K. H. (1980). Participant structures in a reading lesson with Hawaiian children: Analysis of a culturally appropriate instructional event. *Anthropology and Educational Quarterly, 11,* 91–115.

Au, K. H., & Mason, J. M. (1983). Cultural congruence in classroom participation structures: Achieving a balance of rights. *Discourse Processes, 6,* 145–168.

Avelar La Salle, R. (1991). *The effect of metacognitive instruction on the transfer of expository comprehension skills: The interlingual and cross-lingual cases.* Unpublished doctoral dissertation, Stanford University.

Bloom, G. M. (1991). *The effects of speech style and skin color on bilingual teaching candidates' and bilingual teachers' attitudes toward Mexican American pupils.* Unpublished doctoral dissertation, Stanford University.

Boykin, A. W. (1983). The academic performance of Afro-American children. In J. T. Spence (Ed.), *Achievement and achievement motives: Psychological and sociological approaches* (pp. 322–369). San Francisco: W. H. Freeman.

Carter, T. P., & Chatfield, M. L. (1986) Effective bilingual schools: Implications for policy and practice. *American Journal of Education, 95,* 200–232.

Cazden, C. (1988). *Classroom discourse: The language of teaching and learning.* Portsmouth, NH: Heinemann.

Chall, J. (1983). *Stages of reading development.* New York: McGraw-Hill.

Chamot, A. U. (1983). How to plan to transfer curriculum from bilingual to mainstream instruction. *Focus, 12.* (A newsletter avialable from The George Washington University National Clearinghouse for Bilingual Education, 1118 22nd St. NW, Washington, DC 20037)

Cohen, E. G. (1986). *Designing groupwork: Strategies for the heterogeneous classroom.* New York: Teachers College Press.

Cummins, J. (1989). *Empowering minority students.* Sacramento: California Association of Bilingual Education.

Delpit, L. (1986). Skills and other dilemmas of a progressive black educator. *Harvard Educational Review, 56,* 379–385.

Delpit, L. (1988). The silenced dialogue: Power and pedagogy in educating other people's children. *Harvard Educational Review, 58,* 280-298.

Diaz, S., Moll, L. C., & Mehan, H. (1986). Sociocultural resources in instruction: A context-specific approach. In *Beyond language: Social and cultural factors in schooling language minority students* (pp. 187–230). Los Angeles: California State University, Evaluation, Dissemination and Assessment Center.

Edelsky, C., Altwerger, B., & Flores, B. (1991). *Whole language: What's the difference?* Portsmouth, NH: Heinemann.

Erickson, F., & Mohatt, G. (1982). Cultural organization of participation structures in two classrooms of Indian students. In G. Spindler (Ed.), *Doing the ethnography of schooling: Educational anthropology in action* (pp. 133–174). New York: Holt, Rinehart and Winston.

Flores, B. M. (1982). *Language interference or influence: Toward a theory for Hispanic bilingualism.* Unpublished doctoral dissertation, University of Arizona at Tucson.

Flores, B. M. (1993, April). *Interrogating the genesis of the deficit view of Latino children in the educational literature during the 20th century.* Paper presented at the American Educational Research Association Conference, Atlanta.

Flores, B., Cousin, P. T., & Diaz, E. (1991). Critiquing and transforming the deficit myths about learning, language and culture. *Language Arts, 68*, 369-379.

Freire, P. (1985). *The politics of education: Culture, power and liberation.* South Hadley, MA: Bergin & Garvey.

Freire, P. (1987). Letter to North-American teachers. In I. Shor (Ed.), *Freire for the classroom* (pp. 211–214). Portsmouth, NJ: Boynton/Cook.

Freire, P. (1993). *A pedagogy of the city.* New York: Continuum Press.

Freire, P., & Macedo, D. (1987). *Literacy: Reading the word and the world.* South Hadley, MA: Bergin & Garvey.

Gee, J. P. (1989). Literacy, discourse, and linguistics: Introduction. *Journal of Education, 171,* 5–17.

Gibson, M. A., & Ogbu, J. U. (1991). *Minority status and schooling: A comparative study of immigrant and involuntary minorities.* New York: Garland.

Giroux, H. (1985). Introduction. In P. Freire, *The politics of education: Culture, power and liberation* (pp. xi-xxv). South Hadley, MA.: Bergin & Garvey.

Giroux, H. (1992). *Border crossing: Cultural workers and the politics of education.* New York: Routledge.

Giroux, H., & McLaren, P. (1986). Teacher education and the politics of engagement: The case for democratic schooling. *Harvard Educational Review, 56,* 213–238.

Golnick, D. M., & Chinn, P. C. (1986). *Multicultural education in a pluralistic society.* Columbus, OH: Merrill.

Heath, S. B. (1983). *Ways with words.* New York: Cambridge University Press.

Hernandez, J. S. (1991). Assisted performance in reading comprehension strategies with non-English proficient students. *Journal of Educational Issues of Language Minority Students, 8,* 91–112.

Jones, B. F., Palinscar, A. S., Ogle, D. S., & Carr, E. G. (1987). *Strategic teaching and learning: Cognitive instruction in the content areas.* Alexandria, VA: Association for Supervision and Curriculum Development.

Knapp, M. S., & Shields, P. M. (1990). *Better schooling for the children of poverty: Alternatives to conventional wisdom: Vol. 2. Commissioned papers and literature review.* Washington, DC: U.S. Department of Education.

Lamont, M., & Lareau, A. (1988). Cultural capital-allusions, gaps and glissandos in recent theoretical developments. *Sociological Theory, 6,* 153–168.

Langer, J. A. (1986). *Children reading and writing: Structures and strategies.* Norwood, New Jersey: Ablex.

Lareau, A. (1990). *Home advantage: Social class and parental intervention in elementary education.* New York: Falmer Press.

Lucas, T., Henze, R., & Donato, R. (1990). Promoting the success of Latino language-minority students: An exploratory study of six high schools. *Harvard Educational Review, 60,* 315–340.

Macedo, D. (1994). Preface. In P. McLaren & C. Lankshear (Eds.), *Conscientization and resistance* (pp. 1–8). New York: Routledge.

McDermott, R. P. (1977). Social relations as contexts for learning in school. *Harvard Educational Review, 47,* 198–213.

McLeod, B. (Ed.). (in press). *Cultural diversity and second language learning.* Albany: State University of New York Press.

Means, B., & Knapp, M. S. (1991). *Teaching advanced skills to educationally disadvantaged students.* Washington, DC: U.S. Department of Education.

Mehan, H. (1992). Understanding inequality in schools: The contribution of interpretive studies. *Sociology of Education, 65*(1), 1-20.

Menchaca, M., & Valencia, R. (1990). Anglo-Saxon ideologies in the 1920s–1930s: Their impact on the segregation of Mexican students in California. *Anthropology and Education Quarterly, 21,* 222–245.

Moll, L. C. (1986). Writing as communication: Creating learning environments for students. *Theory Into Practice, 25,* 102–110.

Oaks, J. (1986). Tracking, inequality, and the rhetoric of school reform: Why schools don't change. *Journal of Education, 168,* 61–80.

Ogbu, J. (1987). Variability in minority responses to schooling: Nonimmigrants vs. immigrants. In G. Spindler & L. Spindler (Eds.), *Interpretive ethnography of education* (pp. 255–280). Hillsdale, NJ: Lawrence Erlbaum Associates.

O'Malley, J., & Chamot, A. U. (1990). *Learning strategies in second language acquisition.* New York: Cambridge University Press.

Palinscar, A. S., & Brown, A. L. (1984). Reciprocal teaching of comprehension fostering and comprehension-monitoring activities. *Cognition and Instruction, 1*(23), 117–175.

Pérez, B., & Torres-Guzmán, M. E. (1992). *Learning in two worlds: An integrated Spanish/English biliteracy approach.* New York: Longman.

Philips, S. U. (1972). Participant structures and communication competence: Warm Springs children in community and classroom. In C. B. Cazden, V. P. John, & D. Hymes (Eds.), *Functions of language in the classroom* (pp. 370–394). New York: Teachers College Press.

Reyes, M. de la Luz. (1987). Comprehension of content area passages: A study of Spanish/English readers in the third and fourth grade. In S. R. Goldman & H. T. Trueba (Eds.), *Becoming literate in English as a second language* (pp. 107–126). Norwood, NJ: Ablex.

Reyes, M. de la Luz. (1991). A process approach to literacy during dialogue journals and literature logs with second language learners. *Research in the Teaching of English, 25,* 291–313.

Reyes, M. de la Luz. (1992). Challenging venerable assumptions: Literacy instruction for linguistically different students. *Harvard Educational Review, 62,* 427–446.

Sue, S., & Padilla, A. (1986). Ethnic minority issues in the U.S.: Challenges for the educational system. In *Beyond language: Social and cultural factors in schooling language minority students* (pp. 35–72). Los Angeles: California State University, Evaluation, Dissemination and Assessment Center.

Tikunoff, W. (1985). *Applying significant bilingual instructional features in the classroom.* Rosslyn, VA: National Clearinghouse for Bilingual Education.

Tinajero, J. V., & Ada, A. F. (1993). *The power of two languages: Literacy and biliteracy for Spanish-speaking students.* New York: Macmillan/McGraw-Hill.

Trueba, H. T. (1989). Sociocultural integration of minorities and minority school achievement. In *Raising silent voices: Educating the linguistic minorities for the 21st century* (pp. 1–27). New York: Newbury House.

U. S. Commission on Civil Rights. (1973). *Teachers and students: Report V. Mexican-American study: Differences in teacher interaction with Mexican-American and Anglo students.* Washington, DC: Government Printing Office.

Valencia, R. (1986, November 25). *Minority academic underachievement: Conceptual and theoretical considerations for understanding the achievement problems of Chicano students.* Paper presented to the Chicano Faculty Seminar, Stanford University.

Valencia, R. (1991). *Chicano school failure and success: Research and policy agendas for the 1990s.* New York: Falmer Press.

Villegas, A. M. (1988). School failure and cultural mismatch: Another view. *Urban Review, 20,* 253–265.

Villegas, A. M. (1991). *Culturally responsive pedagogy for the 1990s and beyond.* Paper prepared for the Educational Testing Service, Princeton, NJ.

Vogt, L. A., Jordan, C., & Tharp, R. G. (1987). Explaining school failure, producing school success: Two cases. *Anthropology & Education Quarterly, 18,* 276–286.

Walker, C. L. (1987). Hispanic achievement: Old views and new perspectives. In H. T. Trueba (Ed.), *Success or failure: Learning and the language minority student* (pp. 15–32). New York: Newbury House.

Webb, L. C. (1987). *Raising achievement among minority students.* Arlington, VA: American Associates of School Administrators.

Winfield, L. F. (1986). Teachers beliefs toward academically at risk students in inner urban schools. *Urban Review, 18,* 253–267.

Zamel, V. (1982). Writing: The process of discovering meaning. *TESOL Quarterly, 16,* 195–209.

Aboriginal Education: The School at Strelley, Western Australia

KENNETH LIBERMAN

In the regions of Australia settled by people of European descent, traditional Aboriginal civilization has nearly disappeared. In the cities, Aboriginal people are part-European in both mind and parentage and live a life of poverty and powerlessness similar to that of urban blacks and Indians in other parts of the world.[1] In the outlying areas of cattle ranches and sheep stations, the indigenous Aboriginals have been incorporated into the Anglo-Australian society as the work force maintaining the pastoral industries. While they retain some traditional spiritual beliefs and connections with the land, they are dominated in their daily lives by white Australians who are convinced that the Aboriginal civilization is facing destruction and that such an expiration is for the best.

In the remote Australian outback, however, where extreme tropical and desert climates have prevented European settlement, Aboriginal people continue to live a traditionally oriented existence free from many of the forms of racial domination common in the regions of Australia where Europeans have settled. While the economic bases of their lives have changed and Aboriginal people now live in large, government-financed central settlements and must cope with government institutions administering funds and services, their social and religious lives remain traditional. After many decades of an assimilation policy that actively subverted the expression of Aboriginal customs and identity, the Australian government has begun to recognize Aboriginal people's determination to seek their own synthesis of modern and traditional life.

In these remote regions three major forms of institutional domination remain, however, and Aboriginal communities have recently begun to seek self-determination. These areas of institutional control are the political administration of the Aboriginal reserve territories under the authority of the federal Department of Aboriginal Affairs, the health facilities controlled by state and federal departments of health, and the educational establishments installed at the central settlements by the education departments of the Australian states.

The problem, as the Aboriginal people view it, is that too many of the important everyday decisions in their remote communities are being made by European officials who work for one of these three government bureaucracies. At each Aboriginal central settlement, European officials live in a mini-suburb of portable houses, surrounded by high fences. The majority of Europeans do not speak the Aboriginal language and know little about Aboriginal life. In most cases, they remain for only one or two years, and yet they are actively involved in setting administrative policies for the settlements. It takes only a few months for the newest European nurse or school teacher to begin attempting to influence the policies of community management. Aboriginals do not want a large number of Europeans in residence because it is then more difficult for local community leaders to influence decision making. At many settlements Aboriginals have demonstrated their frustrations by rioting.

Wresting control of these community services from the government bureaucracies has been difficult, though the federal Department of Aboriginal Affairs has been more willing to relinquish control than the various state departments of health and education. In most regions, however, Aboriginal people have no land rights to protect them from the massive, internationally based mining developments that have disrupted community cohesion and destroyed important religious sites. In 1978 a confederation of central-desert dialect groups convinced the government to hand over control of their health facilities on an experimental basis, but none of the states or the federal government has been willing to relinquish control of schooling, despite strong pressure from Aboriginal communities in Queensland, the Northern Territory, and Western Australia.

While most Aboriginal families want their children to receive an education, the attendance rate at government-run schools is frequently 20–25 percent and sometimes less. The major objections of the Aboriginal people are that the curriculum, set by people who live in capital cities often 500–1500 kilometers away, is irrelevant to Aboriginal needs, that the teachers are often unable to communicate successfully with students and so retreat into programs consisting mostly of films, and that the community's most talented youth are sent away to more advanced schools in districts where the population is more European. The educational establishment frequently competes with community elders for authority over Aboriginal youth. In some mission settlements, students have been prohibited from eating and sleeping with their families,[2] and many schools have built cafeterias and dormitories which further diminish traditional patterns of authority. For these reasons, schooling is viewed by Aboriginal people as a political issue.

Only the Strelley Aboriginal community in Western Australia has been successful in inaugurating an educational program designed and administered entirely by Aboriginals. Strelley is known in Australia for its history of rugged independence from federal and state control.[3] Community leaders initiated the famous Pilabara Strike of 1946, during which Aboriginal farm workers earning less than two dollars per week walked off the ranches of northwest Australia, commencing a national movement that led to equal wages for Aboriginal workers. The community has had a record of rejecting European assistance if such assistance also meant European control. As a result, it has been mostly self-supporting for the past several decades, at first from mineral production and later from pastoral industries. Because of this tradition, the Strelley community had no school or health facility at its central settlement for many years. Only after convincing the Australian government that it would never accept the establishment of schools except on its own terms did the government consent to grant funds to institute a school program.

Six hundred Aboriginal people live at Strelley and speak some nine dialects of the Western Desert Aboriginal language, the most dominant dialects being *Nyangumarta, Mantjiltjarra,* and *Kukatja*. The community owns and operates several sheep and cattle ranches which it has purchased over the years; its land holdings, unique in Australia, amount to most of the De Grey River's watershed near Port Hedland in northwest Australia. The community desired literacy and mathematics skills to further its development independent of European control, and these skills were viewed in frankly political terms. In the words of one of the elders on the school board: "When the whitefellas come to this country, he bin kill 'em blackfella. Now we learn all this literacy, we win the country back."

Beginning in 1975 with three classes, one at each of the three major camps, and four teachers, the Strelley School now has five ungraded classes of twelve to seventeen students each, three preschools, one "bridging" class for older students, two Nyangumarta literacy classes, and one Mantjiltjarra literacy class. There are also workshops such as motor maintenance, typing, and functional literacy that involve more than 150 students, about half of whom are adults. Students in the five ungraded classes spend ninety minutes each in literacy and in mathematics instruction daily.

The school is governed by an all-Aboriginal school board, unique in Australia. The board retains exclusive control over staffing, sets curriculum priorities, selects students for particular programs, and works to insure that teaching is consistent with the Aboriginal traditions of the community. For example, they have divided class enrollment according to the traditional Aboriginal moeity divisions, the mechanism of social organization whereby the members of a community are divided into two groups (of two subsections each) for the purposes of marriage and association. Selecting class membership on the basis of these divisions insures that patterns of association that disrupt the traditional social organization will not develop.

Most schools at remote Aboriginal settlements are held in exclusive quarters under the influence of European administrators, and Aboriginal parents feel alienated from the school, where they are, for the most part, not needed or wanted. At Strelley, all classes are located in the camps and are held outside or under tin shelters; the pupils and teachers, one European and one

Aboriginal per class, sit on woolen blankets in circles in traditional Aboriginal fashion. Instruction is observed by the local community, which the school board members believe helps to promote community involvement and control. Aboriginal people spend their entire lives out-of-doors, and Aboriginal and European staff alike insist that holding classes on the ground and in the camps instead of inside school buildings or trailers insures that the school will remain an Aboriginal enterprise.

The curriculum emphasizes traditional Aboriginal activities. Mathematics instruction, for example, is presented in the context of fishing and gathering pearls. Literacy classes are based mostly on texts produced at the settlement and deal with elements of everyday Aboriginal life. The adult special workshops cover a variety of practical skills such as motor maintenance and handicrafts; the English literacy classes discuss current issues facing the community. No instruction is given that would conflict with the traditions of the sacred Aboriginal Law, which is maintained throughout the activities at Strelley as the best guarantee of a strong Aboriginal culture.

Aboriginal people wish to modernize on their own terms. They value much that modern life offers them, but they resist domination by government institutions. To the extent that they can educate themselves to manage their own communities (drive the supply trucks, repair their automobiles, answer their own correspondence, maintain electric generators), they can decrease the number of Anglo-Australians who exercise control over their communities. While the education that Aboriginal people seek is European, though adjusted for the Aboriginal context, they believe in the possibility of developing a modern social praxis that retains traditional culture. At Strelley, the elders monitor the progress of all aspects of the school, remove whatever they feel is unnecessarily European, and make proposals for a pedagogy that maintains the Aboriginal culture. While they are uncertain about where all this will lead, Aboriginals recognize the practical necessity of controlling the major institutions of modernization, of which schooling is one. The school at Strelley is the most advanced indigenous attempt to design and administer an Aboriginal version of education.

Bilingual programs in Australia vary widely in both extent and underlying purpose. The Strelley community feels that the introduction of a bilingual program solely for the purpose of better English literacy is morally indefensible. Therefore, bilingualism at the school is advocated as a way of reinforcing traditional identity, and the success of bilingual education at Strelley may be attributed to its acceptance as such by the community.

Shortly after the school was begun, the Strelley school board decided to initiate a bilingual program. Although the Aboriginal language is oral and has no traditional written form, linguists have developed a conventional orthography for the language. Community leaders worried that young people would use their new skills to replace senior members of the community in positions of leadership. This was seen as a threat to the long-term cohesiveness of the community, and the community therefore decided it would be wise to teach older members of the settlement literacy and numeracy. At the same time, the school board concluded that instruction solely in English posed potential problems; introducing instruction in the Aboriginal language would guarantee that the educational program would be compatible with Aboriginal culture. This two-fold strategy of teaching adults as well as youths and providing instruction in their native language and in English has become central to Strelley's vision of Aboriginal education.

After six months of discussion and consultation about the design of a bilingual program, it was decided that literacy skills in the Aboriginal language would be provided first for adults. One of the school board's priorities is to prevent the schooling program from eroding the traditional lines of authority within the community, and it was considered wiser to concentrate first on making adults literate in their own language, and then to have these adults teach the children. They thought that this would allow parents to maintain their children's respect and their authority over them.

The school board selected a number of older, illiterate adults to be the first bilingual students, and those selected had to commit themselves to becoming full-time teachers after they had become literate in the Aboriginal language. The board considered it pedagogically sound to have these adult teachers instruct the classes because they would be the most knowledgeable about the language and would also be of most help in developing educational texts in the Aboriginal language. One of the European teachers reports that having adults who initially were entirely illiterate was an advantage because they were highly motivated and had no previous unhappy school experiences. And because they had just learned literacy skills themselves, they became excellent teachers. Once they had learned to read and write in Nyangumarta, they were taught English literacy skills. Another teacher observed, "Once they become literate in their own language, they storm ahead." Two of the adults acted as trainee linguists and analyzed their own language for the purpose of devising teaching materials. Senior members of the community are developing skills ahead of the youths, and the traditional respect for elders, basic to the political and religious organization of Aboriginal society, is being preserved.

From 1978 through 1979, the adults who had passed the two-year program taught two new adult classes in Nyangumarta, with the occasional assistance of one European teacher. These new adult students — men and women — are now teaching Nyangumarta to the children as part of the regular school program, while additional adult bilingual classes have begun to prepare adult teachers in the other dialects.

Two young people were chosen by the school board to participate in the classes so they could become typists for an extensive Nyangumarta bibliography program. A regular newsletter in both English and Nyangumarta is published at the settlement. More than 50 small books have been written by adult teachers, and some 200 books in several dialects are envisioned. These texts are to replace others provided by the Western Australian Department of Education which the school board feels are inapplicable to Aboriginal communities and oriented toward the assimilation of Aboriginal children into European society.

The school at Strelley has been fully integrated into the everyday life of the community, and nearly every member has been involved with the educational program. Attendance is over 90 percent, and the vitality of the community participants is obvious. The school has evolved into a community center, a focus for community energies. Community problems are discussed among participants in the school program, and classes serve as a forum for discussing and resolving settlement issues. But, what is more important, the school is viewed as a developing institution that will guarantee Aboriginal self-determination in the future.

Other Aboriginal communities have requested government funding for similar programs, but their requests have not been successful. Some Aboriginals at Strelley are concerned that the very success of their program may jeopardize future funding because the government of Western Australia is worried that other settlements may insist on similar educational programs. The governments of Western Australia and Queensland have been reluctant to fund any development that would increase the economic or cultural vitality of the Aboriginal people in fear that a revitalized Aboriginal population may press land claims, particularly in regions where mineral resources are, or may be, located. The attitude of these state governments is that if Aboriginals are to be educated, they should be socialized at the same time into the Anglo-Australian culture. The removal of the most talented students from their communities, however, has severely limited the capability of Aboriginal groups to maintain community cohesion. An Aboriginal civilization that modernizes while retaining its traditional culture poses a permanent political and economic threat to the conservative regimes of Western Australia and Queensland, whose economic prosperity depends on multinational mining developments located on traditional Aboriginal homelands.

Because of this, state governments have opposed funding Aboriginal-initiated and -controlled efforts in education. The Aboriginal community at Noonkanbah in the Kimberley region of Western Australia has received assistance from Strelley in setting up a school program, and part of the Aboriginal community at Alice Springs in the Northern Territory has turned to Survival International, an international native peoples' defense group in London, for assistance in establishing a similar program. As the movement for Aboriginal self-determination grows in all areas of life, Aboriginal control of education in their communities will probably become more prevalent in the future, although education department officials in one state have argued that all Australian students should receive the same education. If the Aboriginal people do succeed in securing more control over their education, then Strelley's educational experiment will most likely be the model for a great many Australian schools.

Notes

1. I have used "Aboriginals" rather than "Aborigines" because Aboriginal people themselves have expressed this preference. Most western publishers, however, opt to reinsert "Aborigines."
2. Robert Tonkinson, *The Jigalong Mob: Aboriginal Victors of the Desert Crusade* (Menlo Park, Calif.: Cummings, 1974).
3. M. Brown, *The Black Eureka* (Sydney: Australasian Book Society, 1976); Kingsley Palmer and Clancy McKenna, *Somewhere Between Black and White* (Melbourne: MacMillan, 1978); D. Stuart, *Yandy* (Melbourne: Georgian House, 1959).

Nicaragua 1980: The Battle of the ABCs

FERNANDO CARDENAL, S.J.
VALERIE MILLER

It is September 1980. Nicaragua is green from winter rains. The countryside that just two weeks ago was bustling with more than 50,000 young volunteer literacy teachers is quieter now. The National Literacy Crusade is over. The peasant-shirt, blue-jean uniforms of the young *brigadistas* ("student-volunteers") can no longer be seen in the far-away hills and valleys. Their footsteps no longer mark the mountain paths between San Rafael and Yall, but their voices and spirit remain, transformed and replaced by those of their students. Local people from Waslale and Wiwill now conduct the community study groups begun by the volunteers. From cotton fields to the jungle valleys, reading and writing continues.

In the cities, the buses overflow, crowded again with teenage faces. Endless registration lines of students surround the high schools and universities. The country begins another school year, which on the surface looks like any other. Yet, Nicaragua will never be the same again. The National Literacy Crusade has broken the patterns of the past and has laid the foundations for the future. In five months, more than 400,000 Nicaraguans learned to master basic reading and writing skills, and tens of thousands of young people and their families learned about rural poverty and peasant culture.

Nicaragua recently celebrated an educational victory that a little over a year ago would have seemed impossible. On August 23, 1980, the nation applauded the success of students and teachers of the National Literacy Crusade. We saluted their achievements, and we also saluted thousands of people who could not stand with us, those who had given their lives in battle to free this land. The National Literacy Crusade was a living tribute to their sacrifice, commitment, and hope. Their dedication and faith in the future made the campaign possible. Their memories live on in each one of us. This article is dedicated to them.

Nicaragua's struggle for self-determination had been going on for many years, but finally exploded on a massive scale in 1978. After decades of foreign domination, inequity, and military repression, the mounting rebellion could no longer be contained. As the battle intensified, young people went to the mountains and joined the liberation forces. Directed and organized by the Sandinista National Liberation Front (FSLN), they fought with an unshakable belief in victory and an uncommon courage against extraordinary odds. Civilians, organized into community-defense committees, added to their force. City people dug up the neighborhood streets to form barricades against tanks and troops. When the tear gas became too thick, housewives set out on their porches specially prepared tubs of bicarbonate of soda water for the young fighters to neutralize the burning chemicals. Women's groups organized clandestine hospitals in their homes. First- and second-graders served as couriers carrying important messages across battle lines. Businessmen led strikes and raised funds for arms. Market women hid ammunition at the bottom of baskets brimming with vegetables and carried out their missions walking confidently between rows of armored cars. Families carved out bomb shelters in their patios, using shovels and spoons. They created homemade hand bombs out of firecrackers and collected rocks to throw against Somoza's machine guns.

Despite this extraordinary display of courage and faith, the war was long and costly. Some 40,000 people were killed, 100,000 wounded, and 40,000 children orphaned. Somoza escaped with all the reserves in the Central Bank except $3.5 million, leaving an international debt of $1.6 billion. Yet, less than one year after victory, the nation was transformed from a violent war zone into one enormous school. The spirit and commitment of hundreds of thousands of Nicaraguans forged in combat became the moving force behind a massive literacy program. Young men and women who had taken up arms and gone to the hills now took up pencils and primers and returned to the mountains.

Where machine guns and bombs had filled the air such a short time ago, the sounds of ABCs and singing could be heard. Along the same paths where young fighters had rushed to battle, young literacy teachers set up blackboards and guided unsteady hands in writing their first words. In cornfields ravaged by war, beside the simple graves of fallen patriots, the literacy volunteers worked the land side-by-side with their adopted peasant families. In bomb-damaged factories, workers taught fellow workers the ABCs. The violence and destruction of yesterday had been replaced by the quiet pride of learning. A new nation was being born. One battle had been won and another begun. In these pages we will describe that second battle by explaining the origins of the campaign and its relationship to development. We will also examine some of the major problems that the Literacy Crusade confronted and the strategies developed to overcome them.

Origins of the Battle

On March 24, 1980, the entire country became engaged in a nationwide learning campaign. Student volunteers went to the countryside to teach literacy and learn the ways of peasant living, while urban workers and housewives taught and learned from people in the cities. The program was designed to help Nicaraguans acquire the skills, understanding, and empathy necessary for participation in a society undergoing rapid transformation.

The spirit that inspired the campaign had its origins in the early part of he century. The 1980 Literacy Crusade grew out of the liberation struggle begun by General Augusto César Sandino. The tensions that led to the struggle were related primarily to efforts to establish an interoceanic canal in Nicaragua. In 1909 Liberal President José Santos Zelays refused to grant canal rights to the United States. As a result, the State Department gave its support to the Conservative opposition which, when it took power, agreed to a permanent U.S. military presence and U.S. control of the economy through management of national bank, railway, and customs operations. In the 1920s the tension between the two parties escalated into open fighting. The buildup of the Liberal army in 1927 posed a serious threat to the Conservative regime. Fearing a loss of power and stability, the United States bolstered the marine presence. By a combination of political promise and military threat, the United States ambassador persuaded both parties to halt the fighting. General elections were agreed to and a National Guard was created to maintain the "peace." U.S. Marine commanders were put in charge of its training and organization, and Anastasio Somoza García was among its chosen officers.

However, General Sandino refused to accept the United States-negotiated accords. For seven years, Sandino and his peasant army battled against foreign intervention. Unable to defeat the increasingly popular general, the marines finally were forced to withdraw in 1933. With their departure, Sandino signed a peace treaty with the government, dismantled his army, and retired to organize peasant cooperatives in the north. The United States installed Anastasio Somoza as the head of the National Guard. In 1934 Somoza had Sandino assassinated, his cooperatives destroyed, and their members and families exterminated.

Throughout Sandino's struggle he had always wanted to assure his people's social and economic development. He set up cooperatives for agricultural production and, when possible, urged his troops to learn to read and write. He was especially proud of their educational achievements:

> I can assure you that the number of our illiterate officers can now be counted on fewer than the fingers of one hand. Unfortunately, due to a shortage of people who can teach, progress among the soldiers has been almost negligible.
>
> When General Pedro Altamirano first joined us he did not know how to read or write but . . . during the fighting and only because I insisted on it, Altamirano learned, stumbling and mumbling as he went along. Despite his age, he has made great strides since then, and now, as amazing as it may seem, he actually knows how to type — even if it is only with one finger.[1]

In the early 1960s, the FSLN took up Sandino's challenge. The struggle for both literacy and liberation was once again alive.

Development and Literacy:
Yesterday

Under Somoza, Nicaragua was run as a family plantation. Development had been narrowly focused on modernizing the economy's agricultural export sector for the benefit of a small privileged minority. The promotion of universal literacy or adult education was irrelevant and potentially threatening. Under this economic system, national development programs were essentially used to enrich Somoza's personal fortune and to buttress the regime's power structure by providing his partners with lucrative business opportunities involving massive graft and corruption. While isolated sectors of the population benefited from the programs, the root causes of economic disparity and political injustice were never addressed. Ultimately, development projects led to the expansion of the government's corrupt patronage system and to the further impoverishment and repression of the majority.

Illiteracy was both a condition and a product of this system. In 1979 a special census revealed that more than 50 percent of the population was illiterate, a figure which soared above 85 percent in some rural areas.[2] This problem was never seriously addressed during the dictatorship because the promotion of universal literacy was neither politically advisable for the maintenance of the system nor economically necessary for its functioning. The development model of export agriculture depended upon a large pool of unskilled workers, and therefore it neither required nor encouraged an educated labor force. Politically, it was unwise for Somoza to undertake a genuine nationwide literacy program. Basic education would have provided the poor and disenfranchised with the potential tools to analyze and question the unequal power relationships and economic conditions under which they had lived. An illustration from the crusade underlines this point. A peasant is speaking during the dialogue section of the lesson:

> Somoza never taught us to read — it really was ungrateful of him, wasn't it. He knew that if he taught the peasants to read we would claim our rights. Ay! But back then, people couldn't even breathe. You see, I believe that a government is like the parent of a family. The parent demands the best of his children and the children demand the best of the parent, but a governor, like a parent, who does not give culture and upbringing to the child, well that means he doesn't love his child, or his people. Don't you agree?[3]

Under Somoza, literacy teaching was used as a cover for counter insurgency operations in the north. The "Plan Waslala," according to the Ministry of Education's own report in 1978, appointed more than 100 literacy teachers to act as spies and identify peasants sympathetic to the FSLN. Many people singled out by this operation later disappeared. Waslala itself was the site of an infamous concentration camp where hundreds of peasants had been savagely tortured and killed.

Development and Literacy: Today

With the recent triumph of the Sandinista Revolution, the meaning of development and education changed radically. The ideas of Julius Nyerere, President of Tanzania, seem especially appropriate for understanding the change. In his writings, Nyerere stresses that development means freedom and liberation. Development means people. But, as he emphasizes, people cannot be developed, human beings can only develop themselves. In the new Nicaragua, we also believe that development means freedom, a freedom that is based on liberation and popular participation. Such a process rests on the redistribution of the nation's power and wealth and on the thoughtful, creative involvement of people in community organization. Development in Nicaragua today requires that all aspects of society be examined and recreated to respond to the needs and aspirations of the majority. It involves a profound transformation of the social system and the creation of structures which promote permanent opportunities for learning and enhance equitable forms of economic and political participation.

We believe that in order to create a new nation we must begin with an education that liberates people. Only through knowing their past and their present, only through understanding and analyzing their reality can people choose their future. Education, therefore, must encourage people to take charge of their lives, to learn to become informed and effective decision makers, and to understand their roles as responsible citizens possessing rights and obligations. A liberating education nurtures empathy, a commitment to community, and a sense of self-worth and dignity. It involves people acquiring the knowledge, skills, and attitudes necessary for their new community responsibilities. Education for liberation means people working together to gain an understanding of and control over society's economic, political, and social forces in order to guarantee their full participation in the creation of the new nation. Literacy and permanent programs of adult learning are fundamental to these goals. We believe they are essential to the building of a democratic society in which people can participate consciously and critically in national decision making. The struggle to achieve these aims is long, and we are just beginning.

Soon after the triumph, the Government of National Reconstruction (GNR) and the FSLN proposed their first development plan. Education and literacy were among its top priorities. The program emphasized economic reactivation and national reconstruction and was founded on four major points. First, it established a socioeconomic policy based on a commitment to full employment, improved social services, universal literacy, land reform, self-sufficiency in basic food stuffs, increased production for the common good, and a mixed economy. Second, it encouraged popular participation through a network of citizens' and workers' associations, a representative legislative body, the Council of State, and a variety of public forums for open debate and dialogue between government and citizens. Third, the program called for the birth and affirmation of the "New Nicaraguan," revolutionary men and women, characterized by sacrifice, humility, discipline, creativity, love, generosity, hard work, and a critical consciousness. Finally, to accumulate the necessary capital for domestic investment and to pay the nation's staggering debt, it emphasized austerity. Salary differentials were drastically reduced, wages controlled, and luxury imports curtailed.

In their development plan, conducting a nationwide literacy campaign was one of the first priorities of the young government. In August 1979, just fifteen days after victory, Nicaragua's Literacy Crusade was born. The first goal of the campaign was to eliminate illiteracy. Specifically, this meant reducing the illiteracy rate to between 10 to 15 percent, establishing a nationwide system of adult education, and expanding primary school coverage through the country. Other important goals were to encourage an integration and

understanding among Nicaraguans of different classes and backgrounds; to increase political awareness and a critical analysis of underdevelopment; to nurture attitudes and skills related to creativity, production, cooperation, discipline, and analytical thinking; to forge a sense of national consensus and of social responsibility; to strengthen channels of economic and political participation; to acquaint people with national development programs; to record oral histories and recover popular forms of culture; and to conduct research in health and agriculture for future development programming.

Specifically, the Crusade was intended to help people acquire basic skills in reading, writing, math, and analytical thinking, and to develop an elementary knowledge of history and civics. Learning materials were chosen to acquaint people with the history of the Revolution, the national development plan, and the emerging political and economic structures. As a whole, the campaign was designed to sensitize the entire country to the problems and rights of the poor and to prepare citizens for their responsibilities in meeting the challenge of national development. The Crusade had one other important function: it gave the young people who had fought and suffered the traumas of the war a channel for their energy and enthusiasm. Their participation as volunteer teachers helped them make the transition between the violence of war and the challenge of transformation.

In its design and implementation, the campaign was eminently political and profoundly spiritual. First, it was aimed at giving the nation's poor and disenfranchised the skills and knowledge they needed to become active participants in the political process. In doing so, it consolidated a powerful new political force and challenged the power of large economic interests. Second, it was spiritual. The act of learning to read and write served to restore and nurture spiritual values which had for so long been suppressed. Dignity and self-worth took on new meaning as people began to gain confidence in themselves and their future. Literacy was considered much more than a basic human right. The FSLN called literacy "an apprenticeship in life because in the process the literate person learns his intrinsic value as a person, as a maker of history, as an actor of an important social role, as an individual with rights to demand and duties to fulfill."[4]

The means to carry out such an ambitious educational challenge emerged from both the philosophical principles and the practical experience of the Revolution. The actual strategies of battle provided a model for educational action. One of the fundamental tenets of the GRN and the FSLN was citizen participation: just as in war, victory rested on active community involvement. Triumph over illiteracy meant citizens learning from citizens, neighbors helping neighbors, an entire nation organized to educate itself. The specific strategy depended upon the network of citizens and labor associations that originally had been organized clandestinely for the war. The actual operation of the literacy struggle followed the same general lines as the liberation struggle — from isolated skirmishes and harassment of the enemy in the pilot project stage, to a national insurrection during the main implementation phase, on to the final offensive of accelerated study, and ultimately to the consolidation of the Revolution through the follow-up program.

The metaphors and terminology of the campaign were purposefully military — "The National Literacy Crusade: Heroes and Martyrs for the Liberation of Nicaragua," "the war on ignorance," "the cultural insurrection," and "the second war of liberation." The literacy warriors, or brigadistas, of the Popular Literacy Army were divided into brigades, columns, and squadrons and were located along six battlefronts identical to those of the war.[5] They joined forces with the Peasant and Workers' Militias and the Urban Literacy Guerillas. Each battle unit chose the name of a fallen combatant as a means of honoring his or her memory.

In no way was the use of military terminology designed to glorify war or violence. Anyone who lived through the horror perpetuated by Somoza's guard was acutely aware that the pain and trauma of violence and repression were not worthy of glorification. On the contrary, the choice of military metaphors was designed to help young volunteers integrate the memories of the past, transforming terms related to the war into positive associations with teaching and sharing. Military terminology also helped the brigadistas see the Crusade as a vital part of the nation's continuing liberation struggle and to understand that, as such, it demanded the seriousness, dedication and discipline of a military offensive. In essence, we wanted to make clear that peace-time battles demanded the same selfless, disciplined commitment as did the war effort; in fact, they demanded more.

The use of military terms and the naming of fallen heroes had a deeply spiritual significance. The Crusade owed its very existence to the Revolution and to the sacrifice of thousands of men and women who fought and died for liberation. By calling forth their names and memories, the young volunteers kept alive the courage and example of their fallen compatriots. A spiritual bond joined the living with the dead. It inspired greater levels of commitment and compassion and it spurred people on in moments of difficulty. Over 40,000 Nicaraguans died in the struggle's violence. The Crusade and its symbols were a living testimony to their sacrifice, dedication, and faith in the future.

The Challenge and the Problems

The challenge confronting the crusade staff would have discouraged most educational planners. At times we were overwhelmed. The lessons of the war, however, provided us with a special source of strength and inspiration. During the insurrection we had learned to take unimaginable risks. We learned about organizing, and about trusting in people's extraordinary capacity for daring, creativity, and perseverance. We were confident that we could translate that spirit into the Literacy Crusade. But, initially, we weren't quite sure how to prepare, organize, and mobilize the large numbers of people necessary for the battle or how to finance it. The problems appeared formidable.

Somoza had left the country destitute. We could not count on public financing. We estimated that we would need to raise approximately $20 million to support the effort. Since the war had affected much of the nation's transportation system, and years of government corruption had impeded the development of a rural infrastructure, new methods had to be devised to maintain communication with the isolated regions of the country, to transport the tens of thousands of brigadistas to the countryside, and to distribute massive amounts of equipment and teaching materials.

The long months of battle had destroyed industry so that supplying even the basic material necessities of the Crusade required herculean efforts. Machinery had to be imported, factories reorganized, cottage industries developed, and materials ordered from foreign markets to provide the necessary uniforms, lanterns, mosquito nets, boots, raincoats, malaria pills, water purification tablets, and study materials. Agricultural production had been interrupted, and scarcity in rural communities was commonplace. Basic foodstuffs first needed to be imported and then distributed to supply the brigadistas.

Because decades of repression had prevented the development of community groups and labor associations, the campaign had to depend on organizations that were still in their infancy for the crucial tasks of mobilizing and supporting the Crusade's volunteer personnel. Long years of neglect had deprived the poor of adequate health care and resulted in high levels of parasitic and skin infections, malaria, and malnutrition. Conditions in rural areas were especially severe. Medical supplies and basic health information would have to be provided to the brigadistas. To mount a campaign of such magnitude, a network of offices needed to be established. Since the number of trained and experienced administrators was limited, the Crusade would have to become a learning laboratory for educational managers.

Once launched, the Crusade confronted another series of problems. The rainy season began in May and continued throughout the duration of the campaign. As a result, many volunteers were isolated, and transportation and communication throughout the country were seriously impaired. Somoza sympathizers and former guardsmen created grave problems and tried to spread fear among the brigadistas and their families in an attempt to paralyze the Crusade. In certain regions, literacy teachers and personnel were threatened and harassed; nine were assassinated.

In the face of such complex difficulties, our inexperience weighed heavily on us. Out of the initial staff of seven, only two had worked in literacy programs, and none had ever been involved in a project of such magnitude. Our strategy for overcoming the team's lack of experience evolved over time. Basically it included study, long hours, hard work, collective problem solving, and hiring experts in adult education.

We spent the first month studying — reading about the experiences of other countries, discussing the small church-sponsored literacy projects that had been attempted in Nicaragua, talking with experts, writing position papers, and outlining a possible primer. We also had to spend time searching for desks and chairs. The Ministry offices had been left empty, and there were times when the team had to take turns using desks and either share chairs or sit on the floor.

To complete our national team, we hired selected experts in education from Argentina, Colombia, Costa Rica, Mexico, Honduras, Puerto Rico, and the United States. During the campaign they were joined by four Cuban specialists who had participated in the 1961 Cuban literacy campaign. As one of their first assignments, they were given a truck to pick up student desks from the university so that they would have a place to sit.

We also requested further technical assistance from a variety of organizations and institutions — UNESCO, the Organization of American States, the World Council of Churches, CELADEC (a Latin American Ecumenical group working in popular peasant education), CREFAL (Regional Center on Adult Education and Functional Literacy for Latin America), and Cuba's Ministry of Education. Cuban teachers who worked in Nicaragua's primary schools participated in the Crusade after classes. Spain, Costa Rica, and the Dominican Republic sent delegations of teachers to participate in the campaign. During the course of the program, additional international experts joined, including people from Canada, Chile, El Salvador, Peru, Spain, and Uruguay. More advisors also came from Colombia, Mexico, and the United States.[6]

At the end of September the core team of seven visited Cuba for a week. We interviewed the former director of the 1961 Cuban Literacy Campaign and spent four valuable days delving into the archives of their Literacy Museum. During October 1979 we organized an intensive one-week planning seminar with a team of experts from Mexico, Colombia, and the United States. After a careful clarification and analysis of the Crusade's proposed plan, we developed some general operational guidelines and began to define program structures and tasks.

As the work intensified, the core team met daily to identify and study specific problems as they emerged, and to seek effective responses. The staff labored fourteen to fifteen hours a day, seven days a week. This combination of commitment, intensive study, group problem solving, and the elaboration of easy-to-follow operational procedures enabled us to overcome many of our initial shortcomings. Before any program could be launched, however, we had to face the legacy of debt, destruction, and corruption left by the dictatorship. Serious problems of financing, health, food, transportation, and communication demanded immediate solutions.

Financing the Crusade

The crusade had to be financed from sources outside the government. We called in two specialists from the Ministry of Planning. After providing them with program details such as the Crusade's proposed scope, duration, and personnel and material needs, they developed a tentative budget calling for approximately $20 million (200 million *cordobas*).

We immediately set up a finance office. Requests for assistance were mailed to governments, institutions, and solidarity groups around the world. Official delegations were sent to the United States and to Europe. In Nicaragua, the Crusade established a program of Patriotic Literacy Bonds and encouraged community fund-raising efforts. Employees from all sectors, public and private, tithed one day's salary each month to the campaign. Marketwomen from Managua and peasants from distant mountain villages came to the national office in order to make their contributions personally. For example, three representatives of the Revolutionary Sports Committee of Chontales, two peasants and one young student, contributed 1,000 cordobas collected from community raffles. Enthusiastic high school students filled the city streets carrying tin cans. Following some of the same tactics used in the insurrection, they set up road blocks — to collect "pennies for pencils" — and called on radio stations to read official declarations of war against ignorance and to make appeals for financial help. Dances, song fests, concerts, and poetry readings all added to the fund-raising effort.

Including cash and materials, some 120 million cordobas were raised. Since the program had been carefully streamlined by cutting out all excess expenses, these funds covered the costs. Catholic and Protestant organizations were the first to contribute. The countries most generous in their donations were the Federal Republic of Germany, Switzerland, Sweden, Holland, and England, although people contributed from all over the world. In this way, they too formed part of the Crusade and shared in its achievements.

Health Problems

For decades, life in the countryside had meant poor health and early death. Malnutrition, malaria, measles, gastroenteritis, and mountain leprosy — a widespread skin infection that causes large scabs and scars — were common and sometimes deadly. To protect the brigadistas, inoculations were given, as well as basic health training which included malaria diagnosis and control. Each teaching squadron was provided with a first-aid kit with supplies sufficient for the duration of the Crusade.

Health problems, however, were more extensive and complicated than anticipated. Many older people attending literacy classes suffered from poor eyesight and therefore had difficulty reading. While eyeglasses had been ordered, their delivery was delayed, causing some people to withdraw, at least temporarily, from the campaign. Other program participants suffered from debilitating illnesses, making attendance sporadic. Volunteers suffered similar ailments. In some cases, disease prevented people from enrolling in the Crusade.

The first-aid supplies which had been carefully calculated to last five months usually ran out within two weeks. When confronted with the extent of illness and disease in the countryside, the brigadistas placed their first-aid kits at the service of the community. Medicine was immediately shared with their adopted peasant families. As a result, new supplies had to be ordered and special medical brigades formed. After a brief intensive training program, some 700 university medical students were placed throughout the country to serve as mobile health teams. Besides providing basic medical attention to volunteers, they also prepared them to give community classes in elementary health education. In addition, the brigades gathered vital information on national disease patterns and health conditions to be used in future health programming.

Food was also a problem. Without the timely organization of an emergency distribution system, food shortages would also have affected the brigadistas' health. Through the Institute of Basic Grain Distribution (ENABAS) volunteers were provided with double rations of basic foodstuffs both to feed themselves and to assist their host families. Weekend visits by parents and care packages from home helped improve the community diet.

Transportation and Communication

Nicaragua's poor transportation system hampered many aspects of the Crusade. Mobilization operations, supply distribution, and communication were all affected. For the March mobilization, brigadistas were dispersed gradually, their departures staggered over a four-day period. To accomplish the massive operation, the Crusade worked in coordination with the Ministry of Transportation and the Farmworkers' Association. They located, employed, and coordinated every available means of transportation — buses, boats, ferries, trains, dump trucks, jeeps, ox carts, horses, mules, donkeys, canoes, rafts, and, finally, feet. Some volunteers had to walk for two or three days to reach their assigned communities. During the campaign, helicopters were used for emergency medical rescues. Vehicles from every ministry and government institution were pressed into service for the distribution of supplies. Food, boots, uniforms, notebooks, pencils, pens, primers, medicine, lanterns, hammocks, and mosquito nets had to be delivered to all 144 municipalities. As winter approached, an emergency plan was instituted to accelerate the distribution process in order to provide sufficient supplies to those areas which would be isolated by the rains.

At the conclusion of the Crusade, the poor networks of roads and almost total lack of bridges exacerbated the problems of demobilization. By August, the winter rains had made many roads and rivers impassable. The lovely streams that the brigadistas had crossed on foot in the dry season had become swollen torrents, and the dirt roads had turned into muddy swamps. What had been a two- or three-day walk in March became a five- or six-day journey.

A carefully orchestrated eight-day demobilization program was put into action. At each point along the way, community organizations provided accommodations and hospitality for the footsore brigadistas. From the farthest sites, the young volunteers walked to area transportation points. From municipal centers, they were transported to department capitals, and then finally to Managua for the August 23rd celebration. Although there were many blistered feet, everyone arrived home safely.

Communication, while always a problem, was greatly improved through a network of forty-eight shortwave radios. Department offices and selected remote municipalities were given radio equipment and their personnel provided with training. A rotating team of volunteers staffed the central office twenty-four hours a day from March 10 to August 22. Besides maintaining communication in technical and administrative matters, the network served as a lifeline in case of medical emergencies.

Establishment of Records

Since government statistics were outdated and notoriously inaccurate, one of the first campaign tasks was conducting a census to establish actual levels of literacy and to ascertain the availability of volunteer teachers. With expert assistance, the census was planned and executed. Teams of volunteer census takers were trained and sent out into the field, and the results tabulated by citizens and labor organizations. Since this was our first experience in mass mobilization, the effort was not without its problems. Because the volunteer response in Managua was much greater than anticipated, not enough public vehicles had been secured for the operation. It was Sunday and all offices were closed. Not wanting to dismiss needed recruits, the Crusade's administrative coordinator borrowed money from his mother to rent private transport. No one was turned away. In all, the volunteers surveyed 1,434,738 people. Since the census tabulation would have absorbed all the nation's computer capacity for two weeks, a group of 2,500 volunteers received special training, and the tabulations were completed in ten days. The results indicated that 722,431 Nicaraguans were illiterate.

In addition, the census gave us a more complete picture of the country's illiteracy levels and their geographic distribution. As the Crusade progressed, however, it became clear that people's notions of illiteracy varied. Some who classified themselves as totally illiterate could recognize the alphabet and read simple words, but could not write. Exact skills were not known until brigadistas gave program applicants a qualifying test. This brief exam was the first in a series of three given during the campaign. The initial test was designed to determine the actual skill level of each participant, beginning with a simple exercise — drawing a straight line. This step was included so that those unable to continue beyond the first question would have some sense of accomplishment and understand that they too possessed the potential to master the alphabet. The next level of skill tested was the ability to write one's name, followed by reading and writing exercises — single words first, then short sentences. The test concluded with a comprehension exercise. People who completed all sections successfully were considered literate, and those who could read and write a few words were classified as semiliterates. Illiterates included people who could not read or write more than their own name.

An intermediate test was given to assess learner progress and diagnose individual study needs. The ability to read and write different syllabic families was determined so that specialized review could be oriented toward practicing those that had not yet been fully mastered. The final exam was administered by the literacy volunteer under the guidance of a technical advisor. It consisted of five parts which tested reading, writing, and comprehension skills. To be considered literate, participants had to write their name, read aloud a short text, answer three questions based on the reading, write a sentence dictated to them, and write a short composition. They were expected to be able to read with comprehension, pronouncing words as a whole and not as a series of isolated syllables. They were to write legibly, leaving appropriate spaces between words, and to spell phonetically. With such skills, participants were prepared within their vocabulary range to read newspapers, application forms, technical information pamphlets, and books.

Records kept on each student included such general information as name, age, sex, date of enrollment, residence, occupation, and past school attendance. A monthly progress chart indicated the lessons and exercises completed in both the primer and math workbook, as well as the total number of sessions attended. Test results for each of the three exams were recorded, as were observations about individual learning difficulties, health problems, and areas of personal interest for future study.

These reports reveal the history and progress of the Crusade. They also indicate the poor conditions under which the majority of Nicaraguans have lived and the tragic human costs of underdevelopment. According to the 1979 census, Nicaragua had an overall illiteracy rate of 50 percent, 30 percent in urban areas and 75 percent in the countryside. Children between ten and fourteen years of age accounted for 21 percent of the illiterate population. In the course of the campaign we discovered other dimensions of the illiteracy problem. As much as we did not want to accept the fact, some people simply did not have the capacity to master reading and writing skills in the campaign. Reports from volunteers and technical advisers indicated widespread learning difficulties and cases of disability. Poor health was the principal cause. Extensive malnutrition handicaps many Nicaraguans, impairing sight and hearing, limiting memory, and often causing early senility. Health statistics indicate that 25 percent of all newborns fall into the high-risk category. Many do not reach five years of age, and those who do suffer serious mental and physical disorders. About 9 percent of the population had severe learning disabilities that prevented them from studying.

Despite debilitating health problems and extreme hardships, 406,056 Nicaraguans learned basic reading and writing skills — an achievement that testifies to the creative power and determination of students and teachers alike. But initial statistics revealed that Nicaragua still had an illiteracy rate of 13 percent to overcome (6 percent urban and 21 percent rural). We believe, however, that by 1981 the rate will decrease as a result of the Crusade's follow-up program and the campaigns in English, Miskito, and Sumo.

Structural Organization: From Mountaintops to Managua

The success of the Crusade's administrative and support structure depended primarily on the participation of the citizen and labor associations. Though we did not know the kind of structure that would facilitate their involvement or exactly how to organize it, we learned much from the process. Since the campaign was an intensive, short-run nationwide project, it required setting up a massive organizational network that could effectively reach from isolated mountaintops down to the neighborhoods of Managua. With that in mind, we tried to develop a system that would be flexible and responsive at the local level and yet maintain a clear central direction and control. A single national coordinating structure took on the general management functions. Operational responsibilities were decentralized through a regional institutional network. In the field, the teachers' organization, ANDEN, and the Sandinista Young People's Association carried out organizational and implementation functions. Citizen groups, labor federations, and public institutions participated and supported the work at all levels. Two national congresses were held which brought together participants and staff to discuss program needs, problems, and solutions. Conferences began at the community level, proceeded to the municipal, on to the departmental, and finally to the national. In all, over 100,000 people participated.

To coordinate the campaign structures, the Crusade functioned in consultation with a National Literacy Commission. Presided over by the Minister of Education, Carlos Tunnerman, the National Literacy Commission, composed of delegates from twenty-five public and private institutions, workers' associations, and citizens' groups, assisted with resource mobilization and coordination. Parallel commissions were established on both the departmental and municipal levels with representatives from the same institutions and organiza-

tions as the national structure. Subcommissions were formed at the comarca and neighborhood levels.

The Literacy Crusade was organized as part of the Ministry of Education and therefore could draw upon any of the Ministry's technical or administrative support services. The campaign itself, however, was coordinated and managed by a single executive structure, the National Coordinating Board, headed by a National Coordinator and consisting of six divisions: Technical/Pedagogical; Production and Design; Technical/Organizational; Public Relations; Financial Promotion; and Administrative. A special subdivision was also established to design and implement the bilingual program.[7]

This administrative and organizational network was complemented by the actual operational structure in the field. The field network was directed by a variety of organizations and coordinated by the Crusade. For the rural work, the Sandinista Young People's Association was responsible for the organization, enthusiasm, and discipline of the teaching brigades. Made up of high school and college students, this group, known as the Popular Literacy Army (EPA), formed the bulk of the rural education corps. The Farmworkers Association (ATC) organized a small but effective teaching unit called the Peasants Literacy Militia (MAC) which worked alongside the EPA.

The Nicaraguan Educators Association (ANDEN) was in charge of the teachers who served as the technical support staff for the brigades and militia. Each squadron of about thirty volunteers was assisted by three professional teachers. ANDEN was also responsible for two of the Crusade's auxiliary activities, the Retaguardia, a summer daycare program for primary school children, and the Quincho Barrilete project, a literacy and basic education program for child street vendors. Cultural brigades for some 450 students were organized by the University and the Ministry of Culture to collect oral histories, promote popular culture, and conduct different types of research studies. In the cities, the volunteers were organized into two main forces: the Urban Literacy Guerillas, coordinated directly by the Crusade and made up of housewives, working students, professionals, and private citizens; and the Workers' Literacy Militia (MOA), coordinated by the Sandinista Worker Federation and composed of factory workers, office personnel, market venders, and government employees.

Pedagogy in Practice: Revolution and Education

In designing the materials and methodologies for the Crusade, the liberation struggle served as inspiration and teacher. Its lessons were many, some pedagogical and some philosophical. Educational experiences carried out over the long years of fighting and community organizing had demonstrated the validity of a variety of teaching approaches and learning principles. Small study groups had met throughout the struggle to analyze, plan, and carry out war-related tasks; clandestine literacy efforts had been conducted as well. Learning in this context had been based on action and reflection. Lessons had a direct, urgent, and immediate application to reality. These experiences had combined such methods and techniques as experiential learning, dialogue, group discussions, and collective problem solving. They also revealed the tremendous creativity and capacity for learning that existed within people regardless of their educational background.

These experiences were enriched by the ideas and practice of Paulo Freire and others. At the beginning of the campaign, Freire had challenged us to create the best learning program we could. He stressed the importance of providing opportunities for learners to practice their creativity and added that within a liberating revolutionary process people would learn to read and write even with mediocre materials. The revolutionary context and methodology were more important than any isolated study program or particular teaching techniques. Literacy, he said, could only "have a genuine meaning in a country which is going through a revolutionary process."[8] With his challenge in mind, we faced two technical questions: how to design literacy materials for use by volunteer teachers and how to translate young people's enthusiasm and commitment into a minimum set of pedagogical skills.

The Crusade's education team attempted to address these questions first by studying Nicaragua's experiences in clandestine literacy teaching and then by analyzing other countries' programs in light of local needs. Cuba's literacy campaign was examined closely, as was that of Peru and those of the African nations of São Tomé and Guinea-Bissau, both of which had been greatly inspired by Freire. His thinking along with many other lines of Latin American thought and experience influenced the campaign, but the most important elements of the program emerged from the reality and needs of Nicaragua and the creativity of the Crusade's national education team. In all, five intense months were spent in developing and pilot-testing materials and methods. The resultant education program was a product of their collective effort. It was founded on dialogue and on a standardized national literacy primer.

We believed, as did Freire, that dialogue is critical to a liberating education and that, combined with a phonetics approach to teaching literacy, it surpasses any other method. Since we were engaged in carrying out a national literacy campaign in the context of profound social transformation, we focused on themes that were concerns of the society at large rather than on narrow issues of interest only to individual communities. Because it offered participants the power of the word and of history, the dialogue was highly political. By expressing their own opinions about their lives, their culture, their past and future, people would begin to develop and strengthen their creativity and analytical abilities as well as to see themselves as makers of culture and history. As Carlos Carrión, the FSLN representative to the Crusade, expressed it:

> The literacy methodology is intrinsically political. How? It's not just that we speak of Sandino or of Carlos Fonseca, or of the Frente Sandinista. The most political, the most revolutionary aspect of this literacy approach is the fact that we are providing scientific knowledge and analytical skills to our brothers and sisters in the fields and factories who do not know how to read or write — the skills to reason, think, compare, discern and the ability to form their own human and political criteria, their own critical framework.[9]

To help volunteers promote the process of dialogue we provided them with concrete, step-by-step guidelines. The five-step process contained a series of suggested questions designed to help participants develop both analytical skills and a profound sense of social responsibility. The questions proceeded from simple to difficult and encouraged the students to describe the contents of a photograph; analyze the situation portrayed; relate the particular situation to the life of the learner, to the community, and to the problems facing them; solve problems around issues identified by the group; and engage participants in transforming reality, committing themselves to solving the problem, and becoming active in the national programs of social change. During the course of the Crusade, however, we came to realize the obvious — that dialogue occurred both during the literacy teaching process itself as well as in the daily living experience, and that the latter was perhaps the richer and more profound exchange. We discovered that photographs needed to be chosen with great care to stimulate a critical discussion. The team had been limited not only by a certain inexperience but also by a lack of photographs from which to choose. After experimenting with line drawings, they discovered that photographs, despite the limited selection, were far more effective in stimulating dynamic discussion.

After twenty minutes or so of dialogue, the direct study of reading and writing skills began — first with a sentence, then a word, and finally a syllabic family. We expanded Freire's single-word approach by using a short phrase or sentence based on the photograph's theme as the starting point for literacy practice. The team felt that a sentence provided a smoother transition from complex discussion to the concrete study of syllables. Because sentences encompassed a whole thought, they were considered more appropriate for adult learning as well as more flexible in generating the study of syllabic families. After reading the sentence, a key word from each phrase was chosen and divided into syllables, from which one family of syllables was selected and studied. For example, in the second lesson the name Fonseca was divided, Fon-*se*-ca, initiating a study of the syllabic family, sa, se, si, so, and su. Writing exercises were introduced and recognition exercises were used to help the participants identify the syllables as phonetic units. As learners mastered the individual syllables, they went on to use them to build new words, thus practicing their creativity and skills in manipulating the written language.

The specific teaching materials we used consisted of the elementary literacy primer, *Dawn of the People,* a teacher's manual, the *Teachers' Guide for Literacy Volunteers,* and an arithmetic workbook, *Math and Economic Reconstruction: One Single Operation.* During the Crusade, teaching games stressing learner creativity, such as a type of syllabic Scrabble, were developed and distributed. In addition, during the entire year of 1980, the national match factory produced all matches in special boxes decorated with the alphabet to be used as letter building blocks.

The primer was divided into twenty-three lessons, each accompanied by photographs and practice exercises, and was organized into three major areas: the history and development of the Revolution; the socioeconomic programs of the Government of National Reconstruction; and civil defense and community participation. Some of the specific lesson themes were "Sandino, guiding force of the Revolution"; "Work is the right and duty of every citizen"; "Spend little, save resources, and produce a lot — that is Revolution"; "The FSLN led the people to Liberation"; "With organization, work, and discipline we will be able to build the nation of Sandino."

The teacher's manual provided step-by-step instructions on the use of the literacy methodology and also contained detailed back-up readings for each of the twenty-three themes. It gave the brigadistas the necessary social, politi-

Ejercicio C

1.- Leamos la oración :

La Reforma Agraria recupera la producción de la <u>tierra</u> para el pueblo.

2.- Leamos la palabra :

tierra

3.- Separemos la palabra en sílabas :

tie   <u>rra</u>

4.- Leamos las sílabas :

rra   rro   rre   rru   rra

5.- Leamos y escribamos las sílabas :

rra   rro   rre   rru   rri

rre   rri   rro   rru

6.- Formemos y escribamos palabras combinando las sílabas conocidas:

cal, and economic information to generate a knowledgeable discussion and dialogue. Since the Crusade was considered a reciprocal learning process, the handbook also outlined a systematic set of study activities for the volunteers. The basis of their learning was their own living and teaching experience. As such, they were responsible for conducting a careful research study of their communities and keeping a field diary of their activities.

A Pedagogy of Shared Responsibility

To prepare the immense teacher corps to use the program's materials and methods, a national training program of short, intensive workshops was conducted. The first training materials explained to the brigadistas their revolutionary educational role as literacy promoters:

> You will be a catalyst of the teaching-learning process. Your literacy students will be people who think, create, and express their ideas. Together, you will form a team of mutual learning and human development. . . . The literacy process is an act of creation in which people offer each other their thoughts, words, and deeds. It is a cultural action of transformation and growth.[10]

Training, therefore, required that all participants take on new educational roles in what we called a pedagogy of shared responsibility. The traditional model of the active, all-wise professor and passive, ignorant pupil was specifically rejected and replaced by one in which the traditional teacher became a type of learning coordinator. The role of the workshop director was one of facilitator, a role that involved motivating, inspiring, challenging, and working with the participants who were encouraged to become active problem solvers. Participants were the foundation and wellspring of the process. Their responsibilities were to explore, research, and create. Small-group study, team teaching, and problem solving affirmed this new relationship. Under the coordination of two facilitators, workshop members were given a variety of educational tasks to accomplish. During the training, they reflected upon the group process and their progress, integrating both theory and practice.

Our primary purpose in training was to have people master the materials and methods while developing skills necessary to solve social problems creatively and sensitively. Methods were chosen to enhance the initiative and imagination with which people acquire and apply knowledge. The specific techniques used were simulations, role playing, group discussions, debates, murals, poetry, drawing, songs, and some artistic forms of expression from Nicaraguan folklore. Each workshop began with an introductory presentation exercise to acquaint participants with each other and to establish a congenial, dynamic learning environment. The participants were initially divided into working teams of about six people each, which formed the principal base of learning for the entire workshop. The small group chose the name of a fallen combatant for their symbol and wrote up his or her biography, hanging it on the wall for others to read. In their teams, participants then discussed the meaning of the Crusade and why they had decided to become volunteers, listing their responses on large sheets of paper and tacking them on the wall for presentation to the group. To conclude the first exercise, they were asked to create some two-line, rhyme-slogans which summarized their discussion. This technique had its roots in Nicaraguan traditional culture, where couplets are a popular literary expression, and in the war. During the long years of struggle, short chants which synthesized and captured the spirit of popular demands and aspirations had been used to animate demonstrations and harass the National Guard.

During the workshop, the rhymes took on a life of their own. Groups used their spare time trying to create new and more imaginative ones. They would practice them together in a corner and in a moment of relative silence between activities shout out their creation with great pride and enthusiasm. They then prepared a carefully written copy of their work so others could join them in shouting their couplet. The effort generated a spirit of lively rivalry and boosted energies when long hours of work became heavy and fatiguing. It also served as a positive means to gauge involvement and comprehension levels. If for example a group didn't understand an exercise or a reading, invariably a humorous couplet indicating their confusion and frustration would surface. At the end of the workshop the walls told the story of training. They were covered by summaries of group discussion and popular poetry.

To implement the training program, a decentralized four-stage model was designed. The program's success depended on its multiplier effect: beginning with seven national trainers, it was expected that in less than four months almost 100,000 people would be prepared. From December to March, workshops were held across the country. The driving force behind the training was the "group of eighty." Forty university students and forty teachers were specially selected for an intensive two-week preparation program and a one-month field experience. From their ranks, forty were chosen to train approximately 600 students and teachers in the next phase. During late February these 600 people prepared more than 12,000 people, most of whom were teachers. They, in turn, conducted the eight-day intensive workshops for thousands of literacy volunteers. Once the Crusade began, permanent training workshops were given for those people who still wished to enter the program. A radio show broadcast twice daily, together with special Saturday seminars conducted by squadron technical advisors, provided a continuing in-service training for the volunteers.

The Continuing Challenge

We are presently involved in designing and establishing a permanent system of adult education. In October 1980 three new Crusades began — in English, Miskito, and Sumo — for Nicaraguans who do not speak Spanish as their native language; and in 1981 we are hoping to launch a Health Crusade along the same lines as the literacy campaign. So much needs to be done. The hundreds of thousands of Nicaraguans who mastered basic reading and writing skills have just begun their studies. Their skills are still fragile.

The Literacy Crusade is only a first step in a long process of education and social creation. For the moment, we are in a transition that began in the final month of the Crusade — a time for people to practice and strengthen their literacy and math skills. The transition program arose from a natural phenomenon occurring in the literacy groups. As the most advanced students finished the primer, they began to concentrate on helping fellow students in mastering skills. When the campaign terminated, outstanding literacy graduates or educated members of the community were chosen to continue the work of the learning group. After being given some basic training by the Crusade's teaching supervisors, the new educational coordinators were provided with a carefully designed teacher's guide and a set of follow-up reading materials that stressed collective study and action as the fundamental basis for community learning. These community learning groups are supported by the network of mass citizen and labor organizations. The work of the coordinators is bolstered by specially selected traveling "promotors" who serve as liaisons to the regional adult education offices and provide the community groups with encouragement, orientation, and extra learning materials when available. Rounding out the transition program is a radio show for the study groups, broadcast twice daily on all national channels.

The challenge for the future is awesome. Expectations are great, problems complex, and resources scarce. In the face of new tasks, the example and lessons of the campaign provide the inspiration and hope for tomorrow. As one young literacy volunteer expressed in August, "The Crusade is like the source of a river of popular knowledge which will flow onward forever."

Life as a Brigadista

Before we conclude, there is one more aspect of the Crusade that needs to be presented — the experience of being a brigadista. Life as a volunteer in the countryside was hard work. Tasks filled the day. Mornings were spent laboring alongside peasant *compañeros;* late afternoons and evenings were dedicated to leading study sessions in homes, patios, or front yards. The experience can best be described by those who were there. We have gathered some quotes which convey how the brigadistas lived and worked and how the campaign touched their lives. No one can explain it better.

> Dear All,
>
> I arrived here on this mountain top yesterday on the back of a mule. . . . We left Saturday from Managua at 3 A.M. in a caravan of 70 buses and dump trucks, about 1,500 university students in all, complete with a gasoline truck and an

army escort to protect us during the 20 hour journey. We spent most of the time singing, shouting cheers, and waving. It was incredible, really! Even though it was nighttime in every village and town along the way, people left their homes to wave at us. Of course, they knew we were members of EPA. Women would offer us oranges and bananas and shout up at us, "Take care! See you when you return. We love you!" They would throw us kisses too. One old man, he must have been at least 70, ran beside the bus smiling up at us shouting EPA, EPA, EPA. I didn't know whether I was crying from the dust, the cold, or the wind, or the emotion I felt at seeing what a revolution can really mean. . . .

Many Hugs, Gabriella

* * *

I am really impressed how some of these kids came prepared and equipped. One of the boys looks like he is ready to fight the crocodile that always shows up in the jungle movies wanting to eat Tarzan. Another one has all the trappings of a walking Boy Scout Store. It's a sure sign of how ignorant most of us are about how people live in the countryside.

The hardest part for the volunteers is the loneliness and isolation, finding themselves suddenly living among strangers with whom, at least up till now, they have little in common. The feeling is one of anguish and insecurity. Thank God because of their political spirit and Christian faith, none of my brigadistas have deserted. Everyday they seem to adjust and find themselves enjoying life here more.

I can understand the horror of some of the parents from the capital when they come to visit their children and find them living in peasant "homes." What I don't understand is why they are so horrified that their kids will have to spend 5 months in these conditions and not that 70 percent of the Nicaraguan people have to suffer this misery their entire lives.

Educational Advisor
Los Santos

* * *

To my literacy teacher and compañero: Guillermo Briones Cisñero

> My friends, Nicaragua is free.
> The oppression of Somoza is defeated
> For with the rumbling of bullets,
>   Anastasio and son ran far away.
> And now with the shouting of ABCs,
>   Ignorance flees and joins them in Paraguay.
> These verses I do recite
>   in honor of Guillermo, my friend and companero
> Because I respect him like no other
>   and love him like an older brother.

Anselmo Hurtado Lopez

* * *

Dear Mom and Dad,

I am fine. I arrived safe and sound but please send me 20 cans of grape juice. The well is filled with mud and the river is far away. . . .

Love, your son

* * *

Dear Folks,

I'm learning a lot. I now know how to milk a cow and plant vegetables. The other day I was with Don Demesio roping a steer but I'm so stupid that I frightened the thing and we had to work twice as hard to catch it again. . . . The rains are constant. The soles of my boots came unglued and I had to sew them with a needle they use to make sacks with.

Love, David

* * *

It's difficult sometimes. Tomasita is smart and wants to study but her baby cries a lot and she can't put him down. I visit her three times a day just on the chance she'll be free but . . . she's only on lesson 4. . . . Camilo doesn't seem to assimilate his sounds very well. Of course he does need glasses. He's 67. . . . Socorro and Joaquina are way ahead on lesson 14 but Julio left to pick coffee and Catalina's in bed with malaria. . . . Vicente has improved incredibly since he fell off his mule. He was really a lazy bum before. But now, with his broken arm, he's quite serious and dedicated, even though he's had to learn to write all over again with his left hand.

Guadalupe from the Brigade Enoc Ortez
in a report to her teaching supervisor

* * *

Eight ex-national guardsmen crossed the border from Honduras yesterday and murdered the literacy teacher Georgino Andrade.

Newsbroadcast, Managua
May 19, 1980

* * *

The struggle is long and sometimes cruel. What's needed above all, my dear friend, is love and commitment. Remember, "the freedom of a people is not won with flowers." We are young and we are called upon to build the new, to create what our heroes and martyrs would have wanted. Put yourself in the place of Georgino Andrade. You wouldn't like it, if out of fear, the cause you gave your life for wasn't continued.

Letter to boyfriend Brigadista
from girlfriend Brigadista

* * *

The Literacy Crusade taught us two things. One, what our own children are capable of doing and of becoming. Two, what our country is like and how gentle and how poor our people are in the countryside.

Mother of three literacy volunteers

* * *

We take our malaria medicine twice a week and we're supposed to use our water purifying tablets. . . . The sicknesses among the children are many. Eight children in the next valley died last month of measles, three from the same family. It's unbelievable the inhuman conditions these people live under. I feel indignation and rage at not being a doctor.

Brigadista
Atlantic Coast

* * *

The Crusade has been carried out by the kids of Nicaragua, the wonderful kids who under the leadership of the *Frente* fought the tyrant — intelligent kids, sacrificing, determined — idealists and realists all at the same time. For me the principal lesson of the campaign is that now Nicaragua knows that it can count on this treasure for its future. Not all the best children died in the war. With the living, we can carry out the other necessary wars to be fought, the war against social injustice, the war against poor health, the war against disease.

The Crusade is over. The People of Nicaragua and the commitment of the *Frente* made it possible. Thanks to their efforts Nicaragua will be totally different in the future. It will be a better nation, a nation that all Nicaraguans deserve. If that's not a triumph, excuse me, but then what the hell do you call a triumph?

Priest,
Squadron Teaching Supervisor

Reflections

Thinking back over the last year, the most important lesson we learned will probably be the most difficult for educational planners to apply. In the final analysis, the success of the campaign depended not on scientifically tested educational theories, or complex planning systems, or even sophisticated curriculum design. The ultimate success of the Literacy Crusade depended on a commitment of the spirit — a commitment of a people and a government born of a liberation struggle. Only that kind of creative force could generate and maintain the levels of sacrifice and dedication required to accomplish such a task.

For when all is said and done, the crusade is not a story of complicated techniques or complex cost-benefit analysis. It is a story of people and the extraordinary potential for liberation and creation that exists within nations.

It is about thousands of problems, big and small. But most of all it is a story about the creative intelligence of people and the courageous sacrifice of thousands of Nicaraguans who gave their lives so that intelligence and creativity could flourish. It is a beginning.

Its promise can probably best be described by the words of a peasant speaking to the mother of his young literacy teacher: "Do you know I am not ignorant any more. I know how to read now. Not perfectly, you understand, but I know how. And do you know, your son isn't ignorant any more either. Now he knows how we live, what we eat, how we work and he knows the life of the mountains. Your son, ma'am, has learned to read from our book."

Notes

1. Quoted in José Román, *Maldito Pais* (Managua: El Pez y La Serpiente, 1979), p. 135.
2. Ministry of Education, *La Educación En El Primar Año De La Revolución Popular Sandinista* (Managua: Author, 1980), p. 162.
3. Auxiliadora Rivas and Asunción Suazo, conversation in literacy class, Masaya, Nicaragua, May 4, 1980.
4. Unpublished Report on Literacy Crusade by FSLN (Sardinista National Liberation Front), December 1979.
5. Brigades were made up of all those brigadistas in one municipality; columns were made up of four squadrons where possible and each squadron contained thirty brigadistas and one to three education advisors.
6. In all, the Crusade's National Office employed the services of the following international experts: 2 Argentinians, 1 Canadian, 1 Chilean, 5 Columbians, 1 Costa Rican, 4 Cubans, 2 Salvadorians, 1 Honduran, 2 Mexicans, 1 Peruvian, 1 Puerto Rican, 4 Spaniards.
7. The Technical/Pedagogical Division had four sections — Curriculum, Research, Training, and Library/Museum — and was designed to provide the educational expertise for the program. The Technical/Organizational Division essentially served as a support-control structure for the literacy promoters and as a liaison to the different sponsoring organizations. It had four sections: Statistics and Census; the Popular Literacy Army (EPA) and the Urban Literacy Guerillas (GUAS); the Mass Citizen and Labor Organizations; and the Internal Technical Secretariat. The Administrative Division was separated into two departments: Logistical Support, which was made up of Supplies, Health, Food Distribution, Transportation, Communication and Maintenance, and Plant Maintenance; and the Department of Administration, which contained Control, Accounting, Personnel, and Budget. The departments and municipalities were each structured along lines similar to the national — Technical/Pedagogical, Statistics and Census, Logistical Support, and Publicity.
8. Paulo Freire in conversion with Fernando Cardenal, Nicaragua, Oct.–Nov. 1979.
9. Carlos Carrión, speech before First Congress of the National Literacy Crusade, June 17, 1980.
10. Cruzada Nacional de Alfabetización, *Cuaderno de Orientacions* (Managua: Ministry of Education, 1979), p. 1.

The photographs in this article were taken during the Literacy Campaign and were provided by the authors.

Tribal Sovereigns:
Reframing Research in
American Indian Education

K. TSIANINA LOMAWAIMA

As we enter the new millenium, scholars who wish to work with American Indian tribes and communities face both new opportunities and new challenges in proposing and carrying out research. Many tribes now require that research proposals be approved by either tribal councils or cultural committees (Nason, 1996a), and growing numbers of tribes are crafting research guidelines and permit protocols (Association of Aboriginal Post-Secondary Institutes, 1996; Hopi Cultural Preservation Office, 1999; Navajo Nation, 1988, 1991a, 1991b, 1993). Rather than simply reject these tribal guidelines and requirements as impediments to academic freedom or as superfluous additions to existing review processes (such as the human subjects review required by most universities and funding agencies), scholars should examine the historic conditions that have led to these contemporary tribal actions. It is important to understand that tribal guidelines are both reasoned and reasonable responses to changes in the balance of power in Indian country in the last few decades. Increasing self-determination in education, as in other areas of life, has enabled tribes to exercise new levels of oversight and responsibility in the review and approval of research protocols. The need for high-quality research in American Indian education is tremendous, and scholars should not view tribal oversight as an unreasonable or debilitating obstacle to doing research.

The history of American Indian education can be summarized in three simple words: battle for power (Lomawaima, 1995).[1] Until recently, American Indian and Alaska Native parents and communities have not held the power to define what education is or should be for their children. For many generations, they have not been allowed to influence, let alone to determine, educational goals, policies, and practices within the schools that their children have been required to attend. Instead, religious proselytizers within the mission schools, federal employees within the Bureau of Indian Affairs[2] (B.I.A.) schools, or the state departments of education that supervise public schools have held the power to determine curricula, pedagogical practices, teacher training and hiring practices, language-instruction policies, disciplinary procedures, and so on. It should come as no surprise, then, that the power to define research in education — its goals, questions, and practices — also has not been in the hands of Native American parents or communities until recently. Beginning as early as the 1930s, when the federal government recognized tribal governments according to a template provided by the 1934 Indian Reorganization Act, and accelerating since the 1950s and 1960s, American Indian parents and communities have struggled to reclaim power over their children's education. Though the struggle is far from over, substantial progress has been made.

In this article, I consider three fundamental questions about the changing circumstances of Indian education and research about Indian education: How has the balance of power in Indian country shifted in the last four decades? How have tribes acted on their concerns about intellectual property and cultural patrimony, and what sort of research review guidelines have they implemented? What does the new balance of power mean for the future of educational research within Native American communities and schools? With discussion and description of governmental powers, especially the characteristics and history of tribal sovereignty, I provide a foundation for understanding shifts in the balance of power over time. I offer several specific examples of tribal requirements for research project approval that illustrate how the rules for doing research have changed. Finally, I examine a few of the challenges and advantages of the changing environment for doing research.

Shifts in the Balance of Power

Power relationships among educational institutions, educational researchers, tribes as semi-sovereign political entities, state governments, the federal government and its bureaus and agencies, and Native parents and children have altered dramatically in the last few decades. When compared to the conditions that existed through the late 1950s, the balance of power has shifted in favor of tribes and native parents.[3] Through the first half of the twentieth century, it was common for Indian children to be removed involuntarily from their homes, enrolled in boarding institutions for five to eight years at a time without visits home, malnourished and abused within the same institutions, or removed from their families without redress or appeal and placed within non-native foster care.[4] Today, Native communities and tribal governments run locally controlled schools, supervise their own social programs, seek protection in federal legislation such as the American Indian Child Welfare Act (P.L. 95-608, 1978), and, increasingly, require that researchers meet tribal requirements or guidelines for conducting research within their communities and schools. Shifts in the balance of power require that scholars who do research among Native communities follow different rules than were current just a few years ago.

In order to understand the new rules for proposing and conducting research involving Native people, scholars must understand the character of the political powers of tribal, state, and federal governments. In order to understand why research rules have changed, scholars must also understand the historical context. This requires knowledge of a broader history than just that of Indian education. Tribes, the states, and the federal government have, since the inception of the United States, been locked in battles over political powers and jurisdictions. All three types of governments — tribal, state, and federal — see themselves to varying degrees as sovereign. Sovereignty, the dictionary tells us, is the fundamental right of a state to self-government and independence (Morris, 1975, p. 1236). Tribes assert an inherent sovereignty that they held prior to the establishment of the United States and, therefore, that cannot be granted by the U.S. government. Most tribes today pragmatically operate within a limited sovereignty that intersects with and is interdependent with state and federal jurisdictions and powers. Nonetheless, sovereignty is the bedrock upon which any and every discussion of Indian reality today must be built.

A few definitions are crucial to understanding the struggle for sovereign powers among tribal, state, and federal governments. To the dictionary definition of sovereignty as a government's inherent right to self-governance and independence, I would add the right to self-education. The United States has long believed in the right of local communities to control local education (Cremin, 1980, 1988).[5] In the United States, tribal sovereign powers have, over time, been subordinated to federal powers and federal jurisdiction. However, the subordination has not been a clean, uncontested process. In 1831, a landmark U.S. Supreme Court decision defined tribes as "dependent domestic nations" (*Cherokee Nation v. Georgia*, 1831). "Dependent" was asserted by Chief Justice John Marshall to mean that tribes were dependent upon the protection and oversight of the federal government. "Domestic" meant that they were encapsulated within the national geopolitical boundaries of the United States. "Nation" still meant nation, but with the prior limitations and circumscriptions — surely an awkward marriage of terms and concepts. The ambivalence and ambiguity inherent in this nineteenth-century definition are with us today.[6]

Despite the ambiguities of tribal sovereignty, some inherent sovereign rights were never given away or delegated to the federal government through treaty or other agreement. These are known as reserved rights, and reserved lands, commonly called reservations, are lands that were reserved by tribes out of their homelands while large tracts were ceded to the federal government. Reserved rights include, for example, in the Pacific Northwest, the right to fish in "usual and accustomed places" whether those places are now within or outside reservation boundaries; in the Great Lakes, the right to hunt, fish, and gather on the lands that were ceded by treaty to the United States; and in the Southwest, rights to reserved water necessary to irrigate crops (*U.S. v. Washington*, 1974, 1975, 1976; *Minnesota et al. v. Mille Lacs Tribe*, 1999; Bowden, 1977).

Other kinds of rights and services were sometimes promised to tribes by the federal government through the treaty process. Treaty guarantees often included the construction of schools and provision of teachers, as well as health care, annuity payments, and rations (Prucha, 1986). Treaty goods and services were promised partly in payment for large tracts of land ceded by tribes to the United States, and partly to accomplish the federal government's goals of assimilating and "civilizing" Native people. It is important to keep in mind that this country was founded on the premise that the Constitution and treaties are the supreme law of the land. Just as the Constitution is a living document that still guides our government, treaties are also living documents; despite being negotiated and ratified in past centuries, they still carry the force of law and are subject to ongoing legal interpretations.

In the balance of power between tribes and the United States, tribal sovereignty confronts federal "plenary power." Plenary power is the power that Congress has assumed over Indian affairs, partly through Constitutional grant, partly through Supreme Court interpretations, and partly through unilateral actions. Congress and the courts have defined plenary power (incorrectly, some would say) as full and complete power over Indian peoples and affairs (see, e.g., *Lone Wolf v. Hitchcock*, 1903). The last two centuries have witnessed a contest between assertions of federal plenary power and assertions of tribal (semi-)sovereignty (Deloria & Lytle, 1983). The low point of tribal sovereignty and the high point of plenary power arguably occurred around the turn of this century. In 1903, the Supreme Court declared in *Lone Wolf v. Hitchcock* that Congress could arbitrarily and unilaterally abrogate any treaty. Also in 1903, the Office of Indian Affairs (O.I.A.) issued administrative regulations — the Short Hair Order and citizenship dress orders — that criminalized long hair on men and Native dress (Hoxie, 1984). Early in this century, Hopi men were incarcerated at Alcatraz for resisting federal authority by refusing to enroll their children in a federal day school, among other issues (James, 1974); pregnant women caught playing cards on a Nevada reservation were forced into hard labor; and indigenous religious beliefs and practices were outlawed (Deloria & Lytle, 1983).

What does this history mean for research? Educational research in the modern academic sense has its own history in American Indian communities, and stems from public and scientific interest in Indian people. The reservation period began in 1867; by 1880, most Native lands had been ceded or seized, and most Americans, not without cause, viewed Indians as the vanishing race.[7] Many Americans believed that Native cultures, and perhaps Native people as well, would soon be extinct given the disastrous demographic trends of the centuries since contact with Europeans (Dippie, 1982; Thornton, 1987). The response of the fledgling field of American anthropology was salvage ethnography, the effort to collect as much information, as many texts, and as many objects as possible as quickly as possible from the Native people.[8]

Once all this information and these materials were collected, they were displayed in public venues such as the 1893 Chicago World's Fair and the 1904 St. Louis Exposition to illustrate progress from the "savage" to the "civilized" races (Breitbart, 1997; Hinsley, 1981; Messenger, 1989). One example of the collecting frenzy: during three field seasons (1879, 1881, and 1884) of expeditions sponsored by the Smithsonian Institution to the Southwest, the pueblo of Zuni was forced to surrender more than ten thousand household items, approximately half of which were pottery. James Stevenson, one of the expedition directors, stated that his purpose was to "illustrate the domestic life and art" of the peoples visited (Hardin, 1989, p. 142). Stevenson, along with his wife Matilda Coxe Stevenson and ethnographer Frank Cushing, were certainly thorough, if indiscriminate, in their zeal. Stevenson wrote to U.S. Geological Survey Director John Wesley Powell:

> As soon as we advance in our catalogue sufficiently to have a better knowledge of what we have, I will forward you a full report — but up to the present we have been so busy collecting that we could only notice the objects casually as we took them in. (Hardin, 1989, p. 142)

Estimates are that between 1850 and 1950, 90 to 95 percent of all objects ever made by an Indian person ended up in a museum collection (J. D. Nason, personal communication, 1993).

Somatology, another subdiscipline within the collecting frenzy, involved the collection of human remains. In 1898, the Smithsonian acquired a collection of human skulls, as well as whole bodies, from the Army Medical Museum. During the same century that the material wealth of Native America was migrating to museums, their human remains were migrating as well. Between 600,000 and 1.5 million human remains found their way to museums through theft or by forceful seizure or as battlefield loot, purchases, gifts, loans, and donations. Curators and cataloguers rarely recorded the family of origin or the means of acquisition (Hinsley, 1981).

Salvage ethnography, the systematic collection of material culture, and the looting of gravesites and goods (either illegally by pothunters or legally by archaeologists) were the most common forms of research in Native communities for most of 150 years. Research activities, then, in the historic long view from the perspective of Native people, have mostly meant an astonishingly high rate of extraction and alienation of cultural property.

Cultural properties have included intellectual property in the form of ethnobotanic knowledge, language texts, and ceremonial esoterica; material property in the form of textiles, pottery, baskets, wood carvings, houses, canoes, masks, and sacred properties; and even the remains of human beings themselves (Messenger, 1989; Ziff, 1996).[9] Linked with this astonishingly high rate of extraction has been a lack of reciprocity (very little attention has been paid to compensating or sharing cultural knowledge with Native communities), and a dismayingly low level of respect for the manufacturers or intelligentsia within the cultures being "studied." As a result, museum curators have earned the distinction of being "the experts" on Hopi pottery, Navajo textiles, or Inuit soapstone carvings. Similarly, archaeologists have for many years presented themselves to the public as the real "stewards" of the Native American past.[10]

For many years researchers have had the distinct advantage of representing the more powerful society, of having the authority of the federal bureaucracy, the federal agent, or the imposed institution (i.e., foundation, hospital, or university) behind them. Until quite recently, the federal assertion of plenary power over tribes has meant that researchers could set their own research agendas, devise their own questions, develop whatever methodology suited their agenda, and do as they pleased without having to consult with or defer to tribal polities. Research has always been deeply implicated in the colonial political context, and educational research is no exception.

In my area of research, Native experiences in federal and mission boarding schools, studies prior to the 1980s tended to "focus on the social, cultural, psychological, or intellectual pathologies of Indian students or the pathologies of the environment"[11] (Lomawaima, 1995, p. 335). If research was not pathology focused, it tended to privilege the evolution of federal policy and the documentation left by federal policymakers and employees (Ryan, 1962; Trennert, 1988). In the last twenty years, however, researchers have attended to the alumni and students from these schools. Native and non-Native scholars have listened to and documented alumni/student feelings, beliefs, and experiences in a respectful, scholarly, and analytical manner (Child, 1998; Coleman, 1993; Haig-Brown, 1988; Hyer, 1990; Johnston, 1988; Lomawaima, 1993, 1994, 1995; McBeth, 1983). These scholars and others like them are turning the tide on a history of research in Indian education that has historically been pathology based, and too often based on generic statements — stereotypes, really — about Indian people. They are reacting against the kind of generalizing research that typically asserts that one particular cultural or learning style supposedly characterizes all Indian children or all Indian learners: as visual, silent, cooperative, field dependent, or right-brained learners. These new researchers understand the need to move past pathology-based and generalizing research.[12]

Changes in the world of academic research about Indian people were arguably catalyzed in 1969 by Vine Deloria, Jr., in *Custer Died for Your Sins*. Deloria called for a new kind of ethical responsibility and obligation toward Native communities among anthropologists (the scholarly researchers most often identified with American Indian communities). He wrote:

> I would advocate a policy to be adopted by Indian tribes which would soon clarify the respective roles of anthropologists and tribes. Each anthro desiring to study a

tribe should be made to apply to the tribal council for permission to do his study. He would be given permission only if he raised as a contribution to the tribal budget an amount of money equal to the amount he proposed to spend in his study. . . . This proposal was discussed at one time in Indian circles. It curled no small number of anthropological hairdos. Irrational shrieks of "academic freedom" rose like rockets from launching pads. . . . But the question is very simple. Are anthros concerned about "freedom" or "license"? Academic freedom certainly does not imply that one group of people have to become chessmen for another group of people. Why should Indian communities be subjected to prying . . . any more than other communities? (Deloria, 1969/1988, pp. 95–96)[13]

The civil rights movement and anti–Vietnam War activism also raised new questions about relations among so-called "races" and ethnic communities, and about social scientists' involvement in research agendas that served national, military, or intelligence purposes. Museum collection and display of sacred objects, cultural patrimony, and human remains came under increased scrutiny, resulting in legislation such as the 1990 Native American Graves Protection and Repatriation Act (NAGPRA, P.L. 101-601).[14] In addition to such federal legislation, more than thirty states have adopted statutes protecting cultural heritage.

As tribal governments have asserted their sovereignty in the decades since the civil rights movements of the 1950s–1960s, the first strides toward self-empowerment have often been strides in educational control and achievement. For example, the 1965 Economic Opportunity Act supported a variety of new educational programs, such as Head Start, Upward Bound, and Indian Community Action Programs (CAP), as well as the 1966 establishment of Rough Rock School on the Navajo reservation.[15] Further, Title I (within the 1965 Elementary and Secondary Education Act, P.L. 89-10) was amended in 1966 to include Bureau of Indian Affairs schools. In higher education, Navajo Community College (recently renamed Diné College) opened its doors in 1969. In 1970, the National Indian Education Association (NIEA) was formed in Minneapolis, Minnesota, and in 1971 the Coalition of Indian-Controlled School Boards (CICSB) was established in Boulder, Colorado. The 1972 Indian Education Act (Title IV of P.L. 92-318) was amended in 1975 to include Johnson O'Malley (JOM) and B.I.A. programs, setting a precedent for limited Indian control of programs and recognizing urban Indian populations, state-recognized, and terminated tribes as eligible for federal educational funds.[16] Members of the Boards of Regents of tribal colleges assembled in Boulder to form the American Indian Higher Education Consortium (AIHEC) in 1972. In 1975, the Indian Self-Determination and Education Assistance Act (P.L. 93-638) increased Indian participation in government programs and established the basis for "638 contracting," whereby tribes or Indian organizations can contract with the B.I.A. to run schools or programs for Indian children. In the last decade, Congress recognized the primacy of Native language preservation with passage in 1990 of the Native American Languages Act (Title I of P.L. 101-477). In 1991, the Final Report of the Indian Nations at Risk Task Force stressed the critical need "to increase the number of qualified American Indian administrators and teachers . . . who possess knowledge of Indian traditions, cultures, and learning styles" (Pavel, 1999, p. 244). The Task Force hearings were "significant events" at which "the voices of Native people were heard, recorded, and reported" (Swisher & Tippeconnic, 1999, p. 297). One result of the Task Force hearings was the convocation of the White House Conference on Indian Education. The White House Conference Report called for more research and outlined needs for "unbiased standardized tests" to better assess student abilities, parental involvement, programs for exceptional students, and alcohol and substance abuse programs (Swisher & Tippeconnic, 1999, pp. 298–299).

John Tippeconnic III, noted scholar of current trends in American Indian education, has summarized the strides toward self-empowerment in the last three decades:

> It is clear that tribal control and Indian control of education are being realized with the federal system, especially by those programs and schools supported by the B.I.A. During the 1994–1995 school year, for the first time in history, there were more tribally controlled schools (93) than B.I.A.-operated schools (92) at the elementary and secondary levels. Today more than 114 tribally controlled schools educate more than 50,000 students. Tribal colleges are probably the most successful examples of Indian control of education. Today more than 25,000 students attend 31 tribal colleges in the United States and Canada. (Tippeconnic, 1999, p. 38)

Tippeconnic also describes increased Native parental and tribal involvement in public school education, but reminds us that ultimate authority for public education still rests with the state, not with tribes.

Meanwhile, Congressional legislation and presidential mandates of the 1970s and 1980s identified tribal self-government and self-determination as the official goals of policy and practice in a wide array of governmental arenas, including education. In 1994, President Clinton issued a memorandum regarding government-to-government relations with tribal governments, which directs federal agencies and bureaus to respect the special political status of tribes, a political status that sets Indians apart as being distinctly different from other ethnic or racial minority groups in this country.

Tribal governments have successfully asserted sovereign rights in land claims cases; in treaty cases over hunting, fishing, and collecting rights; in water rights cases; and in a variety of other issues. The pendulum has begun to swing in the direction of tribal sovereignty, with some serious exceptions, particularly recent U.S. Supreme Court decisions regarding American Indian religious freedoms.[17]

Does this brief historical overview mean that all research among American Indians prior to the 1970s was unethical, unprincipled, exploitative, and bad?

Or that all research since then has had the rosy glow of high principles? Of course not. I have no desire to issue either blanket condemnations or commendations regarding eras of research; common sense tells us we have to judge each researcher on her/his own terms. I argue that we must be cognizant of the reality of power relations in this country. The exercise of power has shaped the course of research in Indian communities. Power has most certainly shaped the attitudes of Indian people and communities toward individual researchers, and toward the whole project of academic and applied research. In recent years, tribal governments have moved decisively to take more power over research into their own hands.

How Have the Rules Changed? Tribal Requirements for Research

In 1995, Professor James D. Nason, then director of the American Indian Studies Center at the University of Washington (Seattle), carried out a preliminary survey of tribes in the western United States and First Nations in western Canada to see who was controlling research activity, and how. The results of his preliminary survey were published in the journal *Tribal Colleges* (Nason, 1996a, 1996b). The first formal written policies he identified were established in 1974 in Canada by the Masset and Hesquiaht Bands in British Columbia, who adopted "Principles of Professional Responsibility" as well as a formal "Application to Do Research" form. Both bands required researchers to "disclose all scholarly or corporate connections, sources of research funding (with original budget), complete project description, and publication plans with anticipated royalties" (1996a, p. 17). In addition, the Hesquiaht principles require that "artifacts, tape recordings, notebooks, and other research results be turned over to the Band; prevent publication of any personal information without Band permission; and restrict publication of anything without prior Band review and comment (with any Band criticism appearing in the publication)"(p. 17). Most of the fifty-three tribes Nason surveyed did not have formal written policies, but 96 percent required research proposals to be submitted for their review and approval. All were interested in seeing other tribes' written policies.

Not all tribal research regulations are as extensive as the Hesquiaht rules, which clearly delineate the major areas of concern to tribes. Nason identified four key problem areas:

1. Inappropriate use of culturally sensitive information, especially spiritual information.
2. Commercial or other exploitive [sic] use of information.
3. Unauthorized infringement of individual, family, or group ownership rights for songs, stories, or other information.
4. Potential conflicts or harm resulting from the research, including the harm that comes from inappropriate interpretation of data, inappropri-

ate intrusions into community life, and breaches of confidentiality and friendship (1996a, p. 19).

Tribes, of course, are not alone in their concerns over ethical, legal, and appropriate research procedures. Before discussing several examples of tribal research policies, we must first ask the question, do researchers need this extra level of review to ensure sensitive and nonharmful research? Do we have procedures within our institutions that we could rely upon to meet tribal concerns? Most of us from academic institutions are already familiar with the research review guidelines and restrictions implemented through university offices or committees for human subject review. These review processes were implemented to protect the subjects of research, as well as the liability of research-sponsoring institutions. Some researchers might question the necessity of further review and restrictions being imposed upon them by tribes.

The human subjects review found at many institutions, however, has some serious limitations from the tribes' point of view. For example, the *Manual of Procedures* for human subjects review published by the University of Arizona exempts some research projects from review in response to concerns about limits on academic freedom:

> The Department of Health and Human Services has issued certain defined limitations concerning rules and regulations for the protection of human subjects that pertain primarily to projects involving history, social and behavioral sciences. *It is a positive response to the numerous objections voiced publicly and in the press by professionals charging the regulation placed unfair limitations on their investigative prerogatives* and stifled incentives to conduct research. The direct result of the action exempts a substantial number of research projects from review by institutional human subjects committees. (Human Subjects Committee, 1997, p. 2, italics added)

In this statement, academic freedom, or "investigative prerogatives," overshadows concern for research subjects. A tremendous amount of research that has focused on Indian people and communities has been in the fields of "history, social and behavioral sciences" (Human Subjects Committee, 1997, p. 2). These are precisely the professionals whom Vine Deloria, Jr., identified in 1969. Tribes and universities are different entities with different concerns. Universities should not necessarily be criticized for protecting their own interests, but certainly researchers should recognize and respect that tribes have interests to protect as well. The internal review processes required by our institutions do not address tribal concerns or interests very well. From tribal perspectives, academic institutional levels of review are not sufficient safeguards, therefore, and tribal levels of review are required.

If we more closely examine the categories of research that are exempted from human subjects review at the University of Arizona, the disparity between the concerns of academic institutions and tribes becomes clearer. According to the *Manual of Procedures*, three categories of exempted research activities are: 1) "research conducted in established or commonly accepted educational settings"; 2) "research involving the use of educational tests, survey procedures, interview procedures, or observation of public behavior"; and 3) "research involving minor subjects under certain circumstances" (Human Subjects Committee, 1997, pp. 2–3).

Educational research in particular leaves tribes vulnerable to potentially insensitive or invasive research procedures that have not been required to pass the scrutiny of internal institutional human subjects review. Additionally, outsiders' evaluations of risk and anonymity may not correspond to a community's internal definitions. Small tribal communities, with high rates of kinship affiliation and intermarriage, are environments in which complete anonymity as a research subject may be impossible to guarantee. The kinds of risks to interpersonal relationships within communities that may result from publication of data without adequate "masking" of participants are often impossible for outsiders to perceive, let alone formally acknowledge (Biolsi & Zimmerman, 1997). Sometimes tribal communities have very different standards for establishing the authority of "experts" who might reasonably speak on certain subjects. In the context of anonymity of informants, Hartman Lomawaima (1989) discussed the necessity within Hopi society of knowing the clan and village affiliation of research participants. Tribal definitions or understandings of the boundaries between "private" and "public" activities may also differ significantly from the understandings of noncommunity researchers.

In short, many university human subject protection policies were drafted based on a very different set of concerns than those that motivate tribes, as summarized by Nason. Most outside researchers simply do not have the kind of cultural, genealogical, and local knowledge necessary to make informed decisions about when the use of culturally sensitive or spiritual information is appropriate or not; when they might be infringing on individual, family, or group ownership rights for songs or stories; or what types of potential conflicts or harm might result from "inappropriate interpretation of data, inappropriate intrusions into community life, and breaches of confidentiality and friendship" (Nason, 1996a, p. 19).

Some universities, including the University of Arizona, have instituted further levels of review for any research proposal that includes American Indian subjects. At the University of Arizona, these proposals must also be reviewed by the American Indian Studies Program staff. This may be a well-meant political strategy and a response to the problems associated with maintaining good relations between the University and the twenty-one federally recognized tribes in our state, but I believe that any review process within the university cannot wholly address the concerns of those outside the university. Academic freedom is a preciously guarded commodity in our world, as well it should be, but do "investigative prerogatives" (Human Subjects Committee, 1997, p. 2) necessarily respect tribal concerns and perspectives? Are research professionals necessarily knowledgeable about tribal concerns and perspectives? Are academic professionals, even if they are Native people, necessarily the best, or the appropriate, representatives of tribal communities vis-à-vis "investigative prerogatives"? I am not convinced that we are.

Power is at the crux of the matter, after all. In Indian America, power means sovereignty, and sovereignty means self-government, self-determination, and self-education. Today — and in the future — sovereignty means that tribes should and will make the rules that researchers must respect and follow. I believe that tribal review does not necessarily mean that high-quality research will be eviscerated, obliterated, impaired, or infringed upon. Instead, tribal review can easily motivate better research, research that will be meaningful and useful to tribal communities. The following examples of tribal research policies illustrate how two U.S. tribes have addressed the world of academic research. They reflect the type of concern that tribes are best suited to identify.

Hopi

The *Protocol for Research, Publications and Recordings*[18] issued by the Hopi Tribe and implemented through the Hopi Cultural Preservation Office (HCPO) clearly identifies why Hopis feel tribally controlled research review is essential: [19]

> The Hopi people desire to protect their rights to privacy and in and to Hopi intellectual resources. Due to the continued abuse, misrepresentation and exploitation of the rights of the Hopi people, it is necessary that guidelines be established and strictly followed. (Hopi Cultural Preservation Office, 1999, p. 1)

The policy statement specifically identifies "commoditization or commercialization" of Hopi intellectual resources as the tribe's preeminent concern. The *Protocol* requires researchers to submit a proposal that addresses tribal concerns, such as possible benefits to the tribe, tribal access to research data and results, and tribal share in publication. Researchers must also explain how they plan to request tribal consent and/or informed consent from individuals asked to participate in the research. A confidentiality agreement must be included if the privacy of consultants is an issue, as well as a discussion of compensation for consultants. When a proposal includes staff support or hiring of on-site research staff, the tribe requests that Hopi preference in hiring and training be followed. The *Protocol* also asks researchers to outline a process whereby the tribe can review and "have input" before research results are published, in order to protect sensitive information. The *Protocol* further reserves for the Tribe the right to 1) assess permit fees; 2) prevent publication of material that is deemed unauthorized or insensitive, or that misrepresents, stereotypes, or harms the safety and welfare of the Hopi people; 3) "require deposit of raw materials or data, working papers or product in a tribally designated repository, with specific safeguards to preserve confidentiality"; and 4) deny a license or permit (Hopi, 1999, pp. 2–3).

The requirement to deposit a copy of all data and raw materials into the tribal archive is an undeniable assertion of ownership of cultural and intellectual properties. The Hopi Tribe's *Protocol* is a concise but powerful statement of tribal sovereignty.

Navajo

The Hopi *Protocol* is three pages long. In contrast, published guidelines of the Navajo Nation, including the pertinent Tribal Council Resolution and the 1988 Navajo Nation Cultural Resources Protection Act, add up to over fifty pages. The Navajo Nation has established extremely detailed guidelines particular to archaeological excavations, to the treatment of sites "whether standing, ruined, or vanished," and to ethnographic research focused on traditional knowledge. The Navajo Nation issues three categories of research permits that address: 1) site visitation, including archaeological research; 2) noncollection inventories, and archaeological and ethnographic inquiries that are associated with identifying historic properties; and 3) archaeological excavation or collection, or ethnographic research conducted by individuals, including any systematic collection of oral information (Navajo Nation, 1993). These guidelines for archaeological and historic preservation research are consistent with the Antiquities Acts of the State of Arizona, regulations published by the Arizona State Historic Preservation Office (SHPO) and the federal Archaeological Resources Protection Act, Native American Grave Protection and Repatriation Act, and American Indian Religious Freedom Act. As a consequence, the permit process can involve many entities — that is, the tribe, the state, B.I.A., and other federal agencies as well.

One of the more interesting aspects of the Navajo Nation's policy is the attention given to the cultural inappropriateness of some of the terminology and procedures required by these interlocking jurisdictions. For example, the Navajo Nation Historic Preservation Department (HPD) and the National Park Service use the term "traditional cultural property." The tribal policy to protect cultural property notes, however, that the phrase "offends many Navajo traditionalists" because the term "property" suggests that sacred places "can be treated as mere commodities" (Navajo Nation, 1991a, p. 1). The guidelines suggest that "traditional cultural property" is an imperfect and obscure translation of the appropriate Navajo term, *hodiyin*, which is more accurately translated as "sacred places." The policy statement acutely recognizes that

> "traditional cultural property" is, indeed, partly a euphemism intended to obscure the "religious" qualities that these places have.... Within the present federal legal framework for historic and cultural preservation, such obscurantism seems necessary to keep such places from being found ineligible for protection under federal preservation law because of the doctrine of separation of church and state. (p. 1)

It is evident that the guidelines published by the Hopi and Navajo Nations speak to shared concerns about commercialization, alienation, and inappropriate dissemination of intellectual property and cultural patrimony. They provide concrete and specific examples of the kind of concerns — fair return, sharing of results, local availability of collected data in tribal archives, translation difficulties, challenges of consistency with federal agency regulations — that tribes are best suited to identify. Given the vast diversity among the Native nations in America, with hundreds of distinct cultures and dozens of surviving languages, the need for local tribal control is clear. Although tribal guidelines may share commonalities of the sort Nason has identified, we cannot assume that tribal research review procedures will align precisely.

Conclusion:
Challenges and Opportunities in Indian Educational Research

This article began by characterizing the history of Indian education as a battle for power, and by observing that the power to define and control education until fairly recently has *not* been in the hands of American Indian/Alaska Native parents or communities. It is imperative to understand Indian education within a matrix of power relations because Euro-American governments, churches, and schools have consistently sought to eradicate Native languages, cultures, and beliefs. The history of scholarly research in Native America has been deeply implicated in the larger history of the domination and oppression of Native American communities, and research in education has not been an exception.

Despite that history — or perhaps more realistically because of it — many Native communities and schools accept the need for high-quality research guided by locally meaningful questions and concerns. We need more research on why and how children succeed; on how local Native control can be meaningfully implemented; on the results of implementing "culturally congruent" teaching pedagogies and curricula; on models of language maintenance and revival; on Native-language curricula; on community-based models of epistemology and community-defined structures of knowledge, and so on. We need more research in Indian education.

If researchers are unfamiliar with the history and current political status of tribes, the requirements of tribal research review may seem daunting or insurmountable. However, scholars should not be discouraged. The power to control local education, to guide local schools, and to govern access to knowledge is something that many Americans have taken for granted for generations. That tribes should now assert their power in similar ways should not be taken as an affront to academic freedom or to the scholarly integrity of research practitioners. Tribal review of research proposals has opened up important new possibilities for truly meaningful research — research that is as informative, revealing, and useful to tribes as it is to academic professionals and disciplinary theories.

Most tribes are small and have limited resources. Because tribes are pragmatic polities, they are the first to recognize the degree to which they must cooperate with and depend upon the skills, professionals, and institutions of the larger society. Tribes welcome assistance if they can participate in setting the terms of that assistance. Participation in decisionmaking is a prerogative of simple dignity and mutual respect, as well as of sovereignty.

To conclude, I propose simple rules for doing research with Indian people. If a researcher wants to know the ethics of doing research in a particular Native community or reservation, they must first ask, then listen. Many tribes have offices or committees, such as the Hopi Cultural Preservation Office, that are experienced in dealing with academic researchers. Smaller tribes may not have the resources of the Hopi or Navajo Nations, but tribal government would still be an appropriate avenue for initial inquiries.[20] Additional resources to assist researchers in making appropriate contacts exist within state and private universities, especially centers or programs of American Indian studies; tribal colleges may have the resources to connect potential researchers with tribes.[21]

If the researcher does more talking than listening in the ensuing dialogue, something is wrong. Tribal governments are often small, understaffed, and poorly funded. They bear all the burdens and responsibilities of local and state governments, without much of these entities' infrastructural support. They are bombarded by federal regulations; complex negotiations with law enforcement agencies, courts, states, and corporations; requests for information from myriad outside entities; and have their own business to accomplish. They may not be able to respond to specific requests, or to meet funding agencies' time lines, so they must be given plenty of lead time. Tribes have too often seen outsiders — teachers, missionaries, federal administrators, researchers, doctors, and "friends" — come and go. Establishing a relationship may take time, and tribal expectations for a long-term commitment are eminently justifiable.

Where tribes have established guidelines for conducting research, researchers must find out the rules and follow them. They should acquaint themselves with tribal history, past social and economic conditions, and the tribe's prior experiences with academic researchers. Understanding current issues and conditions may require extensive research in the published literature, as well as a review of documentary records in local or national archives and conversations with knowledgeable individuals.

Researchers must give something back. The possibilities are almost endless and they must be imagined and negotiated by the researcher(s) and tribe(s) involved. What is given may be concretely tangible: shared royalties, coauthorship, data that is useful to tribal agencies, data and "expert witness" testimony in critical court cases, reproduction of historic photos or documents from distant archives, training and employment for tribal members, mentoring of Native students, the development of educational curriculum or classroom materials, the publication of Native-language texts, improved medical procedures or treatments, or legal assistance. Just as importantly, what is exchanged may be less tangible but even more enduring: friendship, respect, and simple, honest communication.

The possibilities for future research in American Indian education are diverse and challenging. Working together, academic scholars, tribes, Native parents, Native scholars, and schools can improve the educational experiences and opportunities of Native children. Dignity, mutual respect, and sovereignty demand no less.

Notes

1. The term *Indian education* as used within this article typically refers to the colonial education of Native peoples by mission or governmental schools and authorities. The terms Native American, American Indian, and American Indian and Alaska Native are used interchangeably in this article to refer to the Native populations who reside within the boundaries of the United States of America. First Nations Native people within Canada have experienced similar educational situations, but are not discussed here, as their political history and relations with dominion and provincial governments within Canada differ in some fundamental respects from the United States.
2. Before the 1930s, the Bureau of Indian Affairs was known as the Office of Indian Affairs (O.I.A.).
3. American Indians were granted citizenship in 1924, but it took several more decades to acquire the right to vote in local, state, and national elections (Prucha, 1986).
4. It is critical to remember that no generic statement applies to all Indian people. The conditions described here never applied to all Indian children, at all times, in all places. Some boarding schools were relatively humane; some children enrolled voluntarily; some children were removed from abusive Indian parents and homes. What is pertinent to the argument at hand is that the practices described here were not only possible, they were indeed unremarkable through one-and-a-half centuries of U.S. history. Federal agents, mission personnel, and state and local welfare and social agency employees all wielded very real power over Indian adults and children. Reforms were initiated in federal Indian education beginning in the late 1920s as support was shifted to day and public schools, but boarding schools remained an important educational option, and conditions remained substandard for many years due to insufficient funding levels (Adams, 1995; Child, 1998; Hoxie, 1984; Lomawaima, 1993).
4. Exceptions are "specially defined" communities such as American Indians or African Americans (see, e.g., Anderson, 1978, 1988; Lindsey, 1995).
6. For more detailed and developed arguments regarding tribal sovereignty and U.S. Supreme Court interpretations, see Wilkins (1997) and Wilkinson (1987).
7. The theme of the "vanishing American" can be seen in American literature and art, such as James F. Cooper's *The Last of the Mohicans* and James Fraser's monumental sculpture "The End of the Trail," which was created for the Panama Pacific International Exposition in San Francisco in 1915 and is now on display at the National Cowboy Hall of Fame in Oklahoma City (Dippie, 1982).

8. See, for example, the annual reports of the Bureau of American Ethnology (B.A.E.) to the secretary of the Smithsonian Institution, and monographs published by the B.A.E. throughout the twentieth century.
9. I am indebted to James D. Nason, Professor of Anthropology and Curator of New World Ethnology, Burke Memorial Museum, University of Washington, for references and information concerning cultural property and the alienation of American Indian cultural properties and human remains.
10. For an example of archaeological claims to stewardship or ownership of "scientific" knowledge gained from Native sites, see Raymond (1989); for a recent discussion of early American history that heavily privileges archaeological interpretations (and even implies that all Native people resist scientific research), see "The First Americans" (1999).
11. See, for example, Birchard (1970); Krush, Bjork, Sindell, and Nelle (1966).
12. Over the years, many excellent scholars have done exemplary research in American Indian education. Susan Philips (1983) at Warm Springs, Teresa McCarty (1989) and Benally, Lynch, McCarty, and Wallace (1991) at Rough Rock, and Donna Deyhle (1992, 1995) with Navajo and Ute students all come immediately to mind. The list should surely include David Wallace Adams (1988, 1995), Judith Kleinfeld (1973), Jerry Lipka (1994a, 1994b), Lipka and Ilutsik (1995), Ron and Suzanne Scollon (1981, 1983), Karen Swisher (1992a, 1992b, 1994, 1995), Swisher and Tippeconnic (1999), Margaret Szasz (1977, 1988), John Tippeconnic III (1999), Tippeconnic and Jones (1995), Lucille Watahomigie (1994), and Harry Wolcott (1967), as well as many others. Their works reflect the changes that have permeated the world of academic research about Indian people.
13. See Biolsi and Zimmerman (1997) for an outstanding anthology of essays written by Native and non-Native anthropologists and scholars responding to and evaluating Deloria's 1969 challenge.
14. In this act, Congress mandated that all museums receiving federal funds had to inventory and identify all Native American human remains, associated funerary objects, and objects of cultural patrimony. Once completed, inventories were to be distributed to tribes, which can then respond (within a complex series of guidelines and deadlines) by requesting the return, or repatriation, of these materials (*Mending the Circle*, 1996).
14. Rough Rock Demonstration School is a community-based bilingual school established on the Navajo reservation in the isolated rural community of Rough Rock, Arizona (McCarty, 1989).
16. In 1953, Congress passed House Concurrent Resolution (H.C.R.) 108, which allowed the Bureau of Indian Affairs to develop termination plans for selective tribes. "Terminated tribes" no longer were recognized government entities; in effect, they ceased to exist as "tribes." Several tribes, including the Menominee and Klamath, were terminated, with disastrous economic results. In the 1970s, Congress passed legislation abolishing termination, and established a process whereby terminated tribes could once again be federally recognized (Prucha, 1986).
17. Regarding rulings that fail to protect American Indian religious freedom, see *Lyng v. Northern California Cemetery Protective Association* (485 U.S. 439 (1988)) and *Employment Division, Human Resources of Oregon, et al., v. Alfred Smith* (494 U.S. —, 108, L.Ed.2d 876, 110 S.Ct. 1595 (1990)). In *Lyng*, the Supreme Court acknowledged that construction of a logging road would destroy the Native religious life of several northern California communities, but ruled that the federal right to economic return (i.e., logging revenues) from federal lands overrides the Native religious freedoms. In *Oregon v. Smith*, despite prior Supreme Court rulings to the contrary, the Court failed to uphold sacramental use of peyote within the Native American Church as a religious freedom.

18. The research protocol is posted on the web at <http:/www.nau.edu/~hcpo-p/>.
19. To give some sense of the scale of public and scholarly interest in the Hopi Tribe alone, bibliographer David Laird (1977) documented that over 4,000 works had been published about the Hopi.
20. Many tribal governments now have web sites; consult the list maintained by Lisa Mitten, librarian at the University of Pittsburgh, available at <http://www.pitt.edu/~lmitten/indians/html>.
21. Lisa Mitten also maintains a list of tribal colleges, Native Studies programs, and Indian education programs, available at <http://www.pitt.edu/~lmitten/education.html>.

References

Adams, D. W. (1988). Fundamental considerations: The deep meaning of Native American schooling, 1880–1900. *Harvard Educational Review, 58,* 1–28.

Adams, D. W. (1995). *Education for extinction: American Indians and the boarding school experience, 1875–1928.* Lawrence: University Press of Kansas.

Anderson, J. D. (1978). *New perspectives on Black educational history.* Boston: G. K. Hall.

Anderson, J. D. (1988). *The education of Blacks in the south, 1860–1935.* Chapel Hill: University of North Carolina Press.

Association of Aboriginal Post-Secondary Institutes. (1996). Research Proposal Checklist. *Tribal College, 8*(2), 11.

Benally, A., Lynch, R., McCarty, T., & Wallace, S. (1991). Classroom inquiry and Navajo learning styles: A call for reassessment. *Anthropology and Education Quarterly, 22,* 42–59.

Biolsi, T., & Zimmerman, L. J. (1997). *Indians and anthropologists: Vine Deloria, Jr., and the critique of anthropology.* Tucson: University of Arizona Press.

Birchard, B. (1970). *Boarding schools for American Indian youth* (National Study of American Indian Education, Series 2, No. 2). Minneapolis: University of Minnesota Center for Urban and Regional Affairs.

Bowden, C. (1977). *Killing the hidden waters.* Austin: University of Texas Press.

Breitbart, E. (1997). *A world on display: Photographs from the St. Louis World's Fair, 1904.* Albuquerque: University of New Mexico Press.

Cherokee Nation v. Georgia, 30 U.S. (5 Pet.) 1 (1831).

Child, B. (1998). *Boarding school seasons: American Indian families, 1900–1940.* Lincoln: University of Nebraska Press.

Clinton, W. J. (1994). *Memorandum: Government-to-government relations with Native American tribal government, April 29, 1994.* Available at <http://www.usdoj.gov/otj/president.htm>.

Coleman, M. C. (1993). *American Indian children at school, 1850–1930.* Jackson: University Press of Mississippi.

Cremin, L. A. (1980). *American education: The national experience, 1783–1876.* New York: Harper & Row.

Cremin, L. A. (1988). *American education, the metropolitan experience, 1876–1980.* New York: Harper & Row.

Deloria, V., Jr. (1988). *Custer died for your sins.* Norman: University of Oklahoma Press. (Original work published 1969)

Deloria, V., Jr., & Lytle, C. M. (1983). *American Indians, American justice.* Austin: University of Texas Press.

Deyhle, D. (1992). Constructing failure and maintaining cultural identity: Navajo and Ute school leavers. *Journal of American Indian Education 31*(2), 24–47.

Deyhle, D. (1995). Navajo youth and Anglo racism: Cultural integrity and resistance. *Harvard Educational Review, 65,* 403–444.

Dippie, B. W. (1982). *The vanishing American: White attitudes and U.S. Indian policy.* Middletown, CT: Wesleyan University Press.

The first Americans. (1999, April 26). *Newsweek,* pp. 50–57.

Haig-Brown, C. (1988). *Resistance and renewal: Surviving the Indian residential school.* Vancouver: Tillacum Library.

Hardin, M. A. (1989). Zuni pottery: The roots of revival. In L. J. Bean (Ed.), *Seasons of the Kachina* (pp. 133–163) (Ballena Press Anthropological Papers No. 34). Hayward, CA: Ballena Press and California State University, Hayward.

Hinsley, C. M. (1981). *Savages and scientists: The Smithsonian Institution and the development of American anthropology, 1846–1910.* Washington, DC: Smithsonian Institution Press.

Hopi Cultural Preservation Office. (1999). *Protocol for research, publications and recordings: motion, visual, sound, multimedia and other mechanical devices.* Available at <http://www.nau.edu/~hcpo-p/index.html>.

Hoxie, F. E. (1984). *A final promise: The campaign to assimilate the Indians, 1880–1920.* Cambridge, Eng.: University of Cambridge Press.

Human Subjects Committee. (1997). *Manual of procedures.* Arizona Board of Regents on behalf of the University of Arizona. Available at <http://vpr2.admin.arizona.edu/human_subjects/manual2.htm>.

Hyer, S. (1990). *One house, one voice, one heart: Native American education at Santa Fe Indian School.* Santa Fe: Museum of New Mexico Press.

James, H. C. (1974). *Pages from Hopi history.* Tucson: University of Arizona Press.

Johnston, B. (1988). *Indian school days.* Norman: University of Oklahoma Press.

Kleinfeld, J. S. (1973). *A long way from home: Effects of public high schools on village children away from home.* Fairbanks, AK: Center for Northern Educational Research.

Krush, T., Bjork, J., Sindell, P., & Nelle, J. (1966). Some thoughts on the formation of personality disorder: Study of an Indian boarding school population. *American Journal of Psychiatry, 122,* 868–876.

Laird, W. D. (1977). *Hopi bibliography: Comprehensive and annotated.* Tucson: University of Arizona Press.

Lindsey, D. F. (1995). *Indians at Hampton Institute, 1877–1923.* Urbana: University of Illinois Press.

Lipka, J. (1994a). Culturally negotiated schooling: Toward a Yup'ik mathematics. *Journal of American Indian Education, 33*(3), 14–30.

Lipka, J. (1994b). Language, power, and pedagogy: Whose school is it? *Peabody Journal of Education, 69*(2), 71–93.

Lipka, J., & Ilutsik, E. (1995). Negotiated change: Yup'ik perspectives on indigenous schooling. *Bilingual Research Journal, 19,* 195–207.

Lomawaima, H. H. (1989). Commentary. In L. J. Bean (Ed.), *Seasons of the Kachina* (pp. 165–171) (Ballena Press Anthropological Papers No. 34). Hayward, CA: Ballena Press and California State University, Hayward.

Lomawaima, K. T. (1993). Domesticity in the federal Indian schools: The power of authority over mind and body. *American Ethnologist, 20*(2), 1–14.

Lomawaima, K. T. (1994). *They called it Prairie Light: The story of Chilocco Indian School.* Lincoln: University of Nebraska Press.

Lomawaima, K. T. (1995). Educating Native Americans. In J. Banks (Ed.), *Handbook of research on multicultural education* (pp. 331–347). New York: Macmillan.

Lone Wolf v. Hitchcock, 187 U.S. 553 (1903).

McBeth, S. (1983). *Ethnic identity and the boarding school experience of west-central Oklahoma American Indians.* Lanham, MD: University Press of America.

McCarty, T. L. (1989). School as community: The Rough Rock demonstration. *Harvard Educational Review, 59,* 484–503.

Mending the circle: A Native American repatriation guide. (1996). New York: American Indian Ritual Object Repatriation Foundation.

Messenger, P. M. (Ed.). (1989). *The ethics of collecting cultural property: Whose culture? Whose property?* Albuquerque: University of New Mexico Press.

Minnesota et al. v. Mille Lacs Tribe, 119 S.Ct. 1187 (1999).

Morris, W. (Ed.). (1975). *The American heritage dictionary of the English language.* Boston: American Heritage Publishing/Houghton Mifflin.

Nason, J. D. (1996a). Tribal models for controlling research. *Tribal College, 8*(2), 17–20.

Nason, J. D. (1996b). Tribal colleges' role in research. *Tribal College, 8*(2), 20.

Navajo Nation. (1988). *Cultural Resources Protection Act.* Tribal Council Resolution CMY-19-88.

Navajo Nation. (1991a). *Navajo Nation policy to protect traditional cultural property.* Window Rock, AZ: Navajo Nation Historic Preservation Department.

Navajo Nation. (1991b). *Interim fieldwork and report standards and guidelines.* Window Rock, AZ: Navajo Nation Historic Preservation Department.

Navajo Nation. (1993). *Navajo Nation Historic Preservation Department policies, procedures, and requirements for acquiring cultural resources investigation permits.* Window Rock, AZ: Author.

Pavel, D. M. (1999). American Indian and Alaska Natives in higher education: Promoting access and achievement. In K. G. Swisher & J. W. Tippiconnic III (Eds.), *Next steps: Research and practice to advance Indian education* (pp. 239–258). (ERIC Clearinghouse/Rural Education and Small Schools)

Philips, S. U. (1983). *The invisible culture: Communication in classroom and community on the Warm Springs Indian reservation.* New York: Longman.

Prucha, F. P. (1986). *The great father: The United States government and the American Indian.* Lincoln: University of Nebraska Press.

Raymond, C. (1989, July 5). Some scholars upset by Stanford's decision to return American Indian remains for re-burial by tribe. *Chronicle of Higher Education,* pp. A4–A6.

Ryan, C. (1962). *The Carlisle Indian Industrial School.* Unpublished doctoral dissertation, Georgetown University, Washington, DC.

Scollon, R., & Scollon, S. (1981). *Narrative, literacy, and face in interethnic communication.* Norwood, NJ: Ablex.

Scollon, R., & Scollon, S. (1983). Language dilemmas in Alaska. *Society, 20*(4), 77–81.

Swisher, K. G. (Ed.). (1992a). [Special issue]. *Journal of American Indian Education, 31*(2).

Swisher, K. G. (Ed.). (1992b). [Special issue]. *Journal of American Indian Education, 31*(3).

Swisher, K. G. (1994). American Indian learning styles survey: An assessment of teacher knowledge. *Journal of Educational Issues of Language Minority Students, 13,* 59–77.

Swisher, K. G. (1995). The Haskell Indian Nations University model for elementary teacher education. *Journal of Navajo Education, 12*(3), 32–40.

Swisher, K. G., & Tippeconnic, J. W., III. (1999). *Next steps: Research and practice to advance Indian education.* ERIC Clearinghouse/Rural Education and Small Schools.

Szasz, M. (1977). *Education and the American Indian: The road to self-determination, 1928–1973* (2nd ed.). Albuquerque: University of New Mexico Press.

Szasz, M. (1988). *Indian education in the American colonies, 1607–1783.* Albuquerque: University of New Mexico Press.

Tippeconnic, J. W., III. (1999). Tribal control of American Indian education. In K. G. Swisher & J. W. Tippiconnic III (Eds.), *Next steps: Research and practice to advance Indian education* (pp. 33–52). ERIC Clearinghouse/Rural Education and Small Schools.

Thornton, R. (1987). *American Indian holocaust and survival: A population history since 1492.* Norman: University of Oklahoma Press.

Tippeconnic, J. W., III, & Jones, P. (1995). A description of Family and Child Education (FACE): A comprehensive approach to family literacy. *Journal of American Indian Education, 35*(1), 6–9.

Trennert, R. (1988). *The Phoenix Indian School.* Norman: University of Oklahoma Press.

U.S. v. Washington, 384F.Supp.343 (1974), 520 F.2nd676 (9th Cir. 1975), Cert. Denied, 423 U.S. 1086 (1976).

Watahomigie, L. J. (1994). Bilingual/bicultural education at Peach Springs: A Hualapai way of schooling. *Peabody Journal of Education, 69*(2), 26–42.

Wilkins, D. E. (1997). *American Indian sovereignty and the U.S. Supreme Court: The masking of justice.* Austin: University of Texas Press.

Wilkinson, C. F. (1987). *American Indians, time, and the law: Native societies in a modern Constitutional democracy.* New Haven, CT: Yale University Press.

Wolcott, H. F. (1967). *A Kwakiutl village and school.* New York: Holt, Rinehart & Winston.

Ziff, B. (Ed.). (1996). *Cultural appropriation.* New York: Rutgers University Press.

Sites of Strength in Indigenous Research

GREGORY A. CAJETE

There is a movement underway on the part of some Indigenous scholars to "Indigenize" foundational elements of the educational process — that is, to view this process from the perspective of Indigenous thought. The movement is tied to an evolving and increasingly more holistic and comprehensive approach to building Indigenous nations. The exploration of Indigenous sites of strength in this volume is a reflection on the creative possibilities inherent in the introduction of an Indigenized framework to develop a contemporary research paradigm and a philosophy of Indigenous educational research. This creative process incorporates the following elements: gaining first-hand knowledge of community needs through "action research"; developing a comprehensive understanding of the history and "ecology" of a community; implementing strategies for regaining control of local communities; creating models based on lessons learned and application of research practices that work; and cultivating networks for mutual support.

These elements of strength exemplify the belief that Indigenous educational research is best performed when an Indigenous view and purpose are represented in the conceptualization, development, and implementation of research and are guided by the needs and sensibility of Indigenous people. In essence, they present an exploration of a culturally informed alternative for thinking about and enabling the contemporary education of Indigenous people through research. As such, these elements of strength are realized and explored in the following sites:

- *Endogenous research that originates from Indigenous researchers* as they engage important issues in their communities and with their own people;
- *Research that is framed and controlled by Indigenous communities,* and that originates in the aims, goals, and needs of these communities as they themselves identify them;
- The evolution of *Indigenous control of schools,* which includes the creation and implementation of culturally responsive curriculum, language revitalization, and governance situated in the hands of Elders and community members, who are in turn served by the schools;

- The shift from research on the "right" methods to fit the student to the school setting to a focus on *the critical examination of the power relationships, complicity, and hidden curriculum within schools* as a substantive cause of minority students' low academic achievement; and
- The affective dimension and *the mobilization of the whole community in a commitment to a "movement"* through shared vision and purpose, critical literacy, social consciousness, and active political involvement in the educational system as a foundation for transformative change through education.

Each site implicitly advocates for the development of a contemporized, community-based education research process that is founded upon Indigenous values, orientations, and principles, but simultaneously employs the most appropriate methodologies, concepts, and technologies of modern educational research. Educational research provides tools essential to the survival of Indigenous people and communities, but this educational research must be contextualized as part of a greater whole. Every community must learn to integrate the learning that occurs through modern education with the cultural bases of knowledge and value orientations essential to the perpetuation of a community and its way of life. For educational research to be deemed useful by Indigenous people, research must be based in their communities and must be an intimate part of their lives. Understanding the depth of relationships and the significance of participation in all aspects of life are the keys to traditional American Indian education, and these understandings form the foundation of the beliefs about the nature of knowledge (and thus the role of research) that are guiding this inquiry. At the same time, Indigenous community-based educational research presents not only a unique challenge but also creative solutions to educational issues across broader contexts.

Mitakuye Oyasin is a Lakota phrase meaning we are all related, which captures an essence of tribal education because it reflects the understanding that our lives are truly and profoundly connected to other people and to the physical world. American Indian education historically occurred in an integrated social context that developed a sense of the importance of each individual as a contributing member of the social group. Essentially, education in tribal contexts worked to sustain a communal life process. It was a process of education that unfolded through mutual, reciprocal relationships between social groups and the natural world. The process encompasses the importance Indian people place on the continuance of their ancestral traditions; the emphasis they put on respect for individual uniqueness in the diverse expression of spirituality. It facilitates a strong and a contextual understanding of history and culture; requires a strong sense of place and service to community; and forges a commitment to educational and social transformation that recognizes and further empowers the inherent strength of Indian people and their respective cultures.[1] These aspects, although they have been given little credence in mainstream approaches to education and research, form a profound orientation for learning through exploring the multidimensional relationships between humans and their inner and outer worlds.

Indigenous education is, at its very essence, learning about life through participation and relationship to community, including not only people but plants, animals, and the whole of Nature. At an individual level, this relationship involved all dimensions of one's being while providing both personal development and technical skills through participation in the life of the community. In tribal education, knowledge is gained similarly from first-hand experience in the world and then is transmitted or explored through ritual, ceremony, art, and appropriate technology. Knowledge gained through these vehicles is then used in the context of everyday living. Intellectual, social, and spiritual learning unfold in the context of relationships we encounter, experience, and try to understand in order to obtain meaning and orient ourselves. Ultimately, an exploration of traditional Indigenous education is an exploration of a nature-centered and community responsive philosophy of research. Education, in this context, becomes education for "life's sake" (Cajete, 1994) and is founded on environmental learning because it all relates to "the deep ecology" and relationships of place.[2]

Every community must learn to integrate the learning occurring in modern education with the cultural and place-based knowledge and value orientations essential to the perpetuation of a community and its way of life. It is an integrated relational education process that can have a profound meaning for the kind of modern education required to face the challenges of living in the twenty-first century. It has the potential to create deeper understanding of our collective role as caretakers of a world we have collectively been responsible for throwing out of balance.

To begin such a process, orientations of American education must begin to move from a focus only on specialization to integrated knowledge; from a focus solely on structures to an understanding of processes; from objective science to systemic science; and from building to "networking" as a metaphor for knowledge. American education must rededicate its efforts to help Americans understand and appreciate "spirituality" as it relates to the earth and the "places" in which we live. It must engender a commitment to service rather than competition as an espoused social value. It must promote practiced respect for individual cultural and biological diversity. It must engage students in learning processes that fully facilitate the development of their human potential through creative transformation. Among American Indians, education has always included a visionary expression of life. Education has been, and continues to be, a grand story, a search for meaning, essential food for the soul. The role of Indigenous research grounded in Indigenous values and needs is an essential element in the implementation of an educational process grounded in Indigenous sensibility and vision.

Notes

1. Hampton (1988) presents an excellent case for the reassessment of Indian education from the standpoint of traditional orientations mentioned. Hampton also presents an excellent outline of one of the possibilities upon which an Indian education philosophy may be based.
2. Capra (1982) presents a similar thesis in his contention that science must evolve a new paradigm of thought, action, and application to meet the challenges of the twenty-first century.

References

Cajete, G. A. (1994). *Look to the mountain: An ecology of Indigenous education.* Skyland, NC: Kivaki Press.

Capra, F. (1982). *Turning point.* New York: Simon and Schuster.

Hampton, E. (1988). *Toward a redefinition of American Indian/Alaska Native education.* Unpublished paper, Harvard University, Graduate School of Education, Cambridge, MA.

PART THREE

Sites of Survivance

"Survivance" is not a very commonplace term, and it is not necessarily the same as survival. American Indian scholar Gerald Vizenor (1994) defines survivance as "a state in which we are moving beyond our basic survival in the face of overwhelming cultural genocide to create spaces of synthesis and renewal" (p. 53). This evokes the relationships between past, present, and future through themes of remembrance, regeneration, and envisioning. While the term has specific meaning in American Indian and other Indigenous communities because of the genocide they have experienced, we use it to speak to our common humanity and the human need for uplift and spiritual renewal.

As such, the articles in this section highlight and reflect sites of survivance — places and ways in which our humanness seeks knowledge, education, and "something better" for our children and grandchildren. In this way, Sandy Marie Anglás Grande's article, "American Indian Geographies of Identity and Power: At the Crossroads of Indigena and Mestizaje," works toward the "development of an Indigenous theory of liberation." This theory examines issues of identity and sovereignty from a vantage point that embraces the tension between survival and resistance, as well as collaboration between Native and non-Native scholars. Echoing the emphasis on identity in "Education as Transformation: Becoming a Healer Among the !Kung and Fijians," Richard Katz discusses the importance of personal transformation and spirituality in the pursuit of learning through his work with Indigenous community healers in Fiji and the Kalahari Desert. In "Serving the Purpose of Education," Leona Okakok describes the steps one community took to name what they want to have happen in the education of their youth in an effort to renew themselves and remember what is most important. In "'Not Bread Alone': Clandestine Schooling and Resistance in the Warsaw Ghetto during the Holocaust," Susan Kardos shares an example of what this kind of effort was like in the Warsaw Ghetto. She captures the spirit of a people who were facing extermination in their fight for education — their experience reminds us of our human need to survive and to leave our children with knowledge of who they are and about their world. Munir Fasheh's "Community Education: To Reclaim and Transform What Has Been Made Invisible" rounds out this section by contrasting his own experience with "new math" to his mother's math, which he explains is connected to her immediate surroundings and to the "concrete needs of her community." Through this comparison, he comes to new understandings about the nature of power, knowledge, and place.

Bryan Brayboy's concluding essay, "'Yakkity Yak' and 'Talking Back': An Examination of Sites of Survivance in Indigenous Knowledge," reminds us that survivance is a stance, or a way of being in the world, which is explicitly connected to Indigenous peoples' rights to self-determine and live as sovereign nations. His discussion of the link between survival and resistance emphasizes that struggle and strength are an intimate part of our humanity. Brayboy helps us understand that the pursuit of education is an endeavor that eclipses schooling and lies at the heart of individual and community movements for equity, justice, and self-education.

As you read through this section, we ask you to consider the following question, which shaped the development of this book:

- What is survivance and how is it important for education?
- What do you see as the relationship between what makes us human and our desire for learning?
- What are the sites of survivance in your own experience or those of your students and community?

References

Vizenor, G. (1994). *Manifest manners: Post-Indian warriors of survivance.* Middleton, CT: Wesleyan University Press.

American Indian Geographies of Identity and Power: At the Crossroads of Indígena and Mestizaje

SANDY MARIE ANGLÁS GRANDE

> Until Indians resolve for themselves a comfortable modern identity that can be used to energize reservation institutions, radical changes will not be of much assistance. (Deloria & Lytle, 1984, p. 266)

> Our struggle at the moment is to continue to survive and work toward a time when we can replace the need for being preoccupied with survival with a more responsible and peaceful way of living within communities and with the ever-changing landscape that will ever be our only home. (Warrior, 1995, p. 126)

Broadly speaking, this article focuses on the intersection between dominant modes of critical pedagogy[1] and American Indian intellectualism.[2] At present, critical theories are often indiscriminately employed to explain the sociopolitical conditions of all marginalized peoples. As a result, many Indigenous scholars view the current liberatory project as simply the latest in a long line of political endeavors that fails to consider American Indians as a unique population.[3] Thus, while critical pedagogy may have propelled mainstream educational theory and practice along the path of social justice, I argue that it has muted and thus marginalized the distinctive concerns of American Indian intellectualism and education. As such, I argue further that the particular history of imperialism enacted upon Indigenous peoples requires a reevaluation of dominant views of democracy and social justice, and of the universal validity of such emancipatory projects — including critical pedagogy. It is not that critical pedagogy is irrelevant to Indigenous peoples, as they clearly experience oppression, but rather that the deep structures of the "pedagogy of oppression" fail to consider American Indians as a categorically different population, virtually incomparable to other minority groups. To assert this is not to advocate any kind of hierarchy of oppression but merely to call attention to the fundamental difference of what it means to be a sovereign and tribal people within the geopolitical confines of the United States.

Previous examinations of the potential for critical theory to inform Indigenous pedagogy (Grande, 1997, 2000) expose significant tensions in their deep theoretical structures. For instance, insofar as critical theorists retain "democracy" as the central struggle concept of liberation, they fail to recognize Indigenous peoples' historical battles to resist absorption into the "democratic imaginary"[4] and their contemporary struggles to retain tribal sovereignty. In fact, it could be argued that the forces of "democracy" have done more to imperil American Indian nations then they have to sustain them (e.g., the extension of democracy in the form of civil rights and citizenship has acted as a powerful if not lethal colonizing force when imposed on the intricate tribal, clan, and kinship systems of traditional Native communities).

Compounding the tensions between American Indian intellectualism and critical pedagogy is the fact that American Indian scholars have, by and large, resisted engagement with critical theory,[5] and concentrated instead on the production of historical monographs, ethnographic studies, tribally centered curricula, and site-based research. Such a focus stems from the fact that most American Indian scholars feel compelled to address the political urgencies of their own communities, against which engagement in abstract theory appears to be a luxury and privilege of the academic elite. While I recognize the need for practically based research, I argue that the ever-increasing global encroachment on American Indian lands, resources, cultures, and communities points to the equally urgent need to build political coalitions and formulate transcendent theories of liberation. Moreover, while individual tribal needs are in fact great, I believe that, unless the boundaries of coalition are expanded to include non-Indian communities, Indian nations will remain vulnerable to whims of the existing social order.

The combined effect of internal neglect and external resistance to critical pedagogy has pushed American Indian intellectualism to the margins of critical discourse. This reality raises a series of important questions that help form the basis of this discussion:

1. Insofar as critical theory remains disconnected from the work of American Indian scholars, how do its language and epistemic frames serve as homogenizing agents when interfaced with the conceptual and analytical categories persistent within American Indian educational history and intellectualism?
2. How has the resistance of American Indian intellectuals to critical theory contributed to the general lack of analyses on the impact of racism (and, for that matter, other "isms") within American Indian communities?
3. How have the marginalization of critical scholarship and the concomitant fascination with cultural/literary forms of American Indian writing contributed to the preoccupation with parochial questions of identity and au-

thenticity? And, how have these obsessions about identity concealed the social-political realities facing American Indian communities?

While the above questions provide the foundation for a broad discussion of the intersection of critical theory and American Indian intellectualism, I submit that the main source of tension is embedded in their competing notions of identity — one rooted in Western definitions of the civil society and the other in the traditional structures of tribal society.

In terms of identity, critical theorists aim to explode the concretized categories of race, class, gender, and sexuality and to claim the intersections — the borderlands — as the space to create a new culture — *una cultura mestíza* — in which the only normative standard is hybridity and all subjects are constructed as inherently transgressive.[6] Though American Indian intellectuals support the notion of hybridity, they remain skeptical of the new mestíza as a possible continuation of the colonialist project to fuse Indians into the national model of the democratic citizen. There is, in other words, an undercurrent to the postcolonial lexicon of *mestizaje* that seems to undermine the formation of "a comfortable modern American Indian identity" (Deloria & Lytle, 1984, p. 266). More specifically, I argue that the contemporary pressures of ethnic fraud, corporate commodification, and culture loss render the critical notion of "transgressive" identity highly problematic for Indigenous peoples. As such, the primary argument is that critical efforts to promote mestizaje as the basis of a new cultural democracy does not fully consider Indigenous struggles to sustain the cultural and political integrity of American Indian communities.

That being said, it is important to note that American Indian critical studies are perceived by both Indigenous and non-Indigenous scholars as a "dangerous discourse" equally threatening to the fields of critical pedagogy and American Indian intellectualism.[7] After all, American Indian critical studies would compel "Whitestream" advocates of critical theory to ask how their knowledge and practices may have contributed and remained blind to the continued exploitation of Indigenous peoples. Specifically, it would require a deeper recognition that these are not postcolonial times, that "globalization" is simply the new metaphor for imperialism, and that current constructions of democracy continue to presume the eventual absorption of Indigenous peoples. For American Indian intellectuals, the infusion of critical studies would require a movement away from the safety of unified, essentialized, and idealized constructions of American Indianness toward more complicated readings of American Indian formations of power and identity, particularly those that take into account the existence of internal oppression. Specifically, it would compel American Indian intellectuals to confront the taboo subjects of racism, sexism, and homophobia within American Indian communities.

Ultimately, however, this article is not a call for American Indian scholars to simply join the conversation of critical theorists. Rather, it is an initiation of an Indigenous conversation that can, in turn, engage in dialectical contestation with the dominant modes of critical theory. In this way, I hope that the development of an Indigenous theory of liberation can itself be a politically transformative practice, one that works to transgress tribal divisions and move toward the development of transcendent theory of American Indian sovereignty and self-determination. With this in mind, my discussion of the central tension between critical pedagogy and American Indian intellectualism unfolds in four parts. Part one examines formations of identity that have emerged from the dominant modes of critical discourse, paying special attention to the notion of transgression, and the construction of mestizaje as a counter-discourse of subjectivity. Part two examines American Indian formations of identity and the external forces that work to threaten these formations, namely ethnic fraud, cultural encroachment, corporate commodification, and culture loss. Part three examines the intersection between American Indian identity and mestizaje, as well as other models of hybridity generated by American Indian and other scholars of color. The article concludes with a call for the development of a new Red Pedagogy,[8] or one that is historically grounded in American Indian intellectualism, politically centered in issues of sovereignty and tribal self-determination, and inspired by the religious and spiritual[9] traditions of American Indian peoples.

Part I.
Identity, Subjectivity and Critical Theory:
Mestizaje and the New Cultural Democracy

"Critical pedagogy is the term used to describe what emerges when critical theory encounters education" (Kincheloe & Steinberg, 1997, p. 24). Rather than offer prescriptions, critical pedagogy draws from the structural critique of critical theory, extending an analysis of school as a site of reproduction, resistance, and social transformation. It examines the ways that power and domination inform the processes and procedures of schooling and works to expose the sorting and selecting functions of the institution. As it has evolved into its current form(s), critical pedagogy has emerged as both a rhetoric and a social movement. Critical educators continue to advocate an increasingly sophisticated critique of the social, economic, and political barriers to social justice, as well as to crusade for the transformation of schools to reflect the imperatives of democracy.

Critical scholars have, over time, provided a sustained critique of the forces of power and domination and their relation to the pedagogical (Kincheloe & Steinberg, 1997). As defined here, "the pedagogical" refers to the production of identity or the way one learns to see oneself in relation to the world. Identity is thus situated as one of the core struggle concepts of critical pedagogy, where the formation of self serves as the basis for analyses of race, class, gender, and sexuality and their relationship to the questions of democracy, justice, and community.

By positioning identity in the foreground of their theories, critical scholars have fueled as many theories of identity as they have varieties of critical pedagogy. While there are differences between and among these formulations, critical constructions of identity are distinct from both liberal and conservative theories of identity. Such theories are viewed as problematic by critical scholars because of their use of "essentialist" or reductionistic analyses of difference (Kinchloe & Steinberg, 1997; McCarthy & Crichlow, 1993; McLaren, 1997). "Essentialist" analysis refers to the treatment of racial and social groups as if they were stable and homogeneous entities, or as if members of each group possessed "some innate and invariant set of characteristics setting them apart from each other and from 'Whites'" (McCarthy & Crichlow, 1993, p. xviii). Critical scholars argue that essentialism not only undertheorizes race but can also result in a gross misreading of the nature of difference, opening the door for the proliferation of deeply cynical theories of racial superiority, such as Richard Herrnstein and Charles Murray's *The Bell Curve* (1994). While conservatives typically invoke essentialist theories, critical scholars acknowledge that some forms of left-essentialism operate in the contemporary landscape to similarly divisive ends.[10]

In response to the undertheorizing of race by both the Left and the Right, critical theorists advocate a theory of difference that is firmly rooted in the "power-sensitive discourses of power, democracy, social justice and historical memory" (McLaren & Giroux, 1997, p. 17). In so doing, they replace the comparatively static notion of identity as a relatively fixed entity that one embodies with the more fluid concept of subjectivity — an entity that one actively and continually constructs. Subjectivity works to underscore the contingency of identity and the understanding that "individuals consist of a decentered flux of subject positions highly dependent on discourse, social structure, repetition, memory, and affective investment" (McLaren & Giroux, 1997, p. 25). In other words, one's "identity" is historically situated and socially constructed, rather than predetermined by biological or other prima facie indicators.

In addition to calling attention to the relational aspects of identity, the critical notion of subjectivity advances a more complex analysis of cultural and racial identity. It shifts race from a passive product of biological endowment to an active "product of human work" (Said, 1993, p. xix). Critical scholars argue that the rupture of previously rigid racial categories reveals contested spaces or borderlands where cultures collide, creating the space to explore new notions of identity in the resulting contradictions, nuances, and discontinuities they introduce into the terrain of racial identity. Thus, where essentialist scholars examine race, class, gender, and sexuality as discrete categories, critical scholars focus on the spaces of intersection between and among these categories.

The emergence of subjectivity as a socially constructed entity spawned a whole new language about identity. Border cultures, border-crossers, mestíza (Anzaldúa, 1987; Delgado Bernal, 1998); *Xicanisma* (Castillo, 1995); postcolonial hybridities, cyborg identities (Harraway, 1991); and mestizaje (Darder, Torres, & Gutierrez, 1997; McLaren & Sleeter, 1995; Valle & Torres, 1995) are just some of the emergent concepts formulated to explain and bring language to the experience of multiplicity, relationality, and transgression as they relate to identity. Moreover, critical scholars contend that the development of transgressive subjectivity not only works to resist essentialist constructions of identity but also acts to counter the hegemonic notion of Whiteness as the normative standard for all subjects. Such efforts represent the hope and possibility of critical pedagogy as they seek to construct a critical democracy that includes multiple cultures, languages, and voices. Critical pedagogy thus serves both to challenge the existing sociocultural and economic relations of exploitation and to strengthen collective work toward peace and social justice, thereby creating a more equitable democratic order and, by definition, more equitable educational institutions.

From Mestizaje to Mestíza back to Mestizaje

The critical notion of mestizaje (Darder, Torres, & Gutierrez, 1997; McLaren & Sleeter, 1995; Kinchloe & Steinberg, 1997; Valle & Torres, 1995) is arguably among the most widely embraced models of multisubjectivity. Historically speaking, the counterdiscourse of mestizaje is rooted in the Latin American subjectivity of the *mestízo* — literally, a person of mixed ancestry, especially of American Indian, European, and African backgrounds (Delgado Bernal, 1998). Mestizaje is the Latin American term for cultural ambiguity, representative of "the continent's unfinished business of cultural hybridization" (Valle & Torres, 1995, p. 141). With regard to this history, Latin American scholars Victor Valle and Rodolfo Torres write:

> In Latin America the genetic and cultural dialogue between the descendants of Europe, Africa, Asia, and the hemisphere's indigenous populations has been expressed in discourses reflecting and responding to a host of concrete national circumstances. In some cases, mestizaje has risen to the level of a truly critical counter-discourse of revolutionary aspirations, while at other times it has been co-opted by the state. (p. 141)

Thus, it could be argued that the political project of mestizaje originated in Latin America, where the cluster of Spanish, Indian, and Afro-Caribbean peoples were ostensibly "fused" through the violence of genocide into the national model of the mestízo.

In the northern hemisphere, Chicana scholar Gloria Anzaldúa's seminal text *Borderlands, la Frontera: The New Mestíza* (1987) reinscribed the cultural terrain with the language and embodiment of mestíza consciousness. Since the book's publication, mestíza has come to embody a new feminist Chicana consciousness that "straddles cultures, races, languages, nations, sexualities, and spiritualities" and the experience of "living with ambivalence while balancing opposing powers" (Delgado Bernal, 1998, p. 561). Anzaldúa (1987) states, "The new mestíza copes by developing a tolerance for contradictions, a tolerance for ambiguity. She learns to be an Indian in Mexican culture [and] to be Mexican from an Anglo point of view" (p. 79). From this base, a variety of Chicana and other border feminisms have emerged, centered on the social histories and epistemologies of women of color.

More recently, the intellectual left, particularly critical scholars, has incorporated the spirit of the Chicana mestíza in its own search for a viable model of subjectivity. It embraces the emergent discourse of mestizaje and its emphasis on the way in which all cultures change in relation to one another as the postcolonial antidote to imperialist notions of racial purity (di Leonardo, 1991). This radically inclusive construct "willfully blurs political, racial, [and] cultural borders in order to better adapt to the world as it is actually constructed" (Valle & Torres, 1995, p. 149) and embodies the mestízo's demonstrated refusal to prefer one language, one national heritage, or one culture at the expense of others. Leading critical scholar Peter McLaren (1997) summarily articulates mestizaje as "the embodiment of a transcultural, transnational subject, a self-reflexive entity capable of rupturing the facile legitimization of 'authentic' national identities through [the] articulation of a subject who is conjunctural, who is a relational part of an ongoing negotiated connection to the larger society, and who is interpolated by multiple subject positionings" (p. 12). In other words, mestizaje crosses all imposed cultural, linguistic, and national borders, refusing all "natural" or transcendent claims that "by definition attempt to escape from any type of historical and normative grounding" (McLaren & Giroux, 1997, p. 117). Ultimately, the critical notion of mestizaje is itself multifunctional, for it signifies a strategic response to the decline of the imperial West, facilitates the decentering of Whiteness, and undermines the myth of the democratic nation-state based on borders and exclusions (Valle & Torres, 1995).

Insofar as the notion of mestizaje disrupts the discourse of jingoistic nationalism, it is indeed crucial to the project of liberation. As McLaren notes, "Educators would do well to consider Gloria Anzaldúa's (1987) project of creating mestizaje theories that create new categories of identity for those left out or pushed out of existing ones" (McLaren, 1997, p. 537). In so doing, however, "care must be taken not to equate hybridity with equality" (McLaren, 1997, p. 46).[11] As Coco Fusco notes, "The postcolonial celebration of hybridity has (too often) been interpreted as the sign that no further concern about the politics of representation and cultural exchange is needed. With ease, we lapse back into the integrationist rhetoric of the 1960's" (Fusco, 1995, p. 46). These words caution us not to lose sight — in the wake of transgressing borders and building postnational coalitions — of the unique challenges presented to particular groups in their distinct struggles for social justice. In taking this admonition seriously, the following discussion moves into an examination of American Indian tribal identity and some of the current pressures facing Indian communities that, I argue, render the notion of mestizaje somewhat problematic. The question remains whether the construction of a transgressive subjectivity — mestizaje — can be reconciled with the pressures of identity appropriation, cultural commodification, culture loss, and, perhaps more importantly, with Indigenous imperatives of self-determination and sovereignty.

Part II.
The Formation of Indígena:
American Indian Geographies of Power and Identity

Whitestream America has never really understood what it means to be Indian and even less about what it means to be tribal. Such ignorance has deep historical roots and wide political implications of not understanding what it means to be tribal, since the U.S. government determined long ago that to be "tribal" runs deeply counter to the notion of democracy and the proliferation of (individual) civil rights. Throughout the centuries, uncompromising belief in this tenet of democratic order provided the ideological foundation for numerous expurgatory campaigns against Indigenous peoples. The Civilization Act of 1819, the Indian Removal Act of 1830, the Dawes Allotment Act of 1886, the Indian Citizenship Act of 1924, the Indian Reorganization Act of 1934, and the Indian Civil Rights Act of 1968 are just a few of the legal mechanisms imposed to "further democracy" and concomitantly erode traditional tribal structures.

Although five centuries of continuous contact may have extinguished the traditional societies of the precontact era, modern American Indian communities still resemble traditional societies enough that, "given a choice between Indian society and non-Indian society, most Indians feel comfortable with their own institutions, lands and traditions" (Deloria & Lytle, 1983, p. xii). Despite such significant differences, tribal America remains curiously difficult to articulate. Vine Deloria Jr., one of the preeminent American Indian scholars, has written over eighteen books and one hundred articles defining the political, spiritual, cultural, and intellectual dimensions of American Indian life. His expansive body of work serves as testimony to the difficulty and complexity of defining tribal life and suggests the impossibility of encompassing the multiple dimensions of Indianness in a single article. To do so would not only minimize Deloria's and other scholars' work, but also presume that centuries of ancestral knowledge could be transcribed into a single literary form. Similarly, to tease out, list, name, and assign primacy to a particular subset of defining characteristics of Indianness would not only serve to objectify and oversimplify the diversity of Native cultures, but would also force what is fundamentally traditional, spatial, and interconnected into the modern, temporal, and epistemic frames of Western knowledge. Accordingly, the following is merely a sample of existing legal, prima facie indicators of what it means to be American Indian in U.S. society, rather than some mythic view of a unified Indigenous culture or an objectified view of Indian "identity":

Sovereignty vs. Democracy: American Indians have been engaged in a centuries-long struggle to have what is legally theirs recognized (i.e., land, sovereignty, treaty rights). As such, Indigenous peoples have not, like other marginalized groups, been fighting for inclusion in the democratic imaginary but, rather, for the right to remain distinct, sovereign, and tribal peoples.

Treaty Rights: These rights articulate the unique status of Indian tribes as "domestic dependent nations." A dizzying array of tribal, federal, and state laws, policies, and treaties creates a political maze that keeps the legal status of most tribes in a constant state of flux. Treaties are negotiated and renegotiated in a process that typically reduces tribal rights and erodes traditional structures (Deloria & Lytle, 1984; Fixico, 1998).

Dual Citizenship: The Indian Citizenship Act of 1924 extends the rights of full citizenship to American Indians born within the territorial United States, insofar as such status does not infringe upon the rights to tribal and other property. It is a dual citizenship wherein American Indians do not lose civil rights because of their status as tribal members and individual tribal members are not denied tribal rights because of their American citizenship (Deloria & Lytle, 1984).[12]

Federal Recognition: Federal law mandates that American Indians prove that they have continued to exist over time as stable, prima facie entities to retain federal recognition as tribes. Acknowledgment of tribal existence by the Department of the Interior is critical, as it is a prerequisite to the protection, services, and benefits of the federal government available to Indian tribes by virtue of their status as tribes. Therefore, a tribe's existence is contingent upon its ability to prove its existence over time, to provide evidence of shared cultural patterns, and to prove "persistence of a named, collective Indian identity" (USD, Bureau of Indian Affairs, n.d., 83.7).

Economic Dependency: American Indians continue to exist as nations within a nation wherein the relationship between the U.S. government and Indian tribes is not the fictive "government to government" relationship described in U.S. documents, but, rather, one that positions tribes as fundamentally dependent.[13]

Reservations: Roughly two-thirds of American Indians continue either to live on or to remain significantly tied to their reservations and, as such, remain predominantly "tribally oriented" as opposed to generically Indian (Joe & Miller, 1997).

The aggregate of the above indicators positions American Indians in a wholly unique and paradoxical relationship to the United States. These indicators further illuminate the inherent contradictions of modern American Indian existence and point to the gross insufficiency of models that treat American Indians as simply another ethnic minority group. Moreover, the paradox of having to prove "authenticity" to gain legitimacy as a "recognized" tribe and of simultaneously having to negotiate a postmodern world in which all claims to authenticity and legitimacy are dismissed as essentialist (if not racist) conscripts American Indians to a gravely dangerous and precarious space. This reality of Indian existence not only deeply problematizes various postmodern theories' insistence that we move beyond concretized categories, but also reveals their colonizing impulse.[14]

In addition to the (legal) prima facie indicators of American Indianness, there are external forces that further impede and complicate the landscape of American Indian identity. More specifically, the forces of ethnic fraud, cultural encroachment, and corporate commodification work in tandem to call into question the ostensibly liberatory effects of transgression. Such forces pressure Indian communities to define American Indian subjectivity in stable, prima facie measures. In other words, the forces of colonialism and imperialism deeply problematize the postmodern notion of transgression in terms of its abandonment of totality and its emphasis on pluralism and discontinuity. As Steven Best (1989) points out, where critical scholars rightly deconstruct essentialist and repressive wholes, they fail to see how crippling the valorization of difference, fragmentation, and agnostics can be. For the American Indian community, the "crippling" effects have been significant. In particular, the struggle to define "comfortable modern American Indian identities" becomes deeply complicated, enmeshed in the impossible paradox of having to respond to the growing pluralism within their own communities and thus the need to define more fluid constructions of Indianness, while also recognizing that the pressures of identity appropriation, cultural encroachment, and corporate commodification require more restrictive constructions of Indianness. In order to better understand the significance of this paradox, the forces of ethnic fraud, cultural encroachment, and corporate commodification are discussed in greater detail.

Identity Appropriation

In post–*Dances with Wolves* America, it has become increasingly popular to be American Indian. Joane Nagel, a sociologist and expert in the politics of ethnicity, attests that between 1960 and 1990 the number of Americans reporting "American Indian" as their racial category in the U.S. Census more than tripled. Researchers attribute this growth to the practice of "ethnic switching," where individuals previously identifying themselves as "non-Indian," now claim "Indian" as their racial affiliation. She identifies three factors promoting ethnic switching: changes in federal Indian policy; changes in American ethnic politics; and American Indian political activism (Nagel, 1995). Those seminal changes in federal policy referred to by Nagel are the Indian relocation policies of the 1960s and 1970s that led to the creation of urban Indian populations, and the various land-claims settlement of the 1980s, which also led to increases in certain tribal populations.[15] The changes in ethnic politics emanate from the civil rights and Red Power movements that made American Indian identification "a more attractive ethnic option" (Nagel, 1995, p. 956). According to Nagel, these factors helped to raise American Indian ethnic consciousness and encouraged individuals to claim or reclaim their Native American ancestry.

While she makes strong arguments for the three factors she identifies, Nagel ignores the possibility that part of the resurgence may also be due to increasing incidents of identity appropriation, or *ethnic fraud*. Ethnic fraud is the term used to describe the phenomenon of Whitestream individuals who, in spite of growing up far removed from any discernible American Indian community, claim an Indian identity based on the discovery of residuals of Indian blood in their distant ancestries. There is nothing categorically wrong with "discovering" one's ancestral background, but when such claims are opportunistically used to cash in on scholarships, set-aside programs, and other affirmative economic incentives, it becomes highly problematic. Furthermore, there is evidence that such "new Indians" discard their new-found identities as soon as they no longer serve them. For example, studies conducted at UCLA in 1988–1989 and 1993 reveal that of the enrolled 179 American Indian students, 125 did not or could not provide adequate documentation of their tribal affiliation, and that, on average, less than 15 percent of American Indian students were enrolled in federally recognized tribes (Machamer, 1997). More importantly, a significant number of students chose to identify as American Indian only to relinquish this identification by the time of graduation, suggesting that, economic incentives aside, "new Indians" chose to reclaim their Whiteness (Machamer, 1997). Such practices indicate that it is not only popular but profitable to be "Indian" in postmodern America.

In addition to outright identity fraud, American Indian communities also endure the more superficial but equally problematic phenomena of ethnic "vogueing." The seasonal influx of tour buses, church groups, and do-gooders discharges a veritable wave of Whiteness into reservation communities. Armed with their own constructions of Indianness, Whitestream individuals appropriate and try on various elements of Native culture and, in the name of religion, multiculturalism, environmentalism, and radicalism, voyeuristically tour reservation communities like cultural predators loose in Indian theme parks. During these visits, they acquire the usual assemblage of trinkets and souvenirs, and afterwards exit dysconscious[16] of the fact that their adventures have conscripted Native culture as fashion, Indian as exotic, and the sacred as entertainment. While there is a measure of complicity on the part of some American Indians who sell their culture, the overlay of colonialism situates these practices more as products of lost culture, lost economic vitality, and a lost sense of being than as crass indicators of Indian capitalism.

All told, the practice of identity appropriation is believed to have become so widespread that some American Indian organizations have felt compelled to devise statements and enact policies against its proliferation.[17] Even the federal government has recognized the occurrence and ill effects of ethnic fraud. The Indian Arts and Crafts Act, for example, stipulates that all products must be marketed truthfully regarding the Indian heritage and tribal affiliation of the artist or craftsperson. Though this act does more to protect consumers against the purchase of "fraudulent" merchandise, it also protects American Indian artisans from unfair competition by "fraudulent Indian" profiteers.

While such tactics appear to be reasonable in theory, in practice they require the employment of equally problematic essentialist ideology. In other words, in the same moment that particular groups work to determine who is and who is not Indian, they also define fixed parameters of authenticity, reducing the question of Indianness to quantifiable variables and objectified models of culture. It is also difficult to reconcile such contemporary measures with the historical memory that quantifying Indianness is a remnant of the Dawes Allotment Act (1887),[18] in which the U.S. government first introduced blood quantum policies and tribal rolls, and the knowledge that, regardless of how they are defined, measures of authenticity will conjure the same political divisiveness they always have. Finally, insofar as compliance with ethnic fraud policies requires the formation of an Indian Identity Police,[19] enforcement also becomes a dubious enterprise, inviting increased scrutiny from outside agencies.

Cultural Encroachment

The fact that nearly two-thirds of American Indians remain closely tied to their reservations not only points to the continued significance of land in the formation of American Indian identity, but also suggests that a large portion of the Indian population remains fairly segregated from the rest of the nation. Clearly, "Indian Country" persists as both a metaphorical and literal place, undoubtedly shaping the subjectivities of all those who call it home. In other words, living in a physically circumscribed space where literal borders distinguish "us" from "them" must, by definition, shape American Indian consciousness and emergent views of identity and difference. More specifically, the relationship between American Indian communities and the predominantly White border towns not only shapes the ways Indians perceive and construct Whites, but also significantly influences their own views of American Indian identity.

Thus, although reservations exist as a vestige of forced removal, colonialist domination, and Whitestream greed, they have also come to serve as protective barriers and defensive perimeters between cultural integrity and wholesale assimilation. They also serve to distinguish American Indians as the only peoples with federally recognized land claims, demarcating the borders of the only domestic sovereign nations. Though the power of this domestic-dependent-nation status is continually challenged in federal courts, Indians have retained a significant portion of their plenary powers, such as the right to establish tribal courts, tribal governments, and tribal police forces. Ultimately, however, the notion of self-government remains a bit of a farce, since most tribes remain entrenched in untenable relationships with the U.S. government and most reservation economies can only maintain stability with the infusion of outside capital (Deloria & Lytle, 1984).

The dependency on outside capital generates a subordinating effect, leaving American Indians at the virtual mercy of venture capitalists and Whitestream do-gooders. As a result, most reservation communities are overrun by emissaries of White justice, private entrepreneurs, and New Age liberals seeking to forge lucrative careers from predatory practices. Bivouacked in internal and external compounds, enterprising members of the Whitestream wield power and broker services by day, and by night retreat back into the comforts of their bourgeois border towns. As a result, most of the businessmen, teachers, principals, doctors, and health-care providers in reservation communities are White, and most of the laborers, minimum-wagers, underemployed, and unemployed are American Indian.

In spite of the pressures of cultural encroachment, reservation communities continue to work toward becoming sites of political contestation and empowerment. They are learning to survive the dangers of imperialistic forces by employing both proactive strategies that emphasize education, empowerment, and self-determination, and defensive tactics that protect against unfettered economic and political encroachment. Thus, whatever else reservation borders may or may not signify, they serve as potent geographic filters of all that is non-Indian — literal dividing lines between the real and metaphoric spaces differentiating Indian Country from the rest of Whitestream America.

Corporate Commodification

The forces of both ethnic fraud and cultural encroachment operate to create a climate ripe for the corporate commodification of American Indianness. While this commodification takes many forms, it is perhaps most visible in the marketing of Indian narratives, particularly publishing, in which literary/cultural forms of Indian intellectualism have been historically favored over critical forms.

For instance, Indigenous scholar Elizabeth Cook-Lynn (1998) questions why the same editors and agents who solicit her "life story" also routinely reject her scholarly work. She writes, "While I may have a reasonable understanding why a state-run university press would not want to publish research that has little good to say about America's relationship to tribes, . . . I am at a loss to explain why anyone would be more interested in my life story (which for one thing is quite unremarkable)" (p. 121). The explanation, of course, is that the marketable narrative is that which subscribes to the Whitestream notion of Indian as romantic figure, and not Indian as scholar and social critic. Such a predisposition works to favor not only cultural/literary forms of American Indian intellectualism over critical forms, but also the work of "fraudulent" Indians over that of "legitimate" American Indian scholars. Cook-Lynn (1998) argues that, just as the rights to our land remain in the hands of the Whitestream government, the rights to our stories remain in non-Indian enclaves. Deloria (1998) similarly contends that what passes in the academic world as legitimate scholarship on American Indians is often the product of average scholars (often White) advocating a predetermined anti-Indian agenda[20] and "fraudulent" Indians. That such work has been allowed to corner the market raises the question of who controls access to the intellectual property of American Indian peoples. Deloria himself asks, "Who is it that has made such people as Adolph Hungry Wolf, Jamake Highwater, Joseph Epes Brown, Su Bear, Rolling Thunder, Wallace Black Elk, John Redtail Freesoul, Lynn Andrews, and Dhyani Ywahoo the spokespeople of American Indians?" (p. 79). He responds by naming Whitestream America as both patron and peddler of the Hollywood Indian. He writes, "They [the fraudulent Indians] represent the intense desire of Whites to create in their own minds an Indian they want to believe in" (p. 79).

As such, the market is flooded with tragic stories of lost cultures, intimate narratives of "frontier life," and quasi-historic accounts of the Native Americans' plight. Such stories are told and retold as part of America's dark and distant past, a bygone era of misguided faith where cultural genocide is depicted as an egregious but perhaps unavoidable consequence of the country's manifest destiny toward democracy. While I would never argue that stories depicting the truth of Native peoples' tragic experiences (e.g., Indian boarding schools, the Trail of Tears) do not deserve a central place in the telling of American history, such accounts become problematic in the wider context of Whitestream consumption of Indian history.

Why are these stories the ones most often presented as the prime-time programs in the commodified literary network of Indian history? What is gained by focusing on these particular aspects of White domination and Indian subjugation? I argue that such stories serve several purposes, none of which contributes to the emancipatory project of American Indians. First, by propagating the romantic image of American Indians and concomitantly marginalizing the work of Indigenous intellectuals and social critics, Whitestream publishers maintain control over the epistemic frames that define Indians, and thus over the fund of available knowledge on American Indians. Second, such control is underwritten by the understanding that American Indian intellectualism exists as a threat to the myth of the ever-evolving democratization of Indian-White relations, and to the notion that cultural genocide is a remnant of America's dark and distant past. Third, the often oversimplified accounts of Indian history, framed in good-v.-bad-guy terms, allow the consumer to fault rogue groups of dogmatic missionaries and wayward military officers for the slow but steady erosion of Indigenous life, thereby distancing themselves and mainstream government from the ongoing project of cultural genocide. Finally, the focus on Indian history allows the Whitestream to avoid issues facing American Indians in the twenty-first century. As a result, Indians as a modern people remain invisible, allowing a wide array of distorted myths to flourish as contemporary reality — for example, that all the "real" Indians are extinct, that the surviving Indians are all alcoholic-drug addicts who have forsaken traditional ways to become budding capitalists, gaming entrepreneurs, and casino owners — and find their way into public discourse. At the same time these images are circulated, the intensive, ongoing court battles over land, natural resources, and federal recognition are ignored, fueling the great lie of twenty-first century democracy — that America's "Indian problem" has long been solved.

Discussion

The forces of identity appropriation, cultural encroachment, and corporate commodification pressure American Indian communities to employ essentialist tactics and construct relatively fixed notions of identity, and to render the concepts of fluidity and transgression highly problematic. It is evident from the examples above that the notion of fluid boundaries has never worked to the advantage of Indigenous peoples: federal agencies have invoked the language of fluid or unstable identities as the rationale for dismantling the structures of tribal life and creating greater dependency on the U.S. government; Whitestream America has seized its message to declare open season on Indians, thereby appropriating Native lands, culture, spiritual practices, history, and literature; and Whitestream academics have now employed the language of postmodern fluidity to unwittingly transmute centuries of war between Indigenous peoples and their respective nation-states into a "genetic and cultural dialogue" (Valle & Torres, 1995, p. 141). Thus, in spite of its aspirations to social justice, the notion of a new cultural democracy based on the ideal of mestizaje represents a rather ominous threat to American Indian communities.

In addition, the undercurrent of fluidity and sense of displacedness that permeates, if not defines, mestizaje runs contrary to American Indian sensibilities of connection to place, land, and the Earth itself. Consider, for example, the following statement on the nature of critical subjectivity by Peter McLaren:

> The struggle for critical subjectivity is the struggle to occupy a space of hope — a liminal space, an intimation of the anti-structure, of what lives in the in-between zone of undecidedability — in which one can work toward a praxis of redemption. . . . A sense of atopy has always been with me, a resplendent place-

lessness, a feeling of living in germinal formlessness. . . . I cannot find words to express what this border identity means to me. All I have are what Georgres Bastille (1988) calls mots glissants (slippery words). (1997, pp. 13–14)

McLaren speaks passionately and directly about the crisis of modern society and the need for a "praxis of redemption." As he perceives it, the very possibility of redemption is situated in our willingness not only to accept but to flourish in the "liminal" spaces, border identities, and postcolonial hybridities that are inherent in postmodern life and subjectivity. In fact, McLaren perceives the fostering of a "resplendent placelessness" itself as the gateway to a more just, democratic society.

While American Indian intellectuals also seek to embrace the notion of transcendent subjectivities, they seek a notion of transcendence that remains rooted in historical place and the sacred connection to land. Consider, for example, the following commentary by Deloria (1992) on the centrality of place and land in the construction of American Indian subjectivity:

> Recognizing the sacredness of lands on which previous generations have lived and died is the foundation of all other sentiment. Instead of denying this dimension of our emotional lives, we should be setting aside additional places that have transcendent meaning. Sacred sites that higher spiritual powers have chosen for manifestation enable us to focus our concerns on the specific form of our lives. . . . Sacred places are the foundation of all other beliefs and practices because they represent the presence of the sacred in our lives. They properly inform us that we are not larger than nature and that we have responsibilities to the rest of the natural world that transcend our own personal desires and wishes. This lesson must be learned by each generation. (pp. 278, 281)

Gross misunderstanding of this connection between American Indian subjectivity and land, and, more importantly, between sovereignty and land has been the source of numerous injustices in Indian country. For instance, I believe there was little understanding on the part of government officials that passage of the Indian Religious Freedom Act (1978) would open a Pandora's box of discord over land, setting up an intractable conflict between property rights and religious freedom. American Indians, on the other hand, viewed the act as an invitation to return to their sacred sites, several of which were on government lands and were being damaged by commercial use. As a result, a flurry of lawsuits alleging mismanagement and destruction of sacred sites was filed by numerous tribes. Similarly, corporations, tourists, and even rock climbers filed suits accusing land managers of unlawfully restricting access to public places by implementing policies that violate the constitutional separation between church and state. All of this is to point out that the critical project of mestizaje continues to operate on the same assumption made by the U.S. government in this instance, that in a democratic society, human subjectivity — and liberation for that matter — is conceived of as inherently rights-based as opposed to land-based.

To be fair, I believe that both American Indian intellectuals and critical theorists share a similar vision — a time, place, and space free of the compulsions of Whitestream, global capitalism and the racism, sexism, classism, and xenophobia it engenders. But where critical scholars ground their vision in Western conceptions of democracy and justice that presume a "liberated" self, American Indian intellectuals ground their vision in conceptions of sovereignty that presume a sacred connection to place and land. Thus, to a large degree, the seemingly liberatory constructs of fluidity, mobility, and transgression are perceived not only as the language of critical subjectivity, but also as part of the fundamental lexicon of Western imperialism. Deloria (1999) writes:

> Although the loss of land must be seen as a political and economic disaster of the first magnitude, the real exile of the tribes occurred with the destruction of ceremonial life (associated with the loss of land) and the failure or inability of white society to offer a sensible and cohesive alternative to the traditions which Indians remembered. People became disoriented with respect to the world in which they lived. They could not practice their old ways, and the new ways which they were expected to learn were in a constant state of change because they were not a cohesive view of the world but simply adjustments which whites were making to the technology they had invented. (p. 247).

In summary, insofar as American Indian identities continue to be defined and shaped in interdependence with place, the transgressive mestizaje functions as a potentially homogenizing force that presumes the continued exile of tribal peoples and their enduring absorption into the American "democratic" Whitestream. The notion of mestizaje as absorption is particularly problematic for the Indigenous peoples of Central and South America, where the myth of the mestizaje (belief that the continent's original cultures and inhabitants no longer exist) has been used for centuries to force the integration of Indigenous communities into the national mestízo model (Van Cott, 1994). According to Rodolfo Stavenhagen (1992), the myth of mestizaje has provided the ideological pretext for numerous South American governmental laws and policies expressly designed to strengthen the nation-state through incorporation of all "non-national" (read "Indigenous") elements into the mainstream. Thus, what Valle and Torres (1995) previously describe as "the continent's unfinished business of cultural hybridization" (p. 141), Indigenous peoples view as the continents' long and bloody battle to absorb their existence into the master narrative of the mestízo.

While critical scholars do construct a very different kind of democratic solidarity that disrupts the sociopolitical and economic hegemony of the dominant culture around a transformed notion of mestizaje (one committed to the destabilization of the isolationist narratives of nationalism and cultural chauvinism), I argue that any liberatory project that does not begin with a clear understanding of the difference of American Indianness will, in the end, work to undermine tribal life. Moreover, there is a potential danger that the ostensibly "new" cultural democracy based upon the radical mestizaje will continue to mute tribal differences and erase distinctive Indian identities. Therefore, as the physical and metaphysical borders of the postmodern world become increasingly fluid, the desire of American Indian communities to protect geographic borders and employ "essentialist" tactics also increases. Though such tactics may be viewed by critical scholars as highly problematic, they are viewed by American Indian intellectuals as a last line of defense against the steady erosion of tribal culture, political sovereignty, Native resources, and Native lands.

The tensions described above indicate the dire need for an Indigenous, revolutionary theory that maintains the distinctiveness of American Indians as tribal peoples of sovereign nations (border patrolling) and also encourages the building of coalitions and political solidarity (border crossing). In contrast to critical scholars McLaren and Kris Gutierrez (1997), who admonish educators to develop a concept of unity and difference as political mobilization rather than cultural authenticity, I urge American Indian intellectuals to develop a language that operates at the crossroads of unity and difference and defines this space in terms of political mobilization and cultural authenticity, thus expressing both the interdependence and distinctiveness of tribal peoples.

Part III.
Mestizaje Revisited: Critical Indígena and a New Red Pedagogy

To their credit, Whitestream critical scholars recognize the potential for their own subjectivities and locations of privilege to infiltrate the critical discourse, limiting it in ways they cannot see or anticipate. McLaren (1997) writes, "An individual cannot say he or she has achieved critical pedagogy if he or she stops struggling to attain it. Only sincere discontent and dissatisfaction with the limited effort we exercise in the name of social justice can assure us that we really have the faith in a dialogical commitment to others and otherness" (p. 13). It is perhaps this commitment to self-reflexivity and an ever-evolving pedagogy that represents critical pedagogy's greatest strength. Indeed, critical scholars from other marginalized groups such as Gloria Anzaldúa, Hazel Carby, Antonia Darder, Dolores Delgado Bernal, Kris Gutierrez, bell hooks, Rudy Mattai, Cameron McCarthy, Enrique Murillo, Frances V. Rains, and Sofia Villenas have seized upon its openness, transmuting critical theories to fit their own constructions of culturally relevant praxis. Currently, American Indian scholars are also investigating ways to import the message of critical pedagogy without wholesale adoption of its means. While addressing the impact of racism, sexism, and globalization on American Indian communities, some American Indian intellectuals share underlying principles of mestizaje like reflexivity, hybridity, and multiplicity. However, this notion of a transgressive mestizaje may ultimately undermine American Indian subjectivity. Recognizing the common ground of struggle is an important first step in working to define the ways that critical pedagogy can inform Indigenous praxis.

The following discussion excerpts work by American Indian and other scholars of color who have taken the next step: to define locally and culturally relevant praxis based on a broader critical foundation. I contend that such work represents the possibility and future of both American Indian intellectualism and critical pedagogy.

Voices from the Margin

As might be expected, Latino, Latina, African American, and feminist riffs on Whitestream critical pedagogy speak more directly to the concerns of American Indian intellectuals. In particular, other scholars of color have recognized that the experience of oppression often requires the assertion of hyperauthenticity, and thus have worked to refine critical theorists' hard line against essentialism. For instance, though Chicano scholar Enrique Murillo (1997) rejects the notion of essentialism as a means of recalibrating the balance of power, he employs the term *strategic essentialism* to describe the contradictory experience of many scholars of color caught between the different legitimizing forces of the academy and their own communities. There are times, for example, when scholars of color feel compelled to perform a heightened professional or scholarly identity when seeking legitimacy in the academy, and other times when they feel compelled to perform a hyperauthentic or racialized self to gain or retain legitimacy within their own communities. Murillo's notion of "strategic essentialism" is useful in describing the experience of American Indian intellectuals working to balance the fluidity of the postmodern world with the more stable obligations of their tribal communities. In more concrete terms, this means that, as American Indian scholars work to construct and advocate more complex understandings of American Indian identity, such efforts remain haunted by the knowledge that any failure to continually define and authenticate Indianness in stable and quantifiable terms may result in the loss of everything from school funding to tribal recognition. Within this context, strategic essentialism refers not only to choosing multiple subjectivities where power is located in the self, but also to negotiating between chosen and imposed identities where power continues to be located in the oppressor.

Similar to Murillo's variation on the notion of strategic essentialism, Delgado Bernal (1998) defines a culturally relevant theory of knowledge that brings discussions of power and identity into the realm of epistemology. She argues for a model of identity-based epistemology and develops the notion of "cultural intuition" to validate the centrality of cultural knowledge in the processes of research and in the development of a culture's intellectual history. Specifically, Delgado Bernal employs the notion of cultural intuition to legitimate her unique viewpoint as a Chicana researcher conducting research within the Chicana community.[21] Though similar to Anselm Strauss and Juliet Corbin's concept of "theoretical sensitivity" (1990), Delgado Bernal's paradigm extends the realm of cultural intuition to include collective experience and community memory and to stress the importance of participants' inclusion in the research process, particularly in data analysis. She writes, "While I do not argue for an essentialist notion of who is capable of conducting research with various populations based on personal experiences, I do believe that many Chicana scholars achieve a sense of cultural intuition that is different from other scholars" (p. 567). This insightful articulation of the value and power of cultural intuition brings voice and, more importantly, language to the struggles of Chicano and other scholars of color seeking validation, power, and equity in the domain of academic research. Moreover, the notion of cultural intuition buttresses arguments already made by American Indian scholars on behalf of their own communities; specifically, for the right to speak in their own voices, define their own realities, and develop their own intellectual histories.

Voices from Indian Country

While it is important and beneficial to observe the insights of other critical pedagogies, it is crucial to look to one's own intellectual history and sources of cultural intuition in the development of Indigenous theories and praxis. In this effort, the challenge to American Indian scholars is not merely to "resurrect" these histories and sources of cultural intuition, but to construct meaningful bridges and points of intersection between American Indian intellectualism and Whitestream critical pedagogies.

To this end, while American Indian scholars have, by and large, resisted direct engagement with critical theory, many have begun to theorize their own constructions of Indigenous knowledge and American Indian identity.[22] As a collective effort, such work provides increasingly complex views of American Indian history; of the promise and failures of education; of the struggles for language, agency, and sovereignty; and of the need for political and sociocultural coalitions. Their writings strive to achieve interplay between the past, present, and future, and ride the faultline between continuity, resistance, and possibility.

What follows is a sampling of such works, chosen because of their particular relevance to the topic of American Indian identity and identity formation. The selected scholars differ in their methods and approaches, but they share a thematic undercurrent that includes the interplay of coalition, agency, tradition, and identity; the transformation of curriculum and pedagogy; the retention and reinvigoration of Indigenous languages; the intersection of religion and spirituality; and the quest for sovereignty. While each domain merits extensive discussion, such an effort goes beyond the limits of this work. However, insofar as American Indian "identity" is formulated as an aggregate of the above struggles, they will be discussed interdependently with the understanding that, especially for American Indians, religion/spirituality and sovereignty are inextricably woven into the struggles for identity, education, and language, and vice versa.

The Interplay of Coalition, Agency, and Identity

In the first draft of the final report of the Indian Nations at Risk Task Force, Indigenous scholar and activist Michael Charleston (1994) writes of the importance of coalition and its central role in the development of effective American Indian schools and Indian-centered curricula. Rather than the abstract language of critical pedagogy, however, Charleston invokes the Lakota tradition of the Ghost Dance as a metaphor of the need for healing through community, ceremony, sacrifice, and tradition.[23] He writes:

> The new Ghost Dance calls Native and non-Native peoples to join together and take action. It calls us to be responsible for the future of the people of our tribes. It calls us to protect, revive and restore our cultures, our Native languages, our religions and values. It calls us to heal our people, our families, our tribes, and our societies. It calls for harmony and respect among all relations of creation. It offers a future of co-existence of tribal societies with other American societies . . . indeed domination, oppression, and bigotry are exactly what we are overcoming in the new Ghost Dance as we seek to establish harmony and co-existence of tribes with other societies in the modern world. (p. 28)

This spirit of coalition reflects the growing desire among American Indians to work together and form alliances with Native and non-Native forces in a mutual quest for American Indian sovereignty and self-determination. Though Charleston's rendition of coalition reflects the spirit of mestizaje — that is, the blurring of political, racial, and cultural borders in the service of social justice — he carefully relegates such coalition to the realm of sociopolitical action. In other words, the new Ghost Dance calls to Indian and non-Indian peoples to take collective action against U.S. policies that continue the project of colonization and cultural genocide. It is thus not a call for the embodiment, in critical-theoretical terms, of a transcultural, transnational subject that calls into question the very notion of authentic identities (McLaren, 1997), but rather a metaphor for collective political action.

This is not to say that Charleston or other American Indian scholars do not support the notion that identity is constructed through multiple, intersecting, and contradictory elements. Rather, they remain wary of constructionist understandings of identity that, in the process of providing a corrective to static notions of culture, ignore the real possibility of culture loss — that is, the real existing threat of cultural genocide of Indigenous peoples. Hale (2000) is worth quoting at length:

> When (cultural) transformation is conflated with loss . . . the collective trauma is obscured and the brute historical fact of ethnocide is softened. The culprits in this erasure are the Indians' . . . enemies, but even more centrally . . . elites who

embraced classic nineteenth century liberalism cast in the idiom of mestizáje. A homogeneous and individualized notion of citizenship could not be compatible with the rights of Indian communities whose collective histories and identities stood opposed to the dominant mestizo culture. Just beneath the alluring promises to Indians who would accept these individual rights of citizenship was incomprehension, invisibility, and punishing racism for those who would not. (p. 269)

Again, though the contemporary critical project of mestizaje is in many ways antithetical to the Latin American one, both projects ignore the "brute historical fact of ethnocide" and the invisibility of Indians within the broader democratic project. In contradistinction to the critical notion of mestizaje, American Indian scholars seek understandings of identity that not only reflect the multiple and contradictory aspects of contemporary experience, but also maintain a sense of American Indians as historically placed, sovereign peoples. For them, sovereignty is not a political ideology but a way of life (Warrior, 1995). As Charleston (1994) writes, "Our tribes are at a very critical point in our history again. We can stand by and wait for our children and grandchildren to be assimilated into mainstream American society as proud ethnic descendants of extinct tribal peoples. . . . Or, we can protect our tribes, as our ancestors did, and ensure a future for our children and grandchildren as tribal people" (p. 28).

Though it may seem from the above that American Indian intellectuals advocate exclusionary rather than coalitionary tactics, impulses toward isolationism need to be understood in the context of unrelenting threats of cultural appropriation and culture loss. Within this context, it is actually remarkable that American Indian tribal communities remain open and working to define the balance between cultural tradition, cultural shift, and cultural transformation.

Identity Formation and American Indian Tradition(s)

Indigenous scholar Devon Mihesuah (1998) examines the notion of "tradition" in the formation of American Indian identity. Acknowledging that, while traditions are important to maintain, they have always been fluid, she writes:

> An Indian who speaks her tribal language and participates in tribal religious ceremonies is often considered traditional, but that term is applicable only within the context of this decade, because chances are she wears jeans, drives a car and watches television — very "untraditional" things to do. Plains Indians who rode horses in the 1860's are considered traditional today, but they were not the same as their traditional ancestors of the early 1500's who had never seen a horse. (p. 50)

While contemporary life requires most Indians to negotiate or "transgress" between a multitude of subject positions (i.e., one who is Navajo may also be Catholic, gay, and live in an off-reservation urban center), such movement remains historically embedded and geographically placed. Moreover, the various and competing subjectivities remain tied through memory, ceremony, ritual, and obligation to a traditional identity type that operates not as a measure of authenticity, but rather of cultural continuity and survival. For example, current understanding of a traditional Navajo (Diné) woman is that she lives in a hogan, speaks her language, participates in ceremonies, maintains a subsistence lifestyle, nurtures strong clan and kinship ties, serves as a vast repository of cultural and tribal history, participates in tribal governance, wears long hair wrapped in traditional cotton cloth, dresses in long skirts and velvet blouses, and dons the silver jewelry of her family to reside as matriarch of the clan. Such individuals, along with their male counterparts, are typically held in high esteem and are granted a great deal of respect and social power. While the Diné recognize this identity as only one among many accepted as "authentically" Diné, it forms the essence of their tribal identity, serves as the repository of their ancestral knowledge, and roots them as a historically embedded and geographically placed people.

The struggle for American Indian subjectivity is, in part, a struggle to protect this essence and the right of Indigenous peoples to live in accordance with their traditional ways. In other words, regardless of how any individual American Indian may choose to live his or her life as an Indian person, most experience a deep sense of responsibility and obligation to protect the rights of those choosing to live in the ways of their ancestors. The struggle for identity thus also becomes the struggle to negotiate effectively the line between fetishizing traditional identities and recognizing their importance to the continuation of American Indians as distinctive tribal peoples. Insofar as American Indian traditional identities remain tethered to "traditional" practices (such as ceremony) and such practices remain interconnected with the land, the struggle for identity becomes inextricably linked with political struggles for sovereignty and the ongoing battle against cultural encroachment and capitalist desire to control Native land, resources, traditions, and languages. So, while American Indians join the struggle against the kind of essentialism that recognizes only one way of being, they also work to retain a vast constellation of distinct traditions that serve as the defining characteristics of "traditional" ways of being. As Vine Deloria and Clifford Lytle (1983) note, this allegiance to traditional knowledge has protected American Indians from annihilation or its modern counterpart, categoric absorption into the democratic mainstream.

The Transformation of Curriculum and Pedagogy
There is a growing body of work by Indigenous scholars that examines the intersection between the experiences of formal education and tribal culture. Recently, such work has moved away from comparatively simplistic analyses of "learning style" or curriculum content into deeper examination of the interplay between power, difference, opportunity, and institutional structure (see,

for example, Deyhle & Swisher, 1997; Haig-Brown & Archibald, 1996; Hermes, 1998; Lipka, 1994; Pewewardy, 1998). Though such work builds upon the efforts of other scholars of color seeking to define culturally relevant pedagogies (Delpit, 1995; Fordham & Ogbu, 1986; Ladson-Billings, 1995; Trueba, 1988; Watahomigie & McCarty, 1994, for example), American Indian scholars rebuff the undercurrent of democratic inclusion and empowerment that undergirds this work, choosing instead to employ sovereignty as the central struggle in defining relevant praxis.[24]

For example, in her work with Lac Courtie Ojibwe (LCO) reservation schools, Indigenous scholar Mary Hermes (1995, 1998) struggles to define a "culturally based curriculum" where both "culture" and "curriculum" are viewed as fluid, "living" constructs that develop in and through relationship. In her own words, Hermes shifts the research question from "What is the role of culture in knowledge acquisition?" to "What is the role of the school as a site of cultural production?" She argues that research focused on the first question often results in essentialized definitions of culture and the subsequent generation of curricular dichotomies distinguishing "academic" curricula from "cultural" curricula. Instead she seeks answers to the more complicated question, "How can we frame our teaching in an Ojibwe epistemology without representing Ojibwe as a static culture?" (Hermes, 2000). Hermes's question represents a paradigm shift, one that decenters the insertion of a static notion of "culture" into "knowledge" and recenters cultural production as an outcome of the schooling process. In practical terms, such a shift means that community interests not only informed but directed her research methods and outcomes. In her work with Ojibwe schools, she implores educators of American Indian students to recognize culture in the classroom at a deeper level than simply adding content or naming learning styles. She writes:

> I am proposing that we begin to view culture as a complex web of relationships, not just material practices, and enact this in our schools in a way that is central to the curriculum. This could mean, for example, directly teaching tribal history, or simply inviting Elders and community members into the school, regardless of the historical knowledge they bring. (p. 389)

Although Hermes is clearly committed to defining a liberatory praxis based upon a transformative understanding of Ojibwe identity, a goal reminiscent of critical pedagogies, she remains equally committed to the project of American Indian self-determination and sovereignty. Thus, as she advocates an understanding of identity that reflects the fluidity of mestizaje, she also seeks to define a curriculum that remains grounded in the unfolding relationships of tribalness.

In summary, although the development of culturally relevant pedagogy is an objective shared by many marginalized groups, the goal of such efforts for most non-Indian minorities is to ensure inclusion in the democratic imaginary, while the goal for American Indian scholars and educators is to disrupt and impede absorption into that democracy and continue the struggle to remain distinctive, tribal, and sovereign peoples.

The Retention and Reinvigoration of Indigenous Languages

For many American Indian communities, language retention and renewal efforts signify ground zero in the struggle for American Indian sovereignty. Like other aspects of Indigenous experience, there is no single state or uniform condition of Native languages. Some are vibrant like Quechua, which has over one million speakers, and others, like Passamaquoddy, are threatened with extinction. Although ways of speaking and thinking about language shift and language loss may vary within a single community by age, family, life history, gender, and social role, there is a shared sensibility among American Indian peoples that language is inherently tied to cultural continuity — particularly religious and ceremonial continuity — and therefore remains at the core of American Indian identity formation (Anderson, 1998).

Therefore, while many would eschew the oft-implied and "essentialistic" construction of language fluency as a marker of cultural authenticity, there is virtual consensus among American Indian peoples that language loss is tantamount to cultural eradication. Language, in other words, is viewed as a carrier of culture and culture as a carrier of language so that shifts in one reverberate in the other. As such, most tribes work hard to maintain their language through a variety of means, including school, ceremony, community, and family. However, as the traditional structures of community and family erode under the pressures of Whitestream encroachment, tribal members increasingly look to schools to serve as sites of American Indian cultural production and reproduction.

In this effort, American Indian educators looking to develop a critical language of American Indian self-determination and intellectual sovereignty are finding that their own Native languages are replete with metaphors of existence that speak to the lived experience of multiplicity, to the sense of interconnection, and to the understanding that American Indians live not only in relationship with each other, but also with the land. In Quechua, for example, the word for being, person, and Andean person is all the same, *Runa*. This root term has the potential to incorporate the many subcategories of beingness while retaining the same basic reference group, as in *llaqtaruna* (inhabitants of the village) and *qualaruna* (foreigner; literally, naked, peeled). It can be used passively as in *yuyay runa* (one who is knowing or understanding), actively as in *runayáchikk* (that which cultivates a person), or reflexively as in *runaman tukuy* (to complete oneself). Hence, the construct speaks to both the group and the individual and distinguishes in-group from out-group while maintaining the fundamental connection between them. Therefore, it is not a static category or limitation to the sense of Runa as the becoming self

(Skar, 1994). Border crossing and the idea of a shifting identity is, thus, neither new nor revolutionary to this Indigenous community, but rather the way of life of Quechua peoples for over five hundred years.

Conclusion

The work outlined above suggests that while American Indian scholars share many of the same concerns as mainstream critical scholars' development of critical agency, construction of political coalition, and transformation through praxis, they reject the construction of the radical mestizaje and work instead to balance their community's needs to both cross and patrol borders of identity and location. They also retain as the central and common goal the perseverance of American Indians as distinctive and sovereign peoples.

Defining that balance is perhaps the quintessential struggle of American Indian peoples today. It is a deeply complicated and contradictory struggle that reflects the colonialist past and portends an uncertain future. In short, American Indians face an identity paradox. At the same time that pressures to respond to internal crises of identity formation — including racism, sexism, and homophobia — require more fluid constructions of Indianness, pressures to respond to external threats to identity formation — cultural encroachment, ethnic fraud, corporate commodification, and culture loss — require more restrictive constructions of Indianness. Hence, as American Indian intellectuals struggle to awaken Indian communities to the "challenges and cultural politics of (their) own ever-burgeoning multiculturalism" (Vizenor, 1999, p. 3), they must also work to ground the ever-changing present in the historical memories of the past while searching for links to an American Indian future.

Though, as I have demonstrated, there is good reason to remain cautious of the constructs that emerge from dominant Whitestream discourses, there is also much to be learned from engagement with such discourse. As Indigenous scholar Robert Allen Warrior (1995) notes, American Indian intellectuals have remained caught in "a death dance of dependence between, on the one hand, abandoning ourselves to the intellectual strategies and categories of white, European thought and, on the other hand, declaring we need nothing outside of ourselves and our cultures in order to understand the world and our place in it" (p. 123). He observes that only when American Indian intellectuals remove themselves from this dichotomy that "much becomes possible" (p. 124).

To this end, I argue that critical scholars need to broaden their own theoretical scopes to consider the different and, at times, competing moral visions of American Indian peoples. Critical engagement with the intellectual histories of Indigenous peoples could only serve to inform discussions of revolutionary theory and praxis. Specifically, such histories call into question the ongoing assumption of conservative and radical ideologies that democracy, as presently constructed in liberal, capitalist terms, presumes the continued absorption or colonization of Indigenous peoples. American Indian scholars also need to enter the critical dialogue and help reimagine the political terrain surrounding identity. They need to create the intellectual space for the struggle for sovereignty and for their efforts to renegotiate the relationship between sovereign American Indian tribal nations and the current democratic order. The challenge to Indigenous scholars is to define the same kind of balance between cultural integrity and critical resistance in their own quest for American Indian intellectual sovereignty. As Warrior (1995) notes, just "as many of the poets find their work continuous with but not circumscribed by Native traditions of story-telling or ceremonial chanting, we can find the work of (critical studies) continuous with Native traditions of deliberation and decision making. Holding these various factors (sovereignty, tradition, community, process and so on) in tension while attempting to understand the role of critics in an American Indian future is of crucial importance" (p. 118).

Ultimately, I am confident that American Indian and non-Indian critical scholars devoted to the remapping of the political project can together define a common ground of struggle and construct an insurgent but poetic moral vision of liberty, sovereignty, and social justice. It is my hope that this discussion will also serve as the foundation for a new critical theory of Indigenous identity and the development of a new Red Pedagogy.

Notes

1. The term *critical pedagogy* will be used interchangeably with *critical theory* to refer to the diverse body of critical educational theories (i.e., postcolonial, feminist, postmodern, multicultural, and Marxist) that advocate an increasingly sophisticated critique of the social, economic, and political barriers to social justice, as well as crusade for the transformation of schools to reflect the imperatives of democracy. The totality of these theories are viewed by critical scholars as the foundation of liberatory discourse and the political project of liberation. *Project* refers to a collectivity of critique and action or solidarity.
2. For the purposes of this article, American Indian intellectualism is distinguished from purely literary or cultural forms of writing, and refers to intellectual activity that engages in substantive critical analysis from an Indigenous perspective.
3. I use the term *American Indians* to refer to the tribal peoples of North America and *Indigenous peoples* as a more inclusive term to relate to global Indigenous peoples.
4. *Democratic imaginary* refers to the notion that democracy is a never-ending project and continuous pursuit — an imagined concept.
5. The comprehensive literature reviews of Robert Allen Warrior (1995), *Tribal Secrets: Recovering American Indian Intellectual Traditions,* and of Donna Deyhle and Karen Swisher (1997), "Research in American Indian and Alaska Native Education: From Assimilation to Self-Determination," provide adequate evidence of the lack of participation of American Indian scholars within the broader field of critical studies.
6. In the critical discourse the notion of transgressive identity takes the postmodern notion of identity — as a highly fluid construct with intersections among the perceived stable categories of race, class, ethnicity, sexuality, and gender — a step further by indicating that even within categories there is "transgression" or strategies of resistance

that work to destabilize identity. In other words, it is not only that the categories of race, class, gender, and sexuality intersect but also that the categories (e.g., Lesbian, African American, upper class) themselves are highly contested spaces. Moreover, "transgression" is viewed as an inherently subversive and destabilizing construct, where there is constant resistance to any fixed notion of identity.

7. By "dangerous discourse" I mean that American Indian critical studies is viewed in the same spirit that Black feminism was once perceived by Whitestream feminists and African American intellectuals. (Adapting from the feminist notion of "malestream," critical scholar Claude Denis [1997] defines Whitestream as the idea that, while American society is not White in sociodemographic terms, it remains principally and fundamentally structured on the basis of White, Anglo-European experience.)

8. Though Marxist-feminist scholar Teresa Ebert employs the term *Red Pedagogy* to refer to her own work toward revitalizing the Marxist critique in feminist discourse, I use the term as both a historical reference to such empowering metaphors as "Red Power" and the "Great Red Road." Moreover, in the spirit of such venerable Indian scholars and activists as Vine Deloria and Winona LaDuke, I reappropriate the signifier *Red* as a contemporary metaphor for the ongoing political project of Indigenous peoples to retain sovereignty and establish self-determination.

9. I wish to be clear that the terms *spiritual* and *spirituality* in this text do not refer to New Age constructions of some mythic pan-Indian spirituality but rather to the historical presence and persistence within Indigenous belief systems of life forces beyond human rationality.

10. For example, various race-centric theories and certain forms of feminism. Joe Kincheloe and Shirley Steinberg (1997) state that "left essentialists tend to focus attention on one form of oppression as elemental, as taking precedence over all modes of subjugation. Certain radical feminists view gender as a central form of oppression, certain ethnic study scholars privilege race, while orthodox Marxists focus on class" (p. 22).

11. Similarly, Cameron McCarthy (1988, 1995), John Ogbu (1978), Chandra Mohanty (1989), and Henry Giroux (1992) — among others — caution against equating hybridity with equality.

12. The very "protection" typically proffered by citizenship rights (i.e., civil liberties) has often worked to erode traditional structures of tribal life, sometimes pitting Indian against Indian and tribe against tribe. For a more complete discussion of the difference between that which is civic and that which is tribal, see Vine Deloria and Clifford Lytle's *The Nations Within: The Past and Future of American Indian Sovereignty*, or Claude Denis's *We Are Not You: First Nations and Canadian Modernity*.

13. As presently constructed, tribal governments retain many powers of nations, some powers greater than those of states, and some governing powers greater than local non-Indian municipalities (Deloria & Lytle, 1984). In spite of their "sovereign" status, Indian tribes currently rely on the federal government for their operating funds, for the right to interpret and renegotiate their own treaty rights, and for access to the natural resources on their own reservations.

14. By "colonizing impulse" I mean the inherent perhaps unconscious impulse to include or conscript Indigenous (tribal) people into the "democratic project."

15. For example, in Maine, with the setting of land claims in the 1970s Carter administration, many people of varying Indian blood quantums "returned" to the reservation since they had a place to call home. The same thing has happened with the Pequot in Connecticut.

16. Joyce King (1991) defines *dysconcious racism* as an uncritical habit of mind; a form of racism that tacitly accepts White norms and privileges. She contends that such unintended racism does not reflect the absence of consciousness, but rather an impaired or distorted way of thinking about race.

17. For example, in response to the growing phenomenon of "ethnic fraud," the Association of American Indian and Alaska Native Professors has issued a position statement urging colleges and universities to follow specific guidelines in their considerations of admissions, scholarships, and hiring practices. Those guidelines are as follows: 1) Require documentation of enrollment in a state or federally recognized nation/tribe, with preference given to those who meet this criterion; 2) Establish a case-by-case review process for those unable to meet the first criterion; 3) Include American Indian/Alaska Native faculty in the selection process; 4) Require a statement from the applicant that demonstrates past and future commitment to American Indian/Alaska Native concerns; 5) Require higher education administrators to attend workshops on tribal sovereignty and meet with local tribal officials, and 6) Advertise vacancies at all levels on a broad scale and in tribal publications. Contrary to the backlash that this statement received, the association does not promote "policing," nor do they employ exclusionary tactics within their own organization, instead relying on self-disclosure.
18. The Dawes Allotment Act (1887) authorized the president of the United States to allot any reservation according to the following formula: 1) To each head of family, one quarter section; 2) To each single person over 18, one-eighth section; 3) To each orphan under eighteen, one-eighth section; 4) To each other single person under eighteen, born prior to the date of the order, one-sixteenth section (Deloria & Lytle, 1983). In order to allot the land, however, government officials required an efficient method by which to determine who was a "legitimate" member of a given community, which resulted in the beginning of widespread use of tribal rolls and blood-quantum policies.
19. The term *Indian Identity Police* is used by M. Annette Jaimes Guerrero (1996).
20. Deloria (1998) includes among such scholars James Clifton, Sam Gill, Elisabeth Tooker, Alice Kehoe, Richard deMille, and Stephen Farca.
21. Dolores Delgado Bernal (1998) identifies four sources of cultural intuition that together provide the epistemological framework for her analysis of Chicana experience: personal experience, knowledge of existing (academic) literature, professional experience, and the analytical research process itself.
22. See, for example, Elizabeth Cook-Lynn (1998), Michael Charleston (1994, 1998); Vine Deloria (1992, 1998); M. Annette Jaimes Guererro (1996); Mary Hermes (1998); K. Tsianina Lomawaima (1994); Devon Mihesuah (1998); Frances Rains (1998, 1999); Karen Swisher (1998); Gerald Vizenor (1999); Robert Warrior (1995).
23. The Ghost Dance was started in 1890 by Chief Big Foot and his band of Lakota as a means of declaring that the Creator would prevent the total destruction of Native people, alleviate their suffering, and return the people to pre-war days of happiness.
24. The Freirean notion of praxis is best understood as action and reflection upon the world in order to change it or simply as intentional action.

References

Anderson, J. (1998). Ethnolinguistic dimensions of northern Arapaho language shift. *Anthropological Linguistics, 40*(1), 43–108.

Anzaldúa, G. (1987). *Borderlands, la frontera: The new mestíza*. San Francisco: Aunt Lute Books.

Best, S. (1989). Jameson totality and post-structuralist critique: In D. Kellener (Ed.), *Postmodernism/Jameson/critique* (pp. 233–368). Washington, DC: Maisonneuve.

Castillo, A. (1995). *Massacre of dreamers: Essays on Xicanisma*. New York: Plume.

Charleston, G. M. (1994) Toward true Native education: A treaty of 1992 (Final Report of the Indian Nations at Risk Task Force, draft 3). *Journal of American Indian Education, 33*(2), 7–56.

Cook-Lynn, E. (1998). American Indian intellectualism and the new Indian story. In D. A. Mihesuah (Ed.), *Natives and academics: Researching and writing about American Indians* (pp. 111–138). Lincoln: University of Nebraska Press.

Darder, A., Torres, R., & Gutiérrez, H. (Eds.). (1997). *Latinos and education: A critical reader.* New York: Routledge.

Delgado Bernal, D. (1998). Using a Chicana feminist epistemology in educational research. *Harvard Educational Review, 68,* 555–582.

Deloria, V. (1992). *God is Red: A Native view of religion.* Golden, CO: North American Press.

Deloria, V., Jr. (1998). Comfortable fictions and the struggles for turf: An essay review of *The invented Indian: Cultural fictions and government policies.* In D. A. Mihesuah (Ed.), *Natives and academics: Researching and writing about American Indians* (pp. 65–83). Lincoln: University of Nebraska Press.

Deloria, V., Jr. (1999). *For this land: Writings on religion in America.* New York: Routledge.

Deloria, V., Jr., & Lytle, C. (1983). *American Indians, American justice.* Austin: University of Texas Press.

Deloria, V., Jr., & Lytle, C. (1984). *The nations within: The past and future of American Indian sovereignty.* Austin: University of Texas Press.

Delpit, L. (1995). *Other people's children: Cultural conflicts in the classroom.* New York: New Press.

Denis, C. (1997). *We are not you: First Nations and Canadian modernity.* Toronto: Broadview.

Deyhle, R., & Swisher, K. (1997). Research in American Indian and Alaskan Native education: From assimilation to self-determination. In *Review of Research in Education* (pp. 113–183). Washington, DC: American Educational Research Association.

di Leonardo, M. (1991). *Gender at the crossroads of knowledge: Feminist anthropology in the postmodernist era.* Berkeley: University of California Press.

Fixico, D. L. (1998). *The invasion of Indian country in the twentieth century: American capitalism and tribal natural resources.* Niwot: University Press of Colorado.

Fordham, S., & Ogbu, J. (1986). Black students and the burden of "acting White." *Urban Review, 18,* 176–203.

Fusco, C. (1995). *English is broken here: Notes on the cultural fusion in the Americas.* New York: New Press.

Giroux, H. (1992). *Border crossings: Cultural workers and the politics of education.* New York: Routledge.

Grande, S. (1997). *Critical multicultural education and the modern project: An exploratory analysis.* Unpublished doctoral dissertation, Kent State University.

Grande, S. (2000). American Indian identity and intellectualism: The quest for a new Red pedagogy. *Journal of Qualitative Studies in Education, 13,* 373–354.

Guerrero, M. A. J. (1996). Academic apartheid: American Indian studies and "multiculturalism." In A. Gordon & C. Newfield (Eds.), *Mapping multiculturalism* (pp. 49–63). Minneapolis: University of Minnesota Press.

Haig-Brown, C., & Archibald, J. (1996). Transforming First Nations research with respect and power. *International Journal of Qualitative Studies in Education, 9,* 245–267.

Hale, C. R. (2000). Book review of *To die in this way: Nicaraguan Indians and the myth of mestizaje 1880–1965. American Society for Ethnohistory, 47,* 268–271.

Harraway, D. J. (1991). *Simians, cyborgs, and women.* New York: Routledge.

Hermes, M. (1995). *Making culture, making curriculum: Teaching through meanings and identities at an American Indian tribal school.* Unpublished doctoral dissertation, University of Wisconsin–Madison.

Hermes, M. (1998). Research methods as a situated response: Towards a First Nation's methodology. *International Journal of Qualitative Studies in Education, 11,* 155–168.

Hermes, M. (2000). The scientific method, Nintendo, and eagle feathers: Rethinking the meaning of "culture based" curriculum at an Ojibwe tribal school. *International Journal of Qualitative Studies in Education, 13,* 387–400.

Herrnstein, R. J., & Murray, C. (1994). *The bell curve: Intelligence and class structure in American life.* New York: Free Press.

Joe, J. R., & Miller, D. L. (1997). Cultural survival and contemporary American Indian women in the city. In C. J. Cohen (Ed.), *Indigenous women transforming politics: An alternative reader* (pp. 137–150). New York: New York University Press.

Kincheloe, J., & Steinberg, S. (1997). *Changing multiculturalism.* Bristol, PA: Open University Press.

King, J. (1991). Dysconcious racism: Ideology, identity and the miseducation of teachers. *Journal of New Education, 60,* 133–146

Ladson-Billings, G. (1995). "But that's just good teaching!" The case for culturally relevant pedagogy. *Theory Into Practice, 34,* 159–165.

Lipka, J. (1994). Language, power, and pedagogy: Whose school is it? *Peabody Journal of Education, 69,* 71–93.

Lomawaima, K. T. (1994). *They called it prairie light: The story of Chilocco Indian school.* Lincoln: University of Nebraska Press.

Machamer, A. M. (1997). Ethnic fraud in the university: Serious implications for American Indian education. *Native Bruin, 2,* 1–2.

McCarthy, C. (1988). Rethinking liberal and radical perspectives on racial inequality in schooling: Making the case for nonsynchrony. *Harvard Educational Review, 58,* 265–269.

McCarthy, C. (1995). The problem with origins: Race and the contrapuntal nature of the educational experience. In P. McLaren & C. Sleeter (Eds.), *Multicultural education, critical pedagogy and the politics of difference* (pp. 245–268). Albany: State University of New York Press.

McCarthy, C., & Crichlow, W. (1993). *Race and identity and representation in education.* New York: Routledge.

McLaren, P. (Ed.). (1997). *Revolutionary multiculturalism: Pedagogies of dissent for the new millennium.* Boulder, CO: Westview Press.

McLaren, P., & Giroux, H. (1997). Writing from the margins: Geographies of identity, pedagogy and power. In P. McLaren (Ed.), *Revolutionary multiculturalism: Pedagogies of dissent for the new millennium* (pp. 16–41). Boulder, CO: Westview Press.

McLaren, P., & Gutierrez, K. (1997). Global politics and local antagonists: Research and practice as dissent and possibility. In P. McLaren (Ed.), *Revolutionary multiculturalism: Pedagogy of dissent for the new millennium.* (pp. 192–222) Boulder, CO: Westview Press.

McLaren, P., & Sleeter, C. (Eds.). (1995). *Multicultural education, critical pedagogy, and the politics of difference.* Albany: State University of New York Press.

Mihesuah, D. (1998). *Natives and academics: Researching and writing about American Indians.* Lincoln: University of Nebraska Press.

Mohanty, C. (1989). On race and violence: Challenges for liberal education in the 1990s. *Cultural Critique, 14,* 179–208.

Murillo, E. G. (1997, April). *Research under cultural assault: Mojado ethnography.* Paper presented at the annual meeting of the American Educational Studies Association, San Diego.

Nagel, J. (1995). American Indian ethnic renewal: Politics and the resurgence of identity. *American Sociological Review, 60,* 947–965.

Ogbu, J. (1978). *Minority education and caste: The American system in cross-cultural perspective.* New York: Academic Press.

Pewewardy, C. (1998). Fluff and feathers: Treatment of American Indians in the literature and the classroom. *Equity and Excellence in Education, 31,* 69–76.

Rains, F. V. (1998). Is the benign really harmless? Deconstructing some "benign" manifestations of operationalized White privilege. In J. Kinchloe, S. R. Steinberg, & R. E. Chennault (Eds.), *White reign: Deploying Whiteness in America* (pp. 77–101). New York: St. Martin's Press.

Rains, F. V. (1999). Indigenous knowledge, historical amnesia and intellectual authority: Deconstructing hegemony and the social and political implications of the curricular other. In L. M. Semeli & J. Kinchloe (Eds.), *What is Indigenous knowledge? Voices from the academy* (pp. 317–332). New York: Falmer Press.

Said, E. (1985). Orientalism reconsidered. *Race and Class, 26,* 1–15.

Skar, S. L. (1994). *Lives together — worlds apart: Quechua colonization in jungle and city.* New York: Scandinavian University Press.

Stavenhagen, R. (1992). Challenging the nation-state in Latin America. *Journal of International Affairs, 34,* 421–441.

Strauss, A., & Corbin, J. (1990). *Basics of qualitative research: Grounded theory procedures and techniques.* Newbury Park, CA: Sage.

Swisher, K. (1998). Why Indian people should write about Indian education. In D. A. Mihesuah (Ed.), *Natives and academics: Researching and writing about American Indians* (pp. 190–199). Omaha: University of Nebraska Press.

Trueba, E. (1988). Culturally based explanation of minority students' academic achievement. *Minority Achievement, 19,* 270–287.

USD, Bureau of Indian Affairs, 209 manual 8, 83.7. Mandatory Criteria for Federal Recognition. 44 U.S.C. 3501 (et seq.) n.d.

Valle, V., & Torres, R. (1995). The idea of mestizaje and the "race" problematic: Racialized media discourse in a post-Fordist landscape. In A. Darder (Ed.), *Culture and difference: Critical perspectives on the bi-cultural experience in the United States* (pp. 139–153). Westport: Bergin & Garvey.

Van Cott, D. L. (1994). *Indigenous peoples and democracy in Latin America.* New York: St. Martin's Press.

Vizenor, G. (1999). *Postindian conversations.* Lincoln: University of Nebraska Press.

Warrior, R. A. (1995). *Tribal secrets: Recovering American Indian intellectual traditions.* Minneapolis: University of Minnesota Press.

Watahomigie, J., & McCarty, T. L. (1994). Bilingual/bicultural education at Peach Springs: A Hualapai way of schooling. *Peabody Journal of Education, 69,* 26–42.

Education as Transformation: Becoming a Healer among the !Kung and the Fijians

RICHARD KATZ

Among both the !Kung hunter-gatherers of the Kalahari Desert in southern Africa and the farming and fishing people of the outer Fiji Islands, healing is a central community ritual with significance far beyond effecting a cure. I asked an experienced !Kung healer how one learns to heal:

> Becoming a healer is difficult. The boiling energy, the [spiritual] power which lets us heal, is painful. It hurts. We fear it. . . . Before we can heal, we must want the energy to boil up in us, we must want it even though we fear it. When we accept that boiling energy we can heal. But don't let anyone fool you. Boiling energy is painful and the fear can defeat you.

A highly respected Fijian healer said the following about becoming a healer:

> The spiritual power is close at hand here in Fiji. Some of us are called to bring that power to the people for healing. That can be frightening, but the hard part is just beginning. To become a healer we must learn to use that power properly . . . to use it only for healing. We say that to become a healer we must follow the straight path . . . and also find it. That is a long and difficult process.

In this article I present original field data on healing among the !Kung and the people of the outer Fiji Islands.[1] I will draw from these data an interpretation of the education of healers that could be called "education as transformation." The process of transformation, a concept deduced from the ethnographic material that follows, characterizes the education of healers in these two nonindustrial, non-Western societies.[2] Briefly, healers' education involves a transformation of consciousness in which potential healers experience a sense of connectedness, joining a spiritual healing power, themselves, and their community. This transformation establishes the possibility of healing but does not remove healers from the context of daily life. Healing involves the healers' struggle to serve as a vehicle to channel healing to the community, without accumulating power for personal use. That effort affects the inner quality of their lives, transforming them.

While some might consider "education as transformation" merely a pre-scientific precursor to Western approaches, I believe it offers a valid alternative perspective on current Western education. The approach is particularly significant for the community mental health movement, a Western system that most closely parallels !Kung and Fijian healing systems. For example, the healing systems in these two cultures help distribute resources fairly throughout the community, emphasize prevention more than treatment, and make extensive use of community support networks. These elements also represent central goals of Western community mental health programs, though often unrealized.[3] Studying education as transformation can suggest features that may be lacking in the education of community mental health workers. Specifically, I will discuss the education of community psychiatrists, the Western healers who most closely parallel the !Kung and Fijian healers.

Among both the !Kung and the people of the outer Fiji Islands, the education of healers deals with fundamental mysteries and dilemmas. Healers are taught how to respond to uncertainty and confusion, reactions that are accentuated in times of illness and stress. Knowledge of healing is respected, and its practice highly valued. Educating the healer in these two cultures is what we in the West would call a sacred process. While the !Kung and Fijian adaptations to their respective eco-niches differ from the adaptations that characterize the industrialized West, those two cultures present critical psychological and sociocultural perspectives on the education of healers that are strikingly absent in the Western approach. The !Kung and Fijians have much to teach us about the education of healers in a self-healing community.

Accepting Boiling Energy: Becoming a Healer Among the !Kung

In Botswana, Namibia, and southern Angola, there are about 50,000 San people, of whom some 5,000 live primarily as hunter-gatherers. It was in a group of nearly 500 !Kung-speaking San, living as hunter-gatherers in Botswana, in the northwestern Kalahari, that I learned about the education of healers.[4] The !Kung typically live in camps of between ten and thirty people closely related through kinship. Half-a-dozen or so grass-woven shelters, usually forming a half- or quarter-circle, face an open area and physically define the camp.

The economic system of the !Kung is based on sharing collected food resources. Between 60 and 70 percent of the diet by weight consists of wild vegetable foods gathered primarily by women.[5] The men supply the remaining food by hunting small and large game. Local groups neither maintain exclusive rights to resources nor defend territories; a reciprocal access prevails. Frequent visiting among the different groups mitigates the effect of localized shortages. Allied groups cooperate, coming together in a given area when resources permit, living apart when sources of food and water are widely scattered. When food is brought into a camp it is distributed for all to partake.

Resources of all kinds circulate among members of a camp and between camps, so that any one person draws upon the entire community's resources. Little investment is necessary in what could be termed a capital sector of the economy. Elements of the material culture are made easily, with ample leisure time to make them. Since individuals and groups must move to stay close to their food sources, personal property is minimal, usually less than twenty-five pounds per individual.[6] Frequent moves and the !Kung emphasis on sharing keep food accumulation to a minimum. The environment itself is their storehouse.

Accumulation of food has distinct advantages in the Kalahari ecological niche. It is not gathered until needed, and what is collected is immediately distributed and consumed. There is a marked absence of disparities in wealth among the !Kung. No one is supposed to stand out from the rest of the group. If someone were to come back from a successful hunt showing excessive pride, he would be put back firmly in his place, even if the kill were a large animal. With the freshly killed meat still over his shoulder, such an improperly proud hunter would hear the pointed teasing of his camp: "What is it that you have there? What a scrawny little thing! You didn't kill that. It looks so sick and scrawny that it must have fallen dead into your arms."[7] Egalitarianism, including sexual egalitarianism, is the rule.

For the !Kung, healing involves health and growth on physical, psychological, social, and spiritual levels; it affects the individual, the group, the surrounding environment, and the cosmos. Healing is an integrating and enhancing force, far more fundamental than curing or the application of medicine. The healing tradition supports the culture's emphasis on sharing and egalitarianism, its belief in the life of the spirit, and its strong community ties.

The central event in the healing tradition is the all-night dance.[8] Sometimes as often as four times in a month, the women sit around the fire, singing and rhythmically clapping as night falls, signaling the start of a healing dance. The entire camp participates as the men, sometimes joined by women, dance around the singers. As the dance intensifies, *n/um* ("energy") is activated in those who are healers, most of whom are among the dancing men. As n/um intensifies in the healers, they experience *!kia* ("a form of enhanced consciousness") during which they heal everyone at the dance. The dance usually ends before the sun rises the next morning. Those at the dance confront, celebrate, and reaffirm the spiritual dimension of their daily lives. They find it exciting, joyful, and powerful. "Being at a dance makes our hearts happy," the !Kung say.

While experiencing !kia, one can heal. Those who have learned to !kia-heal are said to possess n/um and are called *n/um k"ausi* ("masters of n/um" or simply "healers"). N/um resides in the pit of the stomach and at the base of the spine. As the healer dances, becoming warm and sweating profusely, the n/um heats up, becomes a vapor, and rises up the spine. When it reaches the base of the skull, !kia results. Kinachau, an experienced healer, talks about the !kia experience:

> You dance, dance, dance, dance. Then n/um lifts you up in your belly and lifts you in your back, and then you start to shiver. [N/um] makes you tremble, it's hot. . . . Your eyes are open but you don't look around; you hold your eyes still and look straight ahead. But when you get into !kia, you're looking around because you see everything, because you see what's troubling everybody. . . . N/um enters every part of your body right to the tip of your feet and even your hair.

N/um is held in awe, considered powerful and mysterious. It is this same n/um that the healer "puts into" people in attempting to cure them. So, once heated up, n/um can both induce !kia and combat illness.

As healers learn to control their boiling n/um, they can apply it to healing. They learn to ≠*twe*, ("to heal" or "pull out sickness"). K"au ≠ Dwa describes how one can heal while experiencing !kia: When you !kia, you see the things you must pull out, like the death things that god has put into people . . . you see people properly, just as they are . . . your vision does nor whirl."

!kia intensifies emotions, be they fear, exhilaration, or seriousness. During !kia, !Kung healers perform cures, handle and walk on fire, describe seeing inside the body, and at times report seeing across great distances and traveling to god's village, activities never attempted in an ordinary state. ≠ Toma Zho, a strong healer, spoke of the feeling !kia gives, that of becoming more essential, more oneself: "I want to have a dance soon so that I can really become myself again." A transcendent state of consciousness, !kia alters a !Kung's sense of self, time, and space. A master of n/um says: "When I pick up n/um, it explodes and throws me up in the air and I enter heaven and then fall down." !Kia makes others feel they are "opening up" or "bursting open, like a ripe pod."

Through !kia, a !Kung transcends ordinary life and can contact the realm of the gods and the spirits of dead ancestors. Sickness is a process in which the //*gauwasi* ("spirits") try to carry people off into their own domain. The spirits, sent by the gods, are strong, but not invincible. A struggle ensues between two groups of relatives, those still living and those already dead. Each group wants the sick one for itself, and neither the realm of the living nor that of the spirits is seen as bad. In his or her ordinary state, a !Kung respects the gods and does not argue with them. In !kia, the healer expresses the wishes of the living and goes directly into the struggle. When a person is seriously ill, the struggle intensifies. If a healer's n/um is strong, the spirits will retreat and the sick one will live. This struggle is at the heart of the healer's art, skill, and power.

In their search for contact with transcendent realms and in their struggle with illness, misfortune, and death, the healing dance and n/um are the !Kung's most important allies. Fiercely egalitarian, the !Kung do not allow n/um to be controlled by a few religious specialists, but rather want it spread widely among the group. While they see only increased benefits from having many healers, becoming a healer is a long and painful process, fraught with danger. To educate a healer requires a continuing reconciliation between these opposing needs and desires, which exist both in the community and the healer.

An unlimited energy, n/um expands as it boils. It cannot be hoarded by any one person. At the healing dance, n/um is shared by everyone, all are given healing. As one person experiences !kia at the dance, others likely will follow. The !Kung do not seek !kia for its own sake, but for its healing protection to the individual, the group, and the culture. Nor is healing reserved for just a few persons with unique characteristics; by the time they reach adulthood, more than half the men and a third of the women have become healers.

The dance provides healing in the most generic sense; it may cure an ill body or mind, as the healer pulls out sickness with a laying on of hands; or mend the social fabric, as the dance promotes social cohesion and a manageable release of hostility; or protect the camp from misfortune, as the healer pleads with the gods for relief from the Kalahari's harshness. Healing occurs as the people contact their spirits and gods through the enhanced consciousness of !kia, and receive the profound knowledge the healers gain in their encounters with the gods. The dance also provides training for aspiring healers. It gives healers opportunities for fulfillment and growth, in which all can experience a sense of well-being, and some experience spiritual development.

These integrated functions reinforce each other, providing a continuous source of curing, counsel, protection, and enhancement. One could say the dance is the !Kung's primary expression of "religion," "medicine," and "cosmology" — their primary ritual. For the !Kung, it is an event of great importance, a point of marked intensity and significance. The healing dance is woven into their hunting-gathering life without undermining the execution of everyday responsibilities. !Kia-healing remains harmonious with the different levels of !Kung existence. Its effectiveness depends on this context. The healing dance is public, a routine cultural event to which all have access. The dance establishes community, and it is the community, in its activation of n/um, which heals and is healed.

Long before people try seriously to become healers, they play at !kia-healing. A group of five- and six-year-old children may perform a small healing dance, imitating the actual dance, with its steps and healing postures, at times falling down as if in !kia. A parent or another close relative, always a !Kung healer, is usually one's healing teacher. The teacher remains an ordinary person during the non-!kia state, rather than an intimate of the gods. Healers teach primarily by example and do not demand obedience or a long apprenticeship. Though originally obtained from the gods, n/um now passes regularly from person to person.

To heal depends upon developing a desire to "drink n/um," not on learning specific techniques. The healer's education stresses not the structure of the dancing, but the importance of dancing so one's "heart is open to boiling n/um"; it emphasizes not the composition of the healing songs, but singing so that one's "voice reaches up to the heavens." N/um is not "put into" someone who will not accept it; the student must seek to receive it. While there is conceptual clarity about what happens during !kia, there is experiential mystery at the time of !kia. At its core, the education is a process of accepting boiling n/um for oneself, a difficult process because n/um, painful and mysterious, is greatly feared.

The experience of !kia brings profound pain and fear, along with feelings of release and liberation. In describing the onset of !kia, healers speak again and again of a searing pain in the pit of the stomach and the area between the diaphragm and waist, especially towards the sides. Recalling his first experiences with n/um, a healer says: "N/um got into my stomach. It was hot and painful . . . like fire. I was surprised and I cried."

K"au ≠ Dwa described explicitly other dimensions of this feeling: "As we !Kung enter !kia, we fear death. We fear we may die and not come back!" Fear of death evokes its own special terror for the !Kung, as it does for people in all cultures. When potential healers can face the fact of death and willingly die, they can overcome fear of n/um, and there can be a breakthrough to !kia. The conviction that one is reborn or can come alive again is helpful, if not essential. /Wi, an older healer, describes this death and rebirth: "In !kia, your heart stops, you're dead, your thoughts are nothing, you breathe with difficulty. You see things, n/um things; you see spirits killing people, you smell burning, rotten flesh; then you heal, you pull sickness out. You heal, heal, heal . . . then you live. Then your eyeballs clear and then you see people clearly." The !Kung must give up the familiar to enter mysterious territory, they must die before they can be reborn into !kia.

Various aspects of the dance support students' critical passage to !kia, helping them to regulate the boiling n/um and resultant !kia so that healing can occur. The teacher, with perhaps one or two other healers, probably will be at the dance, trying to put the correct amount of n/um into the student. Others may provide physical support when the onset of !kia makes the student shaky. A most important support and inspiration is the group of women clapping and singing the healing songs. Their singing helps the n/um to boil, and helps regulate the depth of !kia. Finally, the participation of all those present offers support for the transition to !kia.

As they dance ever more seriously into the night, the potential healers' n/um may begin to boil, and !kia becomes imminent. As they feel !kia coming on, the potential healers try to regulate their condition, and they may resist the transition to an altered state. Others help them to overcome their resistance. They try to help students strike a balance between the oncoming intensity of !kia and their fear of it. Experienced healers go as deeply into !kia as they can, but must maintain control over the n/um to use it for healing. If the !kia is coming on so fast that fear escalates and prevents the experience of !kia, students may stop dancing for a while, or drink some water to "cool down" the too rapidly boiling n/um. The n/um must be hot enough to evoke !kia, but not so hot that it provokes debilitating fear. Throughout the dance, extensive physical contact between the potential n/um masters and experienced healers helps the students regulate the n/um. Learning to heal is focused within the dance and is an experiential education. Teaching consists of helping students overcome their fear and then guiding them in using !kia for healing. The physical, emotional, and psychological aspects of teaching are inseparable.

Two variables determine career patterns for !Kung healers — age and experience with n/um. There are important male-female differences in these patterns.[9] /Wi, an experienced male healer, provides an overview of the male pattern: "The n/um of the young man is very painful, like fire. The old ones, the ones in whom the n/um has become weak, their n/um is light because they have given most of it to younger ones who are now struggling with the pain of it. The middle-aged man has power, pulling power, more so than the old man."

The career pattern is fluid, and variations often occur. In the early phase of the career, most males in their late teens and mid-twenties try to become healers and participate in the dances, seeking to drink n/um. Experiencing !kia marks a first turning point in the healer's career, and ends the initial phase. The middle phase is characterized by another turning point, applying !kia to healing. The ability to heal usually comes to the student between the ages of twenty-five and forty and brings recognition as a healer. Those still seeking to become healers between twenty-five and thirty-five feel some tension. But the fact that the community already has enough healers overshadows the dilemmas of anyone whose potential for healing remains ambiguous. If by the age of about forty, one has not yet experienced !kia, it is assumed that one is not meant to become a healer. Accepting that fact is another turning point. One who is not meant to heal is not stigmatized. At a dance, the emphasis is on working with those who can provide healing to the group rather than on working with those who have not yet reached that point — and may never do so.

The experienced phase is characterized by still another turning point, when the healer is considered "completely learned." Such a healer heals dependably, frequently, and strongly. But there is not always consensus on who is "completely learned," and those who are will at times seek further assistance in their healing work.

Old age brings different responses. By the time healers reach their seventies, most retire from active healing, weakened by various ailments. This retirement, however, is neither irreversible nor strictly observed. A few healers continue into their seventies — it is said that their strong n/um keeps them healthy. Nonhealers may continue dancing until old age makes the necessary physical exertion impossible.

The career pattern of female healers is different. Unlike the men's long and difficult search for healing power, it takes only a few days for most women to get n/um, although actual reception of n/um is no less painful. They receive it from old women teacher-healers who visit their camp. Though n/um can be received from early adolescence to late middle-age it lies dormant in women during their reproductive years. The !Kung say that when the n/um boils within, it can be dangerous to the fetus or the nursing child. Women know they cannot develop their n/um fully until childbearing is over.

The education of healers emphasizes psychological and motivational, rather than social or economic, factors. Healers are similar to nonhealers on a broad range of social, economic, and political variables. For instance, Lee suggests that there are no differences between healers and nonhealers in such variables as owning hunting dogs, kin relation, among of travel, or contact with Bantu groups.[10] While healers are not a privileged group, they do differ psychologically from nonhealers in ways that both prepare for healing work and result from that work. For example, T.A.T.-type tests show that healers have easier access to fantasy. Because these fantasies and !kia are both altered states of consciousness, the healers' access to their own fantasy life can be seen as conducive to and affected by !kia. As shown by an adaptation of the Draw-a-Person test, healers have a body image determined more by their internal states than by external anatomical criteria.[11] Although !kia is a very physical experience, it emphasizes processes that ignore or break out of the healer's anatomical boundaries. It is in psychological characteristics, which would predispose them to accepting boiling n/um, that healers are unique. It is a distinction they carry within. "We (!Kung) are not meant to boast of our healing. It is just something we do to help others."

The Straight Path:
Becoming a Healer Among the People of the Outer Fiji Islands

The island nation of Fiji, consisting of 100 inhabited islands and 500,000 people, is situated in the South Pacific, north of New Zealand. Approximately 50 percent of the population is descended from emigrants from southern India who came as indentured servants more than 100 years ago. My data on education of healers deal only with indigenous Fijians, and are limited to a district of rural outer islands, where they live in villages of about 100 people located several hours from each other by foot. There is no electricity, and there are no motorized land vehicles or roads. Outboard engines power some of their open twenty-foot boats.

The Fijians live by subsistence farming and fishing.[12] A village consists of several groups of closely related kin who jointly own land and choice fishing areas, often working them communally. Sharing of resources is highly valued. When Fijians sit down to eat in the village, their doors must always remain open. Whenever anyone passes by, they call out, "Please come in and eat." Fijian social structure is hierarchical, but humility, regardless of status, is valued.

Fijians in the outer islands describe the ideal Fijian in the following way: The most important characteristic is *vakarokoroko* ("respect") — respect for traditions and customs, and for others. A second is *duavata* ("togetherness") — living together, working together, sharing resources. A third is *yalo vinaka* ("kindheartedness") — giving from a kindness and goodness of heart without any expectation of return. A fourth is *dauloloma* ("love for all") — being full of love for all one meets. Becoming a healer means striving toward this cultural ideal. Though the Fijian people are Christianized, aspects of indigenous religion remain, and Fijian healers are the guardians of the indigenous system.

Ceremonial life is essential in Fiji, promoting economic and social exchange and celebrating the religious dimension. Three main elements characterize Fijian ceremonies generally and the healing ceremony in particular: the *Vu* ("ancestors"); the *mana* ("spiritual power"); and the *yaqona* ("a plant with sacred use") that brings this power to humans. Dead ancestors are accessible, generally benevolent, and are felt to be close at hand. Mana, the ultimate power, is an invisible, irreducible force that "makes things happen."[13] As Fijians say, "Mana is mana," and its effects are often described as miraculous. The yaqona is called the "nourishment of the gods."[14] When humans offer yaqona to the ancestors in the correct ritual manner, the channel of communication to the ancestors is opened, and their mana becomes available.

Healers may request the healing influence of mana, but others may subvert the yaqona to request mana to work against someone. Fijians call this latter practice witchcraft.[15] As one healer put it: "You can perform witchcraft because some of the ancestors are not entirely trustworthy." The healing ceremony deals with resolving uncertainty and making comprehensible the unknown. Most important, it is the primary arena in which the forces of good and evil — healing and witchcraft — struggle against each other. Because these forces are ever present, the healer must be educated in the "straight path," to use mana exclusively for healing purposes.

Fijians group sicknesses into two major categories, depending on their etiology. The "true" or "real" sicknesses are caused by natural events. For example, one may have painful joints from being in the cold ocean too long. The second type, "spiritual" sicknesses, are caused either by witchcraft or by some violation of cultural norms, punished directly by the ancestors. While Western medicine is reserved for treating "true sicknesses," both true and spiritual sicknesses are brought to Fijian healers. The same symptom pattern often can express either etiology.

In times of doubt, crisis, or illness the healer is the primary community resource.[16] No problem is excluded from his or her domain, but the majority of cases are illnesses with physical symptoms. Requests for help range from a boy with a swollen neck, to a childless woman who wishes to become pregnant, to a family seeking protection against others' evil intentions, to an entire village wanting to make amends for violating a sacred custom. As one villager remarked about the healer in her village: "He can't get sick, because without him, we would all be lost." Even though healers are highly respected, seen as "hard working" and closer than most to the "Fijian ideal," they remain fully contributing community members.[17] Healers are villagers first and foremost.

The healing ceremony, centering around the ritual exchange of yaqona, typically begins when the patient comes to the healer with a request for help or a cure. The patient incorporates the request within a ritual presentation of yaqona to the healer. The healer accepts the yaqona on behalf of the ancestors from whom he or she draws healing powers. Yaqona may be prepared with water and drunk by the healer. In the healer's act of acceptance, the healing is accomplished. In that moment, the mana is said to become available, making accurate diagnosis and selection of an effective treatment possible. The patient returns after four days for the conclusion of the treatment, or, if necessary, further treatment in the same or some new direction. Herbs and massage are used in about 25 percent of the instances to carry out the healing. Various types of massage can be employed, and there are numerous herbs in the natural pharmacopia, sometimes requiring elaborate preparations.

Yaqona is the ever-present accompaniment and stimulus of Fijian social life. A Fijian elder voiced what is common knowledge: "A Fijian cannot live without the yaqona. It is what makes our village live and work together." During day-to-day social occasions, the mana lies dormant. The healing ritual turns the yaqona into an active channel for the mana. Performing that ritual is one of the healer's many technical skills. Healing also requires substantial interpersonal skills and social sensitivity. Helping a patient may require the understanding and manipulation of belief, but resolving a village crisis may require the political realignment of groups.

Though meant for the protection and healing of humans, mana can be turned by some to opposite purposes. The education of the healer demands that the healer find and stay on what is called the *gaunisala dodonu* ("straight path"). The journey along that path is what enables healers to direct mana toward healing. Though mana is accessible to many, few know how "to begin walking on the path" and even fewer know "how to stay on it." Since being a healer is an achieved role, one is not prepared by birth to travel the straight path. As one healer put it: "It is hard to walk along this straight path because there are many times when we are tempted to stray, and times when we cannot clearly see where the path goes." The path itself is not straight, but the way one travels it should be.

Traveling the straight path means living out certain attributes that characterize the ideal Fijian. The healer's character creates the possibility of healing work, and the development of character marks the continuation and deepening of that work. Information about healing techniques is available only to those with character. There is respect for the technical aspects of healing, but character precedes and provides a context for healing technology.

The following attributes are often mentioned when prescribing the way a healer must live in order to follow the straight path:

> *dauvakadina* ("telling and living the truth"): The amount of truth in each person determines the power of your healing. You must speak to your patients only what you have been told by your guardian ancestor. If you elaborate on that, and add your own opinions, or try to show how much *you* know, you are just lying.
>
> *dauloloma* ("love for all"): In this healing work you should love everybody, whether a relative or foreigner. They are all the same for you. You must help them all because of your love.
>
> *i tovo vinaka* ("proper or correct behavior"): The mana is getting weaker in Fiji because people are not now following ancient customs. We must observe these customs, like the taboos, if our behavior is to be proper.
>
> *sega ni vukivuki* ("humility"): This work is your secret. Showing this work to everybody, even those who do not need your help, is boasting.
>
> *vakarokoroko* ("respect"): Everybody must be respected. Each person deserves our love and help. And the traditional ways of the land must be respected. We show our true nature by such respect.
>
> *sega ni lomaloma rua* ("single-mindedness"): You must firmly and fully believe in your work and faithfully worship your guardian ancestor. Once you decide about something and judge what is right, you must stick by your word and seize the moment to act. No wavering or turning back.
>
> *veiqaravi* ("service"): The power is to be used only for healing and serving others. You cannot use it to harm or kill others, or for your own personal gain, to get money or other things. That must be very clear. If you do, the power leaves you.

Though these attributes are often phrased in terms of the healing work itself, they generally prescribe the way a healer must live.[18]

Almost all prospective healers work first as assistants to established healers. Approximately a third of them are assistants to a healer who has just cured them and offer their help out of appreciation for the cure and respect for the healing power. About half of the healers, at the beginning of their careers, have a close relationship with an experienced healer, who helps the apprentice with difficult cases and provides general guidance. Through his or her behavior, the teacher demonstrates the straight path to the student. By traveling the path, one learns how to walk it.

Healers mark the beginning of their work with a first vision, one that calls them to healing. They place life-changing significance on the experience. Loti's first healing vision — composed of temporally separated segments — is typical:

I was sleeping or maybe just resting a bit. The ancestor of our village appeared to me as a woman. She told me to go to the cliff by the shore and jump on the ancient Fijian canoe that lay in the bay. I went to the cliff. The boat lay beneath, far below. I was afraid to jump . . . but jumped, landing on the deck. The canoe sailed out to sea. Suddenly a sea-snake appeared, and around its neck, hanging by a gold chain, was the mana-box. The ancestor told me to take the box. She said it was for me. But I was very afraid, afraid the snake would bite. I approached carefully, using a long pole from the sail to try to lift the mana-box off the snake's neck. I hesitated more than once, and moved cautiously. I reached out with the pole . . . and failed. I was undecided about continuing on. A second time I reached out with the pole . . . and again failed to get the box. The ancestor said that I must return to the village. "The mana is not for you today," she said. The next day she appeared again. "You have one more chance. Leap onto the canoe and take the mana-box." Again I went to the shore, leaped onto the canoe and soon found myself facing the sea-snake with the mana-box around its neck. This time I did not hesitate. I slipped the mana-box off its neck and didn't even need the pole. The ancestor told me that I was now to use that mana for healing, that I was to begin the healing work. The next morning I awoke somewhat confused. How could I begin to heal, I wondered, since I did not know how to perform the healing ceremony. The ancestor spoke to me again: "Don't worry. You have the mana with you. Use the mana for healing and the ways of healing will come to you."[19]

The ancestor who wishes to provide mana for the healing work appears during that first vision, requesting that the person engage in healing work on his or her behalf. In offering the straight path, the ancestor makes clear what is needed to follow that path. Loti, for example, learns about the importance of being single-minded. The first vision calls for a commitment to use the power of mana only for healing.

These first healing visions, enhanced states of consciousness, vary in detail and in intensity. For some, the vision occurs in a dream state, at times moving into or out of a waking state; for others, the vision occurs while the person is awake, and most often alone. Frequently, the person sees the ancestor, and usually they converse. In many cases, the healer reports leaving his or her body, traveling (often flying) away to contact the ancestor more directly or to see something the ancestor wants to show, such as the traditional canoe in Loti's trip.

Altered states of consciousness in which the ancestors are felt, seen, or heard are common among people of the outer Fiji Islands, whether or not they are healers. Fear dominates encounters between nonhealers and the ancestors. These encounters are brief, and the opportunity for communication is not pursued. The prospective healer's acceptance of the ancestor's communication and the commitment to work in alliance with that ancestor distinguishes his or her experience from that of others. The first vision presents to the healer a new way of being and behaving, a new way of viewing him or herself as one now capable of directing mana toward healing. The vision signals permission to hold a healing ceremony.

In affirming the healing value of the ancestors, the healer shows courage in overcoming a fear that many Fijians believe is "natural." This fear is supported by some urban ministers who say that seeking communication with the ancestors can lead to working with *tevoro* ("the devil") and the practice of witchcraft. The healer must continually disprove that supposition. By engaging in extended communication, the healer creates a relationship that makes healing possible, and by staying on the straight path, he or she counters the presumption of witchcraft.

The first vision lays the foundation of the healing work — the connection with the ancestor who will be the source of power and of the commitment to use that power for healing. It inspires the appearance of the path and sets in motion a process I call "envisioning." Envisioning helps healers to actualize the straight path which unfolds along the lines suggested by the first vision, filling in the details of healing techniques as one works. Envisioning is more than carrying out the intent of the first healing vision. It involves advice and instruction from a teacher, if there is one; subsequent visions; lessons learned from one's patients; and most of all the actual practice of healing and learning to live with that practice in one's community.

The first vision calls on the healer's emotional commitment to healing rather than presenting information about healing technology. The healer must affirm belief in mana without knowing how to conduct a healing ceremony and agree to begin the healing work, trusting that specific healing techniques will come as the work is done. The call is felt as a painful challenge, a necessary responsibility, since Fijians do not seek the healing power. One must try first to refuse the ancestor's request, acceding only when the ancestor insists. Feeling humble and unworthy of the responsibility of power, one also intuits the pain and difficulty that characterize the healing work, a life filled with temptations, tests, and others' suffering. Many, especially those not yet adults, do not take up the healing work immediately after their first vision. Weeks, months, even years may pass. The vision may be reconsidered, its consequences reevaluated. Another strong emotional experience often precipitates the practice, perhaps an unexplained request for healing from a sick person.

Only one phase in the career of the Fijian healer is universal, the first healing vision. The median age for first visions is forty; they commonly occur in mature adulthood, but can occur during adolescence or early adulthood. The first vision marks the entry onto the path, and the career of the healer consists of traveling on and development in that path. The life of the healer is an unfolding of the first vision, and an actualizing of the envisioning process. In traveling the path, the healer's power deepens as the ability to use and live with healing power matures.

A common metaphor of the straight path is a path cut by hand with a bushknife through heavy underbrush of the Fijian forests. In creating the path one must follow, dead ends and shortcuts, torturously difficult passages and relatively easy ones, cause the person's movement to fluctuate in rhythm and speed, sometimes circling back on itself. Western concepts of development, including clear directions, linear progress, and success defined by levels of attainment, do not apply here.

The straight path challenges character, which unfolds amidst confusing situations. Education of the healer deals with subtle movements back and forth along dimensions of character, at increasingly demanding levels. The movement itself releases increasingly potent healing power. But as one travels the path, living out the attributes of character becomes increasingly difficult. The healer is constantly tested — tempted, for example, to charge money for a healing ceremony, to become sexually involved with one's patients, and otherwise to betray the attributes that define the path. Increased power is determined by meeting severe tests.

As the healer accumulates power, he or she begins treating broader problems, such as hostilities between villages. Because the magnitude of power makes it more volatile, harder to control or direct, the healer becomes more vulnerable to practicing witchcraft. Many healers who are considered very powerful are also suspected of witchcraft. Tests of the healer then become even more important.

Popular but sometimes superficial criteria for judging the healer's movement along the path include: the response of clients, the number of clients one sees, the importance of these clients, and the degree to which one's cures are considered "miraculous." The increasing severity of the tests faced and resolved by healers also determines his or her movement. Accessibility of visions to the healer, their frequency, the number and power of the ancestors who visit, and the extent of direct communication between healer and ancestor indicate the healer's movement.

Those criteria that healers use to judge each other are most important, and include a total dedication to healing, expressed in the proper performance of the healing ceremony rather than in achieving specific cures. The healer's understanding, in contrast to knowledge, is most essential. Understanding is associated with the heart rather than exclusively with the mind, a broadly emotional rather than a narrowly cognitive way of knowing.

Of those healers who embark on the journey, not all continue on the straight path. Some give up working with yaqona entirely, as they find the path too demanding, and see themselves as unwilling or too weak to continue. This infrequent outcome typically occurs early in the career, perhaps during the first phase of tests. Others may continue practicing the healing ceremony, though it becomes an empty performance, since their commitment is a pretense. They can harm people by building false expectations, and they are particularly prone to attempt witchcraft.

Becoming a healer in Fiji does not bring economic rewards or increased social status. On a variety of economic and social indicators, healers are the same as nonhealers. However, they do differ in their response and relationship to mana.[20] For example, healers connect mana more frequently with healing than do nonhealers, respect it more, and consider it more powerful than do nonhealers. Healers also feel less surprised, afraid, and anxious when mana comes to them, since for them the experience of mana is more familiar. Fijian healers work hard and contribute fully as respected members of their community. They are given no special privileges in order to perform their healing, which in fact takes little time. Their distinctiveness remains a private affair, a motivation and set of beliefs that prepares them for their healing work, allowing them to work extensively with mana where others cannot.

Education as Transformation

In reflecting on the education of healers among the !Kung and the Fijians, certain principles common to both systems emerge. These principles can be said to describe a model that I call "education as transformation." The concept of transformation is alien to mainstream approaches to education and individual development in the West. But insofar as human illness and healing involve universal psychological processes, we must seriously consider the education of healers in these two cultures and ask whether their education includes essential characteristics absent from our approach.

Several general principles characterize the education of !Kung and Fijian healers, one of which is the healer's experiences of transformation. Becoming a healer depends on an initial transformation of consciousness, a new experience of reality in which the boundaries of self become more permeable to an intensified contact with a transpersonal or spiritual realm. At this juncture, prospective healers experience a sense of connectedness that joins a transpersonal or spiritual healing power, themselves, and their community. But gaining access to the healing power is not enough; healers must then learn to apply that power to healing within the community. This occurs through the process of envisioning, during which the experience of transformation is continually enacted and reaffirmed in the healers' daily lives. Envisioning occurs in the details of ordinary life as the healer's life is transformed from the inside by the healing practice. Thus transformation initiates the intensive phase of becoming a healer and also characterizes the healer's subsequent development.

In these transformations the emphasis is on the psychological process of transition rather than on the nature of barriers crossed or stages reached. Healers move continually between their fear of the transforming experience and their desire to heal others, their search for increased healing power and the difficulty of working with it. The emphasis on transition establishes flexible boundaries between career phases and psychological states.

A second principle is that the experience of transformation, which makes healing possible, does not remove healers from the context of daily living nor diminish their everyday responsibilities. !Kung and Fijian healers are as hardworking in ordinary subsistence activities as nonhealers, and they contribute fully to their communities. The service orientation of the healing work is a third principle. Though healers themselves must become engaged in a difficult educational process, they do so as their community's emissary. The healers' commitment is to serve as vehicles that channel healing to the community rather than to accumulate power for personal use. Healers struggle for a sense of connectedness joining self, community, and the spiritual domain and their commitment to community service guide the unfolding of their healing practice and lives. A fourth principle is that transformation sets in motion an inner development that is not manifested or rewarded by changes in external status. As one old Fijian healer said: "Being a healer is a silent thing."

A fifth principle is the emphasis on character as a critical context for healing and healing technology. It is qualities of heart — courage, commitment, belief, and intuitive understanding — that open the healers to the healing potential and keep them in the healing work. Healing technologies become available only to those with the necessary character. Technologies serve the healing aim, but they do not justify or measure the healing work. A final principle is that the education of healers stresses the proper performance of the healing ritual rather than discrete outcomes. The cure of a patient assumes importance only in the larger context of the community's healing ritual. Proper performance demands that the healer serve as a focal point of intensity, embodying an unswerving dedication to healing and reaffirming the community's self-healing capacity.

Though the term "transformation" has been used among Western psychologists and educators to describe both a process and an outcome, it generally connotes changes that remain within the intra- and interpersonal spheres of a person's life. Change limited to this personal level does not address transformations described by !Kung and Fijian healers, with the accompanying permeability of the self's boundaries to the transpersonal and the resulting restructuring of the sense of self.

Both theoretical and research literature in the West attempt to deal with these transpersonal changes, usually referring to them as "altered states of consciousness."[21] But the framework employed emphasizes these changes of consciousness as states generally divorced from the context of ongoing daily life. Thus the literature misses an essential ingredient of transformation, namely, how it initiates an envisioning process. A second line of consciousness research — commonly known as biofeedback — has examined changes in consciousness more grounded in daily life. These processes, however, are less encompassing than those which occur during transformation.

The core of the model — a radical change in consciousness that is an accepted part of the work and process of daily living — has largely remained a paradox in Western thinking. William James pointed this out when he described transformation as characteristic of "unusual" states, such as religious conversion and dissociative states.[22] The Outward Bound Schools and various recent transpersonal education approaches are examples of educational settings whose aim is transformation.[23] But owing to the brevity of these interventions and their discontinuity with the students' ongoing lives, they often have only short-term effects and so fail to achieve the transformation described in the two cultures.

Several Western theorists have sought to incorporate the idea of transformation into their view of individual development, thereby tying the experience of transformation into the context of daily life. But, again, they differ with the idea of transformation as presented in the model. Two such major theorists are Jung and Erikson.[24] The person who has achieved "wisdom," by Erikson's definition, may briefly contact spiritual realms, receiving some guidance. The person who is "individuated," in Jung's sense, may have longer or more frequent contacts, receiving more extensive guidance. !Kung and Fijian healers, however, have more pervasive contact with and guidance from the spiritual dimension, a contact that is more woven into the fabric of their daily life.

For Erikson and, to a lesser extent, Jung, spiritual factors play an important role in development only in the final stages of adult development. In fact, biological, psychological, and social dilemmas must be met and resolved before the spiritual dilemmas become a major influence in one's life. Similarly, Maslow delineates a "hierarchy of needs." He argues that what might be called spiritual needs become relevant only after a series of "earlier" and "more basic" needs have been met, such as needs for shelter, food, security, and love.[25]

By contrast, among the !Kung and Fijian healers, transformation itself initiates the healers' development. The transforming experience stimulates the solution of biological, social, and psychological dilemmas, whereas, for Erikson and Jung, transformation is more a result of a life's unfolding. Thus the model presents transformation as a life-changing process as well as a description of the unfolding of that changed life.

Fowler's work on "faith development" considers the influence of spiritual factors throughout development and approaches the idea of transformation.[26] But it is not until the final stage, Universalizing Faith, that he deals with a spiritual influence as direct and pervasive as that which occurs among !Kung and Fijian healers. In contrast to the transformation experienced by those healers, which keeps them within the culture's mainstream and close to its ideals, the transformation experienced by Fowler's Universalizers often brings them into conflict with their culture, as they are often seen as subversive. And unlike Fowler's stage of Universalizing Faith, which he describes as extremely rare, becoming a healer in Fiji or among the !Kung is neither uncommon nor at odds with the cultural ideology.

While the idea of transformation is part of some Western approaches to religious education, this idea differs greatly from the !Kungs' and Fijians' in cases where stress is placed on participation in organized religion rather than on changes in daily life. In the West, even when transformation is expressed in a religious approach, it is often outside the mainstream, where education is primarily secular, seeking to move beyond "religion" towards "science."

The idea of transformation is, however, central to a variety of other educational paths, whose influence on mainstream Western education has been practically nonexistent. Some of these approaches, like education as transformation, stress the education of the heart. Examples include the Lakota (Sioux) way of educating healers;[27] the Bhakti path in Hinduism;[28] the Christian devotional life;[29] the Mahayana-Buddhist way of compassion;[30] and the life of the *curandero*.[31] While stressing the way of the heart, education as transformation and these other educational paths, also include the way of the "head" and "hand." The classical Western distinction between thought, feelings, and beliefs is not important in those approaches.

Education of the Community Psychiatrist

The structure of Western societies, characterized by specialization and professionalization, prevents an exact comparison between Western healers and those of the !Kung or the Fijians, but the community psychiatrist offers a reasonable parallel. Community psychiatrists are health professionals in the West who assume medical, social, and psychological responsibilities; they are often called "priests of the new science" or "scientists of the new religion." Though my specific focus is on the community psychiatrist, the implications of education as transformation are relevant to community mental health workers in general. In spite of the fact that community psychiatry has relatively few workers in the community mental health field and comprises a small specialty within psychiatry, community psychiatrists are exemplary community health workers because their discipline shapes the education and practice of other mental health workers such as clinical psychologists and social workers. While there are factors common to all forms of healing, I will stress the role of transformation because I believe the lack of attention paid to this process in the community psychiatrists' education creates problems that interfere with their functioning effectively.[32]

The !Kung and Fijian healer and the community psychiatrist each expresses the dominant values of and respond to needs in his or her respective culture. Each is educated in a culturally appropriate way. In the West, medical school still dominates the education of the community psychiatrist. The psychiatric component of that education stresses a psychoanalytic orientation, as well as a biomedical approach. There is a practicum component, including a residency, usually in a community mental health center. Among medical and psychiatric peers, community psychiatrists are often the ones struggling most actively to respond to the needs of their communities.

In comparison to education as transformation, the education of community psychiatrists, however, does not emphasize a new experience of reality. The psychiatrist learns a new set of values and attitudes, a change that does not require the restructuring of self as experienced by !Kung and Fijian healers. Community psychiatrists learn a "scientific" approach to behavior and human problem solving which stresses their own mastery over a body of concepts and techniques that are the result of their colleagues' collected wisdom. Unlike their !Kung or Fijian counterparts, they do not draw upon transpersonal knowledge and are dependent on what they can conceptualize and control.

The education of community psychiatrists serves to separate them from responsibilities of everyday life in the community. As rare and valued specialists, they are protected and isolated. They literally are hard to reach. The highly differentiated and individualistic nature of Western society makes a sense of unity between self and community impossible. Rather than serving as community emissaries, community psychiatrists often act on the basis of professional commitments. They pursue individual careers, often at odds with what the !Kung and Fijians would see as their healing role. The development of empathy, a skill stressed in the psychiatrist's training, is necessary because of a preexisting gap between healer and client. In fact, the community psychiatrist is at times taught to treat the disease or problem, rather than the person, in order to maintain distance from the patient.

In sharp contrast to the !Kung and Fijian healers, the career growth experienced by the community psychiatrist is expressed by increased status. Achieving status is in fact a major contribution to this growth. Those seeking psychiatric help often judge competence on the basis of the psychiatrist's status, and little attention is given to erasing status differences between "doctor" and "patient." More than their !Kung or Fijian counterparts, psychiatrists are prey to expectations that may exceed their actual competence.

Community psychiatrists are expected to become individual repositories of healing. They are both respected and feared for their personal knowledge. Instead of being continuously available to serve the people, this knowledge serves different masters, including personal gratification. This is in marked contrast to the fact that healing power and knowledge is neither meant to be personally owned nor even controlled by the !Kung or Fijian healer.

Though some young people feel they have been called to medicine, the calling becomes less important, less of a guide to future action as their medical education progresses. Envisioning is a process that is absent from the education of most community psychiatrists, and largely unsupported for the few individuals for whom it plays a role. The profound, continuing influence of the Fijian first vision is rare.

At times, the education of the community psychiatrist has been described as a journey, but the journey is rarely a guiding metaphor. Compared to the !Kung and Fijian healers' careers, the psychiatrists' course follows a logical and linear progression, with clear markers of progress, such as grades, and discrete boundaries of transition, such as becoming a resident or staff psychiatrist. There is more emphasis on sociological transitions, such as career changes, than on the fluctuations in the healing knowledge or power that characterizes education as transformation. Regulating healing knowledge or power is not a focus in the education of psychiatrists. While transition states are of value in themselves in the transformation model, such periods are seen more as delays or sidetracks in the central business of career development for the community psychiatrist.

The "heart" is often seen as a hindrance in the community psychiatrist's education rather than as the foundation of knowledge. This is partly a consequence of a narrow Western definition of heart, which reduces it at times to an "antiscientific" emotionalism. Intellectual skills are stressed; emotions, courage, commitment, and belief are often dismissed as old-fashioned and sentimental. For !Kung and Fijian healers, technology follows in the wake of character. For the community psychiatrist, however, technical knowledge is the main ingredient of education, the measure of educational success, and the sign of competence. It is offered to students with few preconditions that they be prepared to use it properly by dint of character.

A recent movement in the medical community has begun to address some of the very principles proposed in the approach of education as transformation.[33] Internal medicine and community mental health, for example, have taken some important steps toward stressing the importance of caring in health delivery.[34] Even though the importance of education as transformation is beginning to be realized, it plays, at most, a minor role in the education of community psychiatrists.

To what extent are the central features of education as transformation culture-dependent, and embedded in specific demographic, economic, technological, and other sociocultural conditions? !Kung and Fijian societies both differ from the industrial West on all those dimensions.[35] The necessity of describing the !Kung and Fijian material in English can create an illusion of familiarity with these two cultures in the Western reader.[36] The degree to which particular aspects of education as transformation are embedded in the patterns of economic and social adaptation characteristic of !Kung and Fijian life remains an empirical question. While particulars may be culture-specific, there are some general aspects of education as transformation that seem applicable across cultures. Two important examples are the healers' relationship to a source of healing power beyond the self, and their service orientation to the community.

A Western equivalent of "envisioning" is essential, and the community psychiatrist is sorely in need of a community healing ritual. Compared to the

!Kung and Fijian healers, community psychiatrists are placed in a vulnerable position. They are personally expected to produce specific cures without any community support, a situation doomed to failure and sure to promote antagonism between healer and community. Education as transformation suggests ways to reconceptualize the issue of healing so that it entails mutual support between healer and community.[37]

Education as transformation respects both aspects of a dialectic that seem necessary to individual and community health.[38] It supports experiences ordered by the structures of daily life as well as those that occur in transition between and beyond those structures. Education as transformation gives added weight to the experience of transition itself, emphasizing the intrinsic value of the psychological movement that animates that transition. The experience of the transpersonal is intensified during these transitions but not restricted to them. Insights and power received during the transitions are activated only as they are applied within the structure of everyday life. Education as transformation emphasizes the intermingling and the continuum between everyday life and the transpersonal, eschewing any dualism.

Education of the community psychiatrist does not effectively maintain that dialectic. It emphasizes a definition of reality which is based more on structures than transitions, and is confined more to an existence within the person and his or her social environment than beyond the person. Community psychiatrists learn what their culture teaches, but what they learn is inadequate to their tasks. Educated to emphasize the personal accumulation of healing power, they are ill-prepared to meet the overriding need in community mental health for a wide distribution of healing resources and a pervasive collaboration between helper and community. They would be better trained to meet that need if their education stressed a broader definition of reality, which would allow for transformation and for a source of healing beyond the person.

The economic and political power that accompanies Western ways of education usually leads to their domination over an approach based on transformation.[39] If misunderstood, an approach based on education as transformation can encourage such attitudes as passivity and submission to the healer, which might impede access to resources in a modernizing context. But such attitudes are not intrinsic to the model, which stresses the collaborative and communal nature of healing. In fact, one could argue for the particular necessity of education as transformation in the industrialized context, not just for the community mental health worker but for all helpers and teachers charged with the responsibility for the maintenance and growth of their respective communities.

Rappaport suggests that rituals in which we experience a transpersonal bonding are essential for the survival of the human species.[40] He claims that only through participating in such rituals can we overcome our separateness as individuals and know the reality of the transpersonal which enables us to accomplish the communal tasks so essential to the survival of the human community. The present individualism and consequent fragmentation of these communal efforts in industrialized society is well documented.[41] By connecting healing power, healer, and community, education as transformation stresses transpersonal bonding. By describing the special contributions of healer education among the !Kung and the Fijian people, I hope to have demonstrated the value of this non-Western approach, which I believe offers a fundamental, perhaps necessary, resource for healing in and of the human community.

Notes

1. I did fieldwork among the !Kung in 1968 while a member of the Harvard Kalahari Research Group, and fieldwork in Fiji between 1976 and 1978 as part of a team effort with Mary Maxwell W. Katz.
2. Statements about the generalizability of this approach, education as transformation, await a more systematic cross-cultural survey. In combination, the !Kung and Fijian material already presents an interesting picture. Since !Kung social structure is ordered so that spiritual power will be used for healing which is available throughout the community, education of !Kung healers stresses access to that power. Since Fijian culture is not ordered in that way, education of Fijian healers stresses the proper application of the power to healing and the distribution of that healing to the community. Each culture still deals with both aspects of the education of healers: access to the power, and application of the power to healing.
3. See Gerald Caplan, *Principles of Preventive Psychiatry* (New York: Basic Books, 1964); and Julian Rappaport, *Community Psychology* (New York: Holt, Rinehart, & Winston, 1978).
4. This ethnographic summary of !Kung life draws on the work of Richard B. Lee and Irven DeVore, eds., *Man the Hunter* (Chicago: Aldine, 1968); Richard B. Lee and Irven DeVore, eds., *Kalahari Hunter-Gatherers* (Cambridge, Mass.: Harvard Univ. Press, 1976); Lorna Marshall, *The !Kung of Nyae Nyae* (Cambridge, Mass.: Harvard Univ. Press, 1976); and Richard B. Lee, *The !Kung San: Men, Women and Work in a Foraging Society* (Cambridge, Eng.: Cambridge Univ. Press, 1979).
5. Lee, p. 450.
6. Richard B. Lee, "The !Kung Bushmen of Botswana," in *Hunters and Gatherers Today*, ed. M. G. Bicchieri (New York: Holt, Rinehart, & Winston, 1972), p. 363.
7. Personal communication with Richard B. Lee, Dec. 1974.
8. See Lorna Marshall "The Medicine Dance of the !Kung Bushmen," *Africa*, 39 (1969), 347–381; Richard B. Lee, "The Sociology of !Kung Bushman Trance Performances," in *Trance and Possession States,* ed. Raymond Prince (Montreal: Bucke Memorial Society, 1966); also Richard Katz, "Education for Transcendence: !Kia-healing with the Kalahari !Kung," in Lee and DeVore, *Kalahari Hunter-gatherers;* and Richard Katz, *Boiling Energy: Community Healing Among the Kalahari !Kung* (Cambridge, Mass: Harvard Univ. Press, in press). Sections of this ethnographic description have appeared in or are based on material from Richard Katz, *Preludes to Growth* (New York: Free Press, 1973).
9. See Richard Katz, *Boiling Energy;* and Richard Katz and Megan Biesele, "Male and Female Approaches to Healing Among the !Kung," paper delivered at Second International Conference on Hunting and Gathering Societies, Quebec, Sept. 1980.
10. Personal communication with Richard B. Lee, Dec. 1974.
11. The T.A.T. and Draw-A-Person test findings were significant at the .05 level. Due to the small sample size and lack of longitudinal data it was not possible to pinpoint the

relative weight of these differences as criteria of selection for healing and/or effects of healing practice.
12. Valuable ethnographic material on Fiji is provided by Laura Thompson, *Southern Lau, Fiji: An Ethnography* (Honolulu: Bishop Museum, 1940); R. Nayacakalou, *Leadership in Fiji* (Oxford: Oxford Univ. Press, 1975); R. Nayacakalou, *Tradition and Change in the Fijian Island* (Ann Arbor: Univ. of Michigan Press, 1962); Asesela Ravuvu, "Fijian Religion," Unpublished Manuscript, University of the South Pacific, 1976; and Mary Maxwell W. Katz, "Gaining Sense at Age Two in the Outer Fiji Islands: A Cross-cultural Study of Cognitive Development," Diss. Harvard 1981. The Katz reference involves the same district dealt with in this paper: the Thompson and Sahlins references deal with other outer island communities. Dorothy Spencer, *Disease, Religion and Society in the Fiji Islands* (New York: Augustin, 1941) is the most recent work on healing and deals with a group of people on the main island of Fiji.
13. The concept of "mana" plays an important role in the study of religion and its origins. See Mircea Eliade, *Rites and Symbols of Initiation* (New York: Harper & Row, 1965); Emile Durkheim, *The Elementary Forms of Religious Life* (New York: Free Press, 1968); and Raymond Firth, "The Analysis of 'Mana': An Empirical Approach," *Journal of the Polynesian Society*, 40 (1940), 483–510.
14. Yaqona's botanical identification is *Piper methysticum*. It is widely used in the South Pacific, and is also called "kava-kava."
15. Because of confusion in anthropology about the usage of the terms "witchcraft" and "sorcery," I will use the Fijian definition of witchcraft, that is, an activity which involves a specific ceremony.
16. There are in fact a variety of traditional Fijian healers. The one we are considering is called a *dauvagunu*. In the rural area studied, twenty-two out of the twenty-three dauvagunu studied were men. This healer treats the broadest range of problems as well as those most severe. Each of these healers serves about three villages in the outer islands; kinship linkages guarantee the outer island Fijians access to a dauvagunu. One massage healer, often a woman, is found in every one or two villages and frequently two herbalists, usually women, are found in a village.
17. When the Fijian healers were compared with a sample of nonhealers matched on a series of demographic variables, healers were rated as more "respected," closer to the "ideal Fijian," and "harder working." Significance was at the .05 level.
18. Although healers use phrases and describe values that are similar to those of Christian belief, there are many aspects of their ideology that are not identical with Western church doctrine. Where there is an overlap in the two systems, it is impossible to know the origin. Since identifiable Western elements are at present thickly blended with others that do not seem of recent Western origin, and since traditional Fijian legends often exemplify these attributes, it is likely that the attributes were also part of the indigenous system before Christian influence.
19. Richard Katz, Field notes, 1976–78.
20. Reported differences which follow are significant at the .05 level.
21. See Charles Tart, ed., *Altered States of Consciousness: A Book of Readings* (New York: Wiley, 1969); and Tart, *States of Consciousness* (New York: Dutton, 1975).
22. William James, *The Varieties of Religious Experience* (New York: Mentor Books, 1958).
23. Richard Katz and David Kolb, "Challenge to Grow: The Outward Bound Approach," in *Opening the Schools: Alternative Ways of Knowing*, ed. Richard Saxe (Berkeley: McCutchan, 1972); Thomas Roberts, *Four Psychologies Applied to Education* (New York: Halsted, 1975); and Katz, *Preludes to Growth*.
24. Carl Jung, *Symbols of Transformation* (Princeton: Princeton Univ. Press, 1952); Jung, *Two Essays on Analytical Psychology* (Princeton: Princeton Univ. Press, 1972); and Erik Erikson, *Childhood and Society* (New York: Norton, 1964).

25. Abraham Maslow, *Motivation and Personality* (New York: Harper & Row, 1970).
26. Jim Fowler and Sam Keen, *Life Maps: Conversations on the Journey of Faith* (Waco, Tex.: Word Books, 1978).
27. John Fire/Lame Deer and Richard Erdoes, *Lame Deer, Seeker of Visions* (New York: Simon and Schuster, 1972) and John Niehardt, *Black Elk Speaks* (New York: Pocket Books, 1972).
28. Swami Muktananda, *In the Company of a Siddha* (Oakland, Calif.: Siddha Yoga Dham of America [SYDA], 1978).
29. Thomas Merton, *Seven Story Mountain* (New York: Harcourt Brace Jovanovich, 1978).
30. Choygam Trungpa, *Cutting Through Spiritual Materialism* (Boulder, Colo.: Shambala, 1973).
31. Douglas Sharon, *Wizard of the Four Winds* (New York: Free Press, 1978).
32. I base the description of the education of community psychiatrists on the writings of Howard S. Becker, Blanche Geer, Everett C. Hughes, and Anselm L. Strauss, *Boys in White: Student Culture in Medical School* (Chicago: Univ. of Chicago Press, 1963); Gerald Caplan, *Principles of Preventive Psychiatry* (New York: Basic Books, 1964); and Donald Light, *Becoming Psychiatrists* (New York: Norton, 1980), supplemented by observations I made while working for four years in a community mental health center and by reflections on my own training as a community psychologist. Other researchers have discussed factors they believe are common to all forms of healing, such as a rationale or myth which includes an explanation of the cause of the distress and a method of relieving it: see esp. Jerome D. Frank, "Therapeutic Factors in Psychotherapy," in *Psychotherapy 1971: An Aldine Annual*, ed. Joseph D. Matarazzo, Allen E. Bergin, Jerome D. Frank, Peter J. Lang, Isaac M. Marks, and Hans H. Strupp (New York: Aldine, 1971).
33. Howard S. Berlinger and J. Warren Salmon, "The Holistic Alternative to Scientific Medicine: History and Analysis," *International Journal of Health Services*, 10, No. 1 (1980), 133–147.
34. Personal communication with Andrew Billings, June 1980.
35. !Kung and Fijian societies also differ from each other in important ways we have not considered in this paper.
36. A number of studies compound this presumption of familiarity by casting traditional healers into the role of "prescientific" or "untrained" psychiatrists, minimizing their intrinsic validity, for example, Ari Kiev, ed., *Magic, Faith and Healing* (New York: Free Press, 1964); and Robert Edgerton, "A Traditional African Psychiatrist," in *Culture, Disease and Healing: Studies in Medical Anthropology*, ed. David Landy (New York: MacMillan, 1977).
37. Another way in which education as transformation can effect changes in the community mental health system is by supporting multiple healing paradigms. Research suggests not only that people in distress are able to utilize multiple and "conflicting" healing paradigms, but also that this is an effective strategy. See Richard Katz and Edward Rolde, "Community Alternatives to Psychotherapy," *Psychotherapy Theory: Research and Practice*, forthcoming. Rather than focus only on improving the education of the community psychiatrist, one could support, alongside the Western healing system, the development of healing systems that already use education as transformation in the training of their healers. Data on usage of multiple healing paradigms in Fiji suggest ways to increase the likelihood this usage strategy will provide better care: healers from each system recognize the different assumptions of each system and respect the work of each other; they should recognize the limitations and strengths of each system, especially their own; and they should be knowledgeable about making referrals between systems and willing to do so.
38. Victor Turner, *The Ritual Process* (New York: Aldine, 1969); Roy A. Rappaport, "Adaptation and the Structure of Ritual," in *Human Behavior and Adaptation*, ed. N. Blurton-Jones and Victor Reynolds (London: Taylor Francis, 1978).

39. Philip Singer, ed., *Traditional Healing: New Science or New Colonialism* (Buffalo: Conch Magazine, 1977).
40. Roy A. Rappaport, 1978.
41. Peter Berger, Brigitte Berger, and Hansfried Kellner, *The Homeless Mind: Modernization and Consciousness* (New York: Vintage Books, 1973).

I wish to thank the governments of Botswana and Fiji for granting permission to do the research and for their cooperation during the research period. I also want to thank Saiamone Vatu, who made the research in Fiji possible; Ifereimi Naivota, our research associate in Fiji; Ron Crocombe and Asesela Ravuvu, Institute of Pacific Studies, University of the South Pacific, who provided important support; and the many people I lived and worked with in the Kalahari and Fiji, who let me come to them as family and shared their knowledge.

I want to offer further thanks to Irven DeVore and Richard Lee, project directors of the Harvard Kalahari Research Group; and to Richard Lee, my guide and interpreter in the Kalahari. The !Kung research was supported by N.I.M.H. grant #MH 13611.

I appreciate the careful reading of this paper in various of its drafts and thoughtful comments by Marten DeVries, Alan Harwood, Robert Jonas, Mary Maxwell W. Katz, Linda Kilner, Bill Lamb, Mike Murphy, Shelaugh O'Rourke, Susan Pollack, Ed Rolde, Jane Wilner, Holly Zeeb, and the editors of the *Harvard Educational Review,* whose especially sensitive work must remain anonymous.

Finally, there is my debt to the !Kung and Fijian healers with whom I worked who wish to be known only to the community they serve. They taught me about education. This paper seeks to be theirs.

Serving the Purpose of Education

LEONA OKAKOK

Alaska! To many who have never been here, the mere mention of the word brings visions of a vast and barren land, a landscape shaped by the endlessly drifting snow, where the human quest for survival is thwarted at every turn by the malevolent forces of nature. Vast, yes. And though I would not dismiss perceptions of barrenness, cold, and a constant quest for survival, I want to put them in perspective.

When people read about northern Alaska — even excellent material — or come here for a short period of time, they form a perception of our land and people based on experiences having nothing to do with us. For instance, if you come from an area that is rich in varieties of landscape, the flat tundra of the high arctic — no matter how full of life — may seem barren to you. You will not see all the various signs of life that are obvious to longtime residents of the area. The same applies to the perception of cold. If your mind is focused on the seventy-degree temperatures back home, the spring here will seem cold to you — although it may be even warmer than usual to a seasoned resident.

Many non-Alaskans assume that everyone prefers warm weather. But, though warmth is certainly welcomed and appreciated during appropriate times of the year, for a hunting society in the North it is not the weather of choice during critical overland travel time into hunting areas. Our preference, then, depends more on necessity than sensation. Unusual warmth would concern an Alaskan hunter. An early thaw could severely jeopardize travel to his spring hunting sites, threatening his ability to provide food for his family for the coming year. Travel to hunting sites has to coincide with the migration of certain animals through these areas. If the rivers break up early, travel is hampered, at best, and life-threatening, at worst.

But Native people as well are not immune to applying old perceptions to new experience. My mother-in-law visited my husband and me in California while we were attending school there some years ago. Looking through the backyard window of our apartment, she remarked that someone "ought to cut down this tree back here. It just blocks an otherwise beautiful view." To her, a good view allowed one to see far away without obstruction. She did not realize that, in that part of the world, the tree was *a valued part of the view.*

Harvard Educational Review Vol. 59 No. 4 November 1989, 405–422

We all know that we can go through life convinced that our view of the world is the only valid one. If we are interested in new perceptions, however, we need to catch a glimpse of the world through other eyes. We need to be aware of our own thoughts, as well as the way life is viewed by other people. It is my hope that this article will show you a different way of looking at northern Alaska and at us, the Inupiat Eskimos who live here.[1]

Northern Alaska Inupiat Eskimos

The Arctic has been home to the Northern Alaska Inupiat Eskimos for thousands of years. Our history as a people is rich in tradition, passed on through the centuries, generation to generation, by storytellers widely known for their skillful art. These stories and legends both entertain and help us to better understand who we are.[2] Because of the high value we place on the ability to retell these stories and legends accurately, we can better ensure that Inupiat strengths and values are passed on to each succeeding generation.

Oral history and the art of storytelling, highly developed in a society which used it to pass on subsistence techniques and cultural values, is still practiced today, but the critical element in the process — the audience — has changed. Audiences which used to be composed of young and old listeners now usually include only the elders. Our accelerated entry into the twentieth century has brought much confusion. Besides the daily chores critical to life in the Arctic, new and varied concerns, including Western education and religion, vie for the time and interest of the child. Even if children are interested, rarely do they have time to sit quietly, to listen and learn from their elders. The purpose of these long storytelling sessions — that of passing down values and other important elements of our culture — is severely restricted. The elders' role as *the* teachers and resource regarding contemporary life is no longer a given. Now, excellence in the subsistence way of life does not ensure survival in our modern world. The cash economy, Western civilization, and Christianity — concepts which the elders could not teach when they were introduced — emerged as standards against which others judged our life.

Parents, recognizing the inevitable encroachment of the Western way of life upon Inupiat land and culture, reluctantly released their young into the hands of schoolteachers, who assured them that this was best for their child. We respected the judgment of these newcomers to the area — teachers and ministers — because they were authorities on the new way of life. They represented the efforts of the United States Bureau of Education, which, through a contractual arrangement with churches, was committed to providing an education to children within what was then the District of Alaska. We did not realize that their objective was to educate our children enough to reject their own culture and to embrace the "more civilized" Western way of life. With this purpose firmly in mind, Western education began for our young.

The Early Years

In order to show the disruption caused by the displacement of our own educational system, I will briefly sketch the early development of Western education in our area of Alaska, which began in 1889 when the first school was established in Barrow (it was administered by the Presbyterian Church through a contract with the Federal Bureau of Education). This early phase continued until the 1920s, causing changes that affected the whole community: Children were no longer learning the ways of our people at home, and families were severely restricted from taking their children along on extended hunting trips — the children's prime learning experience. Families often had to depend on relatives willing to allow children to remain with them in the village while their parents were on extended hunting leave. Although many elders now gratefully acknowledge their relatives' hospitality back then and recall being treated as children of the household, there was much left to be desired. Certainly there were exceptions, but frequently those who were given the chance to attend school had to continue their basic education — achieving the ability to survive in their world — long after others their age had achieved success as subsistence hunters. The effort to mainstream the Inupiat children into Western society failed.

The focus of education in the North shifted only after local control was initiated in the mid-1970s. No longer were we, as a people, to be forced to assimilate into Western society. Western education *would* serve its purpose, but it would be a purpose determined by our own people.

The District

Eben Hopson, the power behind the formation of the North Slope Borough, our Home Rule Government, said in a speech before the local School Board in December, 1975:

> Possibly the greatest significance of Home Rule is that it has enabled us to regain control of the education of our children.... We must now begin to assess whether or not our school system is truly becoming an Inupiat School system reflecting Inupiat educational philosophies, or are we, in fact, only theoretically exercising political control over the educational system that continues to transmit White urban culture. Political control over our schools must include professional control as well in our academic institutions if our academic institutions are to become an Inupiat School System able to transmit our Inupiat traditions, values and ideas.[3]

In his speech, Mr. Hopson also reiterated the basic purpose behind the formation of the North Slope Borough School District: stopping the assimilation process which had long been advocated by Bureau of Indian Affairs schools as the only way to "civilize" our people.

Steven Patkotok (r) teaches ivory carving to Vernon Rexford.

In assuming control over our educational system, which began after the establishment of the North Slope Borough School District in the mid-1970s, we, the people of the northern countries, have struggled with the problem of Western content and approaches to education in our schools. While seeking to produce students with scholastic achievements comparable to those of other areas of the United States, the board has also sought ways to bring into our schools certain elements of historical and contemporary Inupiat Eskimo culture and knowledge of our natural environment. We have found that the attainment of academic skills in our students is directly related to our ability to successfully introduce Inupiat Eskimo concepts and educational practices into our schools. This paper describes some of our actions in this area. After discussing some important differences between the Inupiat and Western concepts of education, I will describe some of the modifications to our school system and innovations that we have implemented with some success.

The North Slope Borough School District, established in 1972, is the northern-most school district in the United States and encompasses the northern third of Alaska, an area of approximately 88,000 square miles. The district serves nine schools in eight villages with over 1,500 students, a majority of whom are Inupiat Eskimo (Northern Alaska Eskimo). The largest of these villages is Barrow, the northernmost community in the United States. Ipalook Elementary School, the largest of the nine schools, is located here, with a school population of 580 children from ECE (Early Childhood Education) through grade six. (Barrow has a separate junior/senior high school.) The smallest of our schools is Cully School in Point Lay, Alaska, with a total pupil population of forty-six, ECE through twelfth grade. Most of the other schools fall somewhere in between Ipalook and Cully.

What draws these nine schools together is a common heritage, language, and the municipal government under which they were established. We decided that local control was the only way to ensure that our values as Inupiat people were reflected within the school system. Great strides have been made with the formation of the school district and the subsequent redefining of the purpose of education. We had to take a "foreign" system — the Western educational system — and strive to make it work for us. This has not happened without its share of problems, however. The differences between cultures and lifestyles were ignored for far too many years in the hope that what worked for the White population could be made to work for our Native people by mere persistence.

The Role of Local Culture in the Learning Process

We, the indigenous people of the United States, have had to overcome many obstacles in order to acquire basic education. One of the main obstacles was language. Not only were we required to learn to read, at the same time we also had to learn the language we were learning to read in. In the late 1930s and early 1940s, in order to help children learn English, teachers visited Inupiaq parents and instructed them to speak only English to their children. Most parents knew very little, if any, English, so they were effectively being told to sever communication with their children. Parents were willing to comply with this instruction, except that their great love for their children and the necessity to interact with them sustained Inupiaq in the household, thus keeping alive the foundation of our culture. But severe retardation of our native language did take place in time. Besides ordering that English be spoken at home, teachers punished children for speaking their mother tongue in the classroom. I remember clearly catching myself many times speaking in Inupiaq during my first few years in school and feeling guilty for doing so. I was rarely caught and, therefore, rarely punished, but others were not so lucky. Many times we'd hear the whack of the ruler either on the head or the palm of the hand of any student caught being "naughty" and speaking in our language.

But we spoke in our own language in order to survive. Imagine learning to say a word in a language you did not know, and having no earthly idea what that word represented. As hard as learning a foreign language was, however, it was easier than absorbing the content of Western education. The world view of the West, the perspective from which our schoolbooks were written, was totally different from ours. Therefore, understanding what we were learning to read in the English language came very hard. For example, as I was learning to read, one of my earliest realizations was that, in the Western world, grandparents and other relatives are not people you see or visit every day, even when they live nearby in the same town or city. A visit from them is an occasion, a cause for special preparations. This behavior was so foreign to my experience that it took me a long time to understand what I was reading and to realize that extended families are not the norm in the Western world.

In our communities, visiting relatives is a frequent, everyday occurrence, learned in early childhood. Unplanned, spontaneous visits (as opposed to purposeful visits) bond our relationships with relatives and friends. When visiting is unplanned, it does not require a formal invitation; tea or a soft drink is usually served unless it is near mealtime, when visitors will be expected to join in the meal. Other cultural practices, such as the special relationships between grandparents and grandchildren, reinforce these visiting patterns. A high degree of social interaction is the norm in our communities.[4]

During the years my husband and I attended the University of Alaska in Fairbanks, my father's first cousin, an elderly lady, lived right in town, an area where I frequently shopped. When I took my father there for a visit I was soundly scolded for visiting only when I had a purpose — in this instance, taking my father to see her. Although I was living in the same town, I had not nurtured my relationship with my aunt with intermittent, spontaneous visits.

In the western world privacy is considered such a basic right that I am afraid many find it hard to understand the value of spontaneous visits. It is equally hard for us to understand why anyone would want to have so much privacy that developing nurturing relationships becomes very difficult, if not impossible. This is an example of one area where two very diverse cultures have different but equally valid values; members of both cultures have to strive to acknowledge and to understand each other's differences.

Another example of the proliferation of Western concepts and Western "realities" contained within textbooks is the "fact" that the sun rises in the East and sets in the West. This is included in tests that evaluate the child's understanding of the world around him or her. In the Arctic, however, the sun behaves differently. Depending on the time of year, it can do almost anything, six examples of which are: 1) it doesn't rise at all; 2) it peeks through the horizon for a few minutes; 3) it rises in the South and sets in the South a few minutes later; 4) it rises in the East and sets in the West; 5) it rises in the North and sets in the North almost twenty-four hours later; *or* 6) it doesn't set at all. During the whole process of moving from the first instance to the last, so gradual is the sun's movement along the continuum that it is almost imperceptible. You will note that the Western world's "fact" about the sun rising in the East and setting in the West is only one of various northern Alaskan realities. Saying that the sun rises in the East and sets in the West up here would be like saying that a yo-yo with a two-foot string reaches twelve inches. Certainly it does, at some instant, reach the twelve-inch point, but there are infinite points along the string that it also reaches, including being fully wound and fully extended.

> ### My Life
> Baxter Adams, Grade 8
>
> When I was small I went to go camping with my family. When I was one years old I walked. When I was two I learned to talk. When I was three I had lots of fun. When I was four I went to Anchorage. When I was five I went to Seattle. When I was six I went to school. When I was seven I went to a circus. When I was eight I went to Fairbanks. When I was nine I got a first shotgun. When I was ten I got a bike. When I was eleven I got a duck. When I was twelve I got a goose. When I was thirteen my uncle caught a whale. When I was fourteen the crews went down to go whaling. That is my life.

Because the rising and setting of the sun rarely changes in the rest of the United States, it does seem a useful gauge in determining a child's learning. But for children in the far North, there are too many variables for "the" fact of where the sun rises and sets for it to be useful. For Western students, the direction of shadows or looking in the direction of the rising or setting sun are obvious clues to the time of day. But when these clues were presented in schoolbooks, I was always looking also for clues as to the time of year, which, I later realized, even if they were given, would not have helped at all. Although I am a puzzle fan, I was often understandably stumped by what I later learned was no puzzle at all to Western students.

Those of us who experienced these problems during our schooling realized that we had to find a better way to teach our children. We who work at the grassroots level of education — the local PTAs, advisory committees, and school boards — are in a unique position to observe schooling in action. We are often the first to know when something works and when it doesn't.

Contrasting Definitions of Education

To me, educating a child means equipping him or her with the capability to succeed in the world he or she will live in. In our Inupiat communities, this means learning not only academics, but also to travel, camp, and harvest wildlife resources in the surrounding land and sea environments. Students must learn about responsibilities to the extended family and elders, as well as about our community and regional governments, institutions, and corporations, and significant issues in the economic and social system.

"Education" and "schooling" have become quite interchangeable in everyday speech. When we talk of a person being educated we usually mean he or she has gone though a series of progressively higher formal systems of learning. Although a person may be an authority on a subject, we don't usually think of him or her as "educated" if he or she is self-taught. Since all of our traditional knowledge and expertise is of this latter type, the concept of "an educated person" has worked against us as a people, creating conflicting attitudes, and weakening older and proven instructional methods and objects of knowledge. Therefore, we, the North Slope Borough School District School Board, have defined "education" as a life-long process, and "schooling" as our specific responsibility. This is expressed in our Educational Philosophy statement:

> Education, a lifelong process, is the sum of learning acquired through interaction with one's environment, family, community members, schools and other institutions and agencies. Within the Home Rule Municipality of the North Slope Borough, "schooling" is the specific, mandated responsibility of the North Slope Borough School District Board of Education.
>
> The Board of Education is committed to providing academic excellence in the "schooling" environment. This commitment to academic excellence shall focus on the learner, recognizing that each student brings to the "schooling" environment his own interests, learning styles, cultural background and abilities.[5]

We decided that our role is to control the environment of the schooling process: the building, the equipment and materials, the quality of teaching and counseling services — everything about our schools — to ensure that education can take place in the classroom.

Remember that education is also the passing down of a society's values to children. Although I suppose there are people who would disagree, I think teachers pass down values by what they do in certain situations. Showing ap-

Poem
Timothy Oomituk, Grade 8

Me
Excited, Active
Visiting, Talking, Playing
Teachers, Friend, School,
Barrow
Working, Learning, Walking
Laughing, Big

Timothy

Larry Chrestman (l) and Timothy Oomituk (author of poem above) during individual work.

proval to a child for quickly attempting to answer a question — even wrongly — is valuing a quick answer to questions. At home, this same child may have been taught not to say anything until he or she has observed and observed and observed, and feels certain that his or her answer is correct. At home, the parents value accuracy more highly than a quick answer. They know that accuracy may mean the difference between life and death in the Arctic. In grade school, however, many of us learned that the teacher would "reward" us when we spoke up, whether we were right or wrong. Only by hearing our responses could she determine whether or not learning was taking place. If the answer was correct, she would have the opportunity to praise us. If a wrong answer was given, this gave her the opportunity to correct us.

Education is more than book learning, it is also value-learning. To address this issue, we, as a board, have incorporated a cultural component into our new-hire orientation. The bilingual department is an integral part of the orientation, highlighting differences in how our children learn. We hope that awareness lessens the frustration of teaching children who do not respond in ways teachers usually expect.

It is interesting that the root of the English word "educate" is very similar to our Inupiaq concept of education. According to Webster:

> It has often been said that *educate* means "to draw out" a person's talents as opposed to putting in knowledge or instructions. This is an interesting idea, but it is not quite true in terms of the etymology of the word. "Educate" comes from Latin *educare*, "to educate," which is derived from a specialized use of Latin *educere* (from *e-*, "out," and *ducere*, "to lead") meaning "to assist at the birth of a child."[6]

This old meaning of the English word "educate" is similar to our own Inupiat Eskimo word "iñuguq-"[7] — which literally means "to cause to become a person." It refers to someone who attends to the child in the formative years and helps him or her to become a person. In our Inupiat Eskimo society, the first few years of a child's life are a time when they are "becoming a person." Anyone who attends to the child during that time of his or her life is said to cause him or her to become a person, "iñuguġaa."

We Inupiat believe that a child starts becoming a person at a young age, even while he or she is still a baby. When a baby displays characteristics of individual behavior, such as a calm demeanor or a tendency to temper tantrums, we say "he or she is becoming a person." In our culture, such characteristics are recognized and accommodated from early childhood. As each child shows a proclivity toward a certain activity, it is quickly acknowledged and nurtured. As these children and adults in the community interact, bonds are established that help determine the teacher and the activities which will be made available to that particular child. As education progresses, excellence is pursued naturally.

Parents often stand back and let a child explore and experience things, observing the child's inclinations. If a child shows an aptitude for skills that the parents don't possess, they might arrange for their child to spend time with an expert, or an adult may ask to participate in the education of the child. Thus, many adults in the community have a role in the education of our children.

When you hear the word "educate," you may think more often of the primary Webster definition, which is "to provide with training or knowledge, especially via formal education." In the Western tradition, educating children depends heavily on a system of formal schooling with required attendance until a certain age.

Our concept of education has much in common with the Western concept of "child-rearing." It is interesting to us that Eskimo practices of child-rearing are commonly regarded as "permissive," in contrast to Western methods. Our perception is that Western child-rearing practices are overly directive and controlling, essentially interfering and intruding in the development of the child. The development of individuality is constrained and childhood is prolonged in Western society.

Though most of the education in our traditional society was not formal, it was serious business. For us, education meant equipping the child with the wherewithal to survive in our world. Because social interaction is a part of survival in the Arctic, this included education in proper social behavior, as well as in equipping the child with the means with which to make a living. As Robert F. Spencer wrote in his description of traditional North Alaskan Eskimo society: "The educative process . . . succeeded in a remarkable way [to produce] an individual capable of living in the cooperative situation demanded by the social and natural environment."[8]

In the traditional Inupiat Eskimo culture, education was everybody's business. It was okay to admonish, scold, or otherwise correct the behavior of any child, whether or not one was a relative. The success of the child's education depended in large part on how well his or her parents accepted admonishment of their child by other members of their own community. We as a people valued this acceptance highly because we knew that every member of our village was involved in some way with equipping our child for success.

Educating for Success

We need to equip our children for all the choices to be made upon graduation. In the North Slope Borough a majority of our students choose to remain in their villages after graduation. To provide an adequate education for each child, therefore, we need to teach Arctic survival skills, as well as the academic skills needed for success in the Western world.

As stated above, there were problems inherent in the displacement of our traditional educational system with the Western model, which have to be addressed if we hope to make schooling a success for our children. I will now discuss our innovations in several key areas.

Teacher-Student Ratio

Most survival education took the form of one-to-one learning. A "student" had many teachers, each teaching the child during different parts of the day or year. Young boys were taught hunting skills by their father, uncle, grandfather, or another skilled hunter. Young girls learned from their mother, grandmother, or sister all the various skills needed to run a household, feed the family, and keep them warm.

In the Western education model, on the other hand, groups of students are put in a classroom and taught many skills throughout the year by a single teacher. The one-to-one student-teacher relationship is absent, and the assumption is that a single teacher is proficient in *all* the skills to be taught to the whole group.

We have addressed this difference in two ways. First, a low student-teacher ratio helps us to better address the needs of individual students. Second, teacher aides hired from within the community provide critical role models for students, since an overwhelming majority of our classroom teachers still have to be brought in from outside our school district.

Although we can never hope to reach the traditional one-to-one ratio through Western classroom teaching, we can recognize the role of other "teachers" — parents, grandparents, community and church members — in

Reading Hour in Barrow, Alaska. Martha Hopson (r) reads to (counterclockwise) Salomi Ahgeak, Mandy Olemaun, and Asisaun Panigeo.

the child's life and work with them toward the child's successful learning. We also need to recognize that the hours children spend away from the classroom are as much a part of their education as classroom time. This means teaching them how to use any situation as a learning experience. Excellent teachers recognize and teach this already. These are points we need to keep in mind, as a school board, when planning our educational program.

Skills Taught

The traditional education of the Inupiat people focused not merely on survival but on excellence. Although all children were expected to master the basics of subsistence living, the inclinations exhibited by each child were noted and nurtured. All specialties were needed in order for the culture to survive. A storyteller and a philosopher were as integral to the community as a good provider or an excellent seamstress. Once an Inupiat Eskimo child shows an inclination, such as an interest in archery, storytelling, or sewing, that interest is nurtured by all concerned with his "education." He or she may be apprenticed to a relative or another member of the community who is an expert in that field. Certain other areas of education may be deemphasized so that the child may develop his or her talent.

Some years ago, at a gathering of elders for a regional Elders' Conference, Otis Ahkivgak recalled how he developed his hunting skills to the exclusion of learning other things considered equally important:

> You see, when they would have the "nalukataq" [blanket toss] festival I would never pay much attention. I would push along a sled by its stanchions and go hunting down there. That is the reason I don't know the great songs of the "nalukataq" feasts. . . . Although I listened from where the airport is now, when they were singing long and loud I was occupying myself delightfully with the snipes. Although I can try singing them by following my recollection of their singing, I do not know them very well.[9]

Once Western education models were introduced into our culture, the nurturing of individual interests virtually stopped. No matter what the unique interests of the child, all were taught the same subjects, at the same pace, in the classroom.

Although we can no longer deemphasize other subjects a child needs to learn, we can recognize the talent within and use that interest to help the child succeed in other areas. This requires talent and creativity on the part of the teacher. We have excellent, creative teachers, but in order to fully utilize this talent we need to identify policies or regulations that restrict the exercise of their creativity and search for alternatives that fully support teachers.

Another way of attending to the quality of skills taught to the children is through building partnerships within the community. For many years now, departments with the North Slope Borough, such as the Planning, Public Safety, and Health and Social Services departments, have willingly sent employees to classrooms to give talks to students on subjects ranging from secretarial work, to surveying, to management. The children need to see how their studies are applicable to real life: how the command of English is important in secretarial work; the use of calculus in surveying; the role of logic, mathematics, and social skills in management decisions.

Parent Involvement

Another challenge is parent involvement. In our traditional society, once a "teacher" is identified, parents do not interfere. Although they, themselves, may not be experts in whatever is being taught, they have complete faith that the "teacher" will do whatever needs to be done to equip the child with the skills to succeed in our world.

Since Western education was introduced in the Arctic, Western teachers were given the same courtesy previously extended to Native "teachers": they were left to do with the child what they needed to do to educate him or her. After all, the teachers were the experts in the areas being taught, something that they, the parents, knew nothing about. Then, as today, this was often misinterpreted by educators to mean that parents did not care about their child's education, when, in fact, they were doing what they felt was in the best interest of the child.

Parent involvement, or rather the lack of it, is often touted as the problem of educating Native youngsters. What we, as people interested in Native education, need to do, now that we are fully immersed in Western education, is to assure parents that this particular type of education needs parent involvement in order for the child to succeed. Parents will become more involved only when they learn that their knowledge, regardless of the extent of their schooling, is valued and plays an important part in their child's education. Teachers need to reach out to individual parents and to the community. Because school was not a positive experience for some of those who are now parents, going to the school, even for parent-teacher conferences, is often intimidating. We hope that through positive interactions these parents can eventually become not only involved but keenly interested in other aspects of education.

Parent involvement is an important element in another specific area of education in the North: that of passing down the language of our people. As is the case with indigenous languages anywhere in the world, our children are our only hope for the survival of our language. Our cultures, as peoples indigenous to the United States, are unique and to be found nowhere else in the world. Once our languages disappear, we have nowhere else in the world to turn to revive them. Yet there has not been much support for the language preservation programs which Native Americans have been trying to administer. We must make certain that indigenous languages within North America are not allowed to die, and we must employ every humanitarian effort it takes to do so.[10]

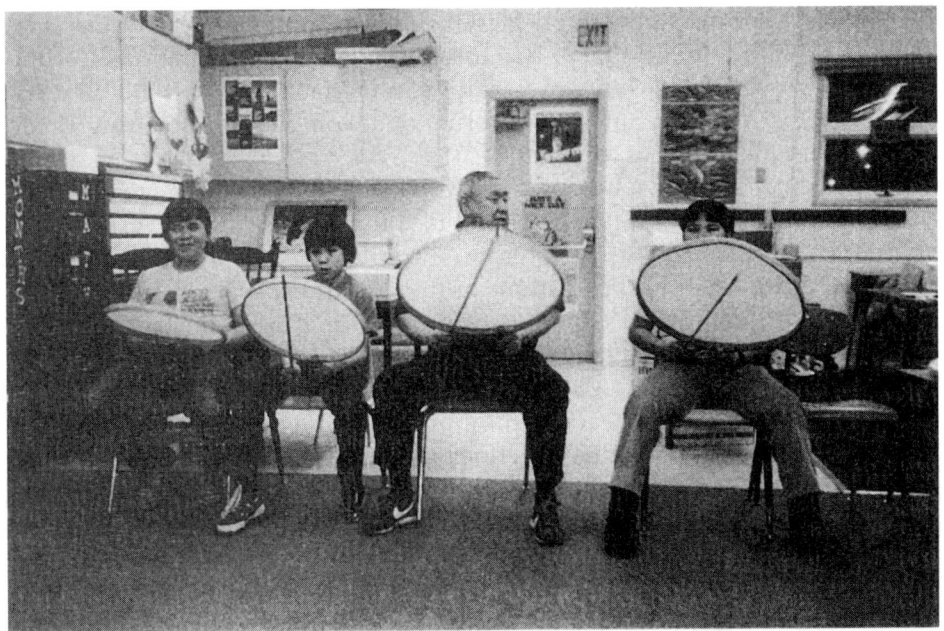

(L to r) Bradford Nageak, Kunneak Nageak, Larry Kaleak (teacher), and Timothy Akpik practice Eskimo drums.

Cultural Identity

Some of our greatest successes in the schooling process can be attributed to the fact that we take advantage of both the historical and contemporary culture of an area. For example, we invite elders into the classroom to tell stories and teach cultural activities (songs, dances, sewing), because in our society respect for elders is a value taught very early in life, and the classroom has become the place where so much of the child's education transpires. Every year, in the North Slope Borough School District schools, elders go to the schools to teach Eskimo dancing. This is one of the most positive and well-attended programs of the whole year. Eskimo dancing is incorporated into the annual Christmas programs at the schools, along with the usual Christmas songs. The children are very enthusiastic about learning and performing these Native dances.

Inupiat people have a long tradition of competitive athletic events, which are integral components of gatherings, celebrations, and trade fairs involving many groups from different parts of the Arctic. These unique sports events, which involve skills of agility, strength, and endurance, are fundamental to work and survival in the Arctic environment. In addition to developing skills, sporting events are used to provide lessons about discipline, patience, good humor, cooperation, and sharing: "A different kind of kid gets involved in the Native games than gets involved in basketball or wrestling. It's something Native kids can excel in, receive self-esteem from, that they get in no other way."[11] In the spring, Native high school children from throughout the state compete in Native Youth Olympics. Top finishers receive invitations to compete in the World Eskimo Indian Olympics in Fairbanks later in the summer, and the Arctic Winter Games, an international competition involving Canadian athletes, held every two years.[12]

In 1984, the North Slope Borough School District Board, recognizing that contemporary Inupiat culture now includes formal institutions, established Student Corporations. This is in response to the rapid growth of public and private institutions and organizations in the last fifteen years.[13] Among these institutions are specialized Native corporations that were mandated in the settlement of Native land claims by an act of Congress (Alaska Native Claims Settlement Act of 1971). Corporations are as much a part of everyday life in Arctic communities as subsistence hunting and fishing. Every child, in order to become capable of making life choices, needs to learn the basics of both realms. We, as a board, recognized that Native village and regional corporations needed employees and board members who are knowledgeable in all areas of corporate management. Thus, Student Corporations, established under the Laws of the State of Alaska, were incorporated into our schools. Children learn about how corporations are established, how proxies operate, and how elections and meetings are held. They also learn to evaluate moneymaking projects and, in the process, hone their decisionmaking skills.

These types of activities within the educational arena serve another, more basic, purpose. After decades of assimilation programs within the educational system that treated local cultures as detriments to the child's education, programs now teach that the culture of the area is *not* a detriment, but is indeed a valuable tool in the schooling of our children.

Bilingual Education

When bilingual education became a reality in the North, many parents and grandparents were very puzzled — and rightly so — by the about-face in the attitude of school staff in regard to speaking Inupiat. Suddenly children were not only allowed to speak Inupiaq in school but actively encouraged to do so. For many, however, this came too late. Parents who had been punished for speaking their native language in schools were raising their children using only the English language to communicate with them. Inupiaq in the home was being replaced by a broken Inupiaq, the English language interspersed with bits and pieces of Inupiaq. During this time, even bilingual education seemed a contradiction in terms to parents who had been persuaded that Native languages inhibit education.

It has sometimes been painfully hard work on the part of the local bilingual department and others interested in the survival of our language and culture to convince parents and the whole community about the need for language revival. But the efforts are paying off. Our district uses a very effective method, the Total Physical Response (TPR) method, of teaching our language to the children. The TPR method involves the whole learner, not just his or her mind. For instance, the teacher walks as he or she is teaching the world "walk," or portrays the emotions when teaching the words for these emotions. Each new word or sentence we hear a child use tugs at the heart, right in there where we hold memories of the times when we had almost . . . almost . . . lost one of the very abilities that make us uniquely who we are.

Addressing Issues

When we talk about educating our children for success we need to examine every facet of schooling to see if it is serving its purpose. Sometimes this requires making some hard decisions. A few years ago we, as a board, reevaluated our philosophy, goals, and policies to make them compatible. After careful research and deliberation we took a bold step. We changed from an individualized learning system to competency-based education. As hard as this decision was, we needed to address the issue of graduates who could not read or write, much less make life choices. We saw that our students were advanced to higher grades not on the basis of skills achieved, but through a process of "social advancement": students were advanced to the next grade even if their skills were not adequate. As a school board, we identified this practice with the way individualized instruction was interpreted and carried out within our district.

Individualized instruction, though very successful in other areas, was never satisfactorily demonstrated within the North Slope. For instance, in some high school classes students were given a book at the beginning of the semester and expected to go as far as possible with it at their own pace. There were no objectives given. The students were only told to read and to do what the text requested they do, with the teacher there as a resource if needed. This was explained to one parent as being individualized instruction. It is instances such as this which alerted us, the Board, to problems within our system which

---

The Dollar Bill

Naomi Ann Itta, Grade 7

Last year, in 6th grade, Mrs. Albert gave all the graduating seniors a dollar bill along with a card.

The dollar bill that I received is very special to me because I liked Mrs. Albert like she was an aunt.

The same day we received the dollar bill, I thanked her by giving her a picture of myself.

At the end of the year I knew that Mrs. Albert was proud of us, not because of the dollar bill, but because of the smile that shined on us like the sun over the ocean.

needed to be addressed, such as teacher accountability. Recently we instituted a competency-based approach to student advancement because we felt that it was more congruent with our traditional educational practices. In the competency-based approach, skills expected to be mastered by students in a certain grade are identified. The students, then, must demonstrate mastery of competencies before they are promoted to the next grade. This approach is similar to our traditional practices in which elders expected children to master certain competencies before they went on to more difficult tasks.

When the Western economic system became a viable way of life in the North, right along with subsistence, we, as Native people, should have felt an ownership of the educational system that taught our children how to survive in our contemporary world, a world which needs people with academic capabilities. But because it is a western educational system, we, as parents and local populace, have found it hard to identify with. We tend to view it still as a foreign system that was thrust on us. The move to mastery learning, a type of education which we identify with, has helped us attain ownership of the educational system in our schools. Since we, as a board, have determined that our children cannot survive in our world without also learning the basics of the Western way of life, we have chosen to teach them that way of life, but in the way that has proven to work in educating generation after generation of our children — through mastery learning.

Although competency-based education was widely supported by the parents because of identification with their own teaching style, others had to be convinced that it was in the best interest of our children. The school district, in order to ensure the success of the program, conducted many in-service programs with teachers and parent groups across our district on the elements of competency-based education, including how content is taught, how learning is assessed, long-range plans for curriculum and instruction, identification of competencies in texts and other instructional material, and lesson design. Now in its third year, it has already proven to be a success. We find that our youngest children are ready for advancement because competencies are identified at the beginning of the year, and the teachers know what the child needs to master in order to advance to the next grade.

With changes in our school system in past years happening so often, we also have had to deal with the fact that our educational system was a mishmash of new ideas which, although these were excellent concepts, were never quite synthesized into a coherent unit or system. What happened was that a group of students were taught using one system for a few years, and then were taught using another system. Because of this lack of continuity we have students in the upper grades who need extra help.

We are currently focusing on providing the very best atmosphere for learning for all children, and doing all we can to remedy the problems some of the older children have because of the deficiencies of earlier systems and the lack of continuity. One of the best ways we have found to address this problem is through enhanced guidance and counseling services. Besides providing counselors in each school site, we also provide a district-wide counselor who travels routinely to all schools, providing individual as well as group counseling. She is also available to travel to villages to help in crisis situations as needed. This coming year we are expanding services to give children better access to guidance and counseling, which may help them deal with difficulties for which they may not be well enough equipped.

Conclusion

In order to provide the best possible education for our children, we need first to identify the desired "product" of our schooling system and then to provide a system through which to acquire that product.

We, as a board, already know that we want young adults capable of becoming productive, happy citizens in whatever world they choose. We then need to make certain that all aspects of the schooling system, especially the environment, are conducive to the achievement of that goal. Above all, we must make certain that cultural differences in the way we view the goals and objectives of programs are addressed. The way different cultures choose to achieve the same goals and objectives varies greatly. We need to take as much care in choosing the system as we do in defining our goals.

We now have an excellent and effective school system in place, based on research that calls for specifying the school mission, educational expectations, curriculum and instruction, and monitoring time on task, student progress, and home-school relations. Profiles of these characteristics have been done on all of our schools in the District. Therefore, we are not as quick to turn to every current trend in education. We are not, however, hesitant to research new ideas. But we take extra effort to make certain the new ideas are compatible with our philosophy. In this way we assure our children the best education we can give them, as well as provide needed stability in programs and goals. Thus, we can ensure that we are, indeed, serving the purpose of education.

Notes

1. "Inupiat" is the plural form of the name we call ourselves, the singular being "Inupiaq." "Inuk," the stem, means "a person." The ending "-piaq" means "real," "most common," or "the most prevalent type." Although the plural form is commonly translated as "the real people," a more accurate translation would be "the most common type of people," or "the people we are most familiar with."

    Although either the singular or plural form can stand alone, sometimes — for more clarity — additional nouns are used:

    If you are talking about one person, you use "Inupiaq" ("An Inupiaq [person] came to see me.")

    If you are talking about a people, you use "Inupiat" ("The Inupiat [people] love to sing.")

When the word is coupled with "Eskimo," which is an easily understood (though non-Inupiaq) word, convention has it take the plural form. Thus we have such sentences as: "She is a fluent Inupiat Eskimo speaker," or "She is a fluent Inupiaq speaker." Both are correct.

The word "Eskimo" is a common term for the circumpolar peoples, who include the Inupiat as well as other groups. We prefer "Inuit" to "Eskimo," but it is less easily recognized by non-Inuit. If we tried to uncomplicate this for the sake of non-Inupiaq speakers, the sentence would begin to lose meaning for Inupiaq-speaking readers. We ask English readers to bear with what seems to be inconsistencies. We are trying, as with everything else, to use a foreign system (English) to get across some Inupiaq concepts and have it make sense to both groups.

2. For more information on passing down values through traditional stories and legends, see Edna MacLean's keynote speech given at the Alaska Bilingual/Bicultural Conference in 1987, available through the State of Alaska Department of Education and Early Development, 801 West 10th Street, Juneau, AK 99801-1878.
3. Eben Hopson speech, December 1975. On file at the Inupiat History, Language and Culture Division of the Planning Department, North Slope Borough, P.O. Box 69, Barrow, AK 99723.
4. For more information on Inupiat extended family relationships, see Rosita Worl and Charles W. Smythe, *Barrow: A Decade of Modernization* (Anchorage: U.S. Department of the Interior, Minerals Management Service, Alaska OCS Region, Socioeconomic Studies Program Technical Report No. 125, 1986); Robert F. Spencer, *The Northern Alaskan Eskimo*, Smithsonian Institution, Bureau of American Ethnology Bulletin 171 (Washington, DC: U.S. Government Printing Office, 1959); or Ernest S. Burch Jr., *Eskimo Kinsmen: Changing Family Relationships in Northwest Alaska*, American Ethnological Society Monograph No. 59 (St. Paul: West, 1875).
5. North Slope Borough School District Policy Manual, Policy AD (Educational Philosophy), Adopted 10/13/76, Revised 8/11/87.
6. *Webster's II New Riverside University Dictionary* (Boston: Houghton Mifflin, 1984), p. 418.
7. Inupiaq words followed by a hyphen are stems that need at least an ending to make sense. For those interested in more information about the structure of the language, please see the introduction to *Iñupiallu Tan illu Uqalu isa Ila ich, Abridged Iñupiaq and English Dictionary*, compiled by Adna Ahgeak MacLean (Fairbanks: University of Alaska, 1980).
8. *The Northern Alaskan Eskimo*, p. 239.
9. Kisautaq (Leona Okakok's Eskimo name), *Puiguikaat (Things You Should Never Forget), Proceedings of the 1978 Elders Conference*, North Slope Borough, 1981, p. 367.
10. For more information on efforts to preserve Alaska Native Languages, contact the Alaska Native Language Center, University of Alaska Fairbanks, Box 757680, Fairbanks, AK 99775.
11. Statement by Reggie Joule, in *Heartbeat: World Eskimo Indian Olympics*, Annabel Lund, writer; Howard Simons, editor; Mark Kelly, photographer; and Clark Mischler, photo editor (Juneau: Fairweather Press, 1986).
12. For more information on these sports, see *Heartbeat*; F. H. Eger, *Eskimo Inuit Games* (Vancouver: X-Press, n.d.).
13. For a description of the recent formation of a profusion of governmental institutions, corporations, boards, and commissions, in our areas, see Worl and Smythe, *Barrow: A Decade of Modernization*.

"Not Bread Alone":
Clandestine Schooling and Resistance in the Warsaw Ghetto during the Holocaust

SUSAN M. KARDOS

Throughout the most trying times in their history — dispersions, forced conversions, state-sponsored massacres, exclusion, discrimination, and mass migration — the Jews have maintained their commitment to education and organized schooling.[1] But no time was more desperate for the Jews than the years of the Holocaust in World War II Europe, and no attempts to sustain education and organized schooling were more poignant than those that occurred secretly and at great peril in the Warsaw Ghetto.

Central questions about the role of education emerge from the stories of the clandestine schools, which were maintained at a time when life for the Jews was shadowed by death and despair: Why have schools? What is schooling for? Should schools prepare students for the future, provide for the present, or preserve the past? For whom should schools be organized — for individuals, for communities, or even for whole cultures? These questions are important to ask — in the United States and around the world — as critics challenge the importance of schooling and wonder about the purpose or relevance of schools as they currently exist. Historians, critical theorists, economists, psychologists, and social scientists have written extensively about the implicit and explicit purposes of schools, highlighting shifting objectives within particular historical or social contexts.[2] One set of answers to the questions posed above can be found in the story of the underground schools in the Warsaw Ghetto. It is a story not only of organized schooling, but also of resistance. It is a story of how schools can be used for individual survival, community continuity, and cultural endurance.

This article examines how the Jews of the Warsaw Ghetto used clandestine schooling to resist Nazi intentions to erase them from the world — not only to eradicate them person by person and community by community, but also to eradicate their entire culture — indeed, their entire history. I first describe the multiple forms of clandestine schooling within the underground network and explain how the schools originated, and then discuss the diversity of schools run by house committees, soup kitchens, orphanages, youth movements, religious groups, and private citizens. I analyze the multiple purposes these schools served, arguing, first, that organized schooling can be characterized as a present-oriented form of resistance, which aided the Warsaw Ghetto Jews in their daily struggles against hunger, chaos, and inhumanity. Organized schooling also served as a future-oriented form of resistance by providing a sense of hope in otherwise desperate and uncertain conditions. Finally, I argue that, for the Jews of the Warsaw Ghetto, clandestine schooling was a form of resistance that was at once past, present, and future oriented. Using examples of curricular content and the activities of the Jewish youth movements in the Ghetto, I maintain that, through the collective action of organized clandestine learning, the Warsaw Ghetto Jews were able to defy the objectives of their oppressors and resist historical and cultural annihilation.[3]

The Warsaw Ghetto

The bomb craters that pockmarked the Polish landscape in September 1939 gave testimony to the three-week *Blitzkrieg*, or lightning war, that befell the country when the Germans attacked. The Nazis immediately issued anti-Jewish decrees and, within a year, walled in a 100-square-block area of the city to form the Warsaw Ghetto. The equivalent of one-third of Warsaw's population, between 400,000 and 500,000 Jews,[4] was squeezed into 2.4 percent of the total area of the city.[5] The original purpose of the Ghetto was to seal off the Jews completely from Poland's economic and cultural life.[6] Initially, although the Jews were fired from all public service jobs, prohibited from being hired by companies owned by non-Jews, and barred from social places such as libraries, theaters, and railroads, they were still permitted to enter and exit the Ghetto. However, on November 15, 1940, all twenty-two entrances to the Ghetto were sealed, and Jews were no longer permitted to leave.[7] In his diary entry for this date, Adam Czerniakow, leader of the *Judenrat* (the Jewish Council governing the Ghetto), wrote, "I was ordered to have 10 of our militiamen posted at each of the street exits from the ghetto by 7 A.M. tomorrow. . . . [Members of the Jewish leadership council] are to block with barbed wire a number of streets which have not been walled up."[8] Two days later he wrote in his characteristically concise style, "November 17, 1940 — Sunday. At the boundaries of the ghetto the *Ordnungspolizei* [German order police]. Throngs of Jews pass by with bared heads."[9] Thus the purpose of the Ghetto shifted. While it was initially intended to humiliate and separate the Jews completely from the rest of the city's population, it now became a means by which to suffocate them, as food was scarce and disease was rampant.

Tens of thousands died of starvation and typhus. In 1941, 43,000 Jews died in the Ghetto; more than 27,000 perished in the first half of 1942, preceding the first mass deportation.[10] For the rest the Ghetto served as a waiting area for those who were later transported to the Treblinka death camp. Although it seems the death rate would have decimated the Ghetto population, the constant influx of Jewish refugees from other provinces kept it crowded. On January 20, 1942, high-ranking Nazi officials met at the Wannsee Conference in Berlin, where they decided to implement the "final solution of the Jewish question" — the extermination of all European Jewry.[11] This decision had immediate consequences for the remaining Ghetto inhabitants; mass deportation to Treblinka began on July 22, 1942. Like much of Nazi-occupied Europe, the Ghetto was rapidly and systematically transformed as part of the grander Nazi objective of the total eradication of Jewish culture and history from the world.[12]

There was nevertheless a sense among the Jews in the Ghetto, at least before they knew of the death camps, that they were glad to be sequestered, "sheltered from harm's way,"[13] and under the direct rule of a Jewish Council rather than the Nazis.[14] Despite the harsh and restrictive decrees issued against the Jews, the random violence and humiliation perpetrated against them, the desperate living conditions, the corruption of the Ghetto police, and the harsh criticism of the Judenrat, the Warsaw Ghetto was the site of an "extraordinary and intense intellectual life."[15] Clandestine religious groups, schools, reading circles, lectures, dramatic programs, and orchestras thrived in the Ghetto.[16] The underground press was strong and integral, particularly the several dozen illegal youth publications that analyzed political issues, outlined educational tasks, urged passive resistance to the Nazis, and laid the foundation for what was to become an armed uprising.[17] The Bundist youth publication *Yugnt Shtime* (*Voice of Youth*) declared:[18]

> The very expression of apathy indicates submission to the enemy, which can cause our collapse morally and root out of our heads our hatred for the invader. It can destroy within us the will to fight; it can undermine our resolution . . . and because our position is so bitterly desperate, our will to give up our lives for a purpose more sublime than our daily existence must be reinforced. . . . Our young people must walk with heads erect.[19]

The youth groups in the Ghetto were responsible for many social, cultural, and political activities and were largely responsible for leading the highly organized and heroic armed Warsaw Ghetto Uprising, which began on April 19, 1943. The Nazis had originally planned to liquidate the Ghetto in three days; however, the Ghetto fighters — mostly from the ranks of the youth groups — defended the Ghetto for five weeks.[20]

. . . Not Bread Alone

While the last and most dramatic story of the Warsaw Ghetto is the uprising, many other forms of resistance were taking place in the Ghetto before the armed revolt. One of the most important arenas of individual and collective resistance was the clandestine school network. When one considers the harsh living conditions of the Ghetto's inhabitants, particularly the children, one wonders why, though expressly prohibited, organized schooling happened nonetheless. In the face of such despair, why did teachers consent to teach and students to learn? An anonymous essayist writing in the Warsaw Ghetto posed a series of similar questions: "Why should one study at all, when uncertain of the day and the moment, with no prospect of to-morrow, not knowing where one shall be, whether one shall eat and what? — How can one, in these circumstances, think of educating children?" This essay, one of many found after the war,[21] sought to answer the question, "What propels youth to schools and learning and bids parents to squeeze out the last penny in order to provide their children with some education, *not bread alone* [author's emphasis]?"[22]

The Jews of the Warsaw Ghetto faced multiple struggles. There was the personal daily struggle against hunger, disease, poverty, overcrowding, and the possibility of deportation, which was intensified by the struggle to maintain a sense of dignity, normalcy, and hope in the face of brutal inhumanity. Then there was the community's struggle to stay organized and cohesive and to maintain social services, political organization, religious life, and governance within the Ghetto walls. Finally there was the broader struggle against historical and cultural eradication and, ultimately, against complete, collective annihilation.

That the Jews of the Warsaw Ghetto enthusiastically organized a variety of forums in which teachers could teach and students could learn illustrates how teaching and learning can be individually and collectively liberatory. Even in the darkest circumstances, teaching and learning can provide participants with the possibility of social and self-determination by transcending the moment and serving as the lifeline between hopelessness and hope.[23]

CLANDESTINE SCHOOLS IN THE WARSAW GHETTO: MULTIPLE FORMS, MULTIPLE ORGANIZING GROUPS

Most schooling for Jewish children ceased when the Nazis bombed Warsaw in September 1939, destroying school facilities. Although the Nazis prohibited schooling for Jews, some schools stayed active for a few months until the last building at 55 Okopowa Street was taken over by the Nazis.[24] From the beginning of the occupation, the Judenrat continually pressed the German authorities for permission to reopen schools. As early as November 1939, then again in December, and once more in May 1940, Adam Czerniakow wrote in his diary about the need for schools. With the exception of some official vocational courses, the requests of the Jewish leadership proved fruitless, and on October 11, 1940, Czerniakow wrote, "There have been rumors that, because of fear of epidemic, Jewish schools will remain closed."[25]

Despite the fact that teaching and learning were perilous acts for Jews in occupied Poland, they persisted. Mary Berg was a teenager from Lodz who

Poetry class in the Warsaw Ghetto, 6–8 Gesia Street. Yad Vashem Photo Archives, courtesy of United States Holocaust Memorial Museum Photo Archives.

fled with her family to Warsaw. She continued her education in Warsaw in a small study circle with teachers and other students from Lodz. On July 12, 1940, she commented in her diary about the proliferation of study groups "in cellars and attics" around the city.[26] She then wrote, "Two . . . schools were discovered by the Germans sometime in June; later we heard that the teachers were shot on the spot, and the pupils had been sent to a concentration camp near Lublin [Majdanek]." Berg went on to describe the "special intensity and warmth" that the grave situation engendered:

> The teachers put their whole heart and soul into their teaching, and all the pupils study with exemplary diligence. There are no bad pupils. The illegal character of teaching, the danger that threatens us every minute, fills us with a strange earnestness. The old distance between teachers and pupils has vanished, we feel like comrades-in-arms responsible to each other.[27]

After the Warsaw Ghetto was sealed off in November 1940, the Nazis continued to forbid the Jews from operating schools for the estimated thirty to forty thousand school-age children who were confined there.[28] Nevertheless, clandestine "children's corners" and kindergartens were in operation; elementary classrooms operated in conjunction with public kitchens; an active network of study groups thrived; religious education persisted; and, in whatever ways possible, youth groups continued their flourishing pre-war intellectual and political activities. Extensive private tutoring, a few clandestine high schools, and hundreds of *komplety* ("complements," or study circles) also existed.[29] Vocational training[30] and university-level programs were offered as well. At their peak, five hundred students were enrolled in medical courses that employed famous lecturers from the Jewish medical faculty of Warsaw University and Krakow University.[31]

These clandestine educational activities in the Warsaw Ghetto engendered the same sort of atmosphere that Mary Berg described. In oral testimony given in 1991, Vladka Meed, a teenage youth movement member, underground activist, and Ghetto survivor, recounts experiencing a similar atmosphere while listening to lectures with other members of her youth group:

> I was a young girl . . . and it was at the time of starvation and typhoid and hunger and constantly peril in the Ghetto, but nevertheless . . . lectures took place in many places and in many houses during the Ghetto period, and the young people used to go there, and they were asking questions. . . . I . . . remember the atmosphere, the elevation, being together with the people and talking about the writer and the character.[32]

The intensity and warmth Berg described was felt by teachers as well. Teacher Ana Natanblut wrote about conversations she had with her friend, researcher and teacher Fanny Boymberg, who was later murdered in Treblinka:

> She gave lessons about her beloved subjects, Latin and history, from early in the morning until late at night. And after all the lessons, she would spend time discussing the material with her female students. She especially worked on old Greek texts and wrote articles, but she also derived pleasure from her discussions with her students, and she used to say that she had never had such joy from her teaching as she had in the Ghetto.[33]

During the second year in the Ghetto, from the fall of 1941 through the summer of 1942, the Judenrat was able to secure permission from the German authorities to open primary schools for no more than five thousand Jewish children. Nevertheless, most clandestine educational activity in the Ghetto continued until the end.

Origins of Schools

The political organization within and outside the Ghetto was composed of complex authority structures, both above- and underground. The loci of authority that were primarily centralized outside the Ghetto — but ultimately determined much of what happened in it — included the occupying German army, the various Nazi forces, the general government of occupied Poland, and the Polish underground. An equally complicated authority structure existed inside the Ghetto. Some groups, such as the Judenrat and the Jewish Police, were recognized by the Germans, while many others were not. Despite the arrests and the flight of Jewish political leaders eastward, some of the organized leadership of the pre-war Jewish community was reestablished in the Ghetto upon its creation.

The sociopolitical structures in the Ghetto created a climate that enabled the clandestine schools to be formed. The youth movements, Ghetto organizations such as Jewish Self-Help and CENTOS (The Jewish Society for the Care of Orphans), cultural organizations such as YIKOR (Yiddish Culture Organizations) and *Tecumah* (dedicated to the "revival" of the Hebrew language), religious organizations, the Judenrat, professional educators, and private Ghetto citizens were all responsible for promoting organized clandestine schooling in the Ghetto.

German education policy in Poland was part of the overall Nazi effort to destroy the intelligentsia (both Polish and Jewish) in the occupied territories; thus, education in occupied Poland was severely restricted for both Poles and Jews. However, once the Jews were ghettoized, the Nazis showed little interest in their political and social activities. An *Oneg Shabbat* essay, entitled "A Preliminary Study in Teaching People During the War," includes an account of the German policy toward schooling during the occupation of Poland.[34] According to the essay, the Germans initially considered dealing with clandestine schools a waste of time because, ironically, they did not see the schools as threatening their primary interest in "demoralizing the masses in order to destroy . . . Jewish culture that is so 'dangerous' to humanity."[35] Therefore, a strong network of underground schools developed in the Ghetto's earliest days.

Clandestine Schooling

House Committees, Soup Kitchens, and Orphanages

House Committees (known also as Building Committees) in the Ghetto organized themselves to provide care and education for small children in "children's corners" and gardens. In the summer of 1941, approximately 4,500 children were under the care of 164 children's corners. Natan Koninski, a teacher and *Oneg Shabbat* contributor, wrote that the youngsters in the children's corners benefited from "competent instructors" and the "company of their peers." The children "spend their time in playing and in games, in learning songs, in exercise, and in listening to interesting stories and instructive talks." According to Koninski, while some children's corners had formally qualified kindergarten teachers, others were taught by lay women or older youth from the apartment houses.[36] For instance, Benjamin Meed, a youth group member, was asked by the elders of his House Committee to help with the children. The program he organized for approximately thirty children included teaching them early literacy skills and Polish songs, and distributing soup.[37]

CENTOS organized soup kitchens and day-care centers, which also provided children with clandestine education. In March 1944, after the liquidation of the Ghetto, Emmanuel Ringelblum (historian, educator, and organizer of the *Oneg Shabbat* Archives) and Adolf Berman (director of CENTOS) made a desperate attempt to report to the world about the activities, events, and tragedy of the Warsaw Ghetto in a communiqué to the Jewish Scientific Institute in New York City. Writing from their hiding places in Warsaw after their escape from the Ghetto, they described many things in the Ghetto, including cultural and educational endeavors. They reported, "Under the mantle of children's kitchens and CENTOS centers, there were formed a network of illegal schools of various ideologies" representing various political, religious, and educational philosophies.[38]

Indeed, in November 1941, teacher Natan Koninski wrote of secret schools fronted by CENTOS kitchens:

> In some kitchens systematic school instruction has now been conducted for a year. Children, grouped according to age and mental development, learned regular school subjects on the basis of a continuous, regular curriculum. Several kitchens conducted the schooling according to the ideological programmes of pre-war times. Thus children were taught the Yiddish or Hebrew languages, studied History of the Jews, [and] literature. Every opportunity was taken to arrange public functions and produce plays or have a convention devoted to Yiddish and Hebrew writers, such as Peretz or Bialik. In kitchens as, for instance, the one at Prosta Street 8, or Nowolipki 68, normal, regular school lessons were maintained and children were getting, apart from the meals, also the so very needed food for the intellect.[39]

Not all kitchens had carefully organized schools; some offered only half-day care programs for the needy and for refugees from all over Poland, and some children were just too ill or malnourished to participate in the programs. Koninski reports that CENTOS ran thirty-five kitchens, boarding houses, and day houses that were responsible for feeding 35,000 homeless, refugee, or otherwise desperate children.[40]

Because of disease and starvation, and because the Warsaw Ghetto was a repository for Jewish refugees from all over Poland, orphans abounded there. Many orphanages organized schooling for their children, but none is more famous than that established by Dr. Janusz Korczak. Korczak, an author and educator, is well known for his child-centered educational philosophy, his commitment to and respect for children, and his final march with his orphans to the deportation site.[41] The orphanage, which existed in Warsaw before the war and later moved into the Ghetto, was set up with a student-run system of justice to which all children and adults were accountable. When the orphanage was moved into the Ghetto, many more children were taken in, and members of the Jewish intelligentsia had jobs as cooks and cleaners as they hid from the Germans. Survivor David Kochalski describes the education program in the orphanage and the access he and the other children had to "all the intelligentsia, teachers, professors, doctors, [and] psychologists . . . who were hiding." He explains, "It was something like a university. . . . We had terrific lectures on everything. . . . All the boys would sit down and . . . every other night another professor would start teaching us."[42]

Having just performed a play, Korczak's children were dressed in costumes when the Nazis arrived to deport them on August 5, 1942. Although only the children were to be deported, Korczak and his assistant, Stefania Wilczynska (Madame Stefa), went with them, marching in lines behind a big green flag carried by one of the boys. This green flag was similar to the one carried by King Matt — the protagonist in one of Korczak's children's stories, *King Matt the First* — as he led a "peaceful crusade" of the children of the world in the name of peace, justice, and an end to all wars. And just as the boy-king is led through the street in chains in the final scene, so too were Korczak and his children led to their demise.[43]

Survivor Erwin Baum remembers his own experience living in Dr. Janusz Korczak's orphanage during the war. Baum had escaped from the Ghetto to get bread the day before Korczak, Madame Stefa, and the rest of the two hundred children were deported. On his way back to the orphanage he came across a woman wailing, "They took the children! They took the children!" Baum ran to the *Umschlagplatz* (assembly point), where the trains deported Jews to Treblinka, and he watched Korczak argue with a soldier, apparently insisting on going on the transport with the children. Baum tried to go too, but was waved away by a German soldier who reprimanded him, "You are not a Jew, get away from here." Baum was left alone with his last hope taken away. He was left to wonder, "What am I going to do without him? How am I going to survive without him?" Fifty-eight years later he says of Dr. Korczak, "I would gladly give half my life for him."[44]

Youth Movements

In the Ghetto, the youth movements established urban *kibbutzim* (communes) in buildings where they conducted intellectual activities, opened high schools, and sponsored lectures and study groups. A Ghetto inhabitant wrote of the youth in *Oneg Shabbat:* "It is no exaggeration to state that the only environment in which political movement still pulsates with life, in which the will to act has not utterly failed and in which action actually takes place — is that of the youth."[45] Emmanuel Ringelblum lectured before a seminar run by a youth group and described his experience in his journal: "When I looked into the glowing faces of youth thirsty for knowledge, I altogether forgot the war [ravaging] the world. The seminars were held directly opposite the [post of the] German sentry who guarded the Ghetto gate . . ."[46] While this is just one small example of the ways in which youth movements valued and actively participated in education, their boldness and defiance illustrate the daily risks the students and teachers took in order to engage in teaching and learning.

Youth movement members who lived in the kibbutzim were able to sustain an active political, cultural, and intellectual life, while maintaining the primary focus on "the teaching of the youth movements' traditional ideologies and values."[47] Survivor Leah Silverstein, one of approximately twenty youths who lived in the kibbutz run by the Zionist youth group *HaShomer HaTzair* (The Young Guardian), describes it as an "oasis in the terrible Ghetto." She remembers: "In the evenings and on *Shabbat* [Sabbath], we used to gather and [have] discussions and . . . presentations by all kinds of literary men who used to come to the kibbutz. So we were politically and intellectually active, in spite of terrible conditions that existed in the Ghetto."[48]

Youth movement members were trained by the youth group leadership as cultural workers and lecturers by attending seminars on political, sociological, historical, and literary subjects. They then traveled to different buildings and repeated these lectures. Vladka Meed was one such youth lecturer. She explains that the purpose of the lectures was to elevate the people, and that the lecturers, who were "proud to belong to this group" of cultural workers, were very "serious about [their] mission."[49]

Societies in the Ghetto other than the youth movements sponsored a wide range of educational and cultural activities. With the help of the residential Building Councils and the Self-Help Organization, the Yiddish cultural organization YIKOR and Tecumah, which was dedicated to the revival of the Hebrew language, held literary meetings and readings in those buildings after curfew.[50] The importance of such activities is represented in an *Oneg Shabbat* essay, which called for an increased number of accessible cultural events in the Ghetto. The author wrote:

> It seems that the present is the worst period in our history. One of the most important tasks in this, our time, is the preservation of spirit in our community. We must undertake everything possible . . . so that our struggle (or rather our wrestling for daily bread) does not exhaust the last, remaining vital force in our nation.[51]

Study Circles, Gymnasia, and Religious Study

In an *Oneg Shabbat* essay entitled "A Preliminary Study in Teaching People During the War," the author, writing about high school–aged children, described clandestine study groups composed of a teacher and a small group of students, which met approximately twelve hours a week for a low tuition fee. The study groups were organized either through private teachers, private citizens, or through the youth movements of political organizations. In the winter of 1940–1941, there was a sharp rise in the number of study groups and the number of students.[52] By 1941 the study groups numbered in the hundreds.[53]

Soon after the formation of the Ghetto, the Jewish teachers began to actively form clandestine study groups, both to earn money and to address what they perceived to be the need for schools, since a large number of Jewish youth at all levels were being deprived of an education. An *Oneg Shabbat* essayist wrote that, in December 1939, "feeling the pinch of necessity, teachers began vigorously to organize youth — mostly without the participation of former headmasters. . . . They came into contact with former students with relative ease and offered them the only feasible option — a clandestine study group composed of former students."[54] There was no shortage of teachers, as discussed in the *Oneg Shabbat* essay "The School System": "We have far too many well-qualified teachers, and an equal or higher number of new candidates. Add to this, that each graduate from secondary education, and each student in more advanced schools, tries hardest to enter the profession due to lack of other sources of income."[55] "A Preliminary Study in Teaching People During the War" reported that in the Ghetto "youngsters study diligently and often show great interest in the course of their work" and "the teachers work very hard and with exceptional honesty, though their material situation is extremely difficult."[56]

This activity, at first economically motivated, was later motivated by other forces as well. Vladka Meed remembers:

> People were going on in the most difficult situations and holding on to life as human beings. . . . Our neighbor . . . in the Ghetto was selling pieces of bread . . . outside of the building of our house . . . and looking out if a German patrol is not passing because in her apartment above us, her daughter was giving lectures to children . . . a small illegal school. This woman did not even think that she is the hero and her daughter didn't think that she is the hero, but they were conducting illegal classes for children, knowing that if a German patrol will . . . catch them, they will be right away not only arrested but also killed. And this is the way people lived.[57]

Joseph Kutrzeba, who came to the Ghetto from Lodz at the age of fourteen, explained that his parents wanted him to continue with his education "no matter what [the] conditions." His father was a prominent teacher, musician, and composer in Lodz, and after the family's arrival in the Ghetto, his father's colleagues, also teachers, organized themselves and their students "almost right away" into komplety. He was part of a study group with two girls, two other boys, and "excellent professors, some of whom were Ph.D.s"[58] He describes the degree of secrecy under which these classes took place:

> Secrecy was most important . . . so we would meet almost every day somewhere else. . . . And before we entered the courtyard, each one of us . . . walked back and forth to make sure that nobody is following [us]. And [we] prearranged knocks on the door. When we studied, there were no manuals so [we] just [had] the professor's memory and written notes. We always had a game of dominos or chess ready in the event someone knocked on the door. Hide the books! And immediately we're just sitting playing the game. So secrecy was very very important because nobody trusted anybody.[59]

He studied "virtually the whole array of high school subjects except those requiring labs" in his clandestine study group, including history, geography, Polish literature ("the great Polish masterworks"), beginning English (which he "adored"), Latin, literature, math, and Hebrew. According to Kutrzeba, the teachers were "stunning" and the education was extremely high quality: "The two years in the Warsaw Ghetto sunk in very deeply. To this day, I know the Latin that was taught."[60]

Study circles were not the only means by which older children could be schooled. The Hebrew *gymnasia* (secondary schools) served students associated with the Zionist *Tarbut* movement, which was a cultural and educational movement dedicated to modern Zionism and the Hebrew language.[61] The youth group *Dror* (Freedom) established a gymnasium in the Ghetto in August 1940 that was based on their ideology of Labor Zionism. At first it was organized for its own members, but it came to include nonmembers as well. Thirteen teachers taught 120 students a traditional curriculum, including Hebrew, Yiddish, Bible studies, singing, art, Jewish history, French, and German, which was replaced with English in the second year of the school's existence.[62]

Religious education also persisted. For example, the religious boys' schools *Yesodey HaTorah* (Foundations of the Torah) and the religious girls' schools *Beis Yaakov* (House of Jacob) reopened soon after the bombardment ended. At their peak, in 1941, forty-six boys' classes employed 132 teachers and four girls' classes employed sixteen teachers at these schools. Eight full *Yeshivot* — religious high schools — were also in operation under the same auspices, serving a total of 3,500 students.[63] In addition to the Yiddishist schools, religious Zionist schools run by the *Mizrachi* (Spiritual Center) organization were also in operation. Finally, many religious youths studied privately with Rabbis, such as the thousand orthodox children studying as part of the "'Patronage' of Torah" study groups established by Rabbi Meshulam Kaminer.[64] On March 18, 1941, Emmanuel Ringelblum described a religious study scene in his journal:

> There's an apartment in a Jewish courtyard where traditional studies are secretly going on. The door of the apartment is opened only to the password (one knock). When you come in, you see a large group of Talmudic students sitting over their studies.[65]

Sanctioned Schools

After a great effort, the Judenrat secured a modest concession from the Nazis and was granted permission to open a small number of sanctioned early primary schools in the Ghetto. On September 5, 1941, Judenrat leader Adam Czerniakow wrote tersely in his diary:

> In the morning at the Community. I am not getting any answers to a number of my letters [to the authorities]. Among other requests I submitted one for au-

thorization of Children's Month. At last permission was given today for opening the elementary schools. I summoned a commission at once and we held a meeting.[66]

Despite the difficult circumstances, the Jewish School Commission saw continued schooling as a necessary investment in the Jewish community's future. By October 1941, six official schools were operating in the children's shelters; by the end of that school year, nineteen were in operation, some of which had previously been underground classes.[67] Meanwhile, the komplety and other covert education activities continued to function separately and clandestinely. In a letter dated December 15, 1941, addressed to possible donors, a special committee of The Patronate of Jewish Cultural Activities in Warsaw articulated the purpose of the organized schools: "Friends and people concerned must now create about the school, and on behalf of it, the right social atmosphere conducive to a healthy education of the Jewish child, for the sake of the future.... We must create what is necessary. This is our duty."[68]

According to Ana Natanblut, a school commission member and teacher, it was the dream of Abraham Wolfowicz, chair of the commission, to "create a unified Jewish school on a democratic basis with a particularly national color."[69] The commission decided that "in all the types of schools, the program should be constructed on a Jewish theme and for the most part teach in Yiddish and Hebrew, depending on the type of school."[70] However, despite the official sanction, day-to-day terror in the Ghetto caused even these schools to have a furtive and perilous aspect to their operation. Czerniakow wrote in his diary about a speech he gave on December 21, 1941, at an official ceremony honoring the Judenrat-sponsored schools: "Somebody reported to the authorities what went on at our school ceremony. The work of a well-known scoundrel."[71]

Despite this peril, Natanblut described the sanctioned schools as places of "celebration" that elicited the same intense devotion from students and teachers as the clandestine schools:

> It was truly crowded and cold and there were no textbooks, but there was an atmosphere of work. The moral climate was uplifted ... and there were no bored teachers or bored students. One's heart would fill with joy and pride when they came to visit a school, and after an interruption of two years time, we once again experienced a true school, with true classes with boards and benches and children learning with a violent desire. People sensed a celebration in the schools.[72]

While the desperate conditions in the Ghetto persisted and Jews were silently dying of hunger and disease, the cultural and educational work of the community still continued. Abraham Wolfowicz found solace in the fact that the schools were taking the first steps "to unite the fragmented Jewish people" despite the fact that the schools actually represented quite different political, philosophical, and religious ideologies.[73] Natanblut further found teachers to be vital in any attempts to overcome the desperation and despair in the Ghetto. She wrote:

> In the days of fear, when the sword of Damocles was hanging over everyone, when hunger and epidemics were our daily bread, when we were sinking into depression because of all of this, the teachers made the effort to build such a school system that shimmered with all the colors of the rainbow in the darkness that had fallen so heavily upon us.[74]

Indeed, Czerniakow commented in his diary on the contrast between the teachers and the desperate conditions under which they taught. On January 20, 1942, he wrote:

> I inspected 4 types of our primary schools. Where the teachers are idealists, the conditions from the educational point of view are . . . satisfactory. On the other hand, in general, the classrooms, corridors, and staircases are very dirty.[75]

By the end of the 1941–1942 school year, the only officially recognized school year in the Ghetto, the nineteen official schools that were fully or partially operational enrolled 6,700 pupils.[76] This number does not include the thousands of students engaged in clandestine study groups, Torah study, and children's corners.[77]

As late as July 5, 1942, less than three weeks before the start of the *Aktion* — the catastrophic deportation of Jews from the Warsaw Ghetto — Czerniakow wrote in his diary about an organized student presentation he attended: "A program was offered by 600 boys and girls from elementary schools. From among the performers I invited to sit at the stand with me a little girl who was made up as Chaplin (great applause)."[78] That, however, was to be among the final joyous occasions for most of the students, their teachers, and even Czerniakow himself.

The Aktion

On July 22, 1942, two and one-half weeks after the joyous moments that the Judenrat leader described in his diary, the Aktion began. Eliminating Warsaw Jewry was another step in the Nazi goal of making Europe *Judenrein* — cleansed of Jews. On that day, Czerniakow was asked by the German authorities to sign a deportation order that would include children. Strongly committed to the Ghetto children but powerless to save them, Czerniakow committed suicide the next day.[79] The Aktion continued for the next seven weeks, until an estimated 265,040 Jews were transported to Treblinka, where most were gassed to death.[80] More than ten thousand Ghetto Jews died or were killed during the Aktion; some (about 11,580) were sent to a *Dulag* (transit camp), from which they were transferred to one of a number of forced labor camps; and some (about 8,000) escaped to the Aryan side of Warsaw.[81] The Ghetto was in chaos; sanctioned schools and other institutions ceased to exist, and the remaining inhabitants were afraid to be out on the streets. After the mass deportations, the Ghetto population was decimated; a mere 55,000 of the 350,000 who were there on July 22 remained.[82] Escapees brought word of mass killings at Treblinka back to the Ghetto, and by the end of August the remaining Jews of Warsaw knew they were doomed to die.[83]

Over the next few months, however, the remaining CENTOS members and teachers organized approximately ten children's clubs in building courtyards with secret passageways between them to avoid getting captured on the streets. Private teachers continued with their komplety as well. Natanblut remembers the gatherings of teachers that took place during this time:

> They did not give in. [Teachers] began to gather weekly in the evenings. Saturday nights and sometimes on Friday nights we would gather in one of the apartments and sit on beds, boxes, windowsills, on the few chairs. In the light of the smelly carbide lamps we would listen to a talk, a recitation, a political bulletin, participate in a discussion, sing together. We would not talk about those things that were looming over us. We would come here to strengthen ourselves. ... The entire remnant of teachers began to come. ... They brought together memories of the school, common interests and common pain.[84]

Despite the continuation of these educational activities, the Aktion marked a monumental shift in all aspects of Ghetto life. In response to the devastation caused by the mass deportations, and within a week of the first one in July, youth movement representatives, many of whom were active in the Ghetto's educational and cultural life, focused their attention on forming the Jewish Fighting Organization. This group would ultimately be responsible for the organized, active revolt against the Germans and their plans for the final liquidation of the Warsaw Ghetto.[85]

WARSAW GHETTO SCHOOLS: MULTIPLE PURPOSES

Why Education?

The questions remain: Given the perilous nature of the activity and the grim conditions in which it was undertaken, why did organized schooling thrive in the Ghetto? What was the purpose of the teaching and learning? The existence and vibrancy of the schools in the Ghetto is particularly remarkable, given the fact that many children became the sole supporters of their families, working as peddlers or in shops. Many children needed to smuggle, beg, or steal food, and school took them away from these survival activities.

It seems that for the Jews in the Warsaw Ghetto, organized schooling in its multiple forms served as a form of resistance that is oriented simultaneously to the past, present, and future. It contributed to individual survival, not only as a means through which to supply food to the hungry (as in the soup kitchens, children's corners, and orphanages), but also as a way to help children and their teachers resist dehumanization and hopelessness by maintaining normalcy and humanity, which seeded hope for the future. Organized schooling also helped the Ghetto society resist decay by sustaining its social, cultural, and political organizations and maintaining community cohesiveness, thus providing a vehicle through which the Jews could resist cultural and historical eradication. They were able to sustain and continue a vibrant cultural, intellectual, and spiritual life, which — within the context of the immediacy of the situation — used a reverence for the past to look toward the future.

Hunger, Normalcy, and Humanity: A Present Orientation

In one sense, organized schools were oriented toward meeting the immediate needs of the children and the community. It was, after all, the paramount goal of soup kitchens to distribute soup and of orphanages to care for orphans. Similarly, in his *Oneg Shabbat* essay, Koninski and others wrote that study circles kept the youth off the streets and provided a livelihood for unemployed, destitute teachers.[86]

An anonymous writer in *Oneg Shabbat* asked, "What propels youth to schools and learning and bids parents to squeeze out the last penny in order to provide their children with some education, not bread alone?"[87] Implicit in this question is the fact that children and adults sought to overcome the immediate, terrible conditions in the Ghetto not only with the essential food and sustenance, but also with teaching and learning. This essayist claims that study, although its practical value might be "questionable," somehow enabled students to persevere in the face of demoralization:[88]

> The Jew, with all his faults, was known for one laudable passion, the one that has kept him from forgetting spiritual life even in the worst, bleakest moments of his life. This passion, the primordial and untamable, keeps swelling in the Ghetto from day to day in inverse proportion to available facilities. It grows despite logic, in defiance of daily events. . . . The young yearn to study on their own, without external spur, not thinking of gain or immediate and future benefit. . . . This phenomenon, in such contrast to the general bestiality, brutalization and demoralization, is the source of power that enables one to persevere, to overcome difficulties and to keep trying and disregarding dangers. . . . The risk . . . is real, not imaginary; . . . the ultimate value, is questionable.[89]

Ghetto survivor Joseph Kutrzeba also described how learning provided students escape from brutalization and entrée into a "different," more normal world. He stated simply, "I wanted to go to school and my parents wanted me to." He recounted that after his komplety lessons he would go to his job for three or four hours a day, delivering telegrams to earn money for his family, and then do homework in the evening: "There was terror and starvation and hunger . . . and yet, for us kids, it was, in a way, it was a salvation. Because what else are you going to do?" He posed this same question later in his testimony — "What do you do with kids under these terrorizing circumstances?"

— and then described the role school played: "At least they enter[ed] for a few hours a day into a different world."[90] Survivor Leah Silverstein echoed the idea that children went to school not only for immediate salvation from a brutal and demoralized existence, but also to actively fight daily apathy and despair. "In terrible times," she said, "and in life-threatening situations, study was the one thing to hold on to. Otherwise you just think about hunger. It is a sort of relief."[91] She further described how the sense of normalcy was maintained:

> There were a lot of activities, you know. People, first of all, all the youth organizations were very active. In addition to this . . . people were trying to hang on to . . . the way of life that they had before they came to the Ghetto and to a certain extent, they succeeded in it. There were . . . cultural organizations. Of course, schooling even was going on in a clandestine form because you were not allowed to have open schools. But schools were existing, . . . even high schools and elementary schools, even universities.[92]

Debórah Dwork, Holocaust historian and chronicler of children's experiences in it, explains how critical it was for the children to maintain some sort of normalcy in an otherwise chaotic and devastated life:

> As we have seen so often before, to go to school, to persevere with one's studies, was a basic tenet of childhood. It was an essential activity that embodied the principal of normality: life would go on, there would be a future after this madness. . . . Many children wished to continue to learn and in extraordinary circumstances they did so.[93]

Chaim Kaplan, another *Oneg Shabbat* contributor, also commented on the drive to maintain some sense of normalcy when he wrote in his diary in 1942 about nursery schools and about older children having lessons, songs, games, stories, and exercises in urban gardens. He wrote, "In short, [schooling was] an arrow in the Nazis' eyes! The arteries of life do not stop pulsing."[94]

Jews also showed their desire to be connected with the world outside the Ghetto and to be counted among the living. The oppressive decrees, the monstrous wall surrounding the Ghetto, the prohibitive travel edicts, and the economic and social separation between the Jews and the rest of Warsaw were unequivocal signals that the Nazis wanted to sever all links between the Jews and the outside world. Holocaust historian Israel Gutman explains:

> The hermetic isolation from human society at large also influenced the quality of life. The Jews of Warsaw felt segregated and abandoned, and the motivations that usually direct a group that strives to be counted among the components of a standard human society disintegrated completely in the Ghetto. There is deep significance to the fact that the Jews were uncertain of what awaited them at the hands of the Nazis. . . . The edicts followed one after the other and left the public in a state of continuous anxiety, which left no time or strength to concentrate on or analyze affairs from a broad or forward-looking perspective.[95]

In the midst of this despair, study was a way for Jews to connect with the living world outside the Ghetto and resist being demoralized and dehumanized. Hundreds of study circles were held in which students took exams and received grades, and Gutman writes that students were "enthusiastic about their studies, which were a kind of link with the great and free world outside."[96] Places such as Janusz Korczak's orphanage brimmed with educational and cultural life. Survivor David Kochalski remembers the humanizing impact that life in the orphanage had on him: "What they tried to do in this orphanage, they tried to make human beings out of us under the worst circumstances, because inside we were like an island. Outside it was hell, a real hell."[97]

Youth group member and Ghetto survivor Ben Meed connects the drive to maintain normalcy through education as a type of "spiritual resistance," that is, "not giving the enemy what he wants," which was "to break you morally, then with hunger, then with disease. And then they want to kill." For Meed the motivation to teach the children came from the desire to "help the children be normal, to be as close as possible to a *life which was*," even though "it's very difficult under the conditions of hunger to be normal." When he taught young children, Meed felt "the singing of the children to be spiritual resistance."[98]

The Ghetto as a "Transient Episode": Hope for the Future

While organized schooling helped some Warsaw Ghetto Jews resist their demise by providing for some of their immediate needs, including normalcy and dignity, there was also a sense that, through their participation in normal activities such as schooling, they could suspend their current state of being, accept the horrors of the Ghetto as a "transient episode," and look completely toward the future.[99]

In his 1997 study of spiritual resistance in the Ghettos and camps, Joseph Rudavsky explored the notion of resistance within the framework of the Jewish conceptions of *Kiddush HaShem* (the sanctification of G-d), usually through martyrdom, and *Kiddush HaHayyim* (the sanctification of life) through living a righteous and joyful life. Rudavsky links the Jews' struggle to maintain normalcy with their struggle for human dignity and hope for the future:

> [The Jews] resolved to conduct their lives not as hunted victims but as human beings who hoped to see a better future, or if they could not survive the war, then at least make the Germans understand that though they might succeed in killing the Jews, they would not succeed in divesting the Jews of their human dignity. The Jews knew that their end might be *Kiddush HaShem*, the sanctity of martyrdom, but while they lived they would implement in their daily activities the age-old principle of *Kiddush HaHayyim*, as they lived meaningful lives, Jewishly and otherwise. They would strive to educate their children, to continue their Jewish studies, to observe their religion, and even to carry on the Zionist struggle for the Jewish Homeland as if the Ghetto were just a transient episode.

Scholars of Jewish law would continue to study and teach; poets, composers, and writers would not permit ghetto life to throttle their creativity, and artists would record the ghetto experience on paper and canvas for future generations.[100]

Joseph Kermish, Holocaust historian and editor of the published *Oneg Shabbat* Archives, further explains this forward-looking stance as passive resistance that grew out of a struggle for normalcy and connectedness to the outside world:

> One of the most interesting and important features of the passive resistance of the Jews in the Ghetto — that struggle so stubbornly and persistently kept up in the will to overcome and carry on — was to maintain a life on a certain cultural standard and to keep up that level in spite of the frightful isolation from the external world; it was marked by great care devoted to providing for a future generation of professional intelligentsia, and by the buildup of a wide network of courses and teaching facilities for higher professional and academic education.[101]

Marian Malowist, a young high school teacher and pedagogue, wrote about the factors that induced Jewish youth to study during wartime, stating that "youth fears it might go astray and wants to accomplish something useful. It expects that the war will end successfully; and then, it will be relatively easy, after having studied in the clandestine study-circles, to obtain a proper school certificate."[102] He posited that youth had some sense of their future that motivated them to study. This was, of course, before the first escapees brought eyewitness accounts from the death camps back to the Ghetto. Ghetto students were further motivated by the promises they received from Polish authorities, at least at first, that their educational certificates and diplomas would be valid after the war.[103] The many students and teachers who stayed engaged in their work based their actions on the hope that the nightmare of the Ghetto would pass.

Explanations based on the hope that a better life would come are inextricably connected to explanations that schooling enabled Warsaw Ghetto Jews to maintain a sense of normalcy and human dignity. However, the many dimensions of the purposes of organized schooling are only fully understood in the context of a discussion of how the Jews collectively used organized schooling as a way to resist historical and cultural obliteration, and how this resistance is at once past, present, and future oriented.

Resistance to Cultural and Historical Eradication: Past, Present, and Future

By prohibiting assemblies of people, religious observance, cultural symbols, celebrations, meaningful work, genuine self-rule, artistic expression, and education, the Nazis sought to snuff out Jewish history and culture in the Warsaw Ghetto and in the world forever. Yet the Jews defied prohibitive edicts by learning, teaching, and sustaining their culture clandestinely, thus realizing the emancipatory possibilities of education. Despite the peril and horrors experienced daily by Ghetto inhabitants, the Jews were able to keep some social, cultural, and political institutions relatively intact. As a result, some semblance of community cohesion was maintained amidst the chaos. Organized schooling in particular served to keep children, adolescents, and adults involved daily in organized community life.

Warsaw Ghetto Jews — students, teachers, parents, and other community members who helped organize and support the various forms of organized teaching and learning — acted collectively to resist cultural and historical annihilation by keeping these very things vibrantly alive in schools, study circles, and youth activities. One example of how the Jews, in their darkest hours, used a reverence for their past to light their future is found in the explicit and implicit content of the curricula of the clandestine schools. Another example is the role the youth movements played in the educational, cultural, and political life in the Ghetto and in their primary role in staging the armed Warsaw Ghetto Uprising.

Curricular Content

Students in clandestine elementary classes and in study circles learned geography, history, math, literature, and Yiddish culture. A document titled "An Outline of Pedagogical Activity in the Alimentation Points on Karmelicka Street 29, Nowolipki Str. 39, and Krochmalna Str. 96" offers insight into the aims of three elementary schools operating out of soup kitchens.[104] In one section, "The Aims of Our Work," the first of eight aims reads, "We strive to turn Alimentation Points into centers to succeed pedagogically and influence children."[105] Other aims included paying attention to the spiritual life of the child, fostering interest in several academic subjects, providing an emotional outlet, implanting a love of and devotion to the Yiddish language and culture, as well as teaching hygiene, cooperation, good behavior, and punctuality. Another section of the document, "Manners of Operation," described such activities as singing, poetry recitation, song enactments, acting out fables, as well as telling or reading certain "suitable tales and literary works." For example, the younger children studied *Pinocchio, Robinson Crusoe*, biblical stories, Greek myths, and tales by Yiddish authors Y. L. Peretz and Sholem Aleichem. The older children also studied stories by these Yiddish authors and by Sholem Asch, as well as novels such as *Uncle Tom's Cabin*.[106]

While these schools clearly had multiple aims, great importance was placed on studying Jewish history and Yiddish literature and culture.[107] According to Yiddish literature scholar Sol Liptzin, literary greats Y. L. Peretz and Sholem Aleichem are purported to be the "awakeners" and "comforters" of Yiddish-speaking Jewry.[108] Where Peretz "stimulated Yiddish creativity and weaned Jewish youth from perilous assimilationist tendencies," Aleichem "brought to light the inner dignity and moral grandeur" hidden beneath the "apparent submissiveness" of the persecuted Eastern European Jews.[109] Peretz, himself a Warsaw native, created simple characters who lived hard lives but were rewarded in this world and in heaven for their piety and self-sacrifice. His works often included a mystical character who symbolized "unexpected help that may come to those who are worthy of extraordinary assistance because they retain faith in fundamental justice that must prevail in heaven and on earth."[110] Aleichem's characters suffered the daily trials of a difficult life, but they exhibited not only an indefatigable will to survive, they did so nobly and heroically, with joy and humor. Liptzin says of Aleichem, "His is a laughter through tears, a stoic humor that surmounts all obstacles and disappointments."[111] Aleichem taught Jews how to "seek liberation from pain in jest" and how to "retain inner dignity and humaneness in a undignified world."[112] Because of their hopeful orientations, Peretz and Aleichem seem appropriate curricular choices for Warsaw Ghetto children. Similarly, in addition to early literacy and daily living skills, children in children's corners and orphanages learned stories, songs, poems, and plays with Jewish historical or cultural themes. Likewise, in addition to their secular subjects, students in study circles and the gymnasia also studied subjects with Jewish historical and cultural relevance.

According to scholar Joseph Kermish, education planners in the Ghetto "aspired to fill their education with the highest humanistic ideals in view of a 'brighter, better future.'"[113] Teacher Ana Natanblut's description of the celebrations put on by the sanctioned schools in honor of the coming of spring in 1942 illustrates the importance of humanistic ideals to the Ghetto educators:

> The Polish school at Gesia 9 presented a performance about how children of different peoples and races loved each other and through this, furthered the brotherhood of all people. The children approached a lonely orphan girl, bringing her presents, joy and love. Each group of children in the presentation sang and danced and dressed in its own way. National differences were not watered down — but that didn't evoke mistrust, but the opposite, more interest and connections with others.[114]

The performances had "deeply ideological content."[115] The school at Nowolipki 68 combined the songs and poems of Yiddish writers such as Chaim Nachman Bialik and Abraham Reisen into a medley as a "march of victorious spring which envelops the world despite the fact that at the beginning, the earth is sunken in ice and the evil winds howl."[116] Natanblut describes the impact these performances had on their audiences:

> The impression was unearthly, either because of the allegorical content which awakened the deepest feelings, be it with song, with the appropriate verses, with beautifully colored costumes, with decorations, or with the play of light and the rhythm of dance.[117]

The Warsaw Ghetto children experienced a profoundly relevant curriculum that was drawn from their Jewish literary tradition and was ideologically charged. This curriculum, as well as religious education, reveals how schooling served as a means through which Ghetto Jews kept their history and culture alive day-to-day and secured its future by instilling it in their youth.

Youth Movements

The youth movements served a similar function through their involvement in educational, cultural, and political activities in the Ghetto. Even before the war, education and political socialization were at the center of Jewish youth group activities, since the groups were youth divisions of predominantly Zionist political and ideological organizations. Holocaust historian Israel Gutman explains that between the two wars "political education in the youth movement did not consummate with commitment only to an ideological line; the dominant foundation of this education was a yearning for radical change — in the existing state of affairs, the nature of the Jew as a human being, and the fate of the Jewish people."[118] In the trying times of Ghetto incarceration, education was an essential means of ensuring the continuation of the movement and its ideology. Though diverse in particular ideologies — including socialist, communist, cultural, or religious — youth groups were united in their belief "that there is going to be a better world," as survivor and youth group member Benjamin Meed stated.[119] These movements were all oriented toward creating a new society based on Jewish ideals, and they believed that their pioneering efforts would come to fruition in the Land of Israel. Moreover, this future orientation had at its heart a reverence for the Jews' historical, cultural, and political past. Indeed, in the Warsaw Ghetto, the youth movements were at the forefront of resistance that took the form of education, cultural events, the underground press, and ultimately the Warsaw Ghetto uprising.

The youth movements took an active role in preserving culture and used organized education to do so. According to Gutman, the youth movements put great emphasis on the spiritual and cultural aspects of their role for two main reasons. First, they feared that the poverty and other Ghetto conditions would permanently damage the psyche of the youth, which they assumed was precisely the aim of the Nazis. In May 1941, the youth organization HaShomer HaTzair's underground paper *Neged HaZerem* (*Against the Current*) published a call for youth leadership and a look toward the future:

> The poverty and total economic deprivation will pass when political conditions change, but the people will not recover from their decline if our youth are blemished and decadent; for only we, the youngsters aged thirteen to eighteen today, are destined to lead the Jewish masses to a different, better future.[120]

Second, the youth movements assumed that in the near future they would be called upon to lead their people, so they had to prepare themselves for the task under the difficult conditions of the Nazi occupation.[121] The September 1941 issue of the Bund youth division's *Yugnt-Shtime* read:

> Our rulers are mistaken in thinking that a draconian prohibition, an official stamp, can nullify cultural values that have been acquired over tens and hundreds of years.... We, the working youth of the people, must assume the task of initiating and directing the cultural and educational endeavor among children and youth ... otherwise our cultural movement among the youth is in danger of spiritual decline.... We must exploit the period of calm to prepare for missions that are sure to come.[122]

It is no wonder that, more than any other group, the youth movements were poised to take leadership roles in many areas of Ghetto life. According to Gutman, the youth groups met the demand for a flexible and adaptable kind of leadership that could cope with trying circumstances and could adjust to the changing leadership needs of the Ghetto community. The youth group leadership was thus able to fill the vacuum left by the large numbers of Jewish political and intellectual leaders who fled Warsaw for the East. Gutman claims that it was the youths' "daring, sensitivity to social injustice, and a willingness to sacrifice [that] advanced the young into the roles they were destined to assume."[123] They were, indeed, fiercely ideological and idealistic.

The underground press was a particularly important forum for education, culture, and resistance for the youth groups. Of the nearly fifty underground publications that appeared in the Ghetto at various times in either Polish, Yiddish, or Hebrew, approximately two-thirds were sponsored by the youth movements.[124] In addition to analyzing Ghetto concerns, the youth papers "presented surveys of innovations in science, book reviews, profiles of famous personalities ... and columns devoted to educational issues raised by the war."[125] They also included editorial columns and information about the political, cultural, and educational activities of the particular sponsoring movement. According to historian and archivist Joseph Kermish, the underground press

> promoted resistance, kindled its readers' spirits, invigorated their will-power, shaped their character, and served as a light to guide their way. It considered its main task to be that of fighting demoralization and despair; it therefore aroused the suffering youth to seek knowledge. Its pages faithfully reflect the youth's growing interest in books, and mainly in serious ones.[126]

Through the underground press, the youth movements served the important function of keeping members of the Ghetto community informed and connected with one another, but they also served the special function of keeping the youth group members closely connected to the various groups' ideals and to one another. Survivors from the youth movements speak passionately about their affiliations with their groups; for example, HaShomer HaTzair member Leah Silverstein attributed members' strength and ability to survive to the "deep moral principles ... acquired in the youth organization." She credited the youth movements with giving them a purposeful aim in life. Silverstein explained, "We had this aim, and we were instilled in good humanistic principles, and in a time of crisis they came to our rescue."[127] Joseph Kutrzeba, a HaShomer HaTzair member for nearly two years, explained simply, "It gave the kids something to believe in."[128] In her analysis of the Polish Zionist youth movements and resistance through education, Erica Nadelhaft writes that the groups offered the youth "an alternative society filled with idealism, learning, and mutual aid and respect" that stood "in opposition to the deterioration of life in the Ghetto and the general decline in moral values."[129]

The youth movements clearly seemed to be hopeful about the future as well. Nadelhaft maintains that

> continuing to educate the young in spite of Nazi prohibitions was thus a form of resistance for the youth movements. They believed that in order to safeguard both the physical and the spiritual existence of Jewish youth they must continue to be active intellectually and culturally. . . . They realized that the Nazis' attack on education was a deliberate attempt to destroy the Jewish people from within, and they acted purposefully and forcefully to counter the blow.[130]

In the days before the Jews of Warsaw found out and recognized that they were doomed to die, they actively worked to avoid becoming demoralized. Survivor Vladka Meed, a youth group member, attributes these actions to her belief that resistance was a reactive response to the particular kind of oppression perpetrated by the oppressor. A community that is resisting, she explains, does so in different ways depending on what the enemy puts before it. Meed says that "resistance was [a way] to hold on to culture and history so that the spirit should not be crushed."[131] Thus, the youth groups not only continued their political activities, but also took on a wide range of social and cultural services.[132] Their members found themselves organizing cultural and educational events, attending and delivering lectures, teaching and caring for younger children, and being part of a vibrant intellectual community that revolved around not only political ideology but also Jewish history, culture, and language.

As an expression of humanity and liberation, education stood in direct resistance to Nazi attempts to dehumanize the Jews of the Warsaw Ghetto and historically and culturally obliterate them. The youth groups stood at the head of this resistance. Because of the strength of their affiliations, their connectedness with one another, and their commitment to issues regarding the "nature of the Jew as a human being and the fate of the Jewish people,"[133] the youth movements were able to unite in collective defiance, first by sustaining this rich intellectual and cultural life and, ultimately, by armed struggle. Leah Silverstein attests that "it was a determination among our group, they are not going to take us alive."[134] After the mass deportations began, escapees and scouts came back to the Ghetto with confirmation of mass killings. It was then that activities of resistance evolved into plans for revolt. Some students and teachers, both secular and religious, continued their studies, but the attention of the Ghetto underground turned toward armed struggle and the formation of the Jewish Fighting Organization.

From Resistance to Revolt

A connection can be traced from the political and cultural underground activities in the Ghetto, including the clandestine schools, to the formation of the Jewish Fighting Organization (*ZOB*).[135] After the mass deportations began, leaders of the Ghetto underground began to meet and lay plans to form the ZOB. The organization's leadership came from the ranks of the youth movement leadership and was commanded by HaShomer HaTzair member Mordechai Anielewicz. In the weeks and months that followed the Aktion, the Jewish Fighting Organization dug trenches, built bunkers, printed leaflets, drew maps, trained members, and smuggled weapons and explosives into the Ghetto. A second Aktion in January 1943 took the Ghetto Jews by surprise. They revolted with small street battles and resistance from within the buildings, but five thousand Jews were deported nonetheless. Still, Nazi attempts to quickly assemble eight thousand deportees were thwarted; some Germans were killed, and the fighting galvanized the resolve of the fighters and of the remaining Ghetto population.[136] On April 19, 1943, German forces armed with weapons and artillery marched into the Ghetto to complete the final liquidation of Warsaw's Jews. They were surprised by the organized, formidable uprising staged by the Jewish Fighting Organization. A poorly armed, ragged collection of about 750 fighters, mostly under the age of twenty-five, successfully fought off German forces from April 19 to May 16, 1943, when the fighting stopped and the Ghetto burned.[137]

Gutman credits clandestine education with having had a part in the successful organization of the armed uprising by the way it

> played a decisive role in the struggle by keeping together a united cadre of people who maintained and cultivated social norms and values during a desperate time. Thanks to the protracted existence of the movements in the underground . . . a consolidated and reliable nucleus stood at the disposal of the Jewish Fighting Organization.[138]

Vladka Meed maintains that "during all the years of the Nazi occupation, resistance took place," but that "in different times, it had different forms."[139] The uprising was the culmination of many smaller acts of resistance, including teaching and learning, and was only possible because of the "inner preparation to stand up against the enemy" created and maintained in clandestine schools, study groups, and in youth group lectures, cultural organizing, and political activity. She explains that in the three years prior to the Uprising, the Jews were preparing and organizing, and the groups that would rise to lead the Jews in revolt stayed "a part of the people" in a grassroots way. While other ghettos showed passive or spiritual resistance, none was able to organize the kind of armed revolt executed by the Jews of Warsaw. Meed attributes this to the fact that "in Warsaw, the ZOB and the underground leadership had a closer relationship with the Ghetto people at a critical time."[140] The Ghetto leadership — both the sanctioned and the underground — was tied into important community organizations, including schools. Furthermore, the youth group leadership was strong and committed. Vladka Meed explains:

> We, the youth, were taken over. We realized that this is an important mission we have to do. Not only for ourselves, but we had a certain idealism. And it was idealism that brought the Uprising. The majority of the organizers and fighters were from the organized youth, and we were raised in justice, humanity, and the belief in mankind.[141]

She added, "But when it comes to deciding our destiny about death, *we* decide in our own way."[142] The clandestine schools of the Warsaw Ghetto helped to provide students, teachers, and the organized community with power, hope, and a sense of humanity. They also served to develop unified group associations and to continue the processes of political socialization, which prepared the youth of the Warsaw Ghetto to lead the best organized and most heroic Jewish armed revolt in the history of the Holocaust.

CONCLUSION

Clandestine schooling helped the Warsaw Ghetto Jews, especially the youth, not only to cling to a sense of normalcy in an abnormal and horrific situation, but also to resist dehumanizing social, political, and physical forces bearing down on them day to day. Schooling also helped them maintain hope for the future. Clandestine schools helped the Jewish community stay organized and cohesive and, by ensuring the continuity of Jewish cultural and historical education, enabled the Jews to resist Nazi attempts at their cultural and historical obliteration. Moreover, the resistance — in its multiple forms and with its multiple purposes — was led by the strength, resolve, and idealism of the organized political youth groups. Ultimately, these groups provided an even greater and more heroic form of organized youth leadership. In her study on Jewish youth groups and resistance through education, Erica Nadelhaft writes:

> Through their educational programmes, cultural events, social-welfare programmes, and other activities, the youth movements were able to preserve their vitality and strength despite the overpowering demoralization and deterioration of ghetto life. Their ability to enclose themselves in their own spiritual world, to cling stubbornly to values and norms of behaviour in spite of all, and their refusal to acknowledge moral decay gave them the strength and determination to survive under Nazi rule. Members remained compassionate, loyal, and above

all, human. It was because of this determined and courageous effort that, when the time for armed resistance came, there existed a united, organized, and morally responsible body of young people willing to make a stand.[143]

For the Jews in the Warsaw Ghetto, schooling promoted resistance in multiple ways. In clandestine schools some Jews (both students and teachers) found relief against hunger, discord, and dehumanization. By aiding in children's and teachers' daily struggles to stay healthy and alive, by providing a sense of normalcy, and by instilling a sense of power and dignity, clandestine schools facilitated participation in a present-oriented resistance. Clandestine schools also facilitated a future-oriented resistance. Teaching and learning are inherently hopeful acts, and the Jews in the Warsaw Ghetto engaged in these acts with a desperate, pleading nod toward the future and the lives they hoped to reclaim when the dark days of the Ghetto were over. As teachers taught and students learned, Ghetto Jews were also engaged in a form of resistance that was at once past, present, and future oriented. They were resisting not only their individual demise and communal decay but also their cultural and historical annihilation. By committing themselves to a curriculum that was built on a shared sense of history, culture, and Jewish nationalism, education in the Warsaw Ghetto became an act of collective defiance. Hersz Wasser was a *Po'alei Zion* (Zion Workers) youth group member and the *Oneg Shabbat* Archive secretary. In an *Oneg Shabbat* essay describing the mission and work of YIKOR, Wasser described its "popular university," which offered Saturday morning lectures on current Jewish topics to hundreds of Ghetto residents. He made an explicit link between education, Jewish culture, and resistance. He wrote, "The intent of the lectures was not just to deepen the interest in science, Jewish history or sociology, but also to strengthen the sense of national dignity and the will to offer resistance."[144]

This story of the clandestine schools in the Warsaw Ghetto during the Holocaust reveals one answer to the essential question, What is schooling for? Survivor accounts woven together with archival evidence bring to life the ways in which schooling can be a form of resistance. This is a story of the relationship between school, community, and culture. It is also a story of courage and heroism — of students and their teachers learning and teaching together in the shadows of despair.

Notes

1. See, for example, Deut. 27:1–8, 31:12–13, found in *Tanakh: A New Translation of the Holy Scriptures According to the Traditional Hebrew Text* (New York: Jewish Publication Society, 1985); Abba Eban, *My People: The Story of the Jews* (New York: Random House, 1968); Chaim Potok *Wanderings* (New York: Alfred A. Knopf, 1978); Raphael Patai, *The Jewish Mind* (New York: Charles Scribner's Sons, 1977).
2. See, for example, John Dewey, *Democracy and Education* (New York: Free Press, 1916); Lawrence A. Cremin, *The Transformation of the School: Progressivism in American Education 1876–1957* (New York: Vintage Books, 1961); David B. Tyack, *The One Best*

System (Cambridge, MA: Harvard University Press, 1974); Patricia Albjerg Graham, "Schools: Cacophony about Practice, Silence about Purpose," *Daedalus, 113*, No. 4 (1984), 29–57; Paulo Freire, *Pedagogy of the Oppressed*, trans. M. B. Ramos (New York: Continuum, 1970); bell hooks, *Teaching to Transgress: Education as the Practice of Freedom* (New York: Routledge, 1994); Alfred N. Whitehead, *The Aims of Education and Other Essays* (New York: Free Press, 1929); Amy Gutman, *Democratic Education* (Princeton, NJ: Princeton University Press, 1987); Richard J. Murnane and Frank Levy, *Teaching the New Basic Skills: Principles for Educating Children to Thrive in a Changing Economy* (New York: Free Press, 1996); James P. Comer, *Waiting for a Miracle: Why Schools Can't Solve our Problems — And How We Can* (New York: Dutton, 1997).

3. It is important to study and understand the Holocaust in terms of the horrific images that comprise it; however, it is also important to resist these images as the only ones. There are also stories of courage, heroism, and resistance, and I seek to illuminate them and move them to the foreground. While this article purports to tell a story of resistance and heroism in the face of Nazi tyranny, it is perhaps also the story of my own resistance to forgetting, to silence, to dehumanization, and to hopelessness.

4. See, for example, Nora Levin, *The Holocaust: The Destruction of European Jewry 1933–1945* (New York: Schocken Books, 1973), p. 208; Israel Gutman, *The Jews of Warsaw 1939–1943: Ghetto, Underground, Revolt*, trans. I. Friedman (Bloomington: Indiana University Press, 1982), pp. 62–65; Anonymous, 1941, "The Jewish Quarter in Warsaw, ARI/PH/10a-2-3," in *Selected Documents from the Warsaw Ghetto Underground Archives, "O.S." Oneg Shabbath* (henceforth *O.S. Archives*), ed. J. Kermish, (Jerusalem: Yad Vashem, 1986), p. 146.

5. Levin, *The Holocaust*, p. 207; I. Gutman, *The Jews of Warsaw*, pp. 60, 62–65; Anonymous, "The Jewish Quarter in Warsaw," p. 146.

6. I. Gutman, *Jews of Warsaw*, pp. 15, 21, 31; Levin, *The Holocaust*, p. 208.

7. Nehemia Titelman, "Setting Up a Closed Ghetto, PH/33-1-8," in Kermish, *O.S. Archives*, pp. 143–145; I. Gutman, *Jews of Warsaw*, p. 48; Levin, *The Holocaust*, p. 208.

8. The *Judenrat* was the Jewish Council, established by the Nazis to receive and implement their dictates. The Council, composed of twenty-four Jewish members, was led by Adam Czerniakow.

9. "Bared heads" refers to the requirement that Jews remove their caps in deference to German guards.

10. Levin, *The Holocaust*, p. 230; I. Gutman, *Jews of Warsaw*, pp. 64–65. See also Ruta Sakowska, "The Warsaw Ghetto," in *The Warsaw Ghetto: The 45th Anniversary of the Uprising*. (Poland: Interpress, 1988), p. 10; "Cable Between Warsaw, London, New York, Tel Aviv, 16 March 1941," trans. L. Silverstein. From the Sikorski Collection, Archives of the YIVO Institute for Jewish Research, RG 493, Folder 174 #1394.

11. "The Wannsee Protocol, Minutes of Discussion 20 January 1942," in *The Holocaust: Selected Documents in Eighteen Volumes, Volume 11: The Wannsee Protocol and a 1944 Report on Auschwitz by the Office of Strategic Services* (New York: Garland, 1982), pp. 18–32.

12. I. Gutman, *Jews of Warsaw*, p. 65.

13. Levin, *The Holocaust*, p. 207.

14. Levin, *The Holocaust*, pp. 206–207; I. Gutman, *Jews of Warsaw*, p. 66.

15. Levin, *The Holocaust*, p. 225. See also Debórah Dwork, *Children with a Star: Jewish Youth in Nazi Europe* (New Haven, CT: Yale University Press, 1991), p. 159. In "Origins of the Education Problems in the Ghetto," *Yad Vashem Bulletin*, No. 12 (December 1962), p. 28, Joseph Kermish describes the intellectual and cultural life in the Ghetto as "filled with a deep spirit of Jewish creativity."

16. "Letter from Adolf Berman and Emmanuel Ringelblum in Warsaw to Jewish Scientific Institute in New York, March 20, 1944," trans. S. Chazen, G. Weiss, and W. Weiss. From the Sikorski Collection, Archives of the YIVO Institute for Jewish Research, RG

493, Folder 180 #1573. See also Joseph Rudavsky, *To Live with Hope, To Die with Honor: Spiritual Resistance in the Ghettos and Camps* (Northvale, NJ: Jason Aronson, 1997); Shimon Huberbrand, *Kiddush Hashem: Jewish Religious and Cultural Life in Poland During the Holocaust,* ed. J. Gurock and R. Hirt, trans. D. Fishman (New York: Yeshiva University Press, 1987); Levin, *The Holocaust;* I. Gutman, *Jews of Warsaw;* Kermish, *Selected Documents from O.S. Archives.*

17. Levin, *The Holocaust,* p. 228; I. Gutman, *Jews of Warsaw,* pp. 144–154.
18. The *Bund* was the Jewish Socialist Democratic Party.
19. Joseph Kermish, "The Underground Press in the Warsaw Ghetto," vol. I, pp. 104–105, as quoted in Levin, *The Holocaust,* pp. 228–229.
20. Levin, *The Holocaust,* p. 352; See also Israel Gutman, *Resistance: The Warsaw Ghetto Uprising* (Boston: Houghton Mifflin, 1994).
21. To understand better the complex political and power structure in the Ghetto, to illuminate the network and organization of underground schools, and to access commentary on clandestine schooling and other cultural events, I relied on the essays and documents of the *Oneg Shabbat* Archives (also known as the Ringelblum Archive), written, compiled, and buried by inhabitants of the Warsaw Ghetto in 1943, under the direction of historian and educator Emmanuel Ringelblum. Of the three collections of materials that were hidden in canisters in the Ghetto during the war, only two were found, one in 1946 and one in 1950. The third, containing material on the underground Jewish Fighting Organization, has never been recovered.

    The *Oneg Shabbat* (Joy of Sabbath) archives, located at the *Yad Vashem* museum in Jerusalem, contain many documents including essays, research surveys and reports, monographs, biographical portraits, announcements, underground periodicals, letters, and materials belonging to the underground organizations. *Oneg Shabbat* was initially intended to be an organization for scientific research, in the tradition of the Vilnius YIVO (Institute for Jewish Research), in which Ringelblum was active before the war. This tradition included interdisciplinary research combining history, sociology, and economics. *Oneg Shabbat* researchers collected data using surveys, questionnaires, guided interviews, and ethnographies that aimed to document the impact the war was having on the Jewish community. Materials were written and collected by an ideologically diverse group of community leaders, economists, educators, and other experts in relevant fields, many of whom came from the ranks of the youth group leadership. Because the compilation of the *Oneg Shabbat* archives was an underground activity, many of the documents are unsigned and undated. The documents I used have been published in a collection called *Selected Documents from the Warsaw Ghetto Underground Archive "O.S." ["Oneg Shabbath"],* ed. Joseph Kermish, trans. M. Z. Prives, Y. Kirshbaum, J. Karsch, S. Katz, L. Reznikoff, E. Shaul, and V. Brown (Jerusalem: Yad Vashem, 1986).
22. Anonymous, "The School System, ARI/74," in *O.S. Archives,* p. 501.
23. This concept of "transcending the moment" was first introduced to me in a personal communication with Eileen de los Reyes, Harvard Graduate School of Education, December 16, 1997.
24. Ana Natanblut, "Shuln in Varshever Geto," trans. P. Parsky, *YIVO Bleter* III, No. 2 (Winter 1947), p. 173.
25. Czerniakow, *Warsaw Diary,* p. 206.
26. Mary Berg, *Warsaw Ghetto* (New York: L. B. Fischer, 1945), pp. 32–33, quoted in Dwork, *Children with a Star,* pp. 181–182.
27. Berg, as quoted in Dwork, *Children with a Star,* p. 182.
28. "The School System," in *O.S. Archives,* p. 501. See also Dwork, *Children with a Star,* p. 201.
29. "The School System," in *O.S. Archives,* p. 503. See also I. Gutman, *Jews of Warsaw;* Dwork, *Children with a Star;* Natanblut, "Shuln in Varshever Geto," p. 173.

30. The *Judenrat* was permitted by the Nazis to open vocational schools for children and adults so that these trained Jews could then work in factories or industries in direct support of the German regime. In addition to the many vocational training activities organized, "the council did not hesitate to deceive the Germans and ran a comprehensive program of [regular academic] classes, including even university-level courses, under the guise of vocational training." I. Gutman, *Jews of Warsaw*, p. 83.
31. Kermish, *O.S. Archives*, p. 460. See also "The School System," in *O.S. Archives*, pp. 513–514.
32. Interview with Vladka (Fagele Peltel) Meed, Transcript of Oral History Interview, 1991, Courtesy of United States Holocaust Memorial Museum (USHMM) Department of Oral History, RG-50.030*153.
33. Natanblut, "Shuln in Varshever Geto," pp. 173–174. See also Genia Silkes, "Letter: Children-Heroes in the Days of Fire, Paris, April 21, 1950," trans. H. Agus, Archives of the YIVO Institute for Jewish Research, RG 1187, Box 3, Folder 39.
34. Anonymous, "A Preliminary Study in Teaching People During the War, PH/13-2-4," in *O.S. Archives*, pp. 468–469.
35. "A Preliminary Study in Teaching People During the War," in *O.S. Archives*, p. 471.
36. Natan Koninski, "The Profile of the Jewish Child, ARI/47," in *O.S. Archives*, p. 389.
37. Interview with Benjamin Meed, February, 29, 2000, New York City.
38. "Letter from Adolf Berman and Emmanuel Ringelblum in Warsaw to Jewish Scientific Institute in New York, March 20, 1944," YIVO Archives. See also Dr. Hillel Seidman, 1943, *The Warsaw Ghetto Diaries*, trans. Y. Israel (Southfield, MI: Targum Press, 1997), Diary Entry October 1, 1942, pp. 142–144.
39. Koninski, "The Profile of the Jewish Child," in *O.S. Archives*, p. 385.
40. Koninski, "The Profile of the Jewish Child," in *O.S. Archives*, p. 385.
41. See Janusz Korczak, *Ghetto Diary* (New York: Holocaust Library, 1978); Betty Jean Lifton, *The King of the Children: The Life and Death of Janusz Korczak* (New York: St. Martin's Griffin, 1997); Larry Brendtro and Denise Hinders, "A Saga of Janusz Korczak, the King of Children" (Essay Review), *Harvard Educational Review*, 60 (1990), 237–276.
42. Interview with David Kochalski, Transcript of Oral History Interview, 1994, Courtesy of USHMM Department of Oral History, RG-50.030*001.
43. Brendtro and Hinders, "A Saga of Janusz Korczak," p. 245.
44. Interview with Erwin Baum, Transcript of Oral History Interview, 1994, Courtesy of USHMM Department of Oral History, RG-50.030*016.
45. Anonymous, "Jewish Youth in Warsaw in the War Years," in *O.S. Archives*, p. 516.
46. I. Gutman, *Jews of Warsaw*, p. 141.
47. Erica Nadelhaft, "Resistance through Education: Polish Zionist Youth Movements in Warsaw, 1939–1941," in *Poles, Jews, Socialists: The Failure of an Ideal*, ed. A. Polonsky, I. Bartal, G. Hundert, M. Opalski, and J. Tomaszewski (London: Littman Library of Jewish Civilization, 1996), p. 227.
48. Interview with Leah Silverstein, Transcript of Oral History Interview, 1996, Courtesy of USHMM Department of Oral History, RG-50.030*363.
49. Interview with Vladka Meed, February, 28, 2000, New York City.
50. I. Gutman, *Jews of Warsaw*, p. 129.
51. Anonymous, "A Call for the Establishment of an Organization for 'Moral Supply in the Warsaw Ghetto,' ARI/88," in *O.S. Archives*, p. 456.
52. "A Preliminary Study in Teaching People During the War," in *O.S. Archives*, p. 472.
53. Kermish, "Origins of the Education Problems in the Ghetto," p. 31.
54. "A Preliminary Study in Teaching People During the War," in *O.S. Archives*, p. 470.
55. "The School System," in *O.S. Archives*, p. 505.
56. "A Preliminary Study in Teaching People During the War," in *O.S. Archives*, p. 473.

57. Interview with Vladka (Fagele Peltel) Meed, Transcript of Oral History Interview, Courtesy of USHMM.
58. Interview with Joseph S. Kutrzeba (Fajwiszys), February, 12, 2000, Rego Park, New York.
59. Interview with Joseph S. Kutrzeba (Fajwiszys), February, 12, 2000.
60. Interview with Joseph S. Kutrzeba (Fajwiszys), February, 12, 2000.
61. Rudavsky, *To Live with Hope*, pp. 52–53.
62. Rudavsky, *To Live with Hope*, pp. 52–53; Nadelhaft, "Resistance through Education," p. 228.
63. Seidman, *Warsaw Ghetto Diaries*, pp. 305–306.
64. "'Patronage' of Torah Study-Groups," in *O.S. Archives*, p. 417; Seidman, *Warsaw Ghetto Diaries*, p. 306.
65. Emmanuel Ringelblum, 1942, *Notes from the Warsaw Ghetto*, ed. and trans. J. Sloan (New York: McGraw-Hill, 1958), p. 138.
66. Czerniakow, *Warsaw Diary*, p. 206.
67. I. Gutman, *Jews of Warsaw*, p. 84. See also "The School System," in *O.S. Archives*, pp. 506–507.
68. "The Patronate of the Jewish Cultural Activity in Warsaw, ARI/217," in *O.S. Archives*, p. 463.
69. Natanblut, "Shuln in Varshever Geto," p. 174.
70. Natanblut, "Shuln in Varshever Geto," p. 174.
71. Czerniakow, *Warsaw Diary*, p. 312.
72. Natanblut, "Shuln in Varshever Geto," p. 180.
73. Natanblut, "Shuln in Varshever Geto," p. 182.
74. Natanblut, "Shuln in Varshever Geto," p. 182.
75. Czerniakow, *Warsaw Diary*, pp. 317–318.
76. I. Gutman, *Jews of Warsaw*, p. 84.
77. I. Gutman, *Jews of Warsaw*, p. 84; Natanblut, "Shuln in Varshever Geto," p. 180; "'Patronage' of Torah Study-Groups, ARII/104," in *O.S. Archives*, pp. 417–418.
78. Czerniakow, *Warsaw Diary*, p. 374.
79. Czerniakow, *Warsaw Diary*, pp. 385; Dwork, *Children with a Star*, p. 173.
80. I. Gutman, *Jews of Warsaw*, pp. 197, 213.
81. "The Aryan side" is a common reference to what lay on the other side of the Ghetto walls, namely communities devoid of Jews.
82. I. Gutman, *Jews of Warsaw*, p. 213.
83. Anonymous, 1942, "The Destruction of Warsaw, II/198," in *O.S. Archives*, pp. 701–703; Anonymous, 1942, "Reminiscences of a Treblinka Escape, ARII/295," in *O.S. Archives*, pp. 710–716; Gutman, *Jews of Warsaw*, p. 223.
84. Natanblut, "Shuln in Varshever Geto," p. 185.
85. I. Gutman, *Jews of Warsaw*, p. 236.
86. Koninski, 1941, "The Profile of the Jewish Child," in *O.S. Archives*, pp. 371–373, 386; "The School System," in *O.S. Archives*, p. 505; "A Preliminary Study in Teaching People During the War," in *O.S. Archives*, p. 468.
87. "The School System," in *O.S. Archives*, p. 501.
88. "The School System," in *O.S. Archives*, p. 502.
89. "The School System," in *O.S. Archives*, pp. 501–502.
90. Interview with Joseph S. Kutrzeba (Fajwiszys), February, 12, 2000.
91. Interview with Leah Silverstein, February 9, 1998, Silver Spring, MD.
92. Interview with Leah Silverstein, Transcript of Oral History Interview, Courtesy of USHMM.
93. Dwork, *Children with a Star*, p. 180.
94. Chaim A. Kaplan, *Scroll of Agony*, quoted in Dwork, *Children with a Star*, p. 189.

95. I. Gutman, *Jews of Warsaw*, p. 115.
96. I. Gutman, *Jews of Warsaw*, p. 95.
97. Interview with David Kochalski, Transcript of Oral History Interview, Courtesy of USHMM.
98. Interview with Benjamin Meed, February, 29, 2000.
99. Rudavsky, *To Live with Hope*, p. 39.
100. Rudavsky, *To Live with Hope*, p. 39.
101. Kermish, *Selected Documents from O.S.*, pp. 458–459.
102. Marian Malowist, 1942?, "Youth and their Education in the Ghetto, ARI/38," in *O.S. Archives*, p. 497.
103. "The School System," in *O.S. Archives*, pp. 501–502, 509.
104. Anonymous, "An Outline of Pedagogical Activity in the Alimentation Points on Karmelicka Street 29, Nowolipki Str. 39, and Krochmalna Str. 96, PH/5-4-3," in *O.S. Archives*, pp. 474–475.
105. "An Outline of Pedagogical Activity in the Alimentation Points on Karmelicka Street 29, Nowolipki Str. 39, and Krochmalna Str. 96," in *O.S. Archives*, p. 474.
106. "An Outline of Pedagogical Activity in the Alimentation Points on Karmelicka Street 29, Nowolipki Str. 39, and Krochmalna Str. 96," in *O.S. Archives*, pp. 474–475.
107. Among the most important aims was teaching students critical hygiene lessons to help them avoid typhus in the disease-ridden Ghetto.
108. Sol Lipzin, *A History of Yiddish Literature* (New York: Jonathan David, 1985), p. 56.
109. Lipzin, *A History of Yiddish Literature*, p. 56.
110. Lipzin, *A History of Yiddish Literature*, p. 62.
111. Lipzin, *A History of Yiddish Literature*, p. 68.
112. Lipzin, *A History of Yiddish Literature*, p. 68.
113. Kermish, "Origins of the Education Problems in the Ghetto," p. 29.
114. Natanblut, "Shuln in Varshever Geto," p. 181.
115. Natanblut, "Shuln in Varshever Geto," p. 181.
116. Natanblut, "Shuln in Varshever Geto," p. 181.
117. Natanblut, "Shuln in Varshever Geto," p. 181.
118. I. Gutman, *Jews of Warsaw*, p. 133.
119. Interview with Benjamin Meed, February, 29, 2000.
120. *Neged HaZerem*, 13/2, Yad Vashem Archive, Underground Press Division, as quoted in I. Gutman, *Jews of Warsaw*, p. 142.
121. I. Gutman, *Jews of Warsaw*, p. 142.
122. *Yugnt-Shtime*, II (September 1941), Yad Vashem Archive, Underground Press Division, as quoted in I. Gutman, *Jews of Warsaw*, p. 142.
123. I. Gutman, *Jews of Warsaw*, p. 133.
124. I. Gutman, *Jews of Warsaw*, p. 152.
125. I. Gutman, *Jews of Warsaw*, p. 153.
126. Kermish, "Origins of the Education Problems in the Ghetto," p. 32.
127. Interview with Leah Silverstein, Transcript of Oral History Interview, Courtesy of USHMM.
128. Interview with Joseph S. Kutrzeba (Fajwiszys), February 12, 2000.
129. Nadelhaft, "Resistance through Education," pp. 218–219.
130. Nadelhaft, "Resistance through Education," p. 229.
131. Interview with Vladka Meed, February, 28, 2000.
132. I. Gutman, *Jews of Warsaw*, p. 121.
133. I. Gutman, *Jews of Warsaw*, p. 83.
134. Interview with Leah Silverstein, Transcript of Oral History Interview, Courtesy of USHMM.

135. I. Gutman, *Jews of Warsaw*, p. 144; "Resistance through Education," pp. 212, 221. See also Interview with Vladka Meed, February, 28, 2000; Interview with Leah Silverstein, February 9, 1998, Silver Spring, MD.
136. I. Gutman, *Jews of Warsaw*, pp. 311–313.
137. I. Gutman, *Jews of Warsaw*, pp. 364–440. See also Levin, *The Holocaust*, pp. 317–361; Simha Rotem, *Memoirs of a Warsaw Ghetto Fighter*, trans. B. Harshav (New Haven, CT: Yale University Press, 1994); Vladka Meed, *On Both Sides of the Wall*, trans. S. Meed (Washington, DC: Holocaust Library in Conjunction with the United States Holocaust Memorial Museum, 1993); Azriel Eisenberg, ed., *Witness to the Holocaust* (New York: Pilgrim Press, 1981), pp. 393–410.
138. I. Gutman, *Jews of Warsaw*, p. 144.
139. Interview with Vladka Meed, February, 28, 2000.
140. Interview with Vladka Meed, February, 28, 2000.
141. Interview with Vladka Meed, Transcript of Oral History Interview, Courtesy of USHMM.
142. Interview with Vladka Meed, Transcript of Oral History Interview, Courtesy of USHMM.
143. Nadelhaft, "Resistance through Education," p. 231.
144. Wasser, Hersz, 1942, "Yiddish Culture Organization 'YIKOR,' Warsaw Ghetto 1940–1942," in *O.S. Archives*, p. 444.

This project has truly been a community effort. Above all, I owe my deepest gratitude to the survivors who gave generously of their time and of themselves to tell me their stories and to critique my retelling. They are Leah Silverstein, Saul Horn, Vladka Meed, Rachel Gurdus, Benjamin Meed, and Joseph S. Kutrzeba (Fajwiszys). Second, I am indebted to the translators and those who helped me find them. I am grateful to the research staffs, archivists, and volunteers of the United States Holocaust Memorial Museum, Washington, DC, and the YIVO Institute for Jewish Research in New York City. Many thanks also to Richard F. Elmore, Leslie Santee Siskin, and Patricia Albjerg Graham, who respectively spurred the conception of this project, encouraged the big ideas, guided the methodology, and saw it through to the end. Finally, thanks to colleagues, friends, and family who believed in the importance of this project and in my ability to complete it. In particular they are Neal Brown, Robert R. Carson, Jr., Dr. David J. Cowen, Alana Feiler, Hillary Johnson, Lesley Nye, and Heather G. Peske. I am also grateful to Adriana Katzew and Tere Sordé Martí, of the *Harvard Educational Review*, for their passionate work on this article.

This article is dedicated to the martyrs and heroes of the Warsaw Ghetto, whom I have come to better understand, to admire, to long for, and to love. It is especially dedicated to the youngest victims — to the students — and their teachers, who learned and taught together in the shadows of despair. They knew that to be counted among the living they needed each other, their history, and their culture. Not bread alone.

Community Education: To Reclaim and Transform What Has Been Made Invisible

MUNIR FASHEH

In describing anyone or anything that cannot survive on its own, Palestinian Arabs in the Galilee say, "It is like an Israeli hen." The difference between the Israeli hen and the indigenous Palestinian hen is that the first cannot survive, grow, or produce eggs without special shots, a special mixture of food, specific temperatures, and a specific schedule; it requires some kind of "scientific and rational" planning and constant support from outside. In fact, any change in the food mixture or in the conditions surrounding the Israeli hen can lead to its inability to produce eggs, at least for a while. In short, if this "technological" hen is taken out of its "artificial and ideological" environment and put into the "real" environment, it will have difficulty surviving.

By contrast, the indigenous Palestinian hen survives because of the characteristics it has developed through the ages, thriving on what it finds in the environment and through its ability to adapt to diverse conditions. It will even consume its own excrement, if need be, in order to survive. These qualities — internal strength, "feeling at home" within the environment, and the ability to adapt to diverse conditions — have helped the indigenous hen to survive for thousands of years.

Human beings and communities require these same qualities for survival and growth; but they also require the qualities of empowerment, creativity, and increased capacity for learning. The role of education in promoting or hindering the development of these qualities is crucial.

I believe that most graduates of the formal educational system within the Palestinian community are like the Israeli hen: their survival depends on external support, and their values are based on artificial, induced, or symbolic qualities. Such graduates live on a special mixture of courses and curricula that are "scientifically and rationally" planned and prepared for them by experts, mainly from abroad. Further, such graduates are in general alienated from their own environment and are mostly blind or insensitive to its basic problems and needs. When the surrounding conditions change, or when real-world situations must be dealt with, such graduates become confused: the "correct" answers and ready solutions they learned in the schools and universities suddenly become useless and meaningless.

The Contrast between My Math and My Mother's Math

The contrast between the educated Israeli hen and the indigenous Palestinian hen parallels the contrast between the mathematics that I studied and taught in schools and universities for more than twenty years and the mathematics of my mother, who is illiterate. This contrast illustrates the importance of one's relationship to the environment, in both the ideological and the real sense.[1]

To borrow an expression from T. J. Jackson Lears, the ideological environment serves to mark "the boundaries of permissible discourse, discourage the clarification of social alternatives, and make it difficult for the dispossessed to locate the source of their uneasiness, let alone remedy it."[2] This environment "functions to 'position' people in the world, to shape the range of possible meanings surrounding an issue, and to actively construct reality."[3] Shaped as it is by existing power relationships, the ideological environment reflects the ideas, perspectives, interests, and behavior of dominant groups and nations, through local elites and urban centers.

The real environment, on the other hand, represents what formal education under these conditions normally marginalizes or excludes. It extends from the immediacies of the historical process as experienced by people, to the social institutions (material, spiritual, and intellectual), productive activities, and cultural traditions that shape people's responses.[4]

It was a drastic event in my life — the 1967 Israeli-Arab war — that caused me to realize certain fundamental things about life, including education and its relation to the environment and the community. That war raised in my mind the first serious challenge to the kind of education — and later to the math — I had been given (and was teaching), both at the school and university levels. In particular, I became aware of my illiterate mother's math.[5]

When the 1967 Israeli-Arab war broke out, I was twenty-six years old, with a master's degree and five years' experience teaching math at various levels. The war shook the foundations of my small, comfortable, and seemingly consistent and meaningful world, a world created by formal, institutionalized education. The war revealed how little we — the formally educated — knew. Almost none of our conceptions, convictions, and expectations matched what was going on. Although I started questioning education in general almost immediately after the war, I did not at that time consider the possible relation of math and physics to many of the problems in today's world, nor did I question the fundamental assumptions upon which math and science were based. In fact, as a result of the war I became more convinced that one task I had as an educator was to expand the use of logic and science in the world through teaching.

I thought that what we needed was more math, a "New Math," as well as better and more diversified ways of teaching it. For six years (1972–78) I was formally involved in math instruction at several levels and in different ways in the schools of the West Bank. But the "New Math" I was in charge of introducing into the schools was, I realized, fundamentally alien, dry, and irrelevant to both students and teachers. In order to overcome this problem, I encouraged the incorporation of cultural concepts, independent avenues of exploration, and personal feelings into the work. I encouraged teachers, for example, to ask small children such questions as, "Which do you like more, five or two, and why?" and not only questions like, "Which is greater, five or two, and why?" I also stressed the idea that most if not all children are logical in their own way and that the job of teachers is to explore and discuss that personal logic. In addition to classroom teaching, I established math clubs, magazines, general discussion meetings, and in-service courses.[6] This approach revitalized the teaching, introduced both structure and logic, and was important in developing creativity and enthusiasm among both teachers and students. It did not yet lead me, however, to question hegemonic assumptions behind the math itself. It was discovery of my mother's math that led me to question such assumptions.

Math was necessary for my mother in a much more profound and real sense than it was for me. Unable to read or write, my mother routinely took rectangles of fabric and, with few measurements and no patterns, cut them and turned them into beautiful, perfectly fitted clothing for people. In 1976, I realized that the mathematics she was using was beyond my comprehension. Moreover, although mathematics was a subject matter that I studied and taught, for her it was basic to the operation of her understanding. What she was doing was math in the sense that it embodied order, pattern, relations, and measurement. It was math because she was breaking a whole into smaller parts and constructing a new whole out of most of the pieces, a new whole that had its own style, shape, and size, and that had to fit a specific person. Mistakes in her math entailed practical consequences, unlike mistakes in my math.

The value of her math and its relationship to the world around her, moreover, was drastically different from mine. My math had no connection to power in the community or the practical world of making things; it was connected solely to symbolic power through the Western hegemonic culture that had engendered it. Without the official ideological support system, no one would have needed my math; its value was derived from a set of symbols created by the hegemony of the dominant culture and by the world of education. In contrast, my mother's math was so deeply embedded in the culture that it was invisible to eyes trained by formal education. Her math had no symbols of power. Its value was connected to concrete and immediate needs and actions.

Seeing my mother's math in context helped me see my math in the context of power. This social context limited her empowerment by minimizing the value of her experience, discrediting her as a woman and an uneducated person, and paying her extremely poor wages for her work. She never understood that social context and was vulnerable to its hegemonic assertions. She never wanted any of her children to learn her profession, sewing clothes; instead, she and my father worked very hard to see that their children were educated and did not work with their hands. As a result, it came as a shock to me when I realized the complexity and richness of my mother's relationship to mathematics. Mathematics was integrated into her world as it had never been integrated into mine. In retrospect, I wish I had learned more about her work and the knowledge embedded in it (though that knowledge was unarticulated) so that I could have combined it with the formal math I had learned. She knew in practice much more than she was able to tell. In contrast, I was able to articulate words and manipulate symbols much more than I was able to put them into practice.

My mother's math was biased toward life, action, production, and personal experience, and it was linked to immediate and concrete needs in the community. My math, on the other hand, was biased toward the manipulation of symbols and theories linked mainly to technological advancement and techniques that usually lead to military, political, and economic power and control. What was lacking in my mother's knowledge was articulated structure and theory, while what was lacking in my knowledge was practice, relevance, and a context. In this sense, neither her knowledge nor mine was a praxis; each form of knowledge lacked one part of the dialectical relationship between life and mental construction, between practice and theory, between the world and our consciousness of it, between reality and our perceptions of it.

I was initially attracted to math and physics because of what I felt to be their role in making the world more intelligible, by finding patterns and relationships and describing them in words, formulas, and theories. It was fascinating for me to realize, for example, that there is a single principle (the law of gravity) that explains falling apples, rising balloons, the rotation of the moon around the earth, and tides. Math and science were attractive because they could help explain phenomena and predict events. I was fascinated by the power of logic to make absolute statements that transcend place, time, and speaker; by the fact that one could reduce a whole system of ideas and statements to very few basic axioms. In addition, math and science enabled people to do such concrete things as build bridges, construct radios, make planes, and facilitate surgery.

I was also attracted to math and science because of the claims made about them: that math and science require higher intelligence than other fields; that science eventually would solve all problems; that math and science enable people to discover objective, universal truths and absolute laws; that expressing ideas in numbers is superior to other forms of expression; that math and science transcend national, racial, and gender boundaries. Furthermore,

I was attracted to math and science because of the claims about their role in improving the human condition, generating tolerance, reducing inequities, and raising people to a higher level of civilization. This was the image of math and science I had internalized and this was the image I preached. Although I was aware that math, science, and technology were also used to produce bombs and pollution, I believed this to be an aberration, an abuse. When pressed to explain the paradox, I responded with the answer that I had internalized: that it was people who abused math and science; at worst, I parroted back the notion that math and science were neutral and thus could be used to any end. I was convinced that the ethical, moral, humanitarian dimension of math and science was both the fundamental role and the norm. In short, I was attracted to study and later teach math and science because they wee associated with things that were pleasurable, ethical, intellectual, and useful, and because of the claims that linked math and science to progress and to the improvement of the human condition.

In 1967, I started to see the practical limits of the education I had been given. The Six-Day War started a process that made the real environment and its power relations more visible. My sense of the intellectual, moral, and humanitarian dimensions of math and science gradually gave way to a sense of the central functions of math and science: creating power and generating hegemony. The stunning Israeli military victory in 1967 was a victory of superior math, science, and technology — not a victory of moral superiority or greater personal courage. The message of the highly sophisticated war planes and bombs was loud and clear. Thus, although it is true that math, science, and technology produce planes, for example, that can transport people for harmless purposes, they frequently produce war planes whose function is to kill and destroy. In almost every country in the world the number of war planes is many times the number of civilian planes. Just as it is misleading to emphasize the protein and other values in meat that has been poisoned, it is deceptive to stress only the technical skills and knowledge one can acquire through education while ignoring its potentially dangerous consequences. In addition to the destructive machinery, certain values and patterns of thinking and behaving that are associated with current models of learning are equally destructive.[7]

My mother's sewing demonstrated another way of conceptualizing and doing mathematics, another kind of knowledge, and the place of that knowledge in the world. But the value of my mother's tradition and of her kind of mathematics and knowledge, though not intrinsically disempowering, was continually discredited by the world around her, by what Paulo Freire calls the "culture of silence,"[8] and by cultural hegemony. Although I was not yet ready to question the theoretical bases of positivistic math and science, this discovery allowed me to recognize the need for a different type of education, and to respect all forms of knowledge and their relation to action.

Formal Education, Hegemony, and Power

The discovery of my mother's math was a discovery about the world and about the relation between hegemony and knowledge. Hegemony does not simply provide knowledge; rather, it substitutes one kind of knowledge for another in the context of a power relationship. Power, in this sense, is almost defined by what is excluded. While I was struggling to make the mathematics I had learned meaningful, what I was seeking was, in fact, in front of me, made invisible to both my mother and me by the education I had been given and that she had desired for me. To recognize my mother's activity as math was for me to recognize that education and knowledge are not only about facts but also about the inner logic of society, both within itself and in relation to outside forces.

The most crucial issue this discussion raises is that of the relation of education to the world it inhabits, the relation of the learner to his or her community and environment. The education I received prepared me to live in a world created by that education and hegemony. It left me blind to its ideological dimension, to the relationship between the knowledge transmitted to me and power. This blindness, which I believe is characteristic of hegemonically educated Third World people, left me unfit to live in the real world and its environment, unaware of its needs and resources. Like the Israeli hen, I was constantly sheltered from events in the real environment, and I looked for support and a sense of worth from outside. My strength did not emanate from internal qualities but from external sources. Hegemony is characterized not only by what it includes but also by what it excludes: by what it renders marginal, deems inferior, and makes invisible. As a result, the effects of hegemonic education make it possible to define the real environment by what formal education marginalizes or excludes.

Hegemony is to be understood here as a form of domination.[9] It often precedes political and military conquests and continues after them. But unlike military conquest, hegemonic conquest permeates almost all spheres, and those being dominated facilitate their own domination. Hegemony is always linked to an ideology that reflects the manners and interests of the invaders and their culture. This ideology embodies certain conceptions, values, language, relations, and interests that are translated into daily practices. Crucial to the hegemonic relationship is the belief of the conquered that the lifestyle and values of the hegemonic group are inherently, naturally, and objectively superior. Hegemony is successful when the invader's ideology is taken or even assumed to be universal and superior; when, like the math I valued, it is believed to transcend class, gender, culture, and national boundaries.

Ideology is a worldview that embodies a particular language and certain conceptions, values, relations, and interests that are translated into daily practices and that produce a certain consciousness. Consequently, the role of intellectuals and institutions is of primary importance, since the reproduction of a hegemonic ideology is achieved through them. Intellectual development in a colonial hegemonic context is designed to provide ideology without a basis in power. This allows intellectuals to participate vicariously in the moral, intellectual, humanitarian, and technical aspects of Western culture, as well as in educational, scholarly, and research activities. The training of colonial intellectuals directs them to derive their sense of worth and status from this vicarious participation, alienating them from their own culture, history, and people. The indigenous population, however, often supports this process by giving status to such intellectuals. Generally speaking, hegemonic education produces intellectuals who have lost their power base in their own culture and society and who have been provided with a foreign culture and ideology, but without a power base in the hegemonic society. I personally have seen this process as I have worked with and observed Palestinian intellectuals over the past twelve years. I have observed that, because they lacked a power base at both ends, these intellectuals tend to sharply overvalue symbolic power and tokens — such as titles, degrees, access to prestigious institutions, and awards — associated with the dominant culture.

Ultimately, I found that the power of Western hegemony rests on the claims of superiority, universality, and ethical neutrality of Western math, positivistic science, technology, and education. These claims of Western superiority extend into social, cultural, moral, political, and intellectual spheres. But continuing to accept Western math, science, and education as universal and authoritative is detrimental to creating a healthier and more humane world. Like any other human activities, math, science, and education need a critical analysis, not only at the implementation and application stage but also, and more important, at the level of the basic premises and values that govern their conceptions, practices, and production.[10]

In short, the 1967 war, its aftermath, and the discovery of my mother's math convinced me that education can do one of two things: it can either introduce hegemony into the community, or it can reclaim and develop what has been made invisible by hegemony.

Education of the second kind, which I refer to in this essay as community education, requires us to use our senses again, to make things visible, and to allow people to speak. Like many other peoples in the Third World, Palestinians have been denied the value of our experience and have been robbed of our voice and sense of self-worth. Value, language, and visibility are at stake here because they have been taken away from a people's fundamental activities. My mother, for example, was unable — and was never given the chance — to articulate her work and her thinking. Meaningful education, or community education, thus reclaims people's lives, their sense of self-worth, and their ways of thinking from the hegemonic structures, and facilitates their ability to articulate what they do and think about in order to provide a foundation for autonomous action.

A Historical Note on Palestinian Education

The roots of the educational system that evolved in the region that includes Palestine go back to Napoleon's invasion of Egypt and Palestine in 1798.[11] Along with the military invasions of the Middle East (which have never ceased since the time of Napoleon), there were also invasions on the economic and sociocultural fronts. Publishing and education were the main avenues for the sociocultural invasions. By the early twentieth century, for example, English, French, German, American, and Italian schools were already active in Palestine, effectively working to gain "converts" to their respective cultures. Since the British occupation of Palestine following World War I, education for Palestinians has been held hostage by outside powers: first by the British and later (since 1948) by some Arab governments (depending on the region) and by Israel.

In spite of its colonialist character, however, formal education helped provide economic security and upward mobility for many Palestinians in the 1950s and 1960s. As a result of losing land and other means of earning a living in 1948, Palestinians turned toward education as a primary means for survival. In spite of the hardships and the impossibility of any central or national planning, by the early 1970s the number of Palestinians studying in universities in proportion to their population as a whole was among the highest in the world.[12] The goal of education was simple and clear: getting degrees in order to get jobs. The types of degrees that Palestinians sought were determined by the professions, areas of specialization, and types of jobs that were available, mainly in neighboring Arab countries. Certain crucial needs — such as those related to the economic development of the community; the intellectual, social, and creative development of children; and the development of relevant research paradigms — were neglected. In addition, needs related to women's issues and to organization, management, and communication skills were ignored. In the 1970s and 1980s, conditions changed significantly. Many types of jobs that were traditionally in demand became less available, which led to growing unemployment among traditionally educated Palestinians. Moreover, formal educational institutions became even less able to function during these years because of military harassment and closure orders.[13] And even when they are functioning, conditions are not conducive to teaching or studying because of increasing class size, shrinking salaries and budgets, escalating fear and harassment of teachers and students, lack of proper facilities, and so forth.

Although the hegemonic trend in formal education has been by far the dominant one among Palestinians, attempts have been made by Palestinians to develop relevant projects and programs in education. More than fifty years ago, for example, a well-known Palestinian educator, Khalil Sakakini, became completely disenchanted with formal education and established a school in Jerusalem that stressed children's intellectual and social growth and happiness, rather than the teaching of a rigid and fixed curriculum. Moreover, evaluation in the school did not depend on grades but rather on achieving competencies by having the children become competent at whatever they did. More recently, there have been attempts to establish the Palestine Open University in Beirut,[14] and certain other non-hegemonic schools and programs in universities in the West Bank. Since 1971 I have personally been involved in various non-formal education activities, both within and outside schools.[15] Most of these attempts, however, were forcibly destroyed, blocked, or marginalized. The beginnings of the Palestine Open University were completely and deliberately destroyed by the Israelis during the 1982 invasion of Lebanon.[16]

There have been many attempts to develop relevant programs in education within the West Bank universities. The Israeli government would not give a permit, however, to An-Najah University to establish a school of agriculture, which would strengthen people's connection to the land and to production. Nor was Birzeit University given a permit (for more than ten years) to establish a school of fine arts, which would promote people's expressions of their culture, hopes, worries, realities, and visions. Nor would Israel allow Bethlehem University to establish a program to train tourist guides, who could open the eyes of tourists to the existence of the Palestinian people and to their reality, history, and culture.

A few small programs dealing with essential needs in the community still exist in some universities, but these programs have been marginalized and limited through measures introduced by the Israeli government, as well as by the formal character of standard education among the Palestinians. These programs include the Community Work Program, the Community Health Unit, the Literacy and Adult Education Program, and the Center for Environment Studies, all at Birzeit University; the Center for Rural Development and Research at An-Najah University; and the Nursing, Hotel Management, Tourist Guides (though not licensed), and Preschool Program at Bethlehem University.

At the school level, the most significant attempt to make education more meaningful has been the program entitled "Education for Awareness and Involvement," which was launched at the Lutheran schools in the Jerusalem area. The purpose of this program, according to one of its pamphlets, is to "help students become more aware of themselves and their community and readying them for involvement in the solution of the problems of their society and its development." In the lower grades and at the preschool level, the Early Childhood Resource Center and the pioneering work in some of the kindergartens in Zababdeh and Beit Sahur represent the main attempt to develop an education that is more meaningful to Palestinian children.

Current Events and Their Impact on Education Among the Palestinians

Just as the impact of the 1967 war started a process that made the real environment and power relations more visible, events since the *intifadeh* in December 1987 are proving that fundamental changes in education are usually not generated from within education itself, and do not happen as a result of preaching, conferences, or resolutions, or by grand designs or expertise on the subject. Rather, such changes are usually generated in response to drastic changes, events, or crises in the environment, by people who are ready to seize the opportunity created by the new conditions and who are competent in recognizing and dealing with the accompanying challenges and needs. At this time no one can completely foresee the full impact of the current conditions on Palestinian society and on education in particular. We can be sure, however, of one thing: that the current conditions and changes will have tremendous consequences, both positive and negative, on Palestinian children and their education.

At the visible level, all educational institutions have been closed by the Israeli government since December 1987 (with the exception of a few weeks).[17] This means the loss, so far, of two academic years for all students. The closure affects 310,000 students at the school level and 18,000 students at the postsecondary level. These numbers represent more than one-third of the total population of the West Bank. More than 13,000 West Bank teachers have been without work for almost two years. By September 1989 there were already two years' worth of preschoolers who did not properly go through the first grade, in addition to this year's new class. Since 1948, education has offered the only path for many Palestinians to make a good living, and clearly, closing schools for such an extended period will have drastic consequences. In addition, all attempts by some private schools and by those operated by the United Nations to distribute educational materials have been considered illegal, and all attempts to teach children at home have been deemed criminal acts under Israeli law in the West Bank.[18]

At the invisible level, the arbitrary use of terror by Israeli soldiers and settlers against Palestinian children will probably have far-reaching effects. What happens to the seven- or twelve-year-old child living in a refugee camp who has been experiencing almost daily the killing or torturing of family members and friends, the beatings and breaking of bones, the breaking into of homes and the destruction of furniture and equipment, living under curfews that extend (sometimes without electricity or water) for weeks and sometimes months? What type of person such a child will become is beyond my ability to imagine.[19] One thing is certain: that these children will internalize this arbitrariness and terror. The most comprehensive and accurate study of children under the *intifadeh* is, by far, the one produced by Anne Nixon of Save the Children in East Jerusalem.[20] The report tracks and details the high percentage of child death, injury, and detention by using extensive case studies, records, and statistical analysis. It also examines collective punishment, and its devastating psychological effects on children and family functioning after one year of the uprising. Finally, the education section of the report examines two primary areas of concern: the denial of the right to education because of school closures, and the schools (when they are open) as a locus of violence.

The Israeli occupation has imposed a climate of terror and misery on the Palestinian people. The corresponding courage, actions, and hope exercised by Palestinians is best described in the words of M. Scott Peck in his book *The Road Less Traveled:* "Courage is not the absence of fear; it is the making of action in spite of fear."[21] He goes on: "Evil is the exercise of political power, that is, the imposition of one's will upon others by overt or covert coercion. . . . I have come to conclude [however] that . . . evil backfires in the big picture of human evolution. For every soul it destroys, it is instrumental in the salvation of others."[22]

Under these conditions, talking about education among Palestinians in the future necessarily means talking about more than just opening schools and going back to the syllabi and tests. It will not be easy, for example, under the old system to control a child who has discovered his power and his dignity. It is not going to be easy to teach history to a child who feels that he or she has been making history. During the past two years, Palestinians have been experiencing a passion of hope and a sense of empowerment as never before. After almost half a century of world silence and inaction concerning the plight of the Palestinians, the children and the very stones have cried out, and their cry has been heard. Palestinians are learning through daily experience that the combination of misery, hope, understanding, creativity, empowerment, and action is exactly what goes into the making of human beings. That is indeed the message they exemplify for education everywhere.

I personally witnessed two events during this period that will help illustrate what Palestinians have been learning. I once watched a boy of seven or eight hiding behind a wall watching several soldiers trying to pull down a Palestinian flag that was hanging over an electric wire. This means of raising the Palestinian flag has been a common practice since the beginning of the *intifadeh:* children attach a flag to one end of a string and a stone to the other end, and then throw it over an electric wire so that the flag will hang high. These actions always draw soldiers, with their sophisticated equipment, to the site of the "crime." On that particular day, the soldiers could not get the flag down through "conventional" means, so they extended a long tube, ignited the top, and burned the flag. After the soldiers left, the boy ran and came back with another boy, threw another flag over the wire, and hid behind the wall — to wait for new soldiers to come. Through this creative, innocent "game" this boy feels empowered, that his actions can make a difference: he can manipulate — almost daily — the fourth-strongest army in the world! That boy is now aware of and able to use the power that exists in every human being.

The second event concerns another common scene in the West Bank and the Gaza Strip. A number of soldiers were harshly beating a young man in his early twenties in the central district of Ramallah. Several women rushed toward the scene shouting and trying to pull the soldiers away from the young man. Suddenly, a woman carrying a baby ran up and started shouting at the young man, "I told you not to leave the house today, that the situation is too dangerous. But you didn't listen; you never listen to me." Then she turned to the soldiers and said, "Beat him; he deserves this. He never listens. I am sick of my life with him." Then back to the man she cried, "I am sick of you and your baby; take him and leave me alone." She then pushed the baby into his arms and ran away. The soldiers were confused. Finally they left the man and went on. A few minutes later, the woman reappeared, took back her baby, told the young man to go to his home, and wished him safety and a quick recovery. I then realized that they were total strangers to one another.

The woman was not acting or pretending; and she was not a superhuman or a hero (as many like to characterize Palestinians today). Nor, on the other hand, was she a subhuman or a member of a non-people (as many Israeli and Western experts have been trying to portray the Palestinians for decades). She was simply acting humanly, as a concerned, responsible, and compassionate human being. Her power and her inspiration stem exactly from this fact and from her understanding that her survival and that of her community are at stake. She acted spontaneously, creatively, and courageously; feeling a sense of community and solidarity beyond the usual uttering of slogans. For this woman, the combination of thinking and acting within a particular context, of praxis, was a natural part of living. It was also obvious that she felt empowered, that she could make a difference. Self-reliance (internal strength, making decisions, and taking action) and mutual help (compassion and communal feeling) could hardly have been combined more clearly within a single event. Her action brings out the hope in human beings: how incredible, how unpredictable, how creative human beings can be.

This woman was practicing a human logic different from the purely rational, mathematical logic that we are taught to consider as the peak of human thought and capability. In this human logic, the conclusion she desired — saving the young man from brutal action — was important; but just as important was that she take some action — she felt a sense of responsibility about going through the process even if it did not lead immediately to a conclusion. Finally, her behavior shows that in order to deal effectively with systems of control, the meaning of words must be produced in the form of action, in the context of action. Some words that gained concrete meaning through her action are solidarity, empowerment, creativity, courage, and human logic. Those people who witnessed this incident also learned a great deal.

Incidents like these help Palestinians rediscover and reclaim their internal strength, their sense of self-worth, and an understanding of the importance of self-reliance for survival and growth. One expression of this development has been the widespread growth of organizations at the grassroots level. Most significantly, many neighborhood committees have been formed to deal with basic problems and needs in the community.[23] The activities of these committees included storing and distributing food, responding to health needs, taking care of the wounded and the needy, communal gardening, teaching children in homes, mosques, and churches, and alerting the community to army raids and settlers' attacks. Popular education dealing with these issues, as well as with school subjects, flourished for a few months after the beginning of the *intifadeh*.

But these neighborhood committees were dealt a severe blow by the Israeli military order of August 18, 1988, which made it a crime for anyone to be involved in popular committees, including those concerned with gardening and teaching children in homes. The penalty for engaging in such activities was up to ten years' imprisonment. This order significantly curtailed the activities of the neighborhood committees.[24] It is actually ironic when one considers the role of home teaching in the survival of the Jews in Europe for many centuries.

In short, the Palestinian *intifadeh* will probably prove to be the most inspiring, far-reaching, and authentic contribution of the Arabs since Islam. There is no historical precedent, for the fight is mainly between trapped young people and one of the strongest and most sophisticated armies in the world today. No one can guess at this point the full impact of the *intifadeh* or the direction which the course of events will take in the future. One thing is definite, however: the impact and consequences will be drastic. The *intifadeh* has already shaken the region — conceptually, socially, psychologically, and economically.

Community Education and the *Intifadeh*

Since the beginning of the *intifadeh,* the Palestinian community in the West Bank and the Gaza Strip has been undergoing a dramatic transformation. New experiences are being lived, new realities created, new needs felt, new problems and challenges faced, new convictions formed, and new mental maps of reality and how to change it are being drawn in people's minds. We need an education that will not impose obsolete, ready, fixed, or irrelevant mental maps of reality on people, but that will help people clarify and develop maps that reflect, as accurately as possible, the world around them and that can help them transform their conditions. Palestinians need an education whose focus is the world of practice and whose purpose is to produce knowledge in the context of action. Like many others, Palestinians have been involved in molding students to make them fit a certain preconceived concept of education. The time and current circumstances are appropriate for reversing this process and building an education that fits the learners.

Events since December 1987 have made Palestinians even more interested in the issue of education, and many are taking a new look at the overall educational practices within the Palestinian community. In response, the Tamer Institute for Community Education has been created to address educational issues that exist under current conditions, as well as to consider issues that will arise in the future.[25] The Institute seeks to affect formal, non-formal, and informal education in new ways.

Education and community transformation in light of the *intifadeh* are among the most serious challenges facing Palestinians today. I have several convictions about the role of education in community transformation, especially in relation to the conditions under which the Palestinian people are now living. First, education should be informed by the real *needs* in the community; prepackaged education should not be allowed to determine the range of *wants* or *demands* that people accept. This obviously means real needs in the community must be identified. In fact, one of the ongoing projects of the Tamer Institute is to identify and prioritize the real needs within the Palestinian community in the West Bank and the Gaza Strip, and at the same time, to identify the new and existing human, technical, and institutional resources that are necessary to meet those needs.

Second, the Palestinian community, like others, needs a feeling of self-worth, empowerment, and self-acceptance. The Palestinian people have been denied the value of their experience and robbed of their voice. Formal education, which usually stresses rote learning and, at best, the acquisition of technical knowledge and skills, ignores the importance of such feelings, and thus creates broken souls. Feelings of self-worth, however, should not be false, superficial, symbolic, or a gift from others; instead, they should emanate from the inner self, from internal strength, and from healthy psychological, intellectual, and spiritual growth. They should be connected to concrete things and, wherever possible, to production that enhances life. The difference between my mother's math and my math again comes to mind.

Producing something, whether materially, socially, culturally, intellectually, or spiritually, is important in building feelings of self-worth and empowerment and in encouraging creativity. A child of six or seven, for example, who learns about language through engaging in writing about something he or she has experienced, felt, or thought about, will recognize language as a means of exploring the environment and expanding his or her world and knowledge. Critical to empowering children is the presence of at least one adult who is ready to listen to or read what the child says or writes, and who will discuss the child's explanation of phenomena, events, and words. Reflecting on one's experience and taking action to change surrounding conditions is the best way to think concretely, meaningfully, accurately, creatively, and thus, effectively and empoweringly.

Of course, education that aims to build feelings of self-worth and empowerment is much more tedious and time-consuming than education that is geared toward teaching technical knowledge and skills. Building self-acceptance is much more difficult than denying one's self-worth; producing something is much harder than consuming it; conceptualizing is much harder than verbalizing; and theory-building is much harder than memorizing and applying theories. In other words, an education that is geared toward empowerment and the wholesome growth of learners is an act of love, while education that aims only at transmitting technical knowledge and skills is basically an expression of laziness.

Third, a main goal of community education is the building of human resources — which is not the same thing as labor force or credentialed people. Human resources (credentialed or not) are people who can perform necessary functions in the community in a competent, creative way and who have not lost the ability to learn. These are people who do not think merely in terms of technical or budgetary issues, but have freed their imaginations from ready and packaged solutions and have acquired the habit of periodically restructuring their lives, both mentally and socially. In fact, an education that is geared toward the building of human resources and empowering people constantly oscillates between life and the mental reconstruction of it. It is not a final and fixed product. Such an education always contains an element of potentiality. It incites people to action as well as to thought. It breaks in from beneath existing structures, so to speak, in order to revitalize them, to restructure them. It is a constant rearrangement of ideas and a constant creation of meanings. This oscillation between life and structure is crucial. Without structure we cannot deal properly with problems and needs; without life (without freedom, spontaneity, creativity, concreteness, and growth) we will soon be dealing with obsolete or marginal problems and needs. This praxis, this constant restructuring of life (both mentally and socially), is at the core of community education.

Conceiving of education as oscillating between life and the mental construction of it means reintroducing practice and context into the learning process. No meaningful learning will take place if the process is devoid of context and practice. For example, in learning how to drive a car one does not start by learning general theories about driving and then applying that knowledge to a particular car in a particular place. Rather, one starts by practicing and learning how to drive a specific car in a specific place, thus learning how to drive any car in any place. In this type of thinking, evaluation means making sure that the learner knows how to drive the car safely and competently; the learner is not given a number measuring his or her relative performance on an irrelevant test. This principle applies to learning any skill or competency. It is a mystery and a pity that this obvious principle more often than not stops at the gates of institutions of formal education.

Building human resources also requires diversity in educational settings, practices, structures, and objectives. Experiences, needs, and interests differ so much from one learner to another that trying to use the same curriculum for all learners is both impossible and undesirable. It is like claiming that one suit should fit all people; those people who do not fit the suit are labeled unfit or failures. Diversity is at the core of life and of learning. The ideal for Palestinian education in the future should not be a fixed, standardized, centralized, rigid curriculum for all (no matter how "Palestinian" that curriculum is). Rather, a curriculum is needed that is flexible and dynamic enough to provide a supportive environment for learners, and to respond to their various needs and to a constantly changing environment. This does not mean that there is no need for a well-structured and strictly executed element of the curriculum to develop specific skills in certain areas. But this should constitute a relatively small part of the curriculum and should be put into practice according to a clear agreement between learners and teachers.

Fourth, networking, communication, and the exchange of ideas and experiences among groups involved in various activities are essential components in community education. Networking and coordination are essential for the following reasons: first, activities in any community are closely interrelated; second, coordination and mutual help avoid duplication and waste, a basic principle in thinking and acting developmentally; and third, because of the oppressive reality that characterizes most societies today, and because of the huge tasks that most societies face, education cannot do the job alone — joining efforts is crucial. Networking and exchanging ideas and experiences should not be confined to individuals and groups within a single community, but should extend across countries, especially within the Third World community interaction.

Fifth, an education that responds to real needs, empowers people, builds networks, raises questions about assumptions and consequences, keeps oscillating between life and structures, and facilitates the transformation of mental and social structures is usually not compatible either with existing economic, political, and social orders or with the dominant values and mental patterns. Real manifestations of this kind of education are usually (and almost everywhere) fought harshly and promptly. The Israeli law of August 1988 criminalizing the teaching of children in homes is one example.

This basic incompatibility of a responsive system of education with the existing order explains a number of otherwise puzzling phenomena: why dictatorial governments in Third World countries don't hesitate to spend lots of money on formal, institutionalized, centralized education and forbid the formation of even small discussion groups outside that formal system; why logics other than Aristotle's are not part of the regular curriculum in schools;[26] why learners are not encouraged to tell their own stories; why people's voices and experiences are rendered inaudible and invisible; why words like hegemony, praxis, compassion, commitment, self-worth, and empowerment are usually absent from or marginal in educational discussions, courses, and schools of teacher training and education.

Conclusion

A basic premise in community education is that social reality will never be completely free of pain or injustice; that prior to and beyond any curriculum, any educational activity, or discussion, there is a concrete and often oppressive and evil reality; and that the purpose of education is not to ignore, conceal, or distort this reality, but to transform it.

The idea of transforming reality is linked to hope, and hope is linked to the belief that change is possible and that we are all responsible for it. Community education embodies the hope that today's technological-military logic and power can be swept away by human logic and human strength. The hope that the *intifadeh* embodies is a hope that transcends the Palestinian situation to reach out to humanity at large. In the big picture of human conflicts, the *intifadeh* is not a struggle between Palestinian young people and Israeli soldiers (although it is taking that form at this point), but rather, it is a fight between human power and technological military power. The victory of the *intifadeh* is not a victory for the Palestinians over the Israelis but a victory for humanity, including both Palestinians and Jews. The *intifadeh* embodies the hope that humanity cannot be crushed indefinitely. Like the wildflower seeds in the Palestinian landscape, humanity can dry up for a while, but with the first rainfall it will bloom all over again. Like a poppy growing up through cement to reach the sunlight and fresh air, humanity strives through oppression to reach toward the light. The role of education in this process is crucial. This is the message that Palestinian children exemplify for education today.

Notes

1. For a further discussion of this point, see Munir Fasheh, "Education as Praxis for Liberation: Birzeit University and the Community Work Programme," Diss. Harvard Graduate School of Education, March, 1988, sec. 2.1.
2. T. J. Jackson Lears, "The Concept of Cultural Hegemony: Problems and Possibilities," *American Historical Review,* 90 (1985), 569–570.
3. Henry Giroux and Peter McLaren, "Teacher Education and the Politics of Engagement: The Case for Democratic Schooling," *Harvard Educational Review,* 56 (1986), 131.
4. See Fasheh, "Education as Praxis for Liberation," sec. 2.1.
5. See Fasheh, "Education as Praxis for Liberation," sec. 1.2.
6. See Munir Fasheh, "Math, Culture and Authority," *For the Learning of Mathematics, 3* (Canada: Concordia University Press, 1982), 2–8.
7. See Christopher Argyris, *Inner Contradictions of Rigorous Research* (San Francisco: Jossey-Bass, 1980); and Paulo Freire, *Pedagogy of the Oppressed* (New York: Seabury, 1970).
8. Paulo Freire, *Cultural Action for Freedom* (Cambridge: Harvard Educational Review, 1970), p. 9.
9. For more details on hegemony see Fasheh, "Education as Praxis for Liberation," Sec. 2.2. For Antonio Gramsci's conception of hegemony see Chantal Mouffe, "Hegemony and Ideology in Gramsci," in *Gramsci and Marxist Theory,* ed. Chantal Mouffe (London: Routledge & Kegan Paul, 1979).
10. See, for example, Argyris, *Inner Contradictions,* and Freire, *Pedagogy of the Oppressed.*
11. Antoine Zahlan, *Science and Science Policy in the Arab World* (London: Croom Helm, 1980).
12. Nabeel Shaath, "High Level Palestinian Manpower," *Journal of Palestinian Studies 1*(2), (1971), 92, 94.
13. For example, prior to the *intifadeh,* Birzeit University was ordered closed seventeen times for long periods.
14. *Palestine Open University Feasibility Study* (Paris: UNESCO, 1980).

15. In addition to establishing math and science clubs at all levels in the schools, and producing magazines in math and science geared to students and teachers, I was involved in a number of other activities. In early 1972, I helped establish the voluntary work group in the Ramallah district (in the West Bank), which mainly involved students and teachers. In 1973, I participated in introducing the Community Work Program into Birzeit University as a requirement for graduation. In this program each student has to work for at least 120 hours in community-related projects during his or her stay at the university. I was involved in 1974 in starting children's activities (for ages 6–13) in the Ramallah and Bireh public libraries, which included programs in drama, art, crafts, mathematical games, simple science experiments, poetry, music, and literature. I helped to develop a course in math for entering college freshman science students, dealing mainly with what is missing in our schools and culture, and also developed a method for teaching math to illiterate adults. In still another area, I wrote a book dealing with the concept and practice of religion in contemporary terms. Finally, I was involved in initiating several student activities at Birzeit University, such as the International Summer Work Camps, where students come from abroad to join Palestinian students for several weeks working on community projects in Palestinian villages and refugee camps. Currently I am involved with two projects: the Economic Development Group, which is concerned with economic development in the West Bank and Gaza Strip, emphasizing self-reliant and people-centered approaches in development; and establishing the Tamer Institute, an institute of community education in the West Bank. The principles underlying the institute's philosophy and practice are these: 1) education is perceived as praxis — it considers context, personal experience, and the producing of something material, social, spiritual, or cultural as primary factors in the educational process; 2) the central goals are the empowerment of people and the changing of structures, both socially and mentally; and 3) the strategy is to work with existing groups and to use existing resources to meet basic needs and solve fundamental problems.
16. The university has since been established under the name of Al-Quds Open University in Amman, Jordan, in 1985.
17. *Palestinian Education: A Threat to Israeli Security?* (East Jerusalem: The Jerusalem Media and Communication Centre, 1989); see also M. Kretzmer, "Class Dismissed," *The Jerusalem Post,* Nov. 25, 1988.
18. Stanley Cohen, "Education as Crime," *The Jerusalem Post,* May 18, 1989. See also *Punishing a Nation* (Ramallah, West Bank: Law in the Service of Man, 1988).
19. Israeli Defense Minister Rabin declared his policy for dealing with the uprising in the following words: "We must put the fear back into the Arabs. We must use force, might, beatings." *The Uprising: Consequences for Health,* pamphlet (Jerusalem: Union of Medical Relief Committees, August, 1988), p. 1.
20. Anne Nixon, *Status of Children in the Uprising* (Stockholm: Save the Children, in press). Available from Save the Children in East Jerusalem.
21. M. Scott Peck, *The Road Less Traveled* (London: Century, 1987), p. 131.
22. Peck, *The Road Less Traveled,* pp. 278–279.
23. Grassroots groups actually started forming in the early 1980s. They included women's committees, medical and agricultural relief committees, and groups working in educational and economic development.
24. Dr. Jad Ishaq, a professor of botany at Bethlehem University, was jailed for six months because of his involvement in community gardening in his hometown, Beit Sahur, in the West Bank. My sister is a teacher of Arabic and mathematics for the first three grades in the Friends' Girls' School in Ramallah, and was teaching about ten children between the ages of four and twelve at our home. She had to stop teaching after the declaration of the order criminalizing teaching children at home.

25. The Arabic word *tamer* means a person who works with dates. In Arabia, dates were a main source of nutrition for many people. They could survive for a relatively long time on dates alone — that is, on what the land produced. In addition to being good, nutritious food, dates are a symbol of spiritual nourishment in the Sufi tradition, where understanding is part of spiritual growth. Part of the work of a *tamer* is transplanting available seeds from one palm tree in order to fertilize another. If this is not done, the dates will be of very poor quality. One main function of the Tamer Institute is to match available resources with real needs, in the hope that the "fertilization" process will yield good "fruit." Any community that ignores this dimension as a main component of its development will eventually build a relationship of dependency on others.

    A teacher, in the Tamer Institute's educational philosophy, is perceived as a *tamer*: providing nourishment for the body, soul, and mind; helping in the survival of the community; and helping "fertilize" what the community needs with what it has. The principles of the Tamer Institute were enumerated above in note 15.
26. See, for example, R. Wozniak, "A Dialectical Paradigm for Psychological Research: Implications Drawn from the History of Psychology in the Soviet Union," *Human Development, 18* (1975), 18–34.

"Yakkity Yak" and "Talking Back": An Examination of Sites of Survivance in Indigenous Knowledge

BRYAN MCKINLEY JONES BRAYBOY

The people of the United States through their governmental agencies, and through the aggression of their citizens have: (1) robbed the American Indian of freedom of action; (2) robbed the American Indian of economic independence; (3) robbed the American Indian of social organization; (4) robbed a race of men—the American Indian—of Intellectual life; (5) robbed the American Indian of moral standards and of racial ideals; (6) robbed the American Indian of a good name among the peoples of the earth; (7) robbed the American Indian of a definite civic status. (Parker, 1916, pp. 254–255)

Parker's work is deeply profound. My purpose in reaching back into the early part of the twentieth century for work is an importance piece of Indigenous Knowledge. I will elaborate on this further in the latter part of this introduction, but it is imperative to note that Indigenous peoples have been making claims about human rights for a long time. What I have to say in this introduction is only made possible by pulling from the past as we look toward the future. One important aspect of this volume is that its editors are making a similar move. They pull from past issues to help us gaze into the future. In the process, the reprinted articles, their volume introduction and section introductions outline one path for us to explore in future scholarship taking up, implementing, and using Indigenous Knowledges as tools of analysis.

Ninety-one years after Arthur C. Parker (1916), a Seneca scholar, "[laid] down seven charges . . . that the [American] Indian makes at the bar of American justice" (p. 254), the United Nations passed a Declaration of Rights for Indigenous Peoples. Unsurprisingly, the "big four" — Australia, Canada, New Zealand, and the United States — were the only four nations to vote against the measure.[1] In part, the UN Declaration stated:

Article 7
1. Indigenous individuals have the rights to life, physical and mental integrity, liberty and security of person.

2. Indigenous peoples have the collective right to live in freedom, peace and security as distinct peoples and shall not be subjected to any act of genocide or any other act of violence, including forcibly removing children of the group to another group.

Article 8

1. Indigenous peoples and individuals have the right not to be subjected to forced assimilation or destruction of their culture. (pp. 4–5)

Indeed, it appears that in many parts of the civilized world, nations have agreed to view its Indigenous inhabitants' human rights as something worth acknowledging, implicitly recognizing that Indigenous peoples still exist as viable, vibrant parts of the fabric of a larger global society. The Declaration serves several other purposes as well, although I only focus on a few of them here. First, it recognizes the devastating influences of colonization and genocide that have been perpetuated against Indigenous peoples.[2] Second, and relatedly, the Declaration makes a statement about the human rights of Indigenous peoples. Namely, it is an international document that asserts the human rights of peoples who have been thought of, in the past and in some cases in the present, as less than human. Finally, the statement moves away from notions of what Anishinaabe scholar Gerald Vizenor calls "victimry." I take victimry to mean the idea that some peoples who have been deeply oppressed and marginalized for long periods of time come to think of themselves constantly as victims and begin to behave in ways that are constantly self-defeating. When this occurs, people lose agency within the larger structural factors to move, define, defy, or resist. They simply become victims and are agents of their own victimry. And while the Declaration is obviously a statement of power, so too is Parker's treatise. Indeed, it was Vizenor (1998) who informed us that "when victims talk back, they stop being victims."

This essay and the edited volume make efforts to begin "talking back," or to stop the victimry by engaging new perspectives on struggle, strength, and survivance. While the editors note that few Indigenous scholars have been published in its pages, there is a potential for Indigenous peoples to talk back here and in the future. In the following pages, I intend to address the ways that we have talked back for millennia, and what our move away from victimry might mean for the future. Before proceeding, I will first outline what I mean by survivance, and then I move into a conversation of what Indigenous Knowledges represent, and what they are not. Along the way, I will attempt to address the ways that Indigenous Knowledges serve as places of power for Indigenous peoples. I also intend to outline three sites of survivance: history, sovereignty, and education. These sites demonstrate the ways that Indigenous peoples talk back and move forward. Finally, I end with some questions to consider over the coming years that are related to the use and integration of Indigenous Knowledge systems in schools and research.

In framing this essay, I rely on Vizenor's (1999) use of the term "survivance." In defining it, Vizenor states in a conversation with Robert Lee:

> Survivance, in my use of the word, means a native sense of presence, the motion of sovereignty and the will to resist dominance. Survivance is not just survival but also resistance, not heroic or tragic, but the tease of tradition, and my sense of survivance outwits dominance and victimry. (p. 93)

The idea of survivance is compelling for Indigenous peoples. Vizenor (1999) connects it to "the notion of sovereignty," which necessarily links the concept of survivance to power and self-determination. In noting that survivance is neither "heroic" nor "tragic," Vizenor leads us to a place where Indigenous peoples act in ways that are directly linked to the ways they have always engaged with the world; with dignity and a belief in their inherent rights to be who they have always been. Vizenor (1999) goes on to elaborate on this and expand the notion of survivance, telling Lee that "survivance is a response; survivance is a standpoint, a worldview, and a presence" (p. 93). In this way, it becomes clear that Indigenous peoples who live, write, and think from a standpoint informed by survivance do so grounded in the belief and knowledge that they can and will "outwit dominance and victimry."

Quechua scholar Sandy Marie Anglás Grande, in her essay in this volume, elaborates on this point by calling on Indigenous intellectuals "to create the intellectual space for the struggle for sovereignty and for their efforts to renegotiate the relationsip between sovereign American Indian tribal nations and the current democratic order." Inupiaq scholar Leona Okakok, in her contribution to this volume, offers ways that the Inupiat peoples of the North Slope in Alaska have used their places to take control of their own educational systems:

> The students, then, must demonstrate mastery of competencies before they are promoted to the next grade. This approach is similar to our traditional practices in which elders expected children to master certain competencies before they went on to more difficult tasks. (p. 262)

Although Grande and Okakok appear on the surface to be addressing different ideas and constituencies, I find that both of these Indigenous scholars are addressing the ways that Indigenous peoples can assert their own takes on education. Grande addresses the intellectual space, while Okakok offers a vision for the schooling space and the educational spaces outside of formal schooling. In these instances, we see a site of survivance located in education.

In examining the role of survivance as something that connects resistance and survival, I find myself perplexed by attempts to tease apart the concepts of resistance and survival. Parker's (1916) quotation that opens this introduction points to the fact that in the United States, the federal government engaged in behaviors that could be tied directly to violations of human rights and genocide. If Indigenous peoples have survived genocide, or the systematic attempt at destroying a group of people based on their origins, as we know we have,[3] then our survival necessitates — carries within it, is inextricably linked to — resistance. In order to survive we have had to resist "dominance" and "victimry"; one cannot survive as an Indigenous person without resisting. Elsewhere I have written about a student who once told me that she was "the descendent of a people who would not die." Indigenous peoples are the descendents of people who would not die, and our survival signals our resistance to be co-opted, assimilated, and destroyed.[4] In reading the essays in this section, it is clear that this is true of all peoples who have had to survive genocide.[5]

Indigenous peoples engage in survivance through survival and resistance, and we are talking back. More than simply talking back, however, we are moving forward, claiming spaces and demanding acknowledgement of sovereignty that has existed since time immemorial.[6] The connections between survival and resistance cannot be complete without a brief examination of the role of power in communities and society. Vizenor (1999) locates survivance as a "notion of sovereignty," while the late Lakota scholar Vine Deloria Jr. (1970) notes that "power cannot be understood outside of its social-political context" (p. 115). Deloria later appears to address power not only as something that necessarily controls individuals or groups of people through physical means, but also addresses the ideological strands of power. Deloria goes even further, noting that power is not something that is necessarily best held by individuals but must be taken up for a group of peoples or by a community. He notes that "power cannot be given and accepted" (p. 123) because it resides in the sovereignty of a group. More succinctly, he writes:

> Sovereignty and power go hand in hand in group action. One cannot exist without the other, although neither can be misused to the detriment of the other. Thus power without a concept of responsibility to a sovereign group is often ruthlessness in disguise. . . . The responsibility which sovereignty creates is oriented primarily toward the *existence* and *continuance* of a group. (p. 123, emphasis added)

As we explore the role of knowledge and knowledge systems in and out of schools around a broadly conceived idea of education, Deloria's wisdom becomes even more central. If we as scholars are to consider the connections between Indigenous Knowledges and sovereignty, as I attempt to do here, then we must realize that our knowledge systems serve as a place of power and a source of continuance of our groups. As such, education becomes "ruthless" in the particular ways that it ignores the rights of Indigenous ways of knowing and attempts to dominate and assimilate groups of people. It is a valuable lesson for us as we move toward articulating Indigenous Knowledges in written forms. Osage scholar Robert Allen Warrior (1995), in writing about Vine Deloria Jr.'s work, notes, "His straightforward warning against making the rhetoric of sovereignty and tradition a final rather than a beginning step remains an important reminder to those who engage in community, federal, and other American Indian work" (p. 97). Importantly, the exploration of Indigenous Knowledges, rooted in sovereignty, can only be a beginning; it is not an end.

To this end, Leona Okakok's essay is particularly poignant. She informs us of the challenges in epistemic clashes, and the wisdom of humility. She writes:

> We all know that we can go through life convinced that our view of the world is the only valid one. If we are interested in new perceptions, however, we need to catch a glimpse of the world through other eyes. We need to be aware of our own thoughts, as well as the way life is viewed by other people.

Implicit in this work is an acknowledgement that many of us are so deeply entrenched in our own ways of knowing that we forget that there are other ways of knowing and that we may be well served by "new perceptions." Okakok reminds us that by seeing other ways of doing things, our ways become clearer; her message is so basic that it is often overlooked. There is brilliance in her work, and her message has implications for Indigenous Knowledges, issues of positionality, and the values that are often associated with the "right" way of doing something. Embedded in Indigenous Knowledge systems, as I understand them, is a sense of humility that allows individuals and communities to draw on the resources of other ways of knowing, doing, and being.

Indigenous Knowledges also force scholars and researchers to be careful in the ways in which they think about, describe, and use "education." Returning to Okakok's article and her definitions of education is informative. She notes, "To me, educating a child means equipping him or her with the capability to succeed in the world he or she will live in." She continues by making a powerful (and political) statement that "Education is more than book learning, it is also value-learning." In Grande's work, and in Susan M. Kardos' article, it is clear that while much of education occurs in schools (whether they are in formal school buildings or in the attics of homes in the Warsaw ghetto), the value-learning that occurs presents an opportunity for marginalized, oppressed peoples to resist, survive, and engage in the process of survivance. Indigenous Knowledges recognize the fact that education is necessarily broad, that it is political, and that it occurs in the everyday ways that we live life.

The articles in this section highlight the ways that sites of survivance occur around education and in and out of schools every day. There are both dangers and possibilities in the recognition that survivance is part of the everyday lives of both those who hold power and those who spend much of their lives fighting unjust rules and standards in schools and life.

Deloria (1970) offers a word of caution, noting that "there is . . . great danger that immoral use of group power or unwitting compromise will destroy the sovereignty of the group and dissipate the power, thus turning fundamental freedoms into licentiousness" (p. 126). Echoing the work of the authors in this section, Deloria points to the moral aspects of education for marginalized peoples. There is hope in these articles as well that is rooted in the fact that Indigenous peoples are still vibrant, viable parts of society. Communities have engaged in the process of equipping their young people with the abilities to survive. Again, we find the wisdom of Indigenous Knowledges in the ways that the Inupiat peoples think about education for their children. Okakok notes that "though most of the education in our traditional society was not formal, it was serious business. For us, education meant equipping the child with the wherewithal to survive in our world." It may be that the greatest gift we can give our children is the ability to "succeed . . . [and] the wherewithal to survive in the world."

As I close my introduction, I want to return to Indigenous Knowledges and their place in the world of education. The authors in this section point to the exceptionality of Indigenous peoples (or other groups, in the case of the Kardos, Katz, and Fasheh articles). By this I do not mean exceptional as in better; I mean exceptional as in different, removed, and separate. I resist the urge to engage in a hierarchical discussion of whose knowledges are better, although I am not so naïve as to miss the fact that much of larger society sees one set of knowledges as "the best" option. I believe that we would do well to heed Mi'kmaq scholar Marie Battiste's (2002) lucid point along these lines. She writes:

> Indigenous scholars discovered that Indigenous knowledge is far more than the binary opposite of western knowledge. As a concept, Indigenous knowledge benchmarks the limitations of Eurocentric theory — its methodology, evidence, and conclusions — reconceptualizes the resilience and self-reliance of Indigenous peoples, and underscores the importance of their own philosophies, heritages, and educational processes. Indigenous knowledge fills the ethical and knowledge gaps in Eurocentric education, research, and scholarship. By animating the voices and experiences of the cognitive "other" and integrating them into educational processes, it creates a new, balanced centre and a fresh vantage point from which to analyze Eurocentric education and its pedagogies. (p. 5)

Battiste notes that we need to move away from binaries and recognize the ways that different knowledge systems extend, complicate, and (at times) contradict others.

In closing, I want to return to the introduction of this volume where the editors note the beautiful artwork on the cover. "Yakkity Yak Ravens" by Sugpiaq/Alutiiq artist Helen Simeonoff highlights the three sites of struggle, strength, and survivance. In the far north, where I currently live, Raven is an important and integral figure in Indigenous Knowledge systems. Raven is a trickster who uses cunning and guile to get what he wants; in the process, others often benefit from his own selfishness. For example, he steals the sun from its owner, drawn by the challenge and the sun's beauty, benefiting people who had lived in darkness. Importantly for this volume, Raven disrupts convenient binaries and points to the everyday contradictions that make up our lives. Raven challenges our conceptions of "good" and "bad" or "good" and "evil." Instead, the lessons Raven brings us are ones that demonstrate the complicated nature of living, knowing, and being. If we are to offer our children "the wherewithal to survive in the world," we would be well served to teach them that life and living are complicated and contradictory. The articles in this volume and the volume as a whole make this point vividly, and I am grateful for it. We would all be well served to resist seeing this volume as the end of addressing this topic and to see it instead as a beginning.

Notes

1. In examining the entire Proclamation, it is evident that it focuses on the rights of Indigenous Peoples and nations in reasserting their power and independence. The Big Four have much to lose from this assertion of rights. These four nations voted against the measure in part because the assertion of group rights "would hinder efforts for economic development and undermine the so-called established democratic norms" that exist in their own countries (Rizvi, 2007, p. 2). The emphasis on individual rights in the four countries takes precedence over group rights, creating a quandary for these nations. As to why it is unsurprising that the Big Four voted against the resolution, I would argue that these countries have the most to lose (discursively) if they agree with the assertion of human rights for their Indigenous peoples. Arthur Manuel, a First Nations leader from Canada was clear on this topic when he stated, "The entire wealth of the United States, Canada, and other so-called modern states is built on the poverty and human rights violations of their Indigenous peoples" (Rizvi, 2007, p. 2). Ultimately, it would be difficult for human rights advocates in these countries to continue pressing nations like China and Iran on their human rights violations, when they are so visibly present in these nations' interactions with Indigenous peoples.
2. Importantly, these issues are quite similar to claims that Parker made in his 1916 piece. The fact that so little had changed in the ninety years since Parker published his commentary are telling. His eloquence was dismissed, and the eloquence of the UN Proclamation has been ignored by the nation states that most need to recognize the human rights of its Indigenous peoples.
3. I am an enrolled member of the Lumbee tribe of North Carolina. In my comments here, I will often use the pronoun "we" in particular points in order to note my own positionality as an indigenous man. I cannot separate myself from the analysis here.
4. This is not to say that we have not changed, adapted, and adjusted over time. Clearly, we have, just as all humans have changed the ways that we interact with the world. Deloria is particularly eloquent here when he writes simply that "no one culture has all the answers." His arguments that Indigenous peoples borrow from others is enlightening and freeing for Indigenous peoples, but it often may not sit well with non-Indigenous peoples. Deloria says, "Whites look at the most profound and sacrificial efforts of contemporary Indians and find them wanting because they, the white, can only relate to the Indians of the past they come to know through movies and television."
5. I fully acknowledge that genocide has been devastating for many communities. I also want to acknowledge that for many Indigenous peoples, our need for survival is rooted in honoring our ancestors who were the victims of disease, starvation, and murder systematically used to destroy our groups. While Indigenous nations have bent, many refuse to break and in this refusal is rooted a sense of survivance that further "outwits victimry and dominance."
6. I am grateful to Malia Villegas for making this point.

References

Battiste, M. (2002). *Indigenous knowledge and pedagogy in First Nations education: A literature review with recommendations.* Ottawa, Canada: Indian and Northern Affairs Canada.

Deloria, V., Jr. (1970). *We talk, you listen: New tribes, new turf.* New York: Macmillan.

Parker, A. C. (1916). The social elements of the Indian problem. *American Journal of Sociology, 22*(2), 252–267.

Rizvi, H. (2007). Native peoples score historic political victory. *TerraViva UN Journal, 15*(166), 1–2.

UN Draft Declaration of Indigenous Rights. (n.d.). Retrieved October 11, 2007, from http://daccessdds.un.org/doc/UNDOC/LTD/N07/498/30/PDF/N0749830.pdf?OpenElement (Note: A final draft has not been posted to the UN's webpage, although this drafted version is the one accepted by the vote on September 13, 2007.)

Vizenor, G. (1998). *Fugitive poses: Native American Indian scenes of absence and presence.* Lincoln: University of Nebraska Press.

Vizenor, G., & Lee, A. R. (1999). *Postindian donversations.* Lincoln, NE: University of Nebraska Press.

Warrior, R. A. (1995). *Tribal secrets: Recovering American Indian intellectual traditions.* Minneapolis: University of Minnesota Press.

About the Contributors

DAVID WALLACE ADAMS is professor emeritus at Cleveland State University and the author of *Education for Extinction: American Indians and the Boarding School Experience, 1875-1928* (1995). His research has appeared in such journals as the *History of Education Quarterly*, *Pacific Historical Review*, *South Atlantic Quarterly*, and the *Western Historical Quarterly*. He is currently writing a multicultural history of childhood in the American Southwest.

PHILIP G. ALTBACH is the Monan University Professor and the director of the Center for International Higher Education at Boston College. He has authored numerous books, most recently *World Class Worldwide: The Transformation of Research Universities in Asia and Latin America* (2007) and *Tradition and Transition: The International Imperative in Higher Education* (2007).

LILIA I. BARTOLOMÉ is an associate professor in the Applied Linguistics Graduate Program at the University of Massachusetts Boston. Her research interests focus on the preparation of effective teachers of second-language learners and teachers' ideological orientations toward language-minority students. She is the author of *Ideologies in Education: Unmasking the Trap of Teacher Neutrality* (in press), and the coauthor of *Immigrant Voices: In Search of Pedagogical Equity* (with H. Trueba, 2000) and *Dancing with Bigotry: The Poisoning of Culture* (with D. Macedo, 2000).

MARIE BATTISTE, a Mi'kmaq educator, is a professor in the College of Education and coordinator of the Indian and Northern Education Program at the University of Saskatchewan. Her research interests span institutional change in the decolonization of education, language, and social-justice policy, and the ethical protection and advancement of Indigenous Knowledge. A technical consultant to the United Nations, Battiste is the coauthor of *Protecting Indigenous Knowledge and Heritage: A Global Challenge* (with J. Y. Henderson, 2000) and the editor of *Reclaiming Indigenous Voice and Vision* (2000).

BRYAN MCKINLEY JONES BRAYBOY is the President's Professor of Education at the University of Alaska Fairbanks and the Borderlands Associate Professor of Educational Leadership and Policy Studies at Arizona State University. His research focuses on the strategies used by American Indian college students to achieve academic success, and the cultural, emotional, psychological, political, and financial costs and benefits of this academic success. He founded the University of Utah's American Indian Teacher Training Program, which prepares Indigenous educators to return to their communities to teach Indigenous children.

GREGORY A. CAJETE, a Tewa Indian from Santa Clara Pueblo, New Mexico, is currently the director of Native American Studies and an associate professor in the Division of Language, Literacy, and Sociocultural Studies in the College of Education at the University of New Mexico. He also teaches at the Institute of American Indian Arts. His work focuses on the design of curricula that is culturally responsive to the needs and learning styles of Native American students. Cajete is the author of five books, including *Look to the Mountain: An Ecology of Indigenous Education* (1994), and *A People's Ecology: Explorations in Sustainable Living* (1999).

FERNANDO CARDENAL, S.J., served as the national coordinator of the Nicaraguan Literacy Crusade and the minister of education for the Sandinista government. He is the current director of the *Fé y Alegría* (Faith and Happiness) school system in Nicaragua. He is a Nicaraguan Jesuit priest and liberation theologian.

MUNIR FASHEH is the founder and director of the Arab Education Forum of the Center for Middle Eastern Studies at Harvard University. He was the director of the Tamer Institute for Community Education in Jerusalem and Ramallah until 1997. A former dean of students and teacher of mathematics, physics, and education at Birzeit University, Fasheh has written six books in Arabic on math, education, society, and religion and edited several publications, including "Emerging and Re-Emerging Learning Communities: Old Wisdoms and New Initiatives from Around the World" (2005).

SANDY MARIE ANGLÁS GRANDE is an associate professor in the education department at Connecticut College and a research consultant for the Ford Foundation. Her research and teaching are inter- and cross-disciplinary, bringing together critical, feminist, Indigenous, and Marxist theories of education with the concerns of Indigenous education. She is the author of *Red Pedagogy: Native American Social and Political Thought* (2004), which has been met with critical acclaim. She has published extensively including "American Indian Identity and Intellectualism: The Quest for a New Red Pedagogy," in *The International Journal of Qualitative Studies in Education* (2000).

JOSIANE HUDICOURT-BARNES is a researcher at the Chèche Konnen Center at the nonprofit education research and development organization, TERC. Her research examines how the cultural capital of Haitian traditions can be used as a resource in academic work. She is the coauthor of "Using Diversity as a Strength in the Science Classroom: The Benefits of Science Talk" (with A. S. Roseberry, 2006) in *Linking Science and Literacy in the K-8 Classroom* (edited by R. Douglas, 2006). She has also published in the *Journal of Research in Science Teaching* (2001), and in *Classroom Diversity: Connecting Curriculum to Students' Lives* (2001).

SUSAN M. KARDOS is the director of the Initiative for Day School Excellence at the Combined Jewish Philanthropies of Greater Boston and a research affiliate of the Project on the Next Generation of Teachers at the Harvard Graduate School of Education. Her work focuses on school organization improvement and leadership, new teacher induction and support, education policy, and Jewish education. She is the coauthor of *Finders and Keepers: Helping New Teachers Survive and Thrive in Our Schools* (with S. M. Johnson & the Project on the Next Generation of Teachers, 2004) and "The Next Generation of Teachers: Who Enters, Who Stays, and Why" in *The Handbook of Research on Teacher Education* (with S. M. Johnson, in press).

RICHARD KATZ is professor emeritus at First Nations University of Canada. He has published widely on healing, and specifically on Indigenous approaches to healing. Katz is the author of *Boiling Energy: Community Healing Among the Kalahari !Kung* (1982) and *The Straight Path of the Spirit: Ancestral Wisdom and Healing Traditions in Fiji* (1999). He is also the coauthor of *Healing Makes Our Hearts Happy: Spirituality and Cultural Transformation Among the Kalahari Ju/'hoansi* (with M. Biesele and V. St. Denis, 1999) and *Nobody's Child* (with M. Balter, 1999).

KENNETH LIBERMAN is a professor of sociology at the University of Oregon. He is the author of *Husserl's Criticism of Reason, with Ethnomethodological Specifications* (2007), *Dialectical Practice in Tibetan Philosophical Culture* (2004), and *Understanding Interaction in Central Australia* (1985).

ABOUT THE CONTRIBUTORS

K. TSIANINA LOMAWAIMA is a professor and the head of American Indian Studies at the University of Arizona. Her research focuses on the history of American Indian education and twentieth-century Native experiences with federal assimilation programs. She is the author of *They Called It Prairie Light: The Story of Chilocco Indian School* (1994), and coauthor of *"To Remain an Indian": Lessons in Democracy from a Century of Native American Education* (with T. L. McCarty, 2006) and *Uneven Ground: American Indian Sovereignty and Federal Law* (with M. L. Archuleta, B. J. Child, and the Heard Museum, 2001).

RICHARD MACLURE is a professor and the former acting dean of the Faculty of Education at the University of Ottawa, where he teaches comparative and international education. His research focuses on basic education, civil society organizations, and youth rights issues in sub-Saharan Africa and Latin America. His work has appeared in *Comparative Education*, *Journal of Latin American Studies*, *Third World Quarterly*, and *Journal of Youth Studies*. He has also worked with international agencies such as USAID and UNICEF.

VALERIE MILLER is senior advisor and cofounder of Just Associates. She has been the policy and advocacy director at Oxfam America, the director of policy and exchange programs at the Institute for Development Research, and an advisor and associate of the Global Women in Politics Program; Women, Law, and Development International; and the Highlander Center. She has also served as a board member of Cenzontle, a Nicaraguan NGO focused on women's economic and political empowerment, and Grassroots International, a U.S.-based group supporting social movements around the world.

LEONA OKAKOK served as the manager of the Arctic Education Foundation, a private scholarship fund, and on the North Slope Borough School District board of education. She is the author of "Why Publish Our Own Material?" in the *Native Press Journal* (1988), and the transcriber and translator of the proceedings of the 1979 Elders Conference in Alaska, titled *Puiguitkaat* (*Things You Should Never Forget*, 1981). She also collaborated with W. Bodfish Jr., on the book *KUSIQ: An Eskimo Life History from the Arctic Coast of Alaska* (1991).

RAMÓN EDUARDO RUIZ is professor emeritus of Latin American history at the University of California at San Diego. He is the author of Triumphs and Tragedy: A History of the Mexican People (1992) and Cuba: The Making of a Revolution (1968). In 1998, he was awarded the National Humanities Award for Lifetime Achievement by President Clinton. His work on Mexico and Latin America is used as a standard reference for many Hispanic scholars. He also served in the Pacific as a second lieutenant in the U.S. Army Air Force during World War II.

About the Editors

MALIA VILLEGAS is Alutiiq/Sugpiaq with family from Kodiak Island and Afognak Island in Alaska and O'ahu in Hawa'i. She is a doctoral candidate in Culture, Communities, and Education at the Harvard Graduate School of Education. Villegas is committed to improving the educational experiences of Indigenous and rural youth and communities. Her specific research interests include Indigenous philosophies of education, community- and place-based education, sovereignty and nation-building, and social and moral development. She is affiliated with the Alaska Native Policy Center at First Alaskans Institute, where she works on research and policy related to Alaska Native education and community development. She will travel to Aotearoa, New Zealand, in 2008 on a Fulbright Fellowship to explore how Maori Indigenous policy and research organizations leverage resources to address community needs. Villegas previously worked in education policy at WestEd on issues of teacher recruitment and retention, urban school reform, and education on the U.S.-Mexico border.

SABINA RAK NEUGEBAUER is a doctoral candidate in Human Development and Education, who holds a master's in Language and Literacy from the Harvard Graduate School of Education (HGSE). Her work emphasizes diagnostic, sociocultural, and pedagogical issues, together with policy agendas that impact English-language learners (ELLs). Before enrolling at HGSE, Sabina worked for the Department of Psychiatry at Yale University and conducted research in Paris and Buenos Aires on language acquisition and disabilities. She also taught children with autism in Richmond, California. Neugebauer has presented papers at several conferences on issues related to bilingualism, learning disabilities, and self-image. She is presently working with the Center for Applied Special Technology (CAST) on a digital literacy intervention specifically targeting ELLs. As a fellow of the Foreign Language and Area Studies and the David Rockefeller Center, Neugebauer has also conducted research in Cusco, Peru, on multilingualism and linguistic capital. She currently leads a project on redefining literacy practices in collaboration with school officials in an Indigenous village in Calca, Peru, where she most recently established a children's library.

KERRY R. VENEGAS is a doctoral candidate in the Communities and Schools Program at the Harvard Graduate School of Education. Previously an alternative education science teacher working with at-risk youth in Colorado, New Mexico, and the Washington, D.C., area, she also served as a Peace Corps volunteer in Bolivia and as an Albert Einstein Distinguished Educator Fellow at the National Science Foundation. Originally from the Southwest, her experience spans the public, private, and nonprofit sectors, including serving as a research consultant for the Harvard Project on American Indian Economic Development. Her research focuses on the experiences and needs of Indigenous at-risk youth and adult learners, especially those who return to complete their secondary education. Venegas has recently been working with Indigenous former street children in the area of career development and healthy life planning through the Bolivian Street Children Project in La Paz, Bolivia, including conducting research into the design and implementation of career development curricula and how it can be used to addresses the multiple cognitive and sociopsychological needs of street children.